The Undivided Sky

The Undivided Sky

The Holocaust on East and West German Radio in the 1960s

René Wolf
Royal Holloway, University of London

© René Wolf 2010

All rights reserved. No reproduction, copy or transmission of this publication may be made without written permission.

No portion of this publication may be reproduced, copied or transmitted save with written permission or in accordance with the provisions of the Copyright, Designs and Patents Act 1988, or under the terms of any licence permitting limited copying issued by the Copyright Licensing Agency, Saffron House, 6–10 Kirby Street, London EC1N 8TS.

Any person who does any unauthorized act in relation to this publication may be liable to criminal prosecution and civil claims for damages.

The author has asserted his right to be identified as the author of this work in accordance with the Copyright, Designs and Patents Act 1988.

First published 2010 by
PALGRAVE MACMILLAN

Palgrave Macmillan in the UK is an imprint of Macmillan Publishers Limited, registered in England, company number 785998, of Houndmills, Basingstoke, Hampshire RG21 6XS.

Palgrave Macmillan in the US is a division of St Martin's Press LLC, 175 Fifth Avenue, New York, NY 10010.

Palgrave Macmillan is the global academic imprint of the above companies and has companies and representatives throughout the world.

Palgrave® and Macmillan® are registered trademarks in the United States, the United Kingdom, Europe and other countries

ISBN 978–0–230–57676–6   hardback

This book is printed on paper suitable for recycling and made from fully managed and sustained forest sources. Logging, pulping and manufacturing processes are expected to conform to the environmental regulations of the country of origin.

A catalogue record for this book is available from the British Library.

A catalog record for this book is available from the Library of Congress.

10 9 8 7 6 5 4 3 2 1
19 18 17 16 15 14 13 12 11 10

Printed and bound in Great Britain by
CPI Antony Rowe, Chippenham and Eastbourne

To Della

Contents

List of Tables	ix
Acknowledgements	x

1 Introduction	**1**
The *Deutsche Welle* programme *'Das Lager'*	1
What do we hear?	4
Aims and objectives	6
Methodology	8
Overview	9
2 Radio and Modernity	**17**
Radio as the agent of modernity	17
Brecht and Benjamin	20
Nazi radio	25
Theoretical approaches	32
Radio and ideology	34
Considerations	40
3 Radio and the Holocaust	**46**
Broadcasts from the Nuremberg Trials	46
Prosecutions after Nuremberg	59
Programmes preceding the Auschwitz Trial	69
Eichmann	83
The Globke issue	84
4 Radio and the Auschwitz Trial	**97**
Preparations	97
On air	101
Broadcasts during the Trial	107
Axel Eggebrecht	126
The aftermath	137
5 Radio and Memory	**146**
Memory makers and memory users	146
Memory makers (East)	154
Memory makers (West)	160
Memory users (East)	167
Memory users (West)	176
Radio: making memory usable	198

6 Radio and History	**202**
A return to the *Deutsche Welle* programme	202
Radio as history	214
Notes	220
Appendix	249
Bibliography	257
Index	268

List of Tables

5.1	Dimensions of programme development	159
5.2	GDR radio listeners	170
5.3	IfD Allensbach Opinion Poll: 'What distinguishes German History?' (May 1995)	173
5.4	Radio listeners in West Germany, 1950	177
5.5	Respondents listening to the radio at least once a day and average daily listening time per listener	178
5.6	NDR radio listeners, 1970	181
5.7	'Which of the following do you consider the correct action by the government of Israel?'	192
5.8	'In your opinion, do you think it is a good thing or a bad thing that the world is reminded of the horrors of the National Socialist concentration camps?'	192
5.9	Persons who have heard of the Auschwitz Trial (1159)	194
5.10	'Why do you want to draw a line under it all?'	195
5.11	How do you view the German soldiers in the Second World War?	196

Acknowledgements

First and foremost my thanks goes to my supervisor Dan Stone, who has been a constant and unerring guide and inspiration; it was through his initiative that I secured a College Research Studentship at Royal Holloway University of London.

Therefore I am grateful to the History Department Royal Holloway for their support, tuition and assistance, in particular Rudolf Muhs, Justin Champion, Penelope Corfield and Pam Pilbeam. I also gratefully acknowledge the funding I received from the AHRB in my third and final year of study.

Many friendly people made my research in the archives very much easier, and I would like in particular to thank Werner Renz at the Fritz Bauer Institute, Walter Roller and Andreas Rühl at the Deutsches Rundfunkarchiv in Frankfurt, and Susanne Höschel and Ingrid Pietrzynski at the DRA in Potsdam-Babelsberg. At the Hessischer Rundfunk I would like to thank Michael Crone, at Südwestfunk Klement Helmholz and at the Norddeutscher Rundfunk Alex Eisenreich (who was more than generous with his transfers from tape to CDs) and Louise Weston at the BBC Written Archives Centre, Caversham.

Last but not least I am greatly indebted to my lovely family, my children Madeleine, Alex and Joey, and above all to my wife Della, as without her none of this would have been possible.

1
Introduction

The *Deutsche Welle* programme *'Das Lager'*, 20 November 1968

On 20 November 1968 the West German national and international radio broadcaster *Deutsche Welle* transmitted a programme entitled 'The Camp' (*Das Lager*). It was introduced by the continuity announcer with the following:

> Announcer: This is *Deutsche Welle* with its programme 'The Political Feature'. Nearly two-and-a-half decades have passed since the terrible events in the concentration camps during the National Socialist era. For the victims, the effects and memories of them are, nevertheless, a living and everyday presence. In connection with the current trials regarding the Auschwitz concentration camp, Siegurt Guthmann talked to former inmates and recounts this in his report 'The Camp'.[1]

The programme itself uses the format of a serious public service broadcast 'feature' which combines interviews and spoken narrative around a number of themes, loosely held together by a short history of the Auschwitz concentration and death camp and the then Third Auschwitz Trial in Frankfurt/Main, starting with the account of one of the first Polish prisoners to arrive in Auschwitz, Miroslav Zalevski. Through simultaneous translation Zalevski remembers being told that the only way out of the camp was through the chimney, but can also recall the inscription (in German) above the kitchen block which read 'There is one way to freedom, its milestones are obedience, truthfulness, following the path of duty, diligence, sacrifice, cleanliness and love of the fatherland',[2] which, the narrator adds, was just one of the many cynical inscriptions of the SS camp guards – the best known one being *'Arbeit macht frei'* (work makes you free) above the main gate.

The first prisoners, however, were not Poles but German criminals, who were transferred from the camp at Sachsenhausen near Berlin, in 1940, among them Bernhard Bonitz, who has just been found guilty of the murder of fellow inmates and sentenced to life imprisonment at the Third Auschwitz Trial. According to the programme, these prisoners were meant to act as 'prisoner-functionaries' or Kapos, in charge of other prisoners and willing tools of the SS.[3] Another such inmate, Josef Windeck, arrived at Auschwitz shortly after Bonitz and went on to become a feared Kapo in the camp; he too received a life sentence in Frankfurt. But the precarious situation of the Kapo was even acknowledged by one of the former prisoners, Dr Tadeusz Paczula:

> You have to distinguish here that the SS man was in a situation which you would call voluntary – the prisoner, even when a professional criminal, was in a predicament here. He was locked up. He was, after all, a prisoner. But among the professional criminals there were some very primitive persons, primitive characters and maybe also people who were mentally not very talented. And they, very willingly, maybe to save or keep their own life, or to improve it, accommodated the orders of the SS.[4]

One of the manifestations of the relationship between Kapo and SS was, according to Paczula, the Kapos' common practice of sending prisoners to or close to the boundary fence to fetch a tool, with the consequence that they would be shot by the SS guard for straying off limits, for which the guard would receive a few days leave, and the Kapo, in return, some food or alcohol.

The narrator points out that the Kapos, like their SS counterparts, deny all knowledge and responsibility for the murders at Auschwitz. A recording of Josef Windeck at the first day of the trial makes rather startling listening not only because of its obvious Freudian slip:

> I have never killed anybody in my whole life and to this day there is not a single drop of blood on my fingers. And you can assure yourself of it that my wife could not go to her grave knowing that she had a husband for a murderer.[5]

Whereas the nature of work was rather unspecified and undirected in the first two years of the camp's existence – and with it the Kapos' role as tormentors of their fellow prisoners much more pronounced, the expansion of the camp in Summer 1942 into death camp (Auschwitz-Birkenau), work camp (Auschwitz I or *Stammlager*) and the various industrial camps (Auschwitz-Monowitz being the largest) meant that most Kapos had to ensure that their work detail remained productive, and the severe ill-treatment subsided somewhat. This, however, was not the case with the two accused, Bonitz and Windeck, as the trial witness Kaminski tells the reporter.

> A meticulous bureaucracy developed around the percentage (about 10–25 per cent) of the new arrivals who were not immediately killed in the gas chambers. The up to 30 subsidiary camps of the 25 German industrial conglomerates needed to keep track of their workforce and deaths were carefully recorded. Dr Paczula, for years the scribe of the 'book of the dead' (*Totenbuch*) at the main camp, recalls that despite most deaths occurring for reasons of starvation, torture or shooting, the causes of death were recorded as tuberculosis, heart attacks or septicaemia. Above all insufficient nutrition led to a state of physical and mental emaciation, its sufferers became known in the camp as *Muselmänner* (Muslims) because of their seemingly fatalistic demeanour and appearance. Paczula struggles to explain this term in its full meaning and feels that the term *Muselmann* has as yet not been clarified by survivors and writers, including himself. It is, he concludes, 'an extreme condition'.[6]

In stark contrast stood the Kapos in Auschwitz. In an astonishing recorded sequence the programme continues with the following:

> Narrator: The Kapos remember the camp differently from the prisoners. On the opening day of his trial before the High Court, Windeck said that he and his like had been living the high life in the concentration camp. Asked about this by us in the corridor of the court, he added:
> Jupp Windeck (speaking in very broad dialect): Well, so much stuff came with the Jews, and we filched from it, of course we did, because we were Germans, and acting as Kapos, we always got ourselves the best from the (possessions) chamber; as a Kapo, if he was German..., that is..., they had... er, by the by, enough to eat and to drink and yes, valuables which they could swap with the civilian, er, workers from Poland and when... well over there is one of those, er, gentlemen, er, prisoners, you can ask him if this is correct!

N: This man, called up repeatedly as witness by Windeck, the Czechoslovak Karel Minz, was not prepared for an encounter with the former camp Kapo. We recorded the following scene:
Karel Minz:(shouting): I can tell you, I could easily hang you, if I didn't mind dirtying my hands!
J.W.(baffled): What (incident) are you talking about?
K.M.: You know!
J.W.: When was this, what, when?
K.M.: In year '42, when I came from Buchenwald.
Other man with Czech accent in background: Sir, this is the hour of truth!
J.W.: No, no, this is this, this is...
K.M.: You once beat me with whip so much, you know!
J.W.: Yes...
K.M.: ...that I don't know how I got back to the block!
J.W.: Listen, for what reason...?
K.M. (enraged, shouting): Why?
J.W.: For what reason would I have done such a thing?
K.M.: Why? I will tell you why!
J.W.: ...for what reason..?
K.M.: You saw me, in the room, that I was smoking, you know....
J.W.: But we were allowed to...
K.M.: Yes, I...
J.W.: But we were allowed to smoke!
K.M.: Yes you were, the SS, but not us.[7]

This incident, Siegurt Guthmann explains, is not about the issue of a cigarette, but about the fact that those who survived carry with them not only the physical but also the mental damage of incarceration, as everything human was trampled on and destroyed in Auschwitz. Even clear-sighted and rational persons such as Dr Paczula, he concludes, have, 'if you listen closely', extreme difficulties coming to terms with their years in the camp. In the closing sequence of the programme, Tadeusz Paczula, recounting his recent visit to the memorial site, finds it hard to believe that such a small space appeared like a vast city to him. 'It is the same but yet it is not the same'[8] he concludes.

What do we hear?

The whole programme, including the continuity announcements, is just over 25 minutes long. It started out originally as a 54-minute programme made by the West German regional public service broadcaster *Hessischer Rundfunk* as part of a series entitled 'Lessons in German' (*Unterricht im Deutschen*). The programme, broadcast after the verdict of the Frankfurt trial had been announced on 26 June 1968, was called 'The camp works like this – Observations from the third Auschwitz Trial in Frankfurt'.[9] The version broadcast on *Deutsche Welle* in November of the same year had national and international audiences in mind, as DW broadcasts were – and are – transmitted on the medium- and short-wave bands.

The brief summary given above cannot do the programme justice. Even a complete transcript would fail to evoke the responses experienced by listening. Why this should be so is one of the great paradoxes of radio. On the one hand most radio listening occurs incidentally and is hardly noticed; while on the other close listening has a profound and immediate effect. In order to analyse the complex relationship between broadcaster and listener several initial distinctions will have to be made.

A radio broadcast relies on sound for the transmission of meaning. But meaning is transmitted without the aim of images or text, and as such it is a *blind* medium.[10] Its codes are exclusively auditory and – as in the case of this study, it would appear – predominantly verbal, and speech remains the fundamental determinant of meaning. But in the carefully constructed sound output of the radio there exists an additional layer of (constructed) meaning which might not be immediately obvious: the context of verbal meaning, sounds and sound effects, silence and music. The additional 'sign-postings' are necessary as the ear is profoundly unreliable as a sensory organ. In fact in studies conducted repeatedly by broadcasting organisations and academics alike on the comprehension of radio programmes, only about 28 percent of listeners could accurately recall what they had heard.[11]

This means that as well as 'Radio as Sound' the faculty of hearing, or the listening process, has to be taken into account. Without the distinctions between listening, overhearing and 'background noise', and even different degrees of listening, allocating 'extended signification' to the semiotic functions of words, sound and music will fail to reveal the radio listening experience. The varying levels of concentration and attention we can apply to radio listening depend therefore, very much on the sound-scape emerging from the radio set.

While the above programme does not appear to require 'radio listening beyond a solely linguistic level',[12] it does seem to invite the listener to do more than just understand words. As we listen to the pauses and contemplative 'ums' and 'ahs' in Paczula's recollection, Guthmann urges us to 'listen closely' (*Aber wer genau hinhört...*) at the end of the programme. The listener's attention is drawn not only by content and intonation of the statements, but is additionally requested by the narrating voice to pay close attention. This 'audio close-up' is just one of the many techniques used by radio journalists to go 'beyond the linguistic level'. Perhaps another one worth mentioning here, in connection with the above programme, is the transcribed sequence between Windeck and Minz: a chance recording, where the unbalanced recording levels of the hand-held microphone reinforce the excitement of the reporter and the people he is recording.

Radio broadcasts have long been a feature of our everyday experience, but rarely – and perhaps surprisingly – have they been considered as a historical source. The above broadcast tells us little of the events and circumstances surrounding the issue of Nazi trials in 1960s West Germany, nor of the debates and controversies that might have been aroused by the media coverage. But the specific interest of a radio programme lies in the fact that it can be consumed 'incidentally', as well as consciously, and by a much wider audience than any other medium. In the German postwar context this makes an investigation into the dissemination of information about the Holocaust on the radio an urgent and important task. Its focus should be on a consideration of the ways in which broadcasters and audiences dealt with the past of the perpetrator nation on the airwaves.

In order to contextualise the above programme, the following chapters offer a systematic and chronological study of the topic of how the Holocaust was represented on East and West German radio in the 1960s, incorporating theoretical considerations, the programmes themselves, background material and audience research up to the date of the transmission date of the broadcast cited above, with particular emphasis on the First Auschwitz Trial (1963–65) in Frankfurt/Main.

Aims and objectives

The aim of this study is to investigate the dissemination of information about the Holocaust on East and West German radio during the 1960s. Whereas the means of dissemination are technical (i.e. radio technology), the research presented here will concentrate particularly on the form, content and the effects of this dissemination. By concentrating on the Nazi crimes trials, it will analyse how radio broadcasts managed to influence historical understanding and consciousness of the Third

Reich and the process of coming to terms with it. There are a number of reasons for this undertaking:

First, as is implied by the book's title of 'The Undivided Sky', the radio's ability to transcend national and geographical boundaries makes it an intriguing focus for a study of the divided Germany. By the 1960s nearly all households in East and West Germany were possessed at least one radio set, making radio broadcasting into the prime instrument for the dissemination of information. While listening habits and the attitudes to radio output had changed somewhat over the period since the radio's inception, the 1960s nevertheless represented the zenith for radio audiences in East and West Germany.

Second, and following on from the above, this investigation will consider the role radio played in the ideological exchanges between the two Germanies. Whereas an obvious assumption would be that much of the broadcast material was aimed at the 'other' side, and that the objective of the respective broadcast authorities was one of ideological subversion, the true picture of the ideological dimension is more complex. While there undoubtedly were some – even substantial – parts of the transmitted output earmarked for this purpose, listening habits of radio audiences did not conform to this model. Therefore the topic chosen, or rather, that emerged from research, is the one of the recent shared past and its treatment on radio.

Third, the 1960s saw the emergence of an active process of 'coming-to-terms-with the past' (*Vergangenheitsbewältigung*) through judicial processes, particularly in the Federal Republic. Broadcasters could hope for large audiences as a result of the public interest created both nationally and internationally by the Eichmann Trial in Jerusalem. The heightened Cold War tensions of the newly built Berlin Wall and the Cuban Missile Crisis are very much in evidence throughout the broadcasts from the trials and surrounding topics. The period in question represents a time of increased 'ideological warfare' around the theme of the Nazi past, which is evident from the large number of programmes it produced.

Additionally, the study will look at the relationship between the broadcaster and the listener as it developed over time, particularly – but not exclusively – in Germany. The treatment of the topic of the Holocaust, as it evolved through ideological contortions of various narratives, engaged the listening public to reflect upon the German past through a series of 'audio-spectacles', epitomised by the sensationalist GDR propaganda broadcasts, which, from today's perspective, could be seen as the forerunners of the commodified Holocaust product.

Methodology

This project has raised some significant methodological difficulties. As the emphasis of research is focussed around individual programmes rather than programming structures and policies (although their influence is analysed), methods used by other commentators were of limited use. Of the little research that there is on radio – and even fewer publications using radio as a historical source – much of its methodology is centred around the *Annales* concept of the *longue durée*[13] or a Habermasian 'public sphere'.[14] Within the framework of this project neither of these concepts appear applicable, as the timeframe does not lend itself to the measurement of long, structural shifts, nor is there any evidence of a wider discourse regarding these specific programmes. Prominence here is given to the listening experience over a short period of time by a chronological arrangement of individual programmes, contrasting and comparing content and form. This sequential system allows for, and shows up, any changes broadcasters had to take into consideration, be it a shift in public opinion or a change in centrally co-ordinated policies. Whereas the impetus for and political slant of the production of these transmissions lies firmly with the journalists and broadcasters, the relationship between the broadcaster and listener carries additional significance here. To explore this, several theoretical models are used, as well as contemplations arising from other media, concentrating on the inter-German discourse on the Nazi past in public service broadcasting. This debate by the 'perpetrator nation' was far more diverse in Germany than in other parts of the world, both in the condemning – mainly by the broadcasters – and of the glorifying (or belittling) of the Nazi past – as voiced by some members of the 'public'. Exploring reception and audiences in this context has to remain speculative, but the model used here does not fall short of conclusions.

Another central aspect of this study is the use of radio programmes as primary historical sources. Whereas logically this seems like a very obvious choice of source material, very little broadcast material has been used in the construction of historical narratives. While to do this using only radio programmes would have been impossible, nevertheless I have attempted to incorporate as many broadcasts as possible, not only to assess their suitability but also – as much as possible – to re-create the listening experience. Therefore transcriptions include the mention of sound effects, music and pauses.

Overview

In the brief overview presented here of the chapters which follow this introduction, the works cited are primarily considered to give an outline of the project using reasonably well-known authors and relevant texts.

The following chapter, 'Radio and Modernity', traces the emergence of the relationship between broadcaster and listener, which will be explored over a number of decades, starting with Bertolt Brecht's pioneering *Radiotheorie* (1927–32), which welcomed the long-overdue (if somewhat antediluvian) invention of the radio.[15] Equally, the German writer and critic Walter Benjamin was an early enthusiast for the new medium and produced some original, if somewhat short, works for radio during the Weimar Republic, which attempted to reinforce their association with science and technology in an age of reason in order to create a populist, critical-practical political consciousness.[16]

But the initial pioneering spirit of the radio was soon tamed by its audience. In contrast to the USA, where radio developed through commercial stations, European state broadcasters had continued to view the medium as a means of educating and informing their citizens, but soon realised that the listener primarily wanted to be entertained. By the mid-1930s this mixture of education, information and entertainment had reached its zenith in the radio output of the German National Socialists and, more importantly, through the production of a cheap, mass-produced radio set, the *Volksempfänger*. 'All of Germany listens to the *Führer* on the *Volksempfänger*'[17] meant that much of the NSDAP's propaganda could penetrate most of the *Reich*, establishing the *Volksgemeinschaft* through the airwaves. A perceptive overview of these early days of German radio of the 1920s and 30s is offered by Konrad Dussel's 2002 publication *Hörfunk in Deutschland*[18] as well as by Kate Lacey's *Feminine Frequencies* (1996).[19] Transcribed excerpts from broadcasts of the time are made available through the publications of the German Radio Archive (DRA).[20]

The wartime experience of radio listening, however, produced a remarkable shift in the audiences' attitude to radio broadcasts, having to distinguish between home and enemy transmissions, and relying on the radio to assess chances of survival. The most comprehensive and analytical work published to date on the popular topic of radio propaganda in the Third Reich is the first publication in the *Zuhören und Gehörtwerden* series, *Radio im Nationalsozialismus*, edited by Adelheit von Saldern and Inge Marßoleck.[21] Additionally a number of biographical reminiscences and diaries about wartime radio listening have been consulted during the course of this study.[22]

Initially, postwar broadcasters and media commentators did not take this shift in the audiences' attitudes into account. In the light of the rise of Fascism and the remarkable reaction to the broadcast of Orson Welles' 'War of the Worlds' in 1938, radio audiences were still viewed as an easily malleable mass, incapable of critical listening. This view is central to the seminal work on radio in the 1940s, Adorno and Horkheimer's 'Culture Industry' chapter in *The Dialectic of Enlightenment*,[23] which has remained remarkably topical despite its emphasis on American radio; the dark, conspiratorial outlook is suitably appropriate for an enquiry into Cold War broadcasting. Adorno remains important throughout this research, not only as a media theorist but also as a commentator and contributor in the debate about the German past and as a voice on the radio.[24] Nevertheless the 'Culture Industry' approach does have its problems in this context. While some of Horkheimer's and Adorno's observations on radio are certainly accurate and insightful, they lack an understanding of the modern European models of broadcasting by continuously equating the Fascist experience with the corporation-controlled networked media 'culture industry' in the USA.

A more recent, more topical model, such as Marshall McLuhan's *Understanding Media* (1964) with its central dictum 'The Medium is the Message', adds some surprisingly original thoughts into the debate around radio broadcasting.[25] Much lauded at the time, McLuhan's publication was also heavily criticised because of its wide, populist approach, which attempted to find unifying formulae.[26] His analyses of radio, particularly of German radio, in the context of this study, appear simplistic at times, but his emphasis on the personal and intimate nature of radio listening forms a cornerstone of this research.

Andrew Crisell's *Understanding Radio* is perhaps the best-known current publication in English to deal exclusively with radio[27] and it is media theorists such as Crissell and Paddy Scannell[28] who offer contemporary insights into radio broadcasting, whilst broader approaches incorporating other media are to be found in Denis McQuail's publications[29] and in the work of systems theorist Niklas Luhmann.[30] Luhmann especially focuses on the specific nature of the dissemination of information through the mass media, which, in the context of this study, is particularly useful. This will be augmented by studies into news comprehension[31] as well as a look at the role ideology plays within broadcast language and the predictability and reassurance regular newscasts produce.[32]

Perhaps the most astonishing part of the DW programme above is the chance meeting between perpetrator and victim. This in itself makes it, one could argue, a valuable historical source. But is it? And of what? Without the context around the Third Auschwitz Trial and the prosecutions of Nazi criminals during the 1960s very little information can be gathered from the broadcast, even less from the above-mentioned sequence. The Nazi war crimes trials, starting with the International Military Tribunal in Nuremberg in 1945–47, and particularly in this context, the later wave of prosecutions in the early 1960s, were pivotal points in post-war history. The importance of the Frankfurt Trials became even more evident after the archival research, which clearly marked them as the main focus of the entire study. Subsequently, the history of 'Radio and the Holocaust' will be explored in chapter 3, starting with the transmissions from the Nuremberg trials 1945–47. Many of the (German language) broadcasts have recently been transcribed and published by the German Radio Archive.[33] The trial broadcasts were, at the time, the most immediate and widest link to the public in Germany, used by the Military authorities and German broadcasters as a powerful tool to establish the new, postwar order. Transcripts from these broadcasts reveal the initial similarities and growing disparities between the programmes from East and West German radio stations, particularly when looking at the interpretations of the origins and roots of National Socialism. Also reflected in the trial broadcasts are surprising insights and reflections on war guilt and repentance; a theme, it can safely be assumed, which found little resonance with the listeners, as was the case with a number of the initial postwar films, such as Wolfgang Staudte's *Die Mörder sind unter uns* (The Murderers are amongst us), and with philosophical contemplations in the form of Karl Jaspers' *Die Schuldfrage*[34] (The Question of Guilt).

It would be difficult to argue that this rejection was indicative of a recalcitrant National Socialist mindset of the general population, but rather than just appeasing the listeners with light entertainment (which, after all, was what the audiences wanted), the 1950s saw the theme of the Nazi past emerge in two, very distinct, versions on the radio: in the GDR the doctrine of anti-fascism was all-pervasive; in West Germany, contrastingly, consumerism prevailed, with the occasional debate around the concept of totalitarianism. This is dealt with effectively in Christoph Classen's *Faschismus und Antifaschismus*,[35] highlighting the pragmatic approaches to Marxism by the SED leadership and their skilled opportunism. For debates around radio in the early Federal Republic, Axel Schildt's *Moderne Zeiten*[36] takes a critical look at broadcasters and broadcast policies, augmented by the standard work on West German broadcasting, Hans Bausch's two volume *Rundfunk in Deutschland*.[37]

As historical sources these broadcasts not only reflect a 'sound-bite' of the time but also allow the historian access to somewhat more spontaneous and otherwise unavailable material,[38] exemplified – to name just one – by the programmes with the commentator and journalist Thilo Koch from the late 1950s, *'Hinter der Mauer des Schweigens'* (Behind the Wall of Silence) for the West German station NDR (*Norddeutscher Rundfunk*).[39] The politics of memory (*Vergangenheitspolitik*) of democratisation through integration (of former Nazis) – to use Norbert Frei's expression[40] – are not evident in most of the surviving programmes of the 1950s West German radio archives. Journalists and commentators, it appears, were at the forefront of hard-hitting investigations.

The programmes of the GDR radio stations are, at least to Western ears, perhaps the most surprising and informative.[41] The vocabulary sounds unfamiliar and the overtly ideological content remains astonishing. Additionally, even at a first encounter, the inferior technological production techniques are clearly audible, such as rough edits and rudimentary experiments with stereo recording.

Whereas the West German programmes fell upon deaf ears, so to speak, and GDR broadcasts dealing with the Nazi past only pointed to the West, it is the relationship between East and West German radio which became a focal point. A very small number of the general public listened to stations from the 'other' side of the 'Iron Curtain', and despite the lack of concrete evidence it is clear that news agencies, security services and journalists regularly retuned their sets to obtain alternative sources. Surviving transcripts and audio tape are indicative of the broadcasters' intentions for the audience they wish to address. By the beginning of the 1960s campaigns of defamation, predominantly but not exclusively from the East to the West, were part of daily broadcasts.[42]

In the context of this time the 'media event' was, without doubt, the Eichmann Trial in Jerusalem. Public opinion regarding Nazi crimes had already undergone a profound change since the 1958 Ulm *Einsatzgruppen* trial, and the spectacular kidnapping of Eichmann in Argentina had aroused even greater interest. But East Berlin had managed to focus international attention on the Adenauer government even before the Jerusalem Trial. The GDR's exposure of Dr Hans Maria Globke, Chancellor Adenauer's personal secretary, as the author of the commentary of the 1935 Nuremberg Race Laws, proved to be a valuable asset in the propaganda against the West. A remarkable number of programmes were made on this topic and some will feature here in this study. These transmissions continued even when the focus in the West had shifted to the upcoming first Auschwitz Trial in Frankfurt in December 1963.

The core of this study is in chapter 4, which contains the analysis of a series of chronologically arranged programmes from East and West German radio stations dealing with the First Auschwitz Trial, which took place between 1963 and 1965. While there have been many academic studies on this topic,[43] including a recent upsurge in English-language publications,[44] none have dealt with Nazi prosecutions in the divided Germany as reported on radio. A recent commemorative exhibition in the *Römer* in Frankfurt and the *Martin-Gropius-Bau* in Berlin produced some highly original sources from the Auschwitz Trial, collected together on an 800-page catalogue[45] and a DVD-ROM which holds over 70 of the 360 hours of the proceeding's audio taped material.[46] Although this audio evidence never formed part of any radio broadcast, it is nevertheless a very welcome addition to the methodological approach of this project as the impact of the voices of victims and perpetrators conveys the tense and chilling atmosphere of the courtroom.

As the much over-used term *Vergangenheitsbewältigung* implies, a 'coming-to-terms-with the past' required an active engagement with the period of the Nazi dictatorship and radio, at least theoretically – and in the opinion of the broadcasters – ideally lent itself to this purpose, as every household in East and West Germany was in the possession of at least one radio set. Moreover the 'consumption' of radio programmes, in as much as such a term can be used, can be incidental and unobtrusive. A controversial radio programme is far less likely to turn the audience against the broadcaster than is television, while remaining effective. Despite the recent change in public attitude, public service radio had not forgotten the unpopularity of the immediate post-war broadcasts and the initial (pre-trial) programmes appear distinctly timid. This carefulness, however, changes through the period of the proceedings as the details of the Auschwitz death camp emerge in the courtroom. By the end of the 1960s the liberal consensus is clearly audible on the airwaves, although in a somewhat ideologically contorted version. 'The battle for hearts and minds' had different connotations in Germany, but the overall rhetoric behind this dictum of Cold War broadcasters remained firmly lodged in the antagonisms of super-power rivalry.

In the context of the Auschwitz Trial – and other NS prosecutions – the resulting verdicts (mild in the West and harsh in the East) were attributed to Cold War tensions[47] and some commentators have argued that a retrospective condemnation of German (in particular West German) justice fails to accommodate the realities of the era.[48] This uncritical acceptance of the justice system and the Trial's verdict, however, does not come across in the radio programmes dealing with the Auschwitz Trial. The enigmatic figure of the Prosecutor-General of Hesse, Dr Fritz Bauer, asserts influence over all commentators, pointing to the inadequacies of the judicial systems. And journalists such as the NDR's Axel Eggebrecht do not shirk from detailed analysis into the nature of German society, anti-Semitism and the problems surrounding the possibility of a meaningful restitution.[49]

The programmes chosen here represent a cross-section of the material found in the archives, selected on the criteria of relevance (to the trials), content (startling or otherwise), prominence of the speakers, technical production and overall coherence. Most of the material cited survived in the form of audio tape. Transcripts were, on the whole, not available and transcription became a laborious and time-consuming, but nevertheless worthwhile process. Additionally the contextualisation of each programme remained important, not so much in terms of programming schedules but in terms of content and consistency. The daily commentaries which were a standard feature of East and West German radio, usually in the form of a three- to five-minute addition after the main newscast, would have been a source of great interest, but unfortunately very few of these were kept. Longer programmes survived, mainly in the form of documentaries and 'features', but also in the form of long reports and recordings of discussions. Together these programmes will represent the historical sources forming the narrative of and around the Auschwitz Trial. The question which arises here of course is: how were they received and What influence did they have?

Radio audience research, or, more precisely, investigations into the perception of specific programmes is virtually impossible. The surprisingly few listeners' letters kept by the various radio stations usually referred to very trivial matters. Only a handful of letters on the topic are to be found at the German Radio Archive in Potsdam-Babelsberg (*Deutsches Rundfunkarchiv*), and these are letters concerning the transmission of Peter Weiss' play *Die Ermittlung* (The Investigation),[50] a play based on the Frankfurt court proceedings, which was performed on stage, radio and television in October 1965.[51] Undoubtedly there must have been some reactions to the often very controversial topics arising from the subject matter of the Nazi past, and it can equally be taken for granted that broadcasters took note of them. By exploring the differences between initial and subsequent programmes, examining the (often very coherent) programming policies of public service broadcasters in Germany as well as using a range of audience research numbers, opinion polls and interviews with the general public, a profile of possible audience reception is drawn up in the penultimate chapter entitled 'Radio and Memory'. Some remarkable qualitative assessments of public opinion were conducted in the form of the1955 *Gruppenexperiment*, a research project led by Friedrich Pollock and Theodor W. Adorno.[52] Surprisingly only one similar study from the following decade remains in existence,[53] whereas a much later study on the transmission of family wartime history, the 2002 *Opa war kein Nazi* (Grandpa was no Nazi), indicates just how flexible and malleable 'public' opinion could be.[54] How much radio played a part in the shifts in opinion which occurred also remains impossible to pinpoint. As many studies have shown, most people do not associate 'listening to the radio' as a specific activity and therefore cannot accurately place and source the received information. Yet radio remains one of the most 'consumed' media for the dissemination of information, and particularly in the divided Germany of the 1960s it was predominant. The model used here to examine the relationship between audience and broadcaster remains a tentative one, but avoids the even vaguer speculation into the 'subliminal' nature of radio transmissions. The building of a 'collective memory' through a wider debate on the radio did not, it appears, take place. Instead the relationship between the broadcaster and the listener – a private sphere – materialises through the introduction of mobile (transistor radio) technology.

To end the study and draw conclusions I return to the *Deutsche Welle* programme cited above, looking more closely at the historical circumstances surrounding the trial and the verdict. The timespan up to the programme's transmission date of November 1968 is one of the most interesting periods of broadcast history and forms a turning point in the postwar German assessment of the past. The final chapter of this book, 'Radio and History', will reflect on the role radio played in this process, focusing in particular on the development of an immediate historical consciousness, and on how the medium is used in the writing of history. By having made a conscious decision to concentrate on the controversial topic of the Holocaust and Nazi crimes trials, methods and processes contained within radio broadcasting and radio listening are explored in their relationship to postwar German society. The juxtaposition of ideological interpretations of the Holocaust and the National Socialist dictatorship exposes the complexities involved in the relationship between broadcaster and listener in the Germanies of the 1960s, revealing an unstable, but gradually increasingly coherent approach to the past.

The initial hypothesis of the title 'The Undivided Sky' – the radio's ability to transcend physical boundaries, and, in the divided Germany of the Cold War, to present an immeasurable opportunity for influence and ideological subversion – now appears somewhat inadequate. In the light of these bipolar interpretations of the Holocaust the process of *Vergangenheitsbewältigung* that established itself in the 1960s owed much to the radio broadcasters and their programmes. As will be shown in the following chapters, this process became an active and involved interchange between audiences and broadcasters – learning and evolving not only through the technological advances of the age, but also using them to come to terms with the complexities of the legal and ethical considerations required for the nation that had perpetrated the Holocaust to embrace genuine repentance and atonement.

2
Radio and Modernity

Radio as the agent of modernity

Modernity, however it is understood, has strong connections to technology. The technological aspects of modernity, or modernisation, are generally viewed as the advances made which distinguish our time from the less technologically advanced antiquity. Or in other words, the awareness of this distinction, modernity as opposed to antiquity, gives rise to a sense of history. Modernity, therefore, can be viewed as the self-conscious placing of oneself in history and the experience of the 'now'. Whether this represents 'progress' or 'decline' is the subject of much debate, but, however viewed, modernity represents technological change and, with it, upheaval. All aspects which contribute to a definition of modernity have this awareness of technological change. In economical, social, cultural and intellectual terms modernity draws a radical distinction between itself and earlier times, emphasising reason and innovation. Detlef Peukert, in his *The Weimar Republic: The Crisis of Classical Modernity* (1991), offers the following definition:

> In an economic sense, modernity is characterised by highly rationalised industrial production, complex technological infrastructures and a substantial degree of bureaucratised administrative and service activity; food production is carried out by an increasingly small, but productive, agricultural sector. Socially speaking, its typical features include the division of labour, wage and salary discipline, an urbanised environment, extensive educational opportunities and a demand for skills and training. As far as culture is concerned, media products dominate; continuity with traditional aesthetic principles... is replaced by unrestricted formal experimentation. In intellectual

terms, modernity marks the triumph of western rationality, whether in social planning, the expansion of the sciences or the self-replicating dynamism of technology, although this optimism is accompanied by sceptical doubts from social thinkers and cultural critics.[1]

Through the *domination of media products,* from newspapers to radio, the ideology of the *triumph of western rationality* is celebrated. The *self-replicating dynamism of technology* announces and advertises itself through media products and although the media themselves become merely functional in this process, they are vital in the procedure of proselytising the new technologies based on scientific reasoning.

Through these technological advances there occurs a separation of time and place, a dislocation (or 'dis-embedding'), which manifests itself through increasingly fast transport and travel systems, at the same time as a compression of space and time through the intrusion and dissemination of 'distant' information.[2] Radio broadcasting, in this context, is the clearest expression of modernity.

But above all, radio, along with most other innovations of modernity, accelerates historical time, increasing the speed of the flow of information and the analysis thereof. Koselleck writes:

> Historical times can be identified if we direct our view to where time itself occurs or is subjectively enacted in humans as historical beings: in the relationship between past and future, which always constitutes an elusive present. The compulsion to coordinate past and future so as to be able to live at all is inherent in any human being. Put more concretely, on the one hand, every human being and every human community has a space of experience out of which one acts, in which past things are present or can be remembered, and, on the other, one always acts with reference to specific horizons of expectation... That historical time occurs within the difference between these two temporal dimensions [past and future] can already be shown by the fact that the difference between experience and expectation itself changes – that is, it is specifically historical.[3]

The analytical investigation between experience and expectations, up until early modern times, Koselleck argues, remained linear, that is to say, nothing fundamentally new could be expected until the Day of Judgement (in Christian terms), and that chronological time would maintain its relationship with historical time. But with the technological and scientific developments of the Enlightenment, modernity changed this linear relationship. The future has become more unknowable and tradition has ceased to be the guiding experience:

> For in Modernity (*Moderne*), as it is shaped by science, technology and industry, the future in fact implies different and new things, which cannot be derived from experience. Precisely the impossibility of foreseeing technical inventions has become a principle derived from experience, and permanently keeps open the difference between past and future.[4]

But this openness to the future was counterbalanced by the development of the modern capitalist industrial society, which heavily relied on predictability and precision. Analyses of the development of work practices in industrial capitalism[5] point to the change from task-orientation to a time-based one; a change which was initially helped with the greater availability of watches, and with a wider availability of radio receivers in the twentieth century the social organisation of time began to depend on technologies such as the radio. This 'domestication of standard national time'[6] on the radio, with constant time-checks and repetitions of schedules on a daily and weekly basis not only furthered capitalist production by bringing the modern industrial world into the home itself, but also offered the reassurance of the consistency of chronological time in the light of a more uncertain future. Whereas it could be argued that chronological (clock) time is the very organising principle of modernity, Koselleck's differentiation between historical and chronological time draws up a useful distinction in how time is experienced, subjective historical time counterbalanced by the objective chronological time.

The subjective experience of time is very much evident when listening to the radio. Whereas the constant reminders of time around the newscasts will remind us how time passes, as soon as a report or programme begins, the pace of time, through the necessary suspension of disbelief, will be experienced differently. The immediacy of the broadcast lifts us out of the immediacy of our own lives, a temporal and spatial dislocation, while firmly lodged in chronological time. And this paradox appears more likely to be the principle of modernity, concurrently dis-organising and structuring. Uncertainty and reassurance, firmly lodged together through technology. The dialectical nature of the radio-listening process is congruent with a 'dialectic of enlightenment'; the positivist belief in progress and reason which is entwined in myth and barbarity.

The following deliberations on theoretical models of radio broadcasting within their historical settings aim to explore as well as to situate the radio into a wider framework of theory and technology. Whereas most models fail to incorporate all aspects of radio broadcasting and the relationship between broadcaster and audience, they nevertheless always add to earlier considerations, and in this way can be viewed as cumulative and progressive.

Brecht and Benjamin

When public radio broadcasting first emerged after the First World War,[7] its immediate importance was far from clear. Having had an experimental phase during the war, the technological equipment was still relatively expensive and cumbersome, and ownership of radio receivers had to be encouraged.[8]

What to broadcast also represented a challenge; should radio be used as an arena of commerce (advertising) or be strictly regulated in the hands of government and authority? The radio, with its disregard for physical and social boundaries, certainly possessed the qualities which could make it an instrument to further mass politics and mass consumption. Early interest in the new medium was limited to a few enthusiasts in the USA, who saw its commercial potential, and in Britain opposition to it came from the newspapers, which led to the formation of the BBC, aiming to keep commercial advertising interests out of the reporting of news.[9]

Theoretical considerations about the nature of broadcasting were few, although regulations were quickly put in place to prevent its misuse.[10] Its use as 'paperless' newspaper was easily understood by Lenin and the Comintern, not only for agitational purposes, but also due to the consistent shortage of paper in the USSR.[11] The Soviet broadcasters were in fact the first to utilise the medium to cover the vast distances to the east by developing short-wave radio. This was extended to broadcasting to the West after 1925 by the Comintern Radio. In Germany listeners' groups quickly formed around these broadcasts, which were being condemned by the government as 'being harmful to family life'.[12] Admired and demonised, the advent of the radio certainly received a popular response, despite (or because of) the absence of theory.

In the atmosphere of technological innovation and renewal of the Weimar Republic the German playwright Bertolt Brecht wrote his *Radiotheorie* (radio theory) between 1927 and 1932. Brecht was initially extremely sceptical of the new medium of radio. After conceding that it was not just a fashionable, but a truly modern invention, he voiced his doubts: it is an 'antediluvian' invention, which had long been forgotten, now rediscovered. Radio, like so many bourgeois inventions, is judged by its possibilities, not by its results, and therefore deemed to be a 'Good Thing'. With this he disagrees. He hopes that through the growth of radio the listeners will realise that, when this caste (the bourgeoisie) managed to broadcast its message around the globe, it would become clear that it had nothing to say.[13] The decision of the German broadcasters not to allow a pluralistic political debate on the airwaves made it politically intolerant. This did not elude Brecht: 'For someone, who has something to say, having no listeners is terrible. But what is worse is having listeners, who can't find anyone to listen to.'[14]

Already encumbered by the existing political and cultural practices of the Weimar Republic, radio broadcasting served up a mixture of information (news) and entertainment, which lent itself readily to propaganda, Brecht noted. The (ideology-forming) cultural institutions are at great pains to convey an education which remains without consequence, culture is assumed to be without ideology and therefore inconsequential. Radio, in this context, remains purely 'decorative' and only through a direct engagement with the audience will the radio become instructive and enlightening.[15]

Brecht's enormously innovative and original radio production about Charles Lindbergh's first solo flight across the Atlantic deserves some attention. In collaboration with the composers Paul Hindemith and Kurt Weill this complex 'multi-media experience' incorporated the radio and the radio listener on stage with the actors and orchestra, at the same time as being broadcast to listeners at home. The interaction is divided between, on the one hand, the performers producing the music and the sound effects and, on the other, the listeners, involved in following the hero, the pilot, by speaking his part (as chorus or individually). This, Brecht believed, would incorporate entertainment with pedagogy, and would change radio broadcasting itself, by encouraging, as he put it, 'a rebellion of the listener' (*Ein Aufstand des Hörers*).[16] Changing the radio from a distribution-machine to a communication-machine was the task of the progressive broadcaster.[17]

But there still remained the crucial problem of what to broadcast. Brecht had likened the arrival of the radio to an artist being given a huge space with nothing to exhibit: 'A difficult job and an unhealthy production'.[18] If indeed the radio, a product of (scientific) western rationality, placed the listener self-consciously in history and the experience of the 'now', then how should this be done?

This complex and paradoxical relationship of the listener with the radio was deliberated on by the German philosopher and critic (and close collaborator of Brecht's at the time) Walter Benjamin, who had a much more positive attitude towards the radio and its technology. Benjamin always strived for a synthesis in cultural-technical developments,[19] and realised that the popularity of the radio depended mostly on keeping the listener entertained.[20]

Whereas Brecht was only briefly involved with the actual radio production with his Lindbergh project (*Ozeanflug*), Benjamin, having rejected a university career, spent a good five years or more in radio, writing and broadcasting for children and adults. Through his friend Ernst Schoen, programme director at the newly established radio service for the south west of Germany SWR (*Südwestdeutsche Rundfunkdienst AG*) in Frankfurt, Benjamin first ventured into broadcasting in 1925. By 1927 he was firmly engaged by radio stations in Frankfurt and Berlin, writing material, according to Schoen's dictum, 'to give each listener what (s)he wants, and a little more (of what we want)'.[21] Benjamin appeared in and wrote over a hundred radio programmes, these included many children's plays – such as *Radau um Kasperl, Das Kalte Herz* – but also programmes of literary criticism on Brecht and Kracauer, as well as experimental programmes, the 'Listening Models' (*Hörmodelle*).[22] This much-overlooked part of Benjamin's work has been explored through the publication of Sabine Schiller-Lerg's extensive investigation into Benjamin's radio work in 1984.[23] Central to Benjamin's understanding of the radio was a theme which late crystallised in his 'The Work of Art in the Age of Mechanical Reproduction': The totalising force of the consumer logic (*Warenlogik*), which he terms *Phantasmagorie*, is upheld and transmitted by technology – such as the radio, and placed within the realm of culture. This 'cultural disguise of production technology' lulls the recipient (listener): Instead of contemplation the new mass audience reacts with consumption and diversion (*Zerstreuung*).[24] The new cultural products emerging in this 'Age of Mechanical Reproduction' all serve a political function through the politicisation of aesthetics, and ultimately, in the aestheticisation of politics, leading to war. To counteract this, and to take a stand, Benjamin's experiments with sound in a 'didactic' setting sail close to Brecht's *Lehrstücke*, but Benjamin saw their function more as self-help than obvious political indoctrination. Engaging the listener to think critically, even in his children's plays, Benjamin involved the (child) protagonist within the world of the radio, reminding the audience of broadcasting studios, microphones, cables and machinery. At all times the listener is reminded that a voice comes through a box, which receives a signal from a transmitter, which was a long distance away, and that at a distance from the transmitter is the studio, where people are speaking into microphones. This 'alienation' technique (*Entfremdung*), or the absence of an encouragement to 'suspend disbelief', was remarkably modern. Benjamin saw the technique of radio production as being closely related to the theatre: For the first time the audience is able to participate actively and practically *as audience* through the reception of the artistic process. 'In relation to the theatre radio represents not only the newer, but also the most exposed technique.'[25] This method of active 'listening with' (*mithören*) is exemplified in his *Hörmodelle*, in which not only speakers, characters and announcers address the listener directly, but also, as part of the programme, incorporate a discussion of the just-listened-to with real or imaginary representatives of the audience.[26]

Although Benjamin viewed the radio as basically populist (*volkstümlich*), in one of his last theoretical considerations about radio, 'Two Types of Populism' (*Zweierlei Volkstümlichkeit*), he argues that the medium of radio best lends itself to explaining and popularising science, by binding the listener to the process of broadcasting and involving the audience with the science of (and on) the radio. But the restrictions of radio technology – the absence of a clearly interactive process – were also the restrictions which lay in the false assumption that a general dissemination of (scientific) knowledge would achieve empowerment. Without application of knowledge there would be no access to power.[27] Therefore Benjamin's conception of 'politicising entertainment' concerned itself with creating a critical-practical political consciousness to accommodate knowledge. This predates by some 10 years his 'The Work of Art in the Age of Mechanical Reproduction' thesis IV, in which he wrote:

> But the instant the criterion of authenticity ceases to be applicable in artistic production, the total function of art is reversed. Instead of being based on ritual, it begins to be based on another practice – politics.[28]

It is perhaps not surprising that, despite the Marxist credentials of both Brecht and Benjamin, Weimar radio was dubbed 'broadcasting for the educated classes' (*Rundfunk für Bildungsbürger*)[29] by radio historians, as the obsession with the radio's potential for education and cultural enrichment led to a neglect of news, current affairs and political analysis.[30] Hans Bredow (1879–1959), the first State Secretary for Broadcasting in the Weimar republic, viewed the possibility of political subversion of the emerging radio transmissions as potentially dangerous[31] and censorship was divided between police and the 'culture councils' (*Kulturräte*),[32] ensuring that Weimar radio remained a 'politics-free zone'.

But a form of ritual remains in the radio-listening process, perhaps because of its immediacy, perhaps because in the secular age listening to the newscast to hear that 'all is well' has replaced the need for prayer/thanksgiving. This reassurance/unsettling dichotomy is at the very heart of the ritual of 'consuming' the news: the same format, order, jingle. For many listeners it is more the observance of the ritual of 'listening to the news' than the content of the news itself. Form becomes content. Therefore the ritualistic aspect of radio news depends on transmitting ideology, of how things should be and are not otherwise or elsewhere.[33]

Thus the radio, by enabling us to 'know what is going on in the world', is instantly creating a worldview that is almost mythical (or antediluvian, to use the term employed by Brecht). And even with a critical distance from the technology and production processes the radio announces the triumph of science and enlightened reason, while at the same time seduces us to accept a mythical world in a daily ritual.

Whereas the cinema (or the theatre for that matter) placed the audience in a darkened auditorium and asked them to suspend their disbelief for a certain period of time, the radio created a world in the listeners' minds, which could act as the conscience, conversation partner, authority figure and educator. The world created by the listening experience pronounced the triumph of technology and reason through its own existence whilst at the same time denying reason a critical stance towards it by lulling the listener into fantasies and affirming the status quo.

With its essentially populist nature, radio broadcasting regulations were very much subject to control by either government in Europe or commercial sponsors in the United States. But neither in Europe nor in the USA did this lead to a free interchange of ideas between the listener and the broadcaster. '[The radio] democratically makes everyone equally into listeners, in order to expose them in authoritarian fashion to the same programmes put out by different stations.'[34]

While this was written in the USA in the late 1930s, at the height of the new commercial stations, cost was a considerable factor – transmitters were infinitely more expensive than receivers – and it was primarily in the interests of the government or the companies owning the stations to have a malleable and acquiescent listening public, which was compliant and bought the advertised products. The ease with which radio can be listened to, the little effort it takes, produces an atmosphere of uncritical obedience:

> Each single manifestation of the culture industry inescapably reproduces human beings as what the whole has made them. And all its agents, from the producer to the women's organisations, are on the alert to ensure that simple reproduction of mind does not lead on to the expansion of mind.[35]

But the voice of the radio had become affirmative and also authoritative. The easy mixture of information and entertainment, which merged news with the 'Viennese waltz and the recipe book' (Brecht), this 'colossal triumph of technology' quietly became an everyday experience. News as entertainment and entertainment as news. Or as Horkheimer and Adorno argue,

> Entertainment is the prolongation of work under late capitalism. It is sought by those who want to escape the mechanised labour process so that they can cope with it again... The only escape from the work process in factory and office is through adaptation to it in leisure time. This is the incurable sickness of all entertainment.[36]

Any critical absorbing of information or an engaging with the broadcaster would be reduced to meaningless chatter, which remains inconsequential.

> The non-committal vagueness of the resulting ideology does not make it more transparent, or weaker. Its very vagueness, the quasi-scientific reluctance to be pinned down to anything which cannot be verified, functions as an instrument of control. Ideology becomes the emphatic and systematic proclamation of what is. Through its inherent tendency to adopt the tone of some factual report, the culture industry makes itself the irrefutable prophet of the existing order.[37]

Nazi radio

After achieving power in January 1933 the Nazis moved quickly to politicise the airwaves. By March Goebbels had secured control of programming, and the post of commissioner of broadcasting (Bredow's former post of State Secretary for Broadcasting) was abolished.[38] Political control of the radio went to the Ministry of Propaganda under the leadership of the NSDAP 'old fighter' Horst Dreßler-Andreß. All press agencies came under state control and were integrated into the Ministry. What is surprising, however, is that the *Gleichschaltung* of the broadcasting authorities and radio stations required remarkably little effort. A recent study revealed that in 1936 the entire radio department in the Propaganda Ministry consisted of only eight persons, and remained at this strength until the outbreak of the war. It has to be assumed, Dussel notes correctly, that there was little resistance to the Nazi propaganda efforts and that they were, on the whole, willingly – and voluntarily – executed.[39]

The effect of the newly politicised radio was enormous. The National Socialists embraced radio technology wholeheartedly. Hitler equated the radio to artillery barrages to 'psychologically wear down the enemy',[40] and (Nazi) party radio enthusiasts called for an end of the 'Bredow System' which they accused of 'Jewish interbreeding and cultural Bolshevism', as well as 'of sabotaging the National Socialist elevation (*Erhebung*).'[41] Radio stations now came under the umbrella organisation of the *Reichsrundfunkgesellschaft* (*RRG*). Additionally, by Autumn 1933, all employers and employees in 'the arts' were organised into a corporate unit, the *Reichskulturkammer,* consisting of sections for Written Word, Press, Theatre, Film, Music, Fine Arts and Radio.[42] This meant that any attempts to hide ideological indoctrination could now be dropped and the radio now achieved its full propaganda function, as the following broadcast from November 1933 by the NSDAP ideologue Julius Streicher illustrates:

> Who is it, who doesn't want peace on earth? Who is it, who exploits disunity between peoples to pursue selfish goals? It is the nation of the Jews (*das Volk der Juden*). It is those people, who, strewn among all other nations, live off the sweat and labour of others. It is those people who promised themselves to be chosen to be the masters of this earth. A chosen nation which eats other nations! Walther Rathenau, a member of the Jewish race, once revealed who pulls the strings of world politics. He wrote: 300 men rule the fate of the earth. 300 men, who know each other, nothing happens without their say. Yes, nowadays nothing happens on this planet without the knowledge of the Jewish people and nothing without the participation of the Jewish race. It was the Jewish people who created disunity among peoples. It is the Jewish people who create

public opinion, as a state within the state. It is the Jewish people who promote eternal strife in the world. The German people have decided to rid themselves of the Jewish yoke in their country. And because the German people have broken Jewish rule in their country, other countries are supposed to give the death knell to the German nation.

In the protocols of the Zionist Congress of Basel it is written: As soon as a non-Jewish state dares to offer resistance to the Jews, we have to be in a position to convince neighbouring states to start a war against it. If the neighbouring states want to join such a nation, we have to unleash a world war. The First World War and its misery has entered our history. There should and must not be a second.

People of Europe! Your arch enemy are the Jewish people! The German nation has dared to confront them. It will see to it that the knowledge of the Jewish foe will become the knowledge of all nations. This understanding will and has to break through, so that the nations will have peace, and can join hands to destroy the might of those people, of whom Christ himself said '[whose] father is the devil.'[43]

The problem of affordable radio receivers was still relatively acute, and the solution was provided by the Ministry of Popular Enlightenment and Propaganda (*Reichsministerium für Volksaufklärung und Propaganda, RMVP*). Under the slogan 'The Führer's voice in every home and factory', a cheap radio set, the *Volksempfänger* (people's receiver) was now made available to all.[44] This was a good-quality radio set which sold in millions. Radio ownership more than doubled from 4,533,000 sets in 1933 to 9,575,000 in 1938.[45] After 1935 loudspeakers were erected in public places to penetrate the public, as well as the private sphere. Radio listening became proscriptive concerning what the listeners should be doing while listening: during light entertainment and music housework could be undertaken; mechanical and undemanding tasks could be done during scientific and cultural programmes; while political programmes had to be listened to without distraction.[46]

In Nazi Germany the radio also became the instrument for the eulogising of 'traditional' family values while simultaneously undermining them, by recruiting family members into the various NS organisations: men into the party or the SS, women into the women's organisation, boys into the Hitler Youth and girls into the BDM (*Bund Deutscher Mädel*). In the party's demand for total loyalty to the Führer the radio simultaneously reinforced and substituted the patriarchal family.[47]

The all-pervasive radio broadcasts became more aggressive and confrontational in tone and content. Streicher's speeches in particular, were popular because of their often vulgar and offensive vocabulary, sparing no-one:

> ...And since time immemorial Satan has been the Jew. (*applause*). And when down there in Italy the head of some international church says, that if one confesses to the race question, to God; just look at it, the Pope is in favour that blacks, Negroes, Mongols, Jews, apes should join together, should mix, he says that's fine as long as they are christened just like I want it [to be]. (*laughter*) So, if one professes to belong to those who are in favour of mixing it all up, as the Jew wants it, and as today the Vatican, then you are pious, then you have religion. But if you belong to those who say: If creation had wanted to mix black with white and green and blue people, then Nature would have taken care of it. If there are people who say, Nature wants separation, so the worthwhile can survive in this world; if you say this, if you say that Jewish race defilement (*Rassenschande*) is race-crime, then you have no religion, then you go to hell. Well, I belong to those, and Farinacci doubly so. In the Vatican's view Farinacci should be burned at the stake (*laughter*)...[48]

Whereas Streicher's rhetoric was colloquial and informal, other party leaders – and this included Hitler – used their speeches to incite hatred as a part of a comprehensive party programme. None of them, however, had managed to acquire the 'fire-side manner' technique which so endeared Roosevelt to the American population; instead Nazi speeches were recorded at rallies with large audiences. It is noticeable that by May 1939 the broadcast language had become increasingly violent, even though war was not expected by most Germans. NSDAP leaders' speeches such as the one by Robert Ley below, could be listened to on the radio,[49] but not read in print:

> And everybody was now convinced that you don't get nothing from nothing, there is no manna from heaven. And I believe it never fell from heaven. I just don't believe it (*applause*). I believe that it was a Jewish concept, like all these visions of paradise dished out to people to keep them from reality. No, the Germans now understood: If this nation wants to have standing in the world, that it needs, that it requires, not out of a quirk of power-politics, but established through

a fundamental right of existence, then it must fight, struggle, work and engage, and keep discipline. And avoid everything that would hamper this struggle. In an instant the nation understood who its enemies were: the worldview of the Jew, the people knew it. There could be no compromise between it and its life-negating world, and there never will be. If other people want to live, the Jews must be destroyed, that is the lesson.[50]

Anti-Semitic rhetoric and fascist ideology on the radio was not, however, restricted to Germany. In the 1930s the USA was also to witness a number of attempts to achieve political indoctrination through wireless broadcasts. Whilst having established its 'voice of authority' in an earlier stage of broadcasting, the quasi-religious broadcasts of Martin Luther Thomas on networked radio were stirring the fascist audiences in America. Theodor W. Adorno's 1943 study of these broadcasts concentrates on form and rhetorical devices, such as revelation and confession, quickly finding the parallels between them and Hitler's. Communism is equated with a Jewish bankers' conspiracy along the lines of the *Protocols of the Elders of Zion*. Under the cloak of being an expression of democracy, Thomas' broadcasts found their audiences in the middle-aged and elderly, lower middle-class people with a strong fundamentalist or sectarian background:

> The ultimate aim of Thomas' propaganda is authority by brutal, sadistic oppression. This is the focal point, the unifying principle that rules his theology and his politics, his psychology and his morals. Among his stimuli the concept of severe punishment in time and eternity is decisive. His descriptions of torture are minute in detail… The future of America of which he warns is depicted in not altogether different terms: 'One of these fine mornings you men and women will rise with no stocks and no bonds and no home and your backs will be placed against a wall with a machine gun bullet in your heart and in your head.' One may well expect that the audience projects this image upon their foes and thus enjoys it. Thomas almost openly professes this ambivalence towards atrocities in one of his anti-Soviet diatribes: 'I want to say that you men and women, you and I are living in the most fearful time in the history of the world. We are also living in the most gracious and the most wonderful time.' This is the agitator's dream, the unification of the horrible and the wonderful, the drunkenness of an annihilation that pretends to be salvation.[51]

What emerges is a reality that is specific to the experience of radio listening. The words of the broadcasts stay with the listener, stored for whatever eventuality, to be transformed into action. In a broadcast from 16 June 1935, transcribed by Adorno, Thomas' anti-Semitic rants are hardly distinguishable from broadcasts in Germany:

> But, my friend, the hour is not far away, when the armies yonder of the Gentile worlds in that great battle of Armageddon, which will come in my opinion in the next great world war, the Jews shall be gathered in that land. They shall be besieged upon every hand, and they shall fall upon their faces, and in their hour of extreme necessity, they will call upon God and God will answer from Heaven; and Jesus Christ, whom they have rejected, their elder brother, shall come with a mighty delivering power.[52]

The legislation which forbade Thomas from being openly anti-Semitic is circumnavigated by putting it into a biblical and religious context. Declaring that 'Communism is nothing more or less than the synagogue of Satan that our Lord spoke about' actually avoids equating Jews with Communism directly, but the implication is there, and it will stay in the listeners' mind.[53] Rhetorical devices work best on the radio as the speaker has the undivided attention of the listener without being seen or interrupted. The listener, on the other hand, experiences a 'cognitive slippage' through the continuous and 'inconsequential' commentary, only vaguely remembering key phrases or concepts.

But in Germany and occupied Europe, Nazi radio broadcasts called openly for murder:

> This is how, people, we will build a new nation. Building a new work, building a social empire, building a Europe where the Jew has no home and nothing to say, but they get a yellow star, and soon they won't even have that, because they will not be here anymore, they will have to vanish, they will have to be destroyed. (*applause*) I say this openly and freely, because I know that there is no other solution. Freeloaders, parasites, lice and fleas and vermin have to be exterminated and nothing else (*applause*). Until then there will be no rest, no peace among men![54]

It is notable, however, that the actual words such as 'kill' ,'murder' and the like are rarely used and euphemisms and metaphors come into play.[55]

During the war the radio listening experience started to require a decoding of ideological content. Military defeats were announced as 'strategic advances' and conquest as 'liberation'. Mihail Sebastian's diaries of his war experiences in Romania make a telling tale,[56] as do Helga Maria Wolf's account of Austrian listeners, *Auf Ätherwellen* (On the Ether Waves).[57] Wherever possible, listeners would tune into as many radio stations as they could, trying to ascertain a coherent and correct picture, as now their lives depended on it. The process of rallying the nation behind the government was the prime objective for domestic broadcasters, but, aware of foreign listeners, and also aiming at them, the wartime public broadcasters of all belligerent nations were producing 'black' and 'grey' broadcasts, which were programmes sounding like the domestic ones of enemy nations, transmitted on identical or nearby frequencies, spreading dis-information. This made it even more difficult to get a clear picture, as well as the abundance of 'enemy' broadcasts, the most well known being Lord Haw Haw, broadcasting to Britain to sway opinion.[58]

The battle on air was conducted not only with newscasts and commentaries, but increasingly with entertainment. The little jazz and dance music that was considered 'Aryan' enough to be played on the German radio was often broadcast to the rest of Europe.[59] Conversely, the BBC and American broadcasters, well aware of the popularity of jazz on the Continent, broadcast as much jazz (and light-hearted commentary) as possible to subvert Nazi ideology. But it produced in the audience a cynicism, which is best summed up by the German author Erich Kästner, who, at the end of the war, wrote in his diary on 30 April 1945:

> It was a quiet day (*ein stummer Tag*). Not only had the Munich radio station shut up, the foreign stations weren't there either. The lies on the air, the coarsest and the subtlest, can be interpreted, the big silence presented a puzzle... During the day the Munich station remained silent for hours. It was as if it was broadcasting silence. Then, at 10 at night, we were sitting in the Waldcafé, it suddenly stirred again. And what did it play? 'Hot' music! First silence without commentary, then un-German jazz without words, what has happened?[60]

The coarsest and subtlest lies could be interpreted, but not silence. The integration of the radio into everyday life was now complete. The running commentary to our daily lives by the radio could not be stopped; stopping it would create a crisis. Had listening to the radio become the only way to place ourselves in history, making us experience modernity? Did the experience of the 'now' depend on the radio receiver?

Theoretical approaches

Despite its title, Brecht's *Radiotheorie* could not really be considered a worked out theoretical model, primarily due to its brevity. The relative absence of theory concerning radio suggests that the incorporation of this medium into our lives was a long overdue process;[61] its very rapid uptake and popularity with listeners so complete that only a few commentators (often working in radio themselves) pondered on the theoretical approaches to the new medium.

Among the theorists attempting to categorise the radio in the postwar period into a system of media was the Canadian Marshall McLuhan (1911–80). The 1964 publication of *Understanding Media* was hailed as one of the most far-reaching and forward-looking works of the time. McLuhan viewed the media as extensions of our human senses, which have a profound effect on our understanding of our immediate environment. We are no more prepared for the advent of radio or television than a member of a 'primitive' society is for literacy. The advent of these 'electric' extensions produces a crisis:

> Electric speed mingles the cultures of prehistory with the dregs of industrial marketers, the non-literate with the semi-literate and the post-literate. Mental breakdown of varying degrees is the very common result of uprooting and inundation with new information and endless patterns of information.[62]

In order to deal with this onslaught of information, and to prevent societal breakdown, an understanding of the media is necessary, whereby the medium and its surrounding technology is taken as seriously as its content, hence *the medium is the message*.

McLuhan distinguishes between high definition 'hot' and low definition 'cool' media depending on the amount of data transmitted to a predominant sense and how much has to be completed by the recipient. Therefore a medium like speech or the telephone could be considered 'cool', as little sensory information is provided and much has to be filled in by the listener. The newspaper, radio and movie, on the other hand, are considered 'hot' as they are 'low in participation' and filled with data.[63] Television is, according to McLuhan, a 'cool' medium, as it engages the viewer and demands an involvement in a process (high in participation). Existing traditions and cultures before the introduction of new media are equally important:

> Nevertheless, it makes all the difference whether a hot medium is used in a hot or cool culture. The hot radio medium used in cool or non-literate cultures has a violent effect, quite unlike its effect in, say, England or America, where radio is felt as entertainment. A cool or low literary culture cannot accept hot media like movies or radio as entertainment. They are, at least, as radically upsetting for them as the cool TV medium has proved to be in our high literacy world.[64]

Radio, McLuhan believes, has had a different background in the USA and Britain because of their long exposure to literacy and industrialism. This 'intensely visual organisation of experience' meant that the 'hot' radio could easily be integrated into the web of other media. But on the European continent, in a 'more earthy and less visual' culture, the 'tribal magic' of the radio resonated the old web of kinship 'once more with a note of Fascism'.[65]

The deeply personal and intimate effect of the radio offers a world of unspoken communication between the broadcaster and the listener. Horkheimer and Adorno view this private sphere as isolating:

> Not only does the mendacious idiom of the radio announcer fix itself in the brain as an image of language itself, preventing people from speaking to each other,... communication makes people conform by isolating them.[66]

But for McLuhan this private experience is 'charged with the resonating echoes of tribal horns and antique drums'[67] which turns the audience into a resonating echo chamber. Whereas this simile suits this study well, further models of McLuhan's analysis are clearly overarching and too self-important. Germany's late industrialisation was 'the rich area of preliterate vitality', which 'felt the hot impact of the radio. The message of radio is one of violent, unified implosion and resonance.'[68] Nevertheless, the 'hot', 'high definition', 'low participation' aspect of the radio will be carried forward in this analysis as the listening process undergoes further examination: 'The ear is hyperaesthetic compared to the neutral eye. The ear is intolerant, closed and exclusive, whereas the eye is open, neutral and associative.'[69]

Despite McLuhan's assertions that 'the effects of the radio are quite independent of its programming',[70] content, especially in the context of this study, is of vital importance. Other media theorists have, particularly in very recent times, commented on the effects the media are creating by the reality they are presenting to the audience. Jean Baudrillard's concepts of *simulacra* and *simulations* are a case in point.[71] For Baudrillard the images and signs with which the audience is bombarded by the modern media represent a fundamental break with modernity, as the representations in the media either mask and pervert basic reality or – when 'the medium has become the message' – is masking the absence of a basic reality or bears no relation to reality whatever and has become its own pure simulacrum.[72] While this could be viewed as an interesting aspect of the current, twenty-first century media saturation, in the context of this study, and in the timeframe of the immediate postwar Germany this model is unsuitable as it necessarily pre-supposes ideological conformity. In order, however, to establish a model which could look at the reality as represented by the media, two vital aspects of radio broadcasting need to be looked at in this context: the system of dissemination of information (news and current affairs) and ideology contained in broadcast language, as listeners in both Germanies had to adjust to new forms and content on the radio.

Radio and ideology

The dissemination of information through the mass media, be it newspapers, radio or television, works as a closed system, that is to say that no immediate interaction takes place between sender and receiver.[73] It is one-way, from sender to receiver. Of course, there are the possibilities of listeners' (readers', viewers') letters and comments, but at the point of reception there is no immediate possibility to respond. But a balance will have to be maintained between the broadcast output and the interest of tuning in. The reality presented must coincide with the listeners' expectations of what reality is or could be. This means, in order to have listeners in the first place, and to continue to have them, the broadcasters have to have an affirmative broadcast output. Affirmation is reached through entertainment: 'To be entertained means to be in agreement'.[74] This is why the mixture and mingling of entertainment and news is so all-important, cultural products placed in time through the hourly news broadcast; reassurance and uncertainty.

But in order not to lose their listeners the broadcasters have a fundamental problem with news broadcasts: the disruption of entertainment must be acceptable within the listeners' expectation of reality. Not only context, tone and presentation are important considerations, but particularly selection. The selection criteria for the news broadcasts must, for the continuation of the broadcasts and continued listening, present the minimum disruption from the everyday experience, yet at the same time create the impression that news is 'new' and relevant. As Luhmann notes, if the listener really expected something new, interesting and newsworthy, the broadcasters could wait until something happens and then broadcast it: 'In this strand [news and in-depth reporting] the mass media disseminate ignorance in the form of facts which must continually be renewed so that no one notices.'[75]

The selection criteria for news broadcasts have to comply with our expectation of the rational in order for 'news' to be relevant and interesting to us:

Surprise, conflicts, quantities and *local relevance* are usually the first priorities of the newscaster, numbers and immediacy of threat of greatest interest to the listener.

The initially reported conflicts will, when looked at more closely, contain some *norm violations*, and the broadcaster will present an evaluation of *norm violations*, including *identifiable names, topicality to previous news items,* and, in some cases, *expressions of opinions*.

These are on the whole carefully pre-selected, not only in terms of political orientation, but also to give an overall picture of the broadcaster's point of view and/or the view of 'their' public. Public opinion in the form of direct contact with the broadcaster (rather than opinion polls) is unlikely to present an accurate picture of a publicly prevailing opinion as editorial or proprietorial influence remains predominant.

All the above selection criteria vary from organisation to organisation, depending on space and time restrictions. All news items therefore will have to be condensed, confirmed, generalised and schematised to fit their individual purpose. Whether an item is deemed 'newsworthy' can fluctuate enormously.[76]

Very few events will dominate the news headlines for long periods of time in all media (the recent events of 11 September 2001 being one such example). When this happens, it is undoubtedly meant to stress the magnitude of an event. But such 'blanket coverage' arouses suspicions and an awareness of the selection process, exposing the framework of current themes and debates as a part of the content of the ideology of the radio (and other media). Whereas Luhmann argues that manipulation, or the suspicion of manipulation, of the mass media is a problem internal to the system, that is to say any manipulated information will be found out in due course and prove counter-productive to its legitimacy,[77] it is doubtful any self-imposed commitment to accuracy would guarantee objectivity. The selection criteria named by him leave enormous scope for manipulation, and accusations of ideological preferences in the selection of news items fall on fertile ground, particularly in the time period of this study (the 1960s). Through the complexities that arise not only through the multiplicity of media outlets, but also through the entanglements of entertainment, reported reality and personal experiences, more communications occur which cannot be communicated. The reality reported in the mass media presents a picture which cannot be deciphered by the Enlightenment's use of reason or by transcendental self-reference. In the latter half of the twentieth century the reality reported on the radio referred to a reality of ideological constructs, be it the non-committal vagueness of 'light entertainment' or the authoritarian voice of totalitarian rhetoric.

The experience of the 'now', the placing oneself in history, in immediate postwar Germany, depended on ideology, or on the successful identification thereof. It required more than just reverting to the functional uses of the radio, such as finding relatives and reports from the military authorities, although this was its immediate and primary function after May 1945. As soon as there was a semblance of 'normality', or peacetime on the radio, through the re-emergence of (seemingly unideological) entertainment, the question of ideology arose again. But a certain 'sublation' (*Aufhebung*) of ideology occurred through the radio reportage from the International Military Tribunal and Nuremburg Trials between November 1945 and October 1947, through the scrutiny and hopeful destruction of National Socialist ideology. Here at the trial of the main war criminals the examination of the power and command structures of the Third Reich exposed the twisted, abnormally transformed, 'anamorphic' worldview contained within the National Socialist doctrine, which, it was hoped, would surely collapse when exposed to the detailed investigations of an international tribunal and the world press. But this relationship of ideology and 'objective' social reality seems more complex, as Slavoj Žižek comments:

> We can now see why anamorphosis is crucial to the functioning of ideology: anamorphosis designates an object whose very material reality is distorted in such a way that a gaze is inscribed into its 'objective' features. A face which looks grotesquely distorted and protracted acquires consistency; a blurred contour, a stain, becomes a clear entity *if we look at it from a certain 'biased' standpoint* – and is this not one of the succinct formulas of ideology? Social reality may appear confused and chaotic, but if we look at it from the standpoint of anti-Semitism,

everything becomes clear and acquires straight contours: the Jewish plot is responsible for all our woes... In other words, anamorphosis undermines the distinction between 'objective reality' and its distorted subjective perception: in it, the subjective distortion is reflected back into the perceived object itself, and in this precise sense, the gaze itself acquires 'objective' existence.[78]

But does exposing this gaze bring us anywhere nearer 'objective reality'? Does analysing and contesting ideology, even to sit in judgement over it, bring us any closer to the truth? This is where the notion of 'sublation' becomes interesting. In the German, the idea of *Aufhebung* implies not only a rescindment or revocation, but also a putting-right or evening-out. Certainly at the end of the war in 1945 it was impossible to achieve this without recourse to ideological terminology such as the use of clichés and stereotypes. These (implicitly or explicitly) are always connected with ideology: certain spheres are automated, others prohibited, true relations de-historicised and with this a secondary reality is created which appears as 'real' and 'objective'.[79]

It is important here to distinguish between the reality presented by the mass media and the reality experienced by the individual. To distinguish, a critical distance from the machine and an understanding of the technology (as was imagined by Benjamin) is not enough anymore. Even a multiplicity of sources from the mass media (as was the war experience) will not necessarily yield a picture of reality.

What has been created is its own system, a series of temporal and spatial displacements, a reality which cannot possibly exist as such, and yet there is a dependence on this illusion, which reassures and frightens at the same time. Yet it is important to bear in mind that – contrary to Baudrillard's assertion – there is a relation between reported and existing reality, but the Enlightenment's starting point of critical self-reference now has been altered, the self-reference cannot be known anymore, it has to be believed.[80] And through the ritual of listening to the radio the Enlightenment's technological advances have produced a reliance on myth and illusion which serves as the 'enlightened', greater, modern picture. But now this reality created by the radio is only in crisis when the transmission stops.

Dealing with the term 'ideology' is hampered by two differing but connected definitions. In Marxist thought, ideology denotes any set of ideas and values which has the social function of consolidating a particular economic order. The function of ideology is to naturalise the status quo, and to represent as immutable features of human nature the particular social conditions which currently exist. Critics of this definition see ideology as an all-embracing political doctrine, which claims to give a complete and universally applicable theory of man, society and political action. The difference between these two definitions could be described as being that the Marxist definition sees ideology embedded (or hidden) in whatever socio-economic system prevails, or that no non-ideological position exists,[81] whereas the opponents of such a view see ideology as something imposed, often by totalitarian regimes. In the course of this study both of these definitions will emerge, as the 'imposed' ideologies of National Socialism and Soviet socialism will be compared to the 'non-committal' ideology of the Federal Republic and the liberal West.

When analysing the content and form of word-based radio programmes, the relationship between language and ideology is of particular interest. The ideological vocabulary is augmented by production techniques and familiar sounds which aim to present the affirmative worldview. Its effects, however appear as short-lived as the ephemeral radio listening experience itself.

Not only was the terminology of the National Socialist ideology deceptively used and constructed, indoctrinating the population over a 12-year period, but it was also immediately 'forgotten', put out of use after 1945. In the GDR the NS terminology was replaced by a Soviet and GDR-specific vocabulary,[82] while in the FRG language saw itself in the tradition of the Weimar Republic. In all three cases the language is German. In other words, the signifiers are the same. Words, and occasionally whole phrases, changed their signification with the changing ideology, thus making the relationship between signifier and signified ideologically dependent. Whereas this situation could be viewed as a historical anomaly, the relationship between language and ideology was closely examined as early as 1929 in a study entitled *Marxism and the Philosophy of Language* by the Russian Formalist V.N. Voloshinov. His work was not considered to be along Stalinist party lines and little is known about the author, who perished in the purges. Many commentators attribute the whole work to M.M. Bakhtin, to whose 'circle' Voloshinov belonged. Language, according to Voloshinov, is inherently 'dialogic': it can only be grasped by its inevitable orientation towards another. Since the building blocks of language, words (or 'signs') are part of a linguistic community where meaning is forever shifting and changing, words themselves represent a focus of struggle and contradiction. Therefore, words have to be investigated by their varied history, as they are forever charged with their own meaning by the social groups and classes and individuals who use them. Language, to Voloshinov, is a field of ideological contention, not a monolithic system; words are the building material of ideology, since without them no values could exist.

How then can broadcast language – and particularly the language of news and in-depth reporting – be analysed? Are there such things as clear ideological markers, which either 'hide' the truth or impose a lie? In the climate of the Cold War, radio broadcasting certainly helped to create an atmosphere of anxiety, a sense of crisis. The mixture of direct propaganda and inconsequential 'light entertainment' meant that the listeners, if critical, could distance themselves from the radio receiver. But subtler techniques, such as the selection of news items and 'factual' reporting (with its 'decomposition of authorial content'), meant that this was not always possible. Rhetorical devices and affirmation of the status quo survived the suspicions of 'news' manipulation and dealt in ideological certainties: the whole process of radio news manufacture to consumption resides now in the ideological framework of doctrine, belief and ritual. In the ritual consumption of news the belief in a reality that lies 'elsewhere' is the important and most influential factor to the effectiveness of the ideology. The 'commodity fetishism' of consuming a newscast must not lie too far outside experienced reality, nor should it be outside the current themes of expectations, but it remains, because it comes from 'out there', firmly from somewhere else, implying that 'we are safe'.

Meaning and comprehension are in a paradoxical relationship in the ritualised radio news consumption. Whereas meaning is not actively or directly interfered with by the broadcasters, studies have also revealed that comprehension of newscasts is remarkably low, often despite repeats and clarifications.[83] The formulaic repetitions in newscast language evoke, when there are no surprises to contend with, a remarkable continuity of concepts, designed not necessarily to inform, but rather to reassure the listener. Even when doubts about the truthfulness of a news report occur – and here Luhmann contends that these doubts can be accommodated within the system of the mass media, providing there are no suspicions of manipulation[84] – the ritualistic mantra of the news spurts out the familiar. In 1977 the East German author Stefan Heym compiled, in an anecdotal essay entitled 'The More in the Mouth, the Emptier the Slogans' (*Je voller der Mund, desto leerer die Sprüche*),[85] a list of nouns (concepts) and their responding adjectives as used in news bulletins. It is remarkable how unchangeable, even in translation and over time, this collection has remained. So 'change' will always be 'drastic', 'an exchange of ideas' 'thorough', 'growth' 'dynamic', 'foundations' 'unshakable', 'decisions' 'far-reaching', and so on. To prove the point he transcribed two consecutive days' newscasts, which were identical except for the identifiable names of politicians and dignitaries.[86] While this suggests a mockery of the intent to inform – and some might argue that the state-run GDR media never had this intention – all evidence suggests that audiences felt that they were well informed and knowledgeable in current affairs. Not only does this suggest that diverse meanings function as 'free-floating' signifiers, whose meaning is fixed by their mode of their hegemonic articulation,[87] but that ultimately these meanings are interchangeable and meaningless. In the context of this study it is noticeable that repetition of news items, such as reports from NS trials, become problematic and tiring to the audiences.

Considerations

In this brief analysis of the early German experience of radio broadcasting and ideology several points are noteworthy. In the context of modernity, in the era of accelerated historical time, there exists a strong notion towards a linear progress. This can be seen throughout nineteenth- and twentieth-century positivism, Marxism included. But this notion rests primarily on the relationship of human beings and nature, through science. The radio, together with other media for the proliferation of information, is certainly a product of science, and also plays a part in the acceleration of historical time. In itself, radio technology has accomplished awe-inspiring feats and has firmly lodged itself into our everyday lives. Life without the radio is unimaginable now. It has become our way (together with TV) of placing ourselves in time and space, our experience of (post) modernity. But the relationship between the technology (adulterated nature) and human beings is far from clear now: who influences whom? And the notion of progress has become problematic, specifically through the assumptions that technological advances carry with them some kind of moral advancement. Martin Jay argues that certainly since the middle of the twentieth century 'the Frankfurt School has jettisoned the triumphalist notion of impending human emancipation.'[88] Therein lies the dialectical and paradoxical nature of Enlightenment reasoning. And, on the other hand, would it be feasible to argue that there exists an unchanging equivalence between progress and barbarity?

The rational responses to the first radio broadcasts certainly bore this out. Both Brecht and Benjamin wanted to remind and encourage the listener about the technology. The rebellion of the listener Brecht envisaged did not happen. Rather, the notion of magic returned: the ritual of listening to the radio, or of watching television, replaces the lost religion, turning it into a process which Adorno terms 'disenchanted enchantment'.[89]

These aspects of the radio did not elude the early programme makers and ideologues. In an analysis of the most popular Nazi radio programme, the *Wunschkonzert*, David Bathrick writes:

> Certainly the radio would play a very special role in the new communication system. In the development of larger goals, radio programmes were seen as having to transcend the pluralism and excessive intellectuality of the Weimar Republic in order to strive for a *Volksbildung* (the formation rather than simply the education of a people) in a larger sense: now they spoke of forming a new folk soul of 'true and genuine life'; of a 'deeper' sense of values than are communicated in the belief systems of bourgeois democracies. This 'metaphysics of the radio', as it was called, suggested an almost religious calling, and it was literally defined as such in a leading media journal: 'The art of the radio (*Rundfunkkunst*) seems to leave the marketplace and return to the church, to a church, which will encompass all its listeners with the same atmospheric powers and which is capable of bridging distances just like the all uniting House of the Lord. Here the central actors are no longer individual destinies, but rather ideas, they are community creating powers which speak forth with the voice in a manner that moves the many.'[90]

The 'religion of modernity' means placing ourselves in time, seeking knowledge through the little ritual. But this ritual isolates more than it brings together; it is deeply entrenched in the laws of the market economy and modernity. In contrast to traditional religion, the consumption of mass media products isolates the individual, offering only false emancipation.

The corporate unity of the authoritative broadcasts with the compliant listener evokes self-congratulatory confirmation of the listeners' views, which are formed by the authority of the broadcast. The news broadcast, which functions as the factual confirmation of the listeners' views, becomes interchangeable with the light entertainment which surrounds it. No critical ability is needed to 'consume' the radio broadcasts. Brecht's 'rebellion of the listener', listening as an active engagement, the ability to analyse information critically, and Benjamin's populist hopes to 'give each listener what (s)he wants, and a little more (of what we want)' have merged only to emphasise and elaborate caricatures and stereotypes of an illusory world that presents itself as reality. You become what you are.

This process, which could be described as 'ideological selection' (selecting the most favourable ideology), occurs in the ritual of listening to the radio. In the extreme case, as described by Horkheimer and Adorno above, of enforced public listening, 'merging with the howl of the sirens proclaiming panic', the ideology is coerced, enforced. But it is equally effective through gentler methods which mix popular (populist) and unchallenging music such as Toscanini and intermittent newscasts. This formula is still very popular today, and was first introduced in one of the Nazis' most popular radio programmes, the *Wunschkonzert*. The words uttered over the radio waves form an 'ideological sound-scape', their meanings are vague through their 'free-floating' signifiers, which give the listener the impression – 'empower' the listener – that through this process they can form an objective opinion.

The merging of entertainment and news probably reached its first zenith with the 1938 broadcast of Orson Welles' dramatic adaptation of H.G. Wells' 'War of the Worlds', which resulted in panic-stricken listeners phoning radio stations to find out about the Martian invasion of the Earth. While this can be seen as a shock theatrical treatment of a literary form for the radio, it nevertheless exemplifies the power and authority of the medium. The illusion created on air might or might not be true, who is to know? The mystery of the ritual leaves us guessing. Entertainment as news and news as entertainment. This was, and to some degree still is, the experience of radio listening.

But can the radio be listened to in a critical way, as envisaged by Brecht and Benjamin? Historically, the rupture in 'corporate listening' occurred during the Second World War. The necessity of having accurate information was essential for survival, especially given the circumstances of so many sources of dis- and mis-information. The plurality of sources did not help in the construction of an accurate picture; in order to achieve this the listener had to become 'critical' again. But the intensity of such an experience destroyed the ritual; reason and rationality only counted if one was to stay alive. For the listeners in the Germany of the immediate postwar years radio had lost its mythical and ritualistic function, and when it did appear, as in the form of 'un-German jazz without words', it caused only astonishment and consternation.

For the Allies and the military authorities this new sobriety among radio listeners was welcome, and was seized upon hastily to start the de-Nazification and re-education programmes. But the ideological entertainment needed to continue and soon the airwaves were filled with jazz and light entertainment again, but the newscasts were not comforting. Once the Nuremberg trials were under way, increasing amounts of documentation showed the deep complicity of the population; the euphemisms of the Nazi language were now exposed to show the full horror of the Hitler regime and the collective guilt of the Nazi organisations. Listening to the news now enraged, embarrassed and shamed, but the way this was expressed in public was through repressed guilt deflected and refracted into self-pity and outrage directed at perpetrators and victims alike; 'perpetrator trauma' as an expression of the non-acceptance of guilt and lack of repentance. Furthermore in many cases the trial broadcasts 'probed the limits of representation' as gruesome detail meant that the critical listening experience was now bound up with relentless self-examination and reminders of an unbearable past.

The new dominant ideologies both tackled this phenomenon through a call for a 'penance through working', which was one of the reasons for the West-German 'economic miracle' of the 1950s and 1960s, and the possibility of establishing a separate East-German Soviet-style state.

Whereas this thematic of 'repression' is explored at length through texts like Alexander and Margarete Mitscherlich's *Inability to Mourn* (1967),[91] recent studies show just how deeply the Nazi ideology had taken root in the German psyche, and a process other than repression took place: the expression of the 'un-public opinion' through a virulent hatred of the opposing ideology (in the West: Hitler not as bad as Stalin; in the East: at least we don't have any fascists) and a 'public' opinion expressed through public figures. The continuing debates in the Bundestag around the issue of statute of limitations of Nazi crimes committed (*Verjährungsdebatte*) returned year after year. For the radio broadcasters this presented a problem: despite the radio's 'one way' communication, broadcasting depends on its listeners. Or, in Bertolt Brecht's words: 'It [the radio] is about a popularity which not only transmits knowledge to the public, but also a public which transmits knowledge.'[92] A response from the listening public had, broadly speaking, to reflect public opinion, but which one? The one expressed by public figures or the ones expressed around the *Stammtisch*? The willingness of the MPs and the Bundestag to forget about the Third Reich was obvious, and international pressure to try war criminals was lessening in the light of continuing Cold War tensions. But, however presented, broadcasters could and would not reflect true public opinion.

The debate of 'working through the past', or 'coming-to-terms-with the past' actually meant much more. As Adorno wrote in 1959:

> The question 'What does working through the past mean?' requires explication. It follows from a formulation, a modish slogan that has become highly suspect during the last years. In this usage 'working through the past' does not mean seriously working upon the past, that is, through a lucid consciousness breaking its power to fascinate. On the contrary, its intention is to close the books on the past and, if possible, even remove it from memory. The attitude that everything should be forgotten and forgiven, which would be proper for those who have suffered injustice, is practiced by those party supporters who committed the injustice. I once wrote in a scholarly dispute: in the house of the hangman one should not speak of the noose, otherwise one might seem to harbour resentment. However, the tendency towards the unconscious and the not so conscious defensiveness against guilt is so absurdly associated with the thought of working through the past that there is sufficient reason to reflect upon a domain from which even now there emanates such horror that one hesitates to call it by name.[93]

The debate around the 'domain from which even now there emanates such horror' had been, in 1959, only briefly touched upon with the trial of the *Einsatzgruppen* in the previous year. After the tribunal at Nuremberg there was reluctance, according to some historians,[94] on the part of the Adenauer government to bring Nazi war criminals to trial. For many, the verdicts at Nuremberg were the final reckoning, the *Schlussstrich*, and for others expressions of war remembrance symbolised the 'coming-to-terms with the past'.[95]

But Germany, East and West, was still a country of refugees, displaced persons, missing PoWs, economic boom and relatively high unemployment. The Nazi past could not be remembered and could not be forgotten. But for the ideology of radio broadcasting this presented no problem:

> The culture industry grins: become what you are, and its deceit consists precisely in confirming and consolidating by dint of repetition mere existence as such, what human beings have been made into by the way of the world. The culture industry can insist all the more convincingly that it is not the murderer but the victim who is guilty: that it simply helps bring to light what lies in human beings anyway.[96]

And here Adorno points to a suspicion which causes some alarm in this context: the innocuous and inconsequential listening experience could diminish – even to the extent of nullifying or reversing – the critical engagement. Was it possible for the German radio programmes dealing with the Holocaust in the 1960s to command enough authority and attention effectively to 'work through the past'? Or was it necessary to shock and disturb, to 'interfere in social reality'?[97]

In the following chapters programmes dealing with the question of justice and retribution concerning the Holocaust will be examined, bearing in mind some of the models explored above. It is evident that all of the theoretical concepts explored here build on each other. However, none of them singly appear to encompass all the processes needed when it comes to a critical engagement with the radio, if such processes are possible at all. But in what follows, the emerging details will further explain at least some of the complexities which lie in the relationship between broadcaster and listener.

3
Radio and the Holocaust

Broadcasts from the Nuremberg Trials

The radio station with the most listeners in the immediate postwar period in Germany was the North-West German Radio (*Nordwestdeutscher Rundfunk, NWDR*), which transmitted to the whole of Northern Germany, the Ruhr and Berlin. During this period the majority of its programmes dealing with the topic of National Socialism were broadcasts from the International Military Tribunal in Nuremberg.[1] At several times during the day the radio station in the vicinity of Nuremberg, the *Süddeutsche Rundfunk* (service Southern Germany), linked up with other public service broadcasters to bring reports and comments throughout the period of the trials.[2] Each of the regional broadcasters had their own reporter, but all were subject to strict scrutiny in accordance with the directives issued by the military authorities. Radio broadcasts in the British zone came under directives – drawn up in 1944 – which met with issues such as the 'Re-education of Germany' (No. 8), the 'Control of Broadcasting' (No. 26) and the 'Control and Censorship of Public Information and Means of Intercommunication' (No. 27).[3] Whereas numbers 8 and 27 regarded the radio as one tool in a wider process of re-education, the envisaged 'control of broadcasting' – a virtual takeover of the German airwaves by the BBC – proved to be too big a task, and by August 1945 some control had returned to the studios of Radio Hamburg/NWDR.[4]

A month earlier, in Berlin, no agreement could be reached between the Soviets and the Western Allies over an integrated radio service, as the Russians refused to vacate the central broadcasting building in the *Masurenallee*.[5] The French also opposed a centralised broadcasting system and it became clear that the radio landscape in occupied Germany would evolve along the lines of the zones of occupation.[6]

As part of the de-Nazification programme of the Allies, the reporting from the war crimes trials was treated with considerable care. This meant that the personnel working in the German public broadcast stations were thoroughly vetted and supervised. Sir Hugh Carleton Greene (who would later serve as the director-general of the BBC from 1960 to 1969) was charged with the establishing of a radio service in the British administered zone by General Major Alex Bishop, head of the Broadcasting Control Unit. Greene insisted that 'no former member of the NSDAP would be employed by the NWDR' and that possible exceptions had to undergo a lengthy investigation process.[7]

It was in the interest of the Allies, and particularly of the Americans, to have a public, rather than a military (secret) trial. Therefore planning for this eventuality involved making provision for about 500 expected international and German newspaper and radio reporters, all of them drawing their information from a central 'Information Control' office in the American zone of occupation. But as part of the Re-education Programme it was decided that the approach of 'Germans reporting to Germans' would be more effective and German journalists (although only five at any one time) were allowed to attend proceedings to follow the trial.[8] The Americans, however, were extremely cautious about granting licenses to the (German) media. No permanent license was issued and reporters had to continually renew permits every three days. But despite having restored the broadcasting facilities, American suspicions were the greatest when it came to radio reporting: for the only place allocated for a radio reporter the Americans insisted that this person had to be a member of the 'Radio Control Branch' of the military 'Information Control Division'.[9] This meant that – at least in the American zone of occupation – the American military authority had the monopoly on reporting. The person chosen by the Americans was a certain Dr Gaston Oulmán, who, in the course of the trial, was exposed as a fraudster and conman, but was kept on by the Americans to avoid a scandal.[10] For a brief period the NWDR, under British control, had employed their reporter Hans Zielinski to file dispatches from Nuremberg, but when his NSDAP membership became known in 1947, he was dismissed.[11] Another NWDR Nuremberg reporter, Elef Sossidi, was requested by the British to change his name to 'Andreas Günther', as listeners might suspect him of being a 'foreign Jew'.[12] The British and the Soviets, along with the French, made sure of the credentials of their reporters by employing (formerly) exiled Germans. The BBC's reporter, transmitting on the BBC wavebands and on Radio Luxembourg's relay, was Eberhard Schütz, an avowed anti-fascist. He was arrested in 1933 for his membership of the

Communist Party (KPD), before fleeing to France and then on to the Soviet Union in 1935. Increasingly critical of Stalin, he was expelled in 1938 and, following a brief stay in Prague, came to London, where he joined the BBC in 1940. In British military uniform and with British press credentials, he was deemed the 'star reporter' of the proceedings, as can be gathered from archival and published evidence.[13] The Soviet-controlled *Berliner Rundfunk* employed, among others, the young (20 at the time), little known but ideologically sound Markus Wolf to report from the IMT.[14]

Even before proceedings began, radio stations were exploring the audience attitudes to the trial, particularly in the Soviet sector. The *Berliner Rundfunk* had reports from the Sachsenhausen concentration camp, a lecture on the question of war guilt, and a recounting of the treatment of the population in Kiev by the German occupying forces in 1943. Later reports from Lublin and Auschwitz were followed by an answer to the listeners' question 'Who is a war criminal?'[15] Other radio stations in the British, American and French zones carried similar programmes, but very little of this material has survived. Some of the reportage and radio lectures of Radio Stuttgart's Fritz Ermath have appeared in printed form,[16] but the majority of the surviving archival material comes from the NWDR. The strong and high-profile reporting and editorial team included names such as Peter von Zahn, Axel Eggebrecht, Karl-Georg Egel and Karl-Eduard von Schnitzler,[17] many of whom actively engaged with the problems of 'working through the past' from the moment transmissions started again from Hamburg. Notable in this context are the reports by Axel Eggebrecht from the Bergen-Belsen trial in Lüneburg[18] as well as von Schnitzler's various analytical programmes on de-Nazification.[19]

Radio stations under American and British control placed a considerable emphasis on the Nuremberg trial reports, broadcasting twice a day (on Radio Frankfurt, for example) for 15 minutes, and carrying additional programmes to regular newscasts (on Radio Munich).[20] East German radio continued to broadcast the reports as part of their news bulletins.[21]

In the short period of time between the end of the Second World War and the beginning of the Cold War, the reporting from these trials began to highlight the differing worldviews of the victors, who had already started to map out their different spheres of influence. But both East and West made use of the trial reports for their re-education/de-Nazification/vospitanie v kulturu programmes.[22] Whereas Western reporters occasionally included some of their own thoughts and listeners' comments in their summaries, the editors of the *Berliner Rundfunk* continued to stress that alongside the individual guilt of the accused it was the capitalist system which was ultimately responsible for the crimes of National Socialism. This was to provide an insight into how the development of public service broadcasting in postwar Germany was to unfold.[23]

At first the reporting from the Nuremberg Trials had a mixed reception. As victors sitting in judgement over the vanquished, the International Military Tribunal was aware that it had to be seen to act fairly and impartially. On 23 March 1946 Eberhard Schütz made the following report for the BBC:

> If one has a conversation today in Germany, be it on the tram or in the street, there appear to be very different opinions about the Nuremberg Trial. There are those who talk insistently of a 'show trial', others who say: 'why waste so much time on gathering this mass of evidence?', and finally there is the growing number of those who, impressed with the objectivity of the Tribunal, know that much more is at stake here. Namely that with this International Military Tribunal a new institution of international law is established, a court to adjudicate crimes between nations, crimes against humanity, a tribunal which cannot rely on precedent, which has to work out its statutes from the best and valued principles of national criminal law. This new institution of international law has survived its baptism of fire here in Nuremberg.[24]

However, not all commentators were willing to give the population this benefit of the doubt. They had been out and about, experiencing the whispering campaigns of some of the unrelenting Nazis, and, to a great extent, the public at large. Here is an excerpt from Radio Stuttgart's Fritz Ermarth's broadcast of 16 October 1946:

> You can hear them, the 'Mr. Exonerated National Socialists', as they walk around nodding to each other: 'Well, yes, things were better under National Socialism'; or 'Of course, Hitler never wanted this'; or 'What we have now is Gestapo terror in a different guise'.
>
> These are things, my dear listeners, which can be heard every day in conversations with our fellow citizens. They brag that they had always maintained times would be terrible if Germany lost the war, the war they had started and wanted to pursue to that last drop of German blood. And [they are] whispering of wars to come between East and West, hoping to experience a miraculous renaissance.

I will not speculate whether this whispering campaign, which can be experienced throughout the country, is organised, or is a spontaneous expression in the guise of democratic hypocrisy of unrelenting National Socialist convictions. But you can feel the spirit of these men with every step, wherever you go in this country.[25]

But the whispering campaign's 'success' was more likely to have been a reaction to the reporting style. Journalists such as Eggebrecht and von Schnitzler expressly intended to make the listener think about their own responsibilities during the time of the Third Reich (Eggebrecht)[26] or to pose fundamental questions about established concepts such as the church, justice, nation, fatherland, etc. (von Schnitzler) as 'reason had been poisoned for the last 12 years'.[27] The accusatory tones in many of the reports from Nuremberg led Markus Wolf, in his 1975 recollections of his broadcast career, to comment that:

A large proportion of the German Nation felt that they were being co-defendants in Nuremberg, rightly or wrongly they felt responsible... I knew that a substantial number of my listeners did not want to hear of these things anymore.[28]

It is interesting to note that the above claim by Wolf is called into doubt in a recent publication about the Nuremberg Trials, countered by the fact that as late as 1949 the Trial documentary film *'Nürnberg und seine Lehren'* (*Nuremberg and its Lessons*) still attracted substantial audiences.[29] Here McLuhan's distinction between the 'intolerant' ear and the 'neutral and associative' eye is clearly identifiable. Listening to the broadcasts clearly struck a more alarming note. In order to deal with the levels of real or imagined complicity, the model of the 'totalitarian system', of the manipulated masses and few master criminals, found popular resonance, as well as critical comment, such as Erik Reger's 1945 article in the newspaper *Berliner Tagesspiegel*:

[The average German] is even proud of his plain stupidity, of this oh so typical German purity of the simpleton, caught up in the net of the Nuremberg criminals. What did they do to us? If only we had known!... The ingenuous eyes roll with the newly-found, young and rosy democratic feeling under a mask of indignation.[30]

But what also emerged from the tribunal was that these crimes could not have been committed by the leadership acting on their own, and there was enough documentation available to incriminate thousands – if not hundreds of thousands. Thus the broadcasts inflamed as much as they pacified, but it remained crucial to the broadcasters that they should continue to fulfil their functions of re-education and de-Nazification. The problem, however, remained how to reach the 'lesser' culprits and also the population at large. Eberhart Schütz's broadcast of the cross-examination of Baldur von Schirach, the NSDAP's youth education leader and Gauleiter of Vienna, on 2 June 1946 gives a good example of the popular admissions of 'guilt' through Schütz's excellent argumentation:

> A few weeks ago I spoke of the problems of responsibility in the Führer state, as is evident in the daily proceedings of the Nuremberg trial. The 21 former leaders of the Third Reich are not being tried as private persons, but as politicians, as representatives of the National Socialist system. Yet they are trying to defend themselves with this very system. The system of the leader (*Führersystem*) relinquishes them from responsibility, the Führer pyramid, which places blind obedience in the stead of responsibility, and where obedience is not so blind, it places loyalty to the Führer against better judgement. This is the mainstay of their defence. So even if defendants such as Frank and Schirach admit to their guilt, it is only admitting to a secondary guilt. One's own guilt, through loyalty and an oath of allegiance, is relinquished by the greater guilt of the Führer, as if criminal responsibility could be done away with...
>
> Let us stop here for a minute. What guilt does Schirach admit to here? Not of complicity to murder, as he denies any knowledge of this. But to educating [youth] to have loyalty to a man, who later turns out to be a murderer. If this admission of Schirach's is to have any meaning, then it is aimed against blind obedience in general, which is based on blind faith in a person, a human, instead of having critical judgement for one's actions.
>
> And what if, when the knowledge of the crimes prevails and fails to justify blind faith and loyalty? Even then Schirach exonerates the German youth of all guilt. In his confession he says he had unlimited power, and he alone carries the guilt of the German youth. Unquestioning obedience, according to Schirach, exonerates all guilt. And thus Schirach even excuses Höß, the murderer of Auschwitz, of any guilt. Hitler and Himmler were the murderers, they gave the orders. Höß is no more than the conscientious, professional executioner.[31]

The problems of collective guilt, which also became a stumbling block at the trial, were nevertheless pursued with great rigour during the trial's dealings with the Nazi organisations. The legal framework of the IMT to pursue crimes against humanity, genocide, war crimes and crimes 'against peace' were established in August 1945 in order to deal with the main war criminals.[32] In December 1945, through the drawing up of Control Council Law No. 10 (*Kontrollratsgesetz Nr. 10*), which aimed at passing future prosecutions to German courts, the crime of membership of a criminal organisation (such as the SS or Gestapo) was added to the above categories, and crimes committed by Germans before May 1945 could be tried retrospectively by legislation passed after that date.[33] At the time of the main trial in Nuremberg, the intended prosecutions of collective 'criminal organisations' was still being given active consideration by the Allies; later disagreements, principally between the Americans and the British, meant that such prosecutions took place under the discretion of the individual military authority.[34] It is hardly surprising that the reports from the IMT were causing unease, as the broadcast of 2 August 1946 about the prosecution of the Nazi organisations by the *Berliner Rundfunk*'s journalist Hermann Deml indicates:

> A thousand little Führers ordered, a thousand imitation Görings looted, a thousand Schirachs filled the youth with hate, a thousand Saukels whipped the slaves, a thousand Streichers and Rosenbergs stirred up hate, a thousand Kaltenbrunners and Franks tortured and murdered, a thousand Schachts and Speers and Funks administrated, financed and supported the Nazi movement. They now will be held accountable at Nuremberg.[35]

He lists the organisations: the government, the NSDAP party leadership, the Gestapo, the high command of the Armed Forces, the SA and the SS, for which he reserves particular contempt:

> Also accused are the SS, especially the Totenkopf organisations, those brutes, and the SD, the hard-core gangsters. Out of the dry material of the files emerges a picture which is choking in its brutality. A report describes in detail the family life of *Lagerkommandant SS Obersturmbannführer* Wilhaus, who had two- to four-year-old children thrown in the air to shoot at, to the encouragement of his own, nine-year-old child with exclamations of 'Oh please, papa, one more time!'. A man to the liking of Himmler, no doubt, [who] said of the SS that it was to be a 'sword without pity'. Such gruesome deeds must

have been referred to by the former SS General Ohlendorf, when he calmly admitted to the murder of 90,000 people and promptly added that 'all liquidations were carried out as humanely as possible'.[36]

Deml ends, however, on a more conciliatory note:

> But for the many thousands of fellow travellers in these organisations, providing they are not guilty of criminal activities and are not fascist propagandists, but on the contrary, have become aware of the overwhelming complicity of the German people, there should be – and this has been stated repeatedly by the anti-fascist parties – an opportunity for redemption and reparation of these war-crimes through steadfast work and the reconstruction of a truly democratic state. The possibility of their exoneration should be possible after the verdict of the International Military Tribunal.[37]

It was far from clear what exactly was meant by the phrase 'opportunity for redemption and reparation' for fellow travellers in 'the construction of a truly democratic state' at the time of the broadcast. The reporters had to tread a fine line here, as many of them had either been in exile or had actively resisted, and from their (own) point of view the majority of the population, who had supported Hitler, had very few redeeming features.

There began to be some divergence in terms of questions relating to how to treat the 'vanquished'; attempts to influence the listeners' opinions in the different zones of occupation was conducted with subtlety and care. Whereas the broadcasts of the BBC's Eberhard Schütz gave the listeners the room to make their own judgements (within the framework of his argument), the *Berliner Rundfunk* started to employ pseudo-Soviet terminology which was to grow in later years. It foreshadowed the obsession in the GDR and the Soviet Union with 'true' or 'real' democracy, 'progressive' nations and, above all, 'anti-fascism'.

The following report, broadcast on 29 September 1946, shortly before the Nuremberg judgement, by Max Seydewitz of the *Berliner Rundfunk*, highlights these concerns:

> Sometimes, my dear listeners, you can get the impression that the anti-fascists have to defend themselves for not having cleared the mountains of rubble in a year, which the main accused here in Nuremberg created through their twelve-year criminal dictatorship and war of plunder. I believe that nobody in the world can take it

as a sign of political maturity and of inner change in our national character, which was diseased by Nazism, if Germans blame anti-fascists for the present need and hardship. [The anti-fascists], who after the collapse of the Third Reich, knuckled down with responsibility, trying, together with all of our people willing to reconstruct with painstaking labour, to rebuild a new, habitable Germany from the gruesome inheritance of the Nazi regime. Those Germans, my dear listeners, who shirk from this reconstruction, and even today are not willing, through their deeds, to endorse the death sentence on the Nazi war criminals, harm Germany's interests more than they can imagine. How the German intellect is judged abroad is evident from a comment by the British MP Errol, who recently returned from a fact-finding mission in Germany. Mr Errol established that the German people, despite all their experiences, had learnt nothing new, and showed no signs of remorse. Their unrepentant attitude is exemplified, says the British observer, by the lack of sympathy for the victims of fascism, who were really the only ones who fought bravely against the criminal policies of the Nazi regime.

The accused of Nuremberg have repeatedly stated during the trial that the German people are co-responsible for the crimes committed by them. The judges and prosecution will hear nothing of this. But still, listeners, none of us must overlook the fact that the question of the complicity of the German people is a subject of lively debate all over the world. We anti-fascists know from experience what the Nazi reign of terror meant, and how difficult it was for the German people under the Nazi dictatorship to act according to one's conscience. But this excuse will not hold anymore today. Today the German people, in their attitude to the Nazi regime and their deeds, are completely free. Today the German people have the opportunity to prove through action that they did not agree with the crimes of the Nazi leaders and their henchmen.[38]

Again and again, the commentary returns to the levels of complicity. It is not surprising that this was foremost in the minds of the broadcasters and the military authorities at this time. While some, like Seydewitz (above), absolved the general public from it – be it only with the promise of future hard work – others, such as Deml, urged participation in the 'anti-fascist' spectrum of political parties, while commentators such as Schütz simply expressed their doubts.

On the whole the verdicts were welcomed by the radio commentators. NWDR reporters claimed that the trial and judgement represented 'a [colossal] change in the development of international law' and that its distinction lay in the fact that 'individual citizens have international duties which supersede national ones'.[39] Markus Wolf commented that the verdict was a 'triumph of justice and freedom over injustice and tyranny'. Gaston Oulmán saw the judges' decision as a 'moral' one, while Peter von Zahn viewed the variety of verdicts, from acquittals and prison to the death penalty, as proof that genuine deliberation took place which could not be said to be 'victor's justice'.[40]

But the topic of collective guilt and complicity which emerged from the trial broadcasts contained particular problems for the radio stations and their audiences. The journalists had to rely on the listeners' willingness to examine their conscience, an undoubtedly painful and traumatic experience for those who did this honestly. Others, as mentioned in the broadcasts, refused to do so, equating postwar reckoning at Nuremberg to the terror of the Gestapo. But for the radio to have this kind of power – to influence, not only ideologically, but morally, with immediate effect – was beset with problems arising from the uses to which it had been put during the war years. While the rise of fascism was still being attributed to the power of the mass media, the public and the authorities continued to view it with suspicion: the authoritative voice, the presenting of 'factual' reports and triumphalist propaganda had bred cynicism. Whether the immediacy of the aural experience was able to eliminate the listeners' doubts was questionable.

A possible model of how the mass media can influence 'public' opinion is put forward by Margot Berghaus in a 1999 edition of the German journal *Rundfunk und Fernsehen* (Radio and Television).[41] Berghaus admits that the sheer volume of interpretations on the effects of the mass media makes it difficult to have a coherent overview, possibly because the parameters of research are not empirically limited.[42] In her three-step model she takes not the medium, but the social environment in which it operates as the starting position, where, through the medium and its content (step two), themes and information form opinion (step three). These, eventually, feed back into the social environment – and, eventually, back to the medium.[43] This model accounts for the lack of empirical evidence of the 'direct' influence of the mass media, as the mediation processes that occur outside the medium, for example in the social environment, absorb and modify. She also views the medium itself as having influence independently beyond its content[44] (similar to McLuhan), and the attitude to the medium itself (in this case the radio) will determine the listeners' judgement on the broadcast content.

This gives some insight into how the above broadcasts might have been received: after the dreadful experiences of the war, the German people, now living in ruins, and dealing with hunger, deprivation, loss and hardship, made it difficult for them to deal with such accusations. Nevertheless, as well as to the necessary 'information' aspect of the radio, it carried commentary and food for thought at a time when the future seemed unsettled. Broadcasters wisely distanced themselves from a type of programming which would not resonate with the public, such as 'obvious' propaganda broadcasts or transmissions which did not reflect the social reality of the listener. The Nuremberg trial broadcasts were addressed to the private individual, as they required private examination. Therefore, as can be noted in the transcripts above, the broadcasters often addressed the listener not only directly, but also showed knowledge of the 'talk in the street' and the 'non-public opinion',[45] including themselves 'as Germans' and appealing to an assumed 'inherent' morality in their listeners. It is difficult to tell how much of what was genuine on the part of the reporters. Markus Wolf admits in his memoirs that the trial documentation certainly surprised him, as he was led to believe, during his exile in Moscow, that the German war crimes consisted solely in the shooting of German and Russian communists.[46] At the NWDR the war experiences of the journalistic staff were in contrast to those of the wider majority: of a total of 118, 23 had been in the resistance, 25 had been persecuted, 21 arrested and a further 14 had been in exile. Only 23 had been war combatants.[47]

The Allies' immediate task was to deal with the effects of the 12-year indoctrination of Nazi propaganda. As early as 1944 Hannah Arendt had noted that after the war identifying a 'good' German would be a task of immense complexity:

> In the meantime it will neither be a question of proving the obvious, which would be that Germans since the times of Tacitus have been latent Nazis, nor to demonstrate the impossibility that all Germans have a Nazi mind-set; it will rather be a matter of contemplating what attitude to take, if possible, to face a nation where the line between criminal and normal citizen, between the guilty and the innocent has been so effectively smudged, so that by tomorrow in Germany no-one will know whether they are facing a secret hero or a former mass murderer.[48]

But ideologically the problems of a thorough de-Nazification presented themselves in a different light. The perpetrators of war crimes, crimes against humanity, and those who, as party members, were complicit in atrocities and bore some criminal guilt were identifiable and known persons. In many cases the prosecution of these people was accepted by the population and the press as something morally and socially desirable in the immediate postwar period. But identifying and differentiating between 'fellow travellers' and bystanders was another matter.

Therefore the task allocated to the broadcasters by the Military High Command in the Western zones was the installation of new values, preferably, 'by Germans for Germans'. The American military governor Lucius D. Clay was keen to see radio broadcasting in German hands and pressed for appropriate legislation as early as 1946, but found that 'the German inability to grasp the concept of democratic freedom showed itself nowhere more than in broadcasting'.[49] Eventually the public service broadcast corporation, modelled on the BBC, became the favoured solution for most radio stations in the Western zones.[50] Radio stations continued to be the subject of close monitoring by the military authorities. A report from 1950 entitled 'One Year of Cultural Radio' by an unnamed scrutiny officer for the US High Command stated the following:

> All [the radio stations in the US zone] considered their programming more or less equally classical and modern, German and foreign authors and topics; all used some (very little) American material, and all endeavoured to a certain extent to use their activities for the reorientation of their audience. In this latter respect, Radio Frankfurt was the most active station...
>
> In brief, the endeavour of cultural radio seems to be:
>
> 1) to purify and revive the old German cultural tradition
> 2) to expose the viciousness of the Hitler era
> 3) to assist in democratic reorientation.
>
> ...It is a well-known fact that the main problem, the root of German reorientation, is the spiritual vacuum existing throughout the German population. Old concepts, traditions, ideals and values have proved false, useless and vicious. New ones have come, often in the same form as the old: in the form of slogans, in the newspapers, through the spoken word. Freedom, democracy, peace are certainly concepts basically attractive to every human being; but it is insufficient merely to proclaim as an ideal the contrary of what proved to be wrong. The new idea has to find a way not only into the ears of the people; it has to be anchored in their hearts and lives. The basic

anchorage has to reach into every sphere of human life, high and low; it has to create a new way of and attitude towards life; and it has to be strong, vital and dynamic enough to be able to change the individual's consciousness to an extent that old ideas drop off automatically. Instead of reminders of the past and abstract discussions of a better future, an incentive has to be given which rouses the initiative and imagination and therewith concentrates and directs the energy to the building of that future. This new idea should be given not in the form of small or large doses of education and lectures, but as an all-comprising, deep-reaching basic idea which appeals to the emotions and minds of the masses to such an extent that they adopt that idea as their own and live according to it...

In short, German radio has a great deal to learn about the effective presentation of its material, in the cultural as in other fields.[51]

In the Soviet Zone there had been an initial call [by the military authorities] to hand in all radio sets, but this was largely unheeded, and soon deemed counter-productive.[52] The centralising policies of the Soviet authorities made use of the radio more rapidly than their Western counterparts to such an extent that those who could do so preferred to listen to the *Berliner Rundfunk* rather than any British, French or American-controlled stations. The friendly continuity of the broadcasters' voices and the radio's utilitarian functions of re-establishing connections amongst the ruins made listening to East German radio reassuring and unthreatening, whereas the Western allied radio seemed brash and authoritative.[53]

However reassuring the broadcasts, the ideological choices appeared stark. Through the incorporation of the Communist International's conception of fascism as 'the dictatorship of the most reactionary and aggressive sections of the German monopoly and finance capital' and its continuation in the Western zones, all questions of complicity in questions such as Hitler's rise to power, the mass membership of the NSDAP and involvement in racial persecution and subsequent genocide could be avoided.[54] This 'sublation' of the Nazi ideology by Stalinism had its desired effect of turning the GDR into a 'bulwark against fascism', seemingly exonerating the population of the GDR wholesale. Broadcasts to this effect were carried on the *Berliner Rundfunk* nationally and on the *Deutschlandsender* (transmitting to the West) such as the following:

> Guilt requires atonement; this is one of the oldest insights of mankind. The German nation as a whole is certainly not guilty of two

world wars. It was forced into them by a relatively small section of the population. The German nation as a whole is also not responsible for the terrible deeds of the SS and the Gestapo in various European countries. The German nation is not a nation of criminals. And yet there exists guilt of a historical nature. Germans submitted to a regime of gangsters, and this criminal system started the Second World War. Our historic guilt is the fact that four million people did not listen when Ernst Thälmann said: 'Hitler – this means war!' The atonement for this guilt was the catastrophe of war and defeat; a heavy atonement indeed.[55]

The ideological confrontation around the issue of the Holocaust had established itself on air.

Prosecutions after Nuremberg

In her introduction to Bernd Naumann's account of the Auschwitz Trial, Hannah Arendt quotes the dismay of witness and Auschwitz survivor Dr Heinrich Dürmayer at the court proceedings: 'I was fully convinced that these people would have to prove their innocence!'[56]

This exclamation is perfectly understandable after even the briefest enquiry into the crimes committed in Auschwitz, as there appeared to be, in the words of witness Dürmayer, 'no one who was not guilty'. But recourse to the law had to be found which did not appear arbitrary or unjust. What had to be considered was the entire Nazi legislation from 1933 to 1945, from the earliest infringements on the civil rights of German Jews to the Nuremberg 'blood' laws of 1935, to the 'Final Solution'. Had 'obeying the law' become a criminal offence? And, if so, which law and when? Did membership of the 'criminal organisations', as defined by the Nuremberg Trials, of the SS and Gestapo constitute an offence worth prosecuting? The Allies' recourse, through the precedent of the IMT, to 'natural law' in 1945 appeared at first controversial, but was deemed sufficient by the international community at the time and gained considerably more authority as a universal measure in later years. The problem that faced not only the Allied military authorities but also the new, re-established German courts when prosecuting war criminals was attempting to establish the motivation behind criminal actions, as it soon became evident that no one carried out atrocities unthinkingly. Therefore, a base motivation of race-hatred resulting in the death of a person or persons could be viewed as constituting murder or accessory to murder, whereas 'obeying a knowingly wrongful order' could be viewed as manslaughter. Who bore the guilt and who was guilty were often different matters. Karl Jaspers, in his 1946 examination of German guilt and complicity, 'The Question of Guilt' (*Die Schuldfrage*), drew distinctions between different types of guilt: criminal, political, ethical and metaphysical. Jaspers, returning from 'inner exile' after the war, made these differentiations in what he believed to be a genuine climate of repentance, but, as it turned out, he was mistaken. The continued emphasis by the authorities on criminal guilt, the only offence which could be unambiguously prosecuted in court, meant that aspects connected to political and moral guilt, in terms of a wider debate around the issues of crimes against humanity (in its literal sense) and genocide, were deemed to be less urgent in the deliberation of justice.[57] In particular, what Jaspers terms 'metaphysical guilt', perhaps the most pressing aspect in the debate about 'coming-to-terms-with the past', proved to be a difficult aspect for the German postwar population to contemplate. Preoccupied with the immediate priorities of food and shelter, deliberating a fundamental solidarity between all humans, as Jaspers argues, appeared to many an impossible task:

> ...if I did not dedicate my life to the prevention of the murder of others, but that I stood by, then I am guilty in a manner which is not discernable in any criminal, political or moral way. The fact that I am still alive when such things happened marks me with an indelible guilt.[58]

Jaspers stood isolated in his analysis of the wider aspects of guilt and complicity. In his correspondence with Hannah Arendt there are distinct signs of resignation and despair concerning the reception of the *Schuldfrage*,[59] and Jaspers' own concerns about the FRG's continued inability to deal with its past found expression in further publications on this topic.[60] It is nevertheless interesting to note that it caused debate, and for some at least, aroused an inner, private examination with the past.

Criminal cases were tried by Allied and German courts under the *Kontrollratsgesetz Nr. 10* and while the military authorities could prosecute in more general terms of interpretation of this law, German courts depended on prosecutions brought by private persons, regarding crimes alleged to have been committed by known individuals. The Allied and German courts did not co-operate with each other.[61] Nevertheless, by mid-1951 5,230 persons had been convicted by German courts under the *Kontrollratsgesetz Nr. 10* in the Western zones[62] and 8,055 by 1949 in the Soviet zone.⁶³ In the Western zones the death penalty was still in operation until 1951,⁶⁴ and in East Germany it was retained until 1987.

But the numbers themselves do not really demonstrate the problems arising from these prosecutions. In the initial postwar period the 'political cleansing' through the process of de-Nazification manifested itself differently according to the respective military authorities. Questionnaires, de-centralisation and a nominal re-education programme were used in the Western zones, whereas rigorous policies of re-education and nationalisation of industry and business in the Soviet zone were seen as dealing with the root cause of fascism, monopoly capitalism. Legal proceedings brought against individuals had the initial effect of evoking self-pity, with individual crimes being glossed over in favour of the idea that a few arch criminals had led the nation astray; many had suffered the loss of loved ones in war and the wanton destruction of the cities. Self-pity was the context for the denial of guilt.⁶⁵

The collective itself further exacerbates the problem arising from an acceptance of a collective guilt: in normal circumstance the guilty one is excluded, expelled from the collective, but the collective cannot exclude itself.⁶⁶ The identified, individual war criminal excused the great mass of fellow travellers from bearing responsibility. Brave attempts such as Wolfgang Staudte's 1946 film *Die Mörder sind unter uns (The Murderers Are Amongst Us)* failed to rouse the public, and many journalists and critics found themselves increasingly isolated for trying to deal with issues such as complicity.

There remained reasons for the West German jurists to pursue Nazi war criminals under the seemingly inadequate German laws of 1871. Through its use of this antiquated legal code, the Federal Republic aimed to show up the illegality of the Nazi legislation as well as its ability to deal with offenders without Allied help.⁶⁷ But many Nazi murderers had been already tried in some form or another by Allied tribunals and were therefore excluded from further prosecution. This issue evolved further during the 1960s in the debate around a proposed statue of limitations for murders committed during the Nazi era when the West German Minister for Justice, Ewald Bucher, in an attempt to justify the limitation to twenty years, uttered the remark:' We have to learn to live with murderers.'⁶⁸

There were also many technical and organisational problems in trying to bring prosecutions before the courts. According to a recent estimate, the total number of persons involved in the murder of the Jews alone was in excess of 200,000.⁶⁹ Persons investigated during the Allies' de-Nazification programmes could not be investigated again and many documents were inaccessible in the atmosphere prevailing during the early Cold War period. The initial lack of prosecutions in the early 1950s still requires some explanation. In an interview with North German Radio (NDR, successor to the NWDR) in 1963, Dr Fritz Bauer rejected the thesis that the files were inaccessible at the time and that therefore prosecutions could not go ahead.[70] It was rather, according to Bauer, the procedural difficulties of finding an authority – in this case a prosecutor's office – which would be responsible for crimes committed outside current German borders, as under current legislation the locality of the crime, and the perpetrator, had to be on German soil. Initially, no prosecutor was responsible for the exceptional circumstances of Cold War Europe.[71] Additionally, bizarre circumstances, such as the defendants' bench in Nuremberg seating only 16, led to the Americans to shy away from prosecuting larger groups. 'More could not be prosecuted as there were no chairs.'[72] There was also the unwillingness of the politicians to initiate proceedings. When Chancellor Konrad Adenauer bade farewell to the American High Commissioner John McCloy in the early 1950s, he thanked him for doing the dirty work of sentencing the Nazi war criminals.[73] This 'dirty work' of 'fouling the nest' by prosecuting 'one's own' fell sharply after 1951, both in the GDR and the FRG: In the West proceedings dropped from 2,495 in 1950 to a mere 238 in 1957, resulting in 809 and 43 convictions respectively.[74] In the GDR there were 331 convictions in 1951, 23 in 1955 and none in 1956.[75]

The political will to deal with the Nazi past appeared to be waning. In the Federal Republic this manifested itself in continuous parliamentary debates around the limitation of prosecutions for manslaughter and accessory to murder, which, according to existing law, stood at 15 years. Thus any proceedings dealing with such offences committed in the period up to 8 May 1945 could not be prosecuted after May 1960. Moves by the Social Democratic opposition to have this amendment postponed for four years were defeated in a parliamentary vote. Despite the reinstatement of many old Nazis into public office through the '131 Law' – a judicial interpretation of paragraph 131 of the *Grundgesetz* (Constitution) – and calls for a general amnesty by the Bavarian CSU, Fritz Bauer, in the above interview, praises the younger generation for their curiosity. Assisted mainly by the publication of several excellent commentaries on the topic, such as Gerald Reitlinger's *'The Final Solution'* (*Die Endlösung*).[76] This led to a noticeable increase in interest and public support for further prosecutions.[77] In addition, occasional surprise revelations and verdicts in NS trials helped the efforts to achieve a centrally co-ordinated office to collate information and prepare prosecutions and, in anticipation of the lapsing of the manslaughter charge, the Regional Justice Administrations Central Office for the Investigation of National Socialist Crimes (*Zentrale Stelle der Landesjustizverwaltungen zur Aufklärung von nationalsozialistischen Gewaltverbrechen*) was set up in Ludwigsburg, Southern Germany, on 6 November 1958.[78]

Almost simultaneously several prominent NS trials were being held, starting with the Schörner trial in the Autumn of 1957. This trial revealed, in accordance with the law of Germans committing crimes against other Germans, that the Wehrmacht not only committed mass executions of civilians in the occupied territories, but also shot their own troops. In the following year, proceedings against the *Kommandant* of the Buchenwald concentration camp, Martin Sommer, revealed the true horror and unbound violence of the camp system. The trial of members of *Einsatzgruppe A* running concurrently in Ulm was revealing hundreds of hitherto unprosecuted individuals, who were guilty of massacres in Lithuania and the Baltic states. The Ulm trial was the first investigation carried out by chief public prosecutor Erwin Schüle, who had spent months in the archives in order to research the activities of the *Einsatzgruppen*, as the former director of police, Bernard Fischer-Schwerder, had hampered his original enquiries.[79] Schüle and the Stuttgart state prosecutor Erich Nellmann decided to intensify their efforts after realising the extent and magnitude of the crimes committed, and also in response to a seeming apathy – not to say antipathy – towards to their investigations. Judiciary and politicians alike appeared to be waiting for the statue of limitations for manslaughter and accessory to murder to take effect – particularly in the Ulm trial. Outraged by this, in an article in the *Stuttgarter Zeitung*, Nellmann proposed wide-ranging powers for the new authority, the *Zentrale Stelle*, in order to allow it to deal with a wide range of crimes committed beyond German soil.[80] However, the *Zentrale Stelle*'s efforts were often undermined by an unwilling judiciary, which had remained thoroughly un-de-Nazified; a fact that was often pointed to by 'revelations' from the GDR's campaign against former Nazi hanging judges.[81]

The seeming unwillingness to prosecute in the 1950s also had ideological reasons and repercussions. In the GDR, up to the time of Stalin's death in 1953, matters had to be dealt with in accordance with Moscow. With regard to Nazi war crimes prosecutions, this resulted in the so-called 'Waldheim' trials of 1950. The KPD (later SED) had made demands for

> ...a complete liquidation of remnants of the Hitler regime and the Hitler party; co-operation of all decent Germans in the tracking down

of hidden Nazi leaders, Gestapo agents and SS bandits; complete cleansing of all public offices of active Nazis; apart from the punishing of the main war criminals by the court of the United Nations, the most severe punishment of those Nazis, who incriminated themselves by taking part in Hitler's high treason, by German courts.[82]

This demand had been drawn up by the Central Committee (ZK) of the Buchenwald KPD inmates, issued on 11 June 1945, and held great sway. Accordingly, 15,038 persons had been kept in internment camps under Soviet military supervision. Of these, 10,510 were sentenced by the military to prison terms to be administered by German authorities. A remaining 3,442 persons were transferred to the East German authorities in 1949 to be sentenced by the courts. The suspected war criminals were kept in Waldheim prison, Saxony, and were tried at the regional court (*Landgericht*) Chemnitz (Karl-Marx-Stadt) between 26 April and 14 July 1950. The speed of these proceedings was astonishing – 142 cases a day – and the sentencing – without defence lawyers or admission of the public – harsh. Prosecutors, judges and jurors were selected from the party leadership and the Soviet authorities had made it clear that they considered the defendants' guilt to have been made clear by what was written in the files. Thus, the majority received sentences of between 15 and 25 years, 947 received sentences of ten to 15 years, 146 life imprisonment and 33 were sentenced to death, with 24 being executed. A bizarre twist in this episode remains unexplained: the relatives of those executed were informed that they had died a 'natural' death and exactly how these 24 met their end is still a mystery.[83] Whereas there were doubtless serious war criminals among the sentenced, serious flaws in the proceedings were discovered as early as 1956, and by 1964 none of those originally sentenced remained in prison.

Thus 1951 appeared to be a year, in both East and West Germany, when the matter of war crimes prosecutions was deemed closed, or at least to have been dealt with decisively for the time being. The number of prosecutions fell drastically after the 'Waldheim' trials in the GDR, and this is now viewed, by many commentators, as a period of Stalinisation of the GDR judiciary. This is not to say that the prosecutions of Nazis in East Germany were not taken seriously. According to many observers, on the whole, with the exception of the Waldheim trials, they were conducted in accordance with national and international standards.[84]

Whereas the newspapers in the GDR were obliged to report any Nazi war crimes trial, this was not the case in the West. Despite a continuing steady trickle of prosecutions of former Nazis, and increasing media coverage, overall public interest in the Federal Republic remained minimal. Heiner Lichtenstein reported from a trial against an Auschwitz doctor at a court in Münster, in 1960:

> 14 November 1960, regional court Münster. On that particular day began the proceeding against Dr med. Johann Paul Kremer, a noted professor of medicine at the university of Münster. The charge is murder and accessory to murder in the concentration camp Auschwitz. There, on the ramp in 1942, he allegedly, with a movement of the thumb, chose to send people to the gas chambers or to be subjected to medical experiments in which tissue samples were extracted from their stomach, liver and spleen without the use of any anaesthetic. The same year Kremer returned to Münster, where he resumed his activities at the Institute of Anatomy. He also remained there after the war, until his past caught up with him in the late 1950s. He was temporarily suspended from duty. The university wanted to wait for the result of the investigation. I was a young free-lance journalist at the time for WDR [West Deutscher Rundfunk] Münster and wanted to report on this case. On this dim, grey and wet November morning I arrived at court over an hour early to secure a place on the press benches. There will be a crush, I thought. And there will be representatives from the university, many students and other interested parties. I was very wrong. There were three observers on the press benches, the university was not represented and in the court room itself were a few pensioners who while away their days in courts. For the court officials 14 November 1960 was just a day like any other. No one saw a difference between this and any other legal proceeding.[85]

While public indifference appeared to be striking, observers like Lichtenstein had the ability to make a difference. A steady focus on the trials on the part of broadcast journalists in particular enhanced the levels of public interest. The spectacular kidnapping and trial of Adolf Eichmann in Jerusalem in 1961 brought 'forgotten' Nazi war crimes to the attention of the world and to a new generation of Germans, while giving fuel to a renewed ideological offensive from the GDR, which had its own agenda.

During this period the mass exodus of professionals and dissidents from East to West Germany, which had begun to happen at the very moment of the FRG's inception in 1949, was starting to accelerate.

Economic hardship and the restrictions of a one-party state led 144,917 GDR citizens to 'go west', approximately 200,000 in 1960, and a further 159,000 up to the building of the Berlin Wall on 13 August 1961.[86] Under the auspices of Albert Norden, KPD founder member, resistance fighter and SED functionary, the ideological offensive against the 're-Nazified' Federal Republic started in 1960. The department HA IX/11 of the Ministry for State Security (*Stasi*) was in the possession of countless files of the past of many prominent West Germans, and by selective leaks the information trickled over to the West German press, first in the form of leaflets naming individuals, later in the form of the 'brown book' (*Braunbuch*), with lists of names with a Nazi past.[87]

The impact was considerable, but the initial sensationalist headlines eventually gave way to more serious investigations. The debate about the Nazi past divided along the following ideological lines. For the GDR, the rise of Hitler and the Nazi state was clear evidence of the excesses of monopoly capitalism. The racial constituent of German fascism was an interchangeable element of a corporatist, anti-Bolshevik ideology. Therefore they saw the continuation of a free-market economy in West Germany as synonymous with the continuation of National Socialism. In the GDR the problem had been solved radically by instituting 'real existing socialism', modelled on that found in the Soviet Union. It is difficult to assess to what extent this view was genuinely believed by the population or the leadership, especially when confronted with the very selective leaking of the Stasi's Nazi archive, persistent emigration and the general unwillingness to co-operate with the West's attempts to bring war criminals to justice.

In the Federal Republic the GDR was viewed with great suspicion. While aware that some of the files in their possession might incriminate high-ranking officials and prominent citizens, there was also awareness that sometimes these 'leaks' consisted of forged documents. The prosecution of former Nazis was conducted as carefully as possible, and according to the strict letter of the law. However, it must be stressed that while the efforts of the *Zentrale Stelle* were impeccable, other organisations and officials were more reluctant to co-operate, a process very well described in Auschwitz survivor Herrmann Langbein's attempts to bring proceedings against the Auschwitz torturer Boger.[88] There were other considerations, often overlooked in this context: In Germany, as the 'frontline' of the Cold War, the rabid anti-communism of the ex-Nazis and wartime generation was often welcome by the NATO partners, particularly the USA. It appeared expedient to overlook the past in favour of containing the present Soviet threat. While this could not be admitted openly, it certainly was the underlying tone of the 1950s in West Germany.

Proceedings against the former adjutant of Auschwitz, Robert Mulka, and others had been co-ordinated by Fritz Bauer in Frankfurt and the Vienna Auschwitz Committee under Hermann Langbein. In March 1958 state prosecutors in Stuttgart received a letter from a former inmate of Auschwitz – identified with the initials A.R., with the concentration camp number 15465 – concerning the whereabouts of the former investigator of the 'Political Section' of Auschwitz and torturer Friedrich Wilhelm Boger, and requesting that an investigation should be undertaken with a to commencing proceedings against him. Whereas the officials took their time over this matter, a copy had also been sent to Hermann Langbein at the international Auschwitz committee in Vienna. Through his efforts, Fritz Bauer and the newly established *Zentrale Stelle*, swift action was taken. By 8 October Boger had been arrested and held on remand. But the case of Boger itself had its peculiarities, as Langbein noted:

> In court, Boger said that he had received a phone call a few days before his arrest. It was the police, and they were asking if this was *the* Boger of the Political Section at Auschwitz. When he answered in the affirmative to this question, they hung up. 'If I had felt guilty, I could easily have fled' – this statement of Boger's on the first day of the trial was never contradicted.
>
> A chain of coincidences led to the German judiciary developing an interest in Wilhelm Boger. He had been on the Allied list of war criminals, is mentioned more than once in expert literature, escaped from American imprisonment and should have been sought by the law. But Boger had been living under his own name since 31 August 1949, known to the authorities.[89]

But Dr Fritz Bauer had a greater prosecution in mind, that is to say, not just the prosecution of Boger, but a total of 26 persons, whose names were revealed to the authorities through a file smuggled out of Poland by the *Frankfurter Rundschau* journalist Thomas Gnielka. This file contained the names and activities of the notorious Auschwitz guards, together with the lists of those they had shot 'while attempting to escape'. In late 1960 there was a major breakthrough: the arrest of the last commandant of Auschwitz, Richard Baer, who had been living under an assumed name and working as a forestry worker. The legal complexities of such a case, which involved many authorities from a number of countries, including the GDR, took its time. By the time the case came to trial in late 1963, two of the defendants, including Baer, had died while awaiting trial, and another two had been excused on medical grounds.[90]

The Frankfurt prosecution, in accordance with the West German judicial system, allocated three prosecuting counsels, the main West German team of state prosecutors under the guidance of Fritz Bauer and two *Nebenkläger* (literally: adjunct prosecutor), denoting prosecutors who, as additional prosecutors, can represent different victims against the same defendant. In the Auschwitz trial the two additional prosecutors were representing victims from 12 different countries and victims and their relatives now living in the GDR. Representing citizens now living in other Western countries was the adjunct prosecutor Henry Ormond, and the lawyer acting for the five GDR citizens bringing charges against Mulka and others was Professor Dr Friedrich Karl Kaul.

Through a series of extraordinary events it had been possible for Kaul to gain his legal qualifications in Germany, first just before 1933 and then again just after 1946, after having spent most of the war in American internment camps. Because of a shortage of un-implicated lawyers in Berlin after the war, he was one of a select few who were able to practice law in both East and West Germany. As a committed communist and a member of the SED Kaul often represented 'fighters for peace' and 'patriots', and after the ban on communists in public service in West Germany in 1951 represented the KPD against the Federal Constitutional Court (*Bundesverfassungsgericht*). Kaul could, according to *Der Spiegel* magazine, 'expose, with the intuition of a diviner and the obstinacy of a rhinoceros, all subterranean contradictions which occur when the right to the free opinion is called on to exercise justice'.[91]

But by 1961 the West German Federal Court decided that Kaul's SED membership was contrary to a jurist's impartiality and excluded him from practicing in the West. After the arrest of Adolf Eichmann Kaul had been speculating about representing the interests of Jewish GDR citizens in Jerusalem, but these plans did not come to fruition as the Israeli Supreme Court abolished the legal framework for an adjunct prosecutor.[92]

In the light of the 'ideological offensive' against the Federal Republic the SED leadership decided to force the issue. In an underground publication of lists of prominent Nazis still in public service in West Germany it emerged that Erwin Schüle, head of the *Zentrale Stelle*, had joined the SA in 1933 and the NSDAP in 1935. During the war he had been ordinance officer in the siege of Leningrad, involved in the 'scorched earth' policy and in charge of 'special punishment squad' (*Sonderstrafkompanie*), infantry division 253.[93] To quote the *Braunbuch*:

> The past of the present chief public prosecutor was recommendation enough for Bonn to engage him with much propaganda effort as the person responsible for the *Zentrale Stelle* investigation of Nazi crimes. The role intended for him was sought out from the start by the Federal Republic, to continue their systematic policy of protecting Nazi and war criminals in the guise of the *Zentral Stelle*. There has not, as a matter of fact, been one prosecution since the establishing of the *Zentralstelle*, which dealt with the desk-murderers, who could, with the stroke of a pen, send thousands and tens of thousands to their deaths.[94]

This was, of course, a great setback for Schüle and the *Zentrale Stelle*. He was suspended from duty and remained the nominal head of the agency until his move to the *Bundesgerichtshof* (Appeal Court) in 1966. He himself was never implicated in any crimes, but the international embarrassment this caused for the FRG had the desired effect: the GDR adjunct prosecutor Kaul was now admitted to the Auschwitz Trial, although recent research shows that Kaul had to convince his superiors to let him attend the proceedings in Frankfurt and only got permission to do so two days before the trial began.[95]

Continuing exposés from the GDR came thick and fast. As early as 1961 Walter Ulbricht had decided that a judicial confrontation with the Federal Republic would prove most rewarding, particularly in light of the half-hearted Nazi crimes prosecutions.[96] A month before the beginning of the Auschwitz trial the politburo of the Central Committee of the SED decided that, apart from a series of attempts to discredit West Germany, efforts would be made to 'transform the Auschwitz trial into a tribunal against I.G. Farben',[97] the conglomerate of petrochemical companies which produced the *Zyklon B* gas for the gas chambers and which had a factory in the subsidiary camp of Auschwitz-Monowitz employing slave labour.

Programmes preceding the Auschwitz Trial

In 1997 the German Radio Archive (*Deutsches Rundfunkarchiv*, DRA) published a catalogue of every existing programme dealing with the National Socialist past. Under the title 'Persecution of the Jews and

Jewish life under the conditions of the National-Socialist dictatorship', this two-volume publication concentrates exclusively on the 1,453 audio materials and radio broadcasts which are today kept in 14 different archives in Germany.[98] Each numbered entry appears by date of broadcast, title, origin (by radio station), length (in minutes) and a brief synopsis, as well as author/producer, spanning the years 1947–1990. The first in this series covered the years 1930–1946,[99] and broadcasts from the Nuremberg Trials were made available in a previous publication of the DRA.[100]

As is noted by the authors of this publication, the majority of broadcasts were not kept, as a matter of course, as magnetic audio tape was still expensive and the idea of building a 'radio archive' for spoken word or documentary programmes had hardly been considered at that time. Very few scripts of newscasts and commentaries, light entertainment and chat shows were kept – the exception being the GDR radio daily political commentaries for the years 1954 to 1964 (inclusive). The existing archival collection represents only a small fraction of what was actually broadcast, although it can be assumed that programmes with this particular theme were subject to careful consideration and not easily discarded. Newspapers and radio listings magazines (such as the West German *Hör Zu* and the East German *Rundfunk und Fernsehen*) revealed very little. A programme such as the 'Sunday Commentary' (*Kommentar am Sonntag*) could have been about anything as the details were not known beforehand for inclusion in any publications. Most of the journalists did not keep their daily or weekly commentary scripts,[101] many have since died and one approached for an interview by the author refused. Furthermore, some clips, parts of programmes and interviews, speeches and debates, some of them not listed in the above-named publication, were buried in the archives, or rather on a reel of magnetic tape. Because often as many as 10–15 of these segments can be on one reel, discovery can be accidental and serendipitous. There are also some trial recordings, such as the 1966 Horst-Fischer trial in Leipzig, where only one programme of 17 minutes is listed, but an additional 70 hours of recordings are in the archives, with no sign of them ever being broadcast or even listened to by anyone after the initial recording.[102]

When dividing the broadcasts into their respective East and West German origins – the proliferation of radio stations and frequencies notwithstanding – surviving and archived radio programmes on this topic are relatively few. For the period before 1960 there are a total of 61 recordings, six from the GDR and 55 from the FRG, even fewer for the period before 1958 (24 in total, four East, 20 West).

But the East–West contrast is at its most obvious when considering the 1960s and later periods. The 'ideological offensive' of the GDR leadership was initiated during this time under the auspices of Albert Norden, politburo member and propaganda expert. This meant, as far as radio programming was concerned, that the output from the East increased considerably, even though a first glance at the numbers might not suggest it. In the decade between 1960 and 1970 the archives contained a total of 20 surviving programmes from the East, which were broadcast on four separate stations (*DDR I, DDR II, Deutschlandsender* and *Berliner Rundfunk*), transmitting on the FM (VHF), MW and LW wavelengths. But, unlike their West German counterparts, the production of these programmes was centralised and frequencies shared, so that a production of *Berliner Rundfunk* would simultaneously be on the DDR I frequency, with perhaps a repeat later in the day on the *Deutschlandsender* and a schools programme on *DDRII*.[103]

West German radio stations, in comparison, aired a total of 203 programmes in the same time-span, from 13 different stations. While this appears to be a significant difference in favour of the broadcasters from the FRG, it has to be remembered that with the exception of the *Deutsche Welle* and *Deutschlandfunk* stations, all broadcasters were increasingly regionally limited by the introduction of the FM frequency, which meant that most transmitters had a maximum 50-mile radius, with intermittent relay masts. Also production was local and sharing production facilities or airing another station's material unusual, despite the establishing of the ARD (*Arbeitsgemeinschaft der öffentlich-rechtlichen Rundfunkanstalten der Bundesrepublik Deutschland* – 'Consortium of public-law broadcasting institutions of the Federal Republic of Germany') in 1950, which tended to concentrate on television.

The period 1970–1980 sees a slight increase in the number of West German programmes on the topic of the NS past – 207 – and fewer from the East – 11. The following decade (1980–1990 inclusive, a total of 11 years) reflects the increased general interest and debate around the Hitler dictatorship: 954 programmes from West German stations and 46 from the GDR.

Therefore strict adherence to the numbers of programmes will yield little insight, not only because of the limited amount of archive material, but also because of the incompatible production and broadcast methods. What can be said about numbers, however, is that in the decade from 1960 to 1970 the increased output from the GDR was part of a concerted effort of the SED's campaign against the 're-Nazified' Federal Republic. The much higher figure for the number of West

German programmes corresponds with the general level of increased public interest in this topic.

The programmes which are in the archives, however, are invaluable examples of a mixture of a 'coming-to-terms-with the past' and propaganda, political oneupmanship and vitriolic accusations. Despite this, to doubt the sincerity of the broadcasters of wanting, or being prepared to engage meaningfully with the Nazi past would be a mistake. In the run up to, during the proceedings of, and after the Auschwitz trial, the language and style of the radio programmes remains serious and professional throughout.

Radio programmes and sound recordings, not only as historical records but also as a medium for dealing with the past, have the advantage of achieving a very direct engagement with the listener. The aural experience, hearing the voices of victims and perpetrators, makes for a closeness and involvement no written text could offer. Furthermore, style and production technique can enhance or detract where mere voices seem inadequate. This, of course, also points to the dangers of using sound recordings and radio for historical evidence. The world presented on air is scripted and edited, measured and tweaked. The distance needed to 'de-construct' radio reality requires clarity, attention and critical awareness; precisely the very things the 'hot' and 'low participation' medium of radio professes to do for you.

The programmes selected in the following part represent a variety of types of programmes, from interviews and commentaries to documentaries and 'features'. Initially, they will be arranged more or less chronologically, but two 'media events' during this period – the Eichmann Trial and the exposing of Chancellor Adenauer's secretary, Dr Hans Maria Globke – will each be the subject of their own sections before there is a return to the theme of the Auschwitz Trial in the next chapter.

In the GDR the awareness of the National Socialist past was tied closely to the legitimacy of the regime. As stands to reason, the opposition to the Nazi dictatorship had claims to leadership in postwar Germany.[104] However, this was not as clear-cut as it might appear. Communists and socialists had been persecuted, incarcerated and murdered throughout the 12 years of the Third Reich, but the legitimacy of the 'anti-fascist' resistance rested on superpower rivalry and political positioning after May 1945.[105] Other 'resistance' fighters, such as the followers and admirers of the plotters of 20 July 1944, had been part of the Nazi regime and held only a limited claim to power in the Western zones of occupation.

There had been, in the period from 1933 to 1945, clandestine organisations and committees of the German Communist Party (KPD) in the concentration camps, most notably in Sachsenhausen and Buchenwald. Other communists had fled into exile to Moscow or were being trained at Comintern schools as instructors and 'cadres' in charge of the 're-education' of German prisoners of war. Walter Ulbricht, future leader of the GDR, had been in Moscow throughout and arrived in Berlin with the Red Army in April 1945. Stalin's pragmatism towards Marxist doctrine and military opportunism was not lost on Ulbricht and the 'Moscow' KPD. Whereas the formerly incarcerated KPD leadership – the Buchenwald Central Committee (ZK) – had somewhat mellowed in their attitude towards religious and social democrat fellow Germans from their time in the camps,[106] the complete reorganisation of the communist party along its own principles – as independent from Moscow – was unthinkable for the 'Ulbricht Group', Stalin and the CPSU. With the help of the Red Army and Soviet Military authorities the Ulbricht Group managed to contain the 'old communists', partially by a massive membership drive, and partially by further incarcerating some of the old guard.[107] By September 1945 Ulbricht had managed to secure a numerical superiority of new cadres over 'old communists'.[108] Despite this, the myth of the 'Buchenwald ZK' was too valuable a propaganda weapon to be discarded. The antifascist resistance in the concentration camps were held up as the legitimate heirs of the new Germany.

The following transcript of a broadcast, first aired on the *Berliner Rundfunk* in 1955, contains all of the elements of myth and ritual, combining a solemnly spoken oath with chant-like answers. The 'Oath of the Prisoners of Buchenwald', written in April 1945 in the KZ Buchenwald, is spoken by the then popular radio presenter and newscaster Horst Preusker, the replies by unknown persons (presumably some of the former inmates):

HP: Us Buchenwalders: Russians, French, Poles, Czechs, Slovaks and Germans, Spaniards, Italians and Austrians, Belgians and people from the Netherlands, English, Luxemburgers, Romanians, Yugoslavs and Hungarians fought the SS. Against the Nazi criminals for our own liberation. We are driven by an idea, our cause is just, ours is the victory. In many languages we conducted our fight hard and with many sacrifices, and this fight is not over yet. Our comrades' murderers are still alive, the sadistic torturers still walk about freely. Therefore we swear, in front of the eyes of the world, here on the parade ground in the place of fascist horrors: only when the last perpetrator is in front of the judges of nations will we cease our fight.

All: We swear it.
HP: The extermination of Nazism is our slogan (*Losung*).
All: We swear it.
HP: Our aim is the building of a new world of peace and liberty.
All: We swear it.[109]

Despite the unknown first broadcast date, attached in the reel casing was a note of release authorisations (for broadcast?) which listed five dates between 1955 and 1967 for this particular programme.

Buchenwald concentration camp was held in particularly high esteem among anti-fascists, not only because of its clandestine communist resistance and 'red' Kapos, but also because it had 'liberated' itself, or, to be precise, after the evacuation death marches of Winter 1944/45 the SS handed the camp over to the KPD-dominated camp Kapos. The remaining 21,000 inmates had 'taken over' the camp on 11 April 1945.[110] This 'self-liberation' (*Selbstbefreiung*) was another theme which was often aired on GDR radio. On the same reel of tape, archived but not listed in the DRA publication, former Buchenwald inmate Richard Kuchardzyk said the following in an interview dated April 1956:

> The camp was free. 21,000 people from 24 nations, their lives saved through this battle. The liberation of the camp on 11 April 1945 was the crowning glory of the illegal resistance of all nations under the leadership of the KPD. Here the working class proved – through this victory over the fascist barbarity in Buchenwald – that it was the leading power in the struggle against war and fascism, proof of proletarian internationalism.[111]

And here emerges a trend in the policies of the SED of the 1950s: by placing the party and the working class at the vanguard of the struggle, the majority of the victims, Jews, were seen at best as fellow sufferers, at worst – and this was particularly true for the Polish Jews – as second-class citizens not worth consideration.[112] Within the Central Committee of the party this led, as early as April 1945, despite a strong element from the Buchenwald group recognising the suffering of Jewish fellow inmates, to some overtly anti-Semitic sentiments, expressing themselves in such phrases as: 'Jewish immigrants don't belong to the working class', 'cosmopolitanism' (a derogatory term) 'only strengthening Jewish capitalists.'[113]

The complexities arising from such sentiments were startling: on the one hand several of the KPD/SED leadership were Jewish in origin, yet the glamour attached to the myth of resistance fighters was undoubtedly linked to the Buchenwald ZK and other former communist camp inmates. Coupled with the Zionist struggle in Palestine this became an emotive issue within the SED.[114] The fact that the Jews in Palestine were fighting the British 'imperialists' was, in Marxist-Leninist doctrine, a liberation struggle and worthy of the support of the Soviet Union and all progressive humanity,[115] but at the same time, descriptions from Moscow of Jews as 'cosmopolitans without a fatherland' and the beginnings of the Soviet anti-Semitic campaign (culminating in Stalin's 'Doctors' Plot') were part of a Cold War rhetoric which had to distinguish between the Jewish worker and the reactionary Jewish capitalist[116] – not a distinction made by the Nazis.

Following the establishment of the state of Israel the party line changed. A campaign in the guise of 'anti-cosmopolitanism' denounced Jews as the wreckers of proletarian internationalism, (bourgeois) 'cosmopolitanism – the ideology of the transatlantic thieves'.[117] An essay with this title came from the pen of Albert Norden, a founder member of the KPD who had spent the years from 1933 to 1945 in exile in Paris, Prague and New York. The son of a German rabbi, he became a spokesman for the East German regime in 1949, and after a brief discredited period in the early 1950s, emerged as a member of the GDR politburo in the position of Secretary for Agitation in 1955. As the head of the National Front for a Democratic Germany and a member of the Committee for German Unity (*Ausschuss für Deutsche Einheit*), he was in charge of the GDR's propaganda campaign against the West,[118] and his involvement in the output of East German radio cannot be understated.

Norden's skill lay in balancing the SED's and Moscow's often-changing view of the West and international relations by arousing the suspicion of 'pro-Nazi' sympathies of capitalist countries and accusations of meddling and subversion.

But after 1956 the SED's apparent anti-Semitic sentiment was on the wane, as evidenced in the radio output of the GDR. Programmes on Anne Frank,[119] on the anniversary of the *Reichskristallnacht*,[120] on the anti-Semitic scriptwriter Eberhard Taubert[121] and on the crimes of the Mayor of Lodz, Werner Ventzki[122] have survived in the Berlin archive of the DRA. However, most of these broadcasts had additional topicality, such as the popularity of the Anne Frank book, the anniversary of the *Kristallnacht* being marred by desecrations of Jewish cemeteries in West Germany, and Eberhart Taubert being employed as a speechwriter and chief strategist by the Bavarian CSU leader Franz Josef Strauß.

However, there is a much more impressive collection of programmes that were produced by the West German radio stations of this period, even if they are somewhat more difficult to locate, as they are stored in the archives of the respective broadcasters. They represent the height of the radio age in the Federal Republic, a time in which the relationship between listener and broadcaster had 'normalised'.[123] Radio Bremen, in numerical terms, appears the most prolific here with a series of 45 30-minute programmes, of which 26 have survived in the archives, under the overall title 'Emigration of the Spirit' (*Auszug des Geistes*).[124] Broadcast weekly and spanning most of the year 1959, Irmgard Bach interviewed German academics and intellectuals who had left Germany in the 1930s, some to return, and some who remained in exile. The interviewees included Hannah Arendt, Leo Löwenthal, Karl Landauer, and Hans Rothfels, among others.

The *Südwestfunk* (SWF), the broadcasting corporation for the South West of the Federal Republic, based in Baden-Baden, also produced a number of highly interesting and topical programmes, employing historians such as Martin Broszat[125] and Joseph Wulf.[126] The WDR (one of the successor station to the NWDR) in Cologne aired a much debated three-hour programme by Hans Günther Adler on Auschwitz.[127]

A programme selected here for closer analysis is the four-part documentary and discussion feature by the Hamburg NDR station 'Behind the Wall of Silence' (*Hinter der Mauer des Schweigens*),[128] which was aired in weekly instalments during February and March 1960. The format is unusual for its time: the broadcasts consist of conversations between the (print and radio) journalist Thilo Koch and the Viennese filmmaker Peter Schier-Gribowsky, reviewing his 70-minute television film '*...as if it was a Part of You*' ('*...als wär's ein Stück von Dir!*'),[129] broadcast on the national first television channel ARD in September 1959. This 'bi-media' approach has several advantages in this context, as the clips chosen by Schier-Gribowsky are discussed not only in the context of his film, but also as 'sound-samples' for radio use (by their own admission). Additionally, the subject matter of the film – and therefore of the radio broadcast – had gained in topicality by the recent desecrations of Jewish cemeteries and the daubing of Nazi graffiti on the synagogue in Cologne. The themes of each broadcast are clearly signposted: the first programme deals with the state of present historical enquiry, the second with victims and perpetrators, the third with political activism and the last is an investigation into public opinion in West Germany today, entitled 'An anti-Semitism without Jews' (*Ein Anti-Semitismus ohne Juden*). The series is framed with a four-minute sound recording (in the first and the last programme) of interviews with passers-by in a Frankfurt street, being asked a variety of questions regarding the Third Reich and the Holocaust.[130]

On the current state of historical enquiry Koch and Schier-Gribowsky agree: not enough is being done. Some have knowledge of the past, some don't, some want to know, others don't, many are uninterested. Facts and figures are readily available, but in Germany, and for Germans, it is not simply that. The problems that arise from the investigation into the very recent past, and the dilemmas facing the (German) historian, are related eloquently by the director of the Munich *Institut für Zeitgeschichte*, Dr Helmut Krausnick. Accounting for one's actions during the Nazi dictatorship, so Krausnick argues, is connected deeply with an enquiry of this nature, not only for those who have (consciously) lived through it, but also for the younger generation as one's actions in the present are inextricably drawn from lessons of one's own and of one's parents' past.[131] This is why (German) contemporary history is deeply entwined with political education as the veil of falsified worldviews and propaganda has to be lifted through rigorous and scientific research:

> We not only ask: What crimes occurred? But also: How could they occur? And by asking this question, the National-Socialist era presents an object lesson par excellence, a wealth of lessons. The persecution of the Jews, which resulted in, in today's estimate, between 4 and 6 million victims, this persecution was the result of a [particular] mind-set, a demand of the individual to place loyalty to the party and submission to the party leadership above conscience. This setting aside of conscience through the *Führerbefehl* made the NS terror what it was, a totalitarian state. And whoever did not fit into this picture of the totalitarian state was vermin, and vermin was to be exterminated. But if you submitted to the claims of totalitarianism, then you became a tool, an instrument of the rulers in [the execution of] their crimes. Consequently the question of [obeying] an order and of conscience became the key aspect in the discussion of this system. Because we can see what happens when a totalitarian state claims not only political leadership, but also monopolises the intellect and morals of a nation.
>
> The fact that the individual during the National-Socialist time was challenged in all these aspects elevates this time from the interesting to the significant, significant for all humanity...[132]

The 'national' aspect of historical research for the benefit of 'all humanity' is again subject to controversies among German historians.[133] While

Krausnick's analysis conforms to the historical interpretations of the time, the moderators express concern about accessibility of such work. Apart from the Institute's journal, the *Vierteljahrshefte für Zeitgeschichte*, little else is on offer, particularly for the non-academic public – notwithstanding the success of the Anne Frank book and school visits to memorial sites.

In his next clip Schier-Gribowsky introduces Dr Hendrik Van Dam, general secretary of the central council of Jews in Germany, who points to the fact that through this ignorance the 'anti-Semitism without Jews' has become a problem not for Jews but for Germans, as the narrow-mindedness and bigotry of a reactionary part of the population are stumbling blocks to peace and social cohesion.[134]

Trying to assess the opinion of Jews in Germany proves quite difficult as only 30,000 have decided to remain there. Of these more than 20 per cent were resident in old people's homes. The interview with Blanca Israel (Mosse?),[135] an 89-year-old Jew in Hannover, reveals astonishing spirit. As a member of Berlin 'high society' in Imperial Germany and the Weimar Republic and the wife of one of Hindenburg's officers, she and her husband stayed in Berlin until March 1943,[136] when they were transported to the Theresienstadt camp. There her husband was murdered, along with most of her family. The closing stages of the war brought her to Switzerland, after having been exchanged along with other *Theresienstädters*, for some high-ranking Nazis, through an acquaintance of Himmler's.[137]

Her son, who had arranged for her to emigrate to the USA, eventually persuaded her to return to Germany. Today, when she hears Germans professing to not having known anything at the time, she is sceptical. 'I doubt whether I can believe that.'[138]

The second in the series of programmes begins with interviews with younger members of the German Jewish community, who, on the whole, were not as conciliatory as the older generation, as their experiences of postwar Germany had been somewhat different. A Mrs Lillienstern from Hannover recalls sitting in a café in Hamburg in the summer, her concentration camp tattoo being stared at by a woman at the next table, who finally remarked: 'What a nice souvenir from the *Reeperbahn*!' When Mrs Lilienstern explained that this was not the result of a frivolous visit to a tattoo parlour in St Pauli, but her concentration camp number, the woman replied: 'How terrible, couldn't they have put it somewhere else!'[139] This and other experiences led the Lilienstern family to leave Germany for the Netherlands.

In his attempt to find perpetrators who were willing to be interviewed, Schier-Gribowsky was less successful. However, he managed to find the former *Kommandant* of the concentration camp Westerbork (Netherlands), Albert Gemmeker, who quite openly, albeit with reservations, talked about his SS career, in his flat in Düsseldorf in May 1959. At the time of broadcast, this was the first and only (sound-recorded and broadcast) interview with a former *Kommandant* of a concentration camp, and even today, when some comparisons are possible,[140] it is still a rare insight into the petty officialdom which surrounded such posts, given added emphasis by the sound recording.

Having trained as a salesman Gemmeker found himself unemployed during the Depression, and then joined the police force:

> A.G.: I wanted to, at least, return to something like the profession I had trained for, and there existed the possibility to become an administrator in the civil service (*Verwaltungsbeamter*). But these posts had been filled, erm... in most of the authorities where the positions had been, and during this time the enlargement of the state police took place, and I was pointed in that direction, so in this manner, as an administrator (*Verwaltungsbeamter*), I came to the Gestapo. I took the usual [career] path, from assistant to secretary to chief-secretary, and finally to inspector, that was already during the war, and as a police inspector – as administrator (*Verwaltungsbeamter*) – service in the Netherlands, and that was in about August 1940, where I worked, for approximately two years, in the personnel department, until one day, when I got an order to take over a camp in the Netherlands, a so-called 'hostage camp' (*Geisellager*).
>
> P.S.-G.: Yes, and now I ask you, why do you think this order came to you? Was this a coincidence or did it have to be [that way]? How do you view this today?
>
> A.G.: Well, I would describe it as a coincidence, because personnel had no other candidates, and as I said, that there were special reasons, for instance that I was particularly suitable for this, or such, I don't think that these were the reasons, because I had never done this before and there was no evidence that I was suited for such a post.
>
> P.S.-G.: So what can be deduced from this is that it would have been possible, in today's view, that you could have become *Kommandant* of another camp, say of Buchenwald, or Dachau or Auschwitz, or others. Or wouldn't that have been possible?
>
> A.G.: That was within the realm of possibilities, but I would have had to have been released from my command in Holland and transferred to a different unit. (long pause)...

P.S.-G.: Herr Gemmeke, how did you run the camp Westerbork, an exclusively Jewish camp?

A.G.: (Pause and sigh)... Obviously there has to be order in such a camp, everything had to work properly, and my predecessor had already established something like camp regulations, which in my opinion were incorrect, so that I got together with the leading inmates, who had practically formed a kind of self-government in the camp, and with these gentlemen, five in number, worked out new camp regulations.

P.S.-G.: And they were Jews?

A.G.: Yes, they were Jews. The regulations stipulated that families could stay together, that, as much as possible within the barracks, the families were in eight blocks of flats, although I must add that because of the great number of persons, large collection-barracks (*Sammelbaracken*) served [the majority of] inmates. So what we did was, though men and women were separated, men to the right and women to the left or vice versa, but this was only at night-time, so that during the day everybody could be with their relatives. But it has to be mentioned that a darker side (*Schattenseite*) came into all this in the form of the transports, and everything that had to do with that. We personally tried to eliminate the transports by attempting to establish work, I would even say [light] industry, which could have led to the camp being re-classified from transit to work camp, so that the inmates would not be transported anymore, but stayed there.

P.S.-G.: Did you know, Herr Gemmeke, where these weekly transports of 1,000 people were going to?

A.G.: Where to, yes, I knew. The destination was Auschwitz.[141]

Gemmeke is insistent that he had no idea what went on in Auschwitz. When questioning superiors about rumours he had heard, they were dismissed as enemy propaganda. In 1949 he was sentenced to ten years' imprisonment, but he did not serve the full term. Schier-Gribowsky asks him how he feels about the sentence:

A.G.: I would like to put it like this: at the time I told the judge, in no way do I feel guilty, as I did what was possible. On the other hand, I can understand that for the people of the Netherlands, who of course only knew that I was in command of a camp for Jews, and did not know what went on there, whether it was good or bad, it would have been inconceivable for them to let me go unpunished, and further, that these people, whether they were in my camp or elsewhere, suffered so much injustice, that for me at least, er, I couldn't really blame others for my incarceration.[142]

As the end of this conversation Gemmeke states that as a result of his experiences with Jews in the camp he could never again be an anti-Semite, and he would never choose the same career path again.

The interview is mesmerising and chilling, and both Thilo Koch and Peter Schier-Gribowsky comment on this. Gemmeke's striving for a job in the administration has all the hallmarks of the 'desk-murderer' – filing and murder are purely administrative duties, and any inklings of guilt are pacified by the excuse of 'having made it as bearable as possible', a statement that comes across as unbelievable.

Jeanette Wolff, SPD member of the Bundestag, recalls her wartime experience of deportation and concentration camps at the start of the third instalment of the series. Despite the hardship and suffering she decided to stay in her native Berlin to build up new, democratic structures and today remains hopeful, but has grave doubts about the constitution's ability to withstand an onslaught from extremism, such as the neo-Nazis.[143]

This threat, according to Thilo Koch, does not come from the wives and families of the former Nazi leadership, but seems to exist independently. There are about 20 neo-Nazi publications such as *'Der Weg'* and *'Der Ring'* available in the FRG, which all appear to have money behind them, but Peter Schier-Gribowsky believes that most of the financial backers might live abroad.

One organisation, however, which he found on his travels, was the Ludendorff Movement, headed by the widow of former First World War General Erich von Ludendorff, Dr Mathilde Ludendorff. The 'Society for the knowledge of God' (*Bund für Gotterkenntnis*) central tenets consist of a series of *völkisch* ideas, condemning anything to do with the Bible. The movement was, in the 1930s, a rival to the National Socialists, and Mathilde Ludendorff cited her (very outspoken) opposition to Hitler as proof of her integrity. Nevertheless this movement is deeply racist and particularly anti-Semitic. Schier-Gribowsky managed to locate Mathilde Ludendorff, but she refused to be interviewed. He did, however, interview an ardent follower of the movement, a certain A.E. Meyer, who goes to great length to explain the movement's virtues.[144]

Another former victim of the National Socialist terror, Kurt Bachmann, voices his concerns about the reintegration of former SS members into public life and industry. This includes figures like the SS general

Heinz Reinefarth, who had massacred the population of Warsaw and then gone on to sit in the *Landtag* in Kiel and become the mayor of Westerland on the island of Sylt. But the programme's presenters note that people like Wolff and Bachmann continue to have an unshakable trust in the democratic process.[145]

In the final programme Koch and Schier-Gribowsky reflect on the present (January 1960) situation. In an interview recorded for the radio, the chairman of the Berlin Jewish community, Dr Heinz Galinski, reminds the listeners that the term 'neo-Nazi' is really a misnomer. This is not a new 'anti-Semitism' – there have been over 1,000 desecrations of Jewish cemeteries between 1950 and 1959 in the Federal Republic and the recent occurrences in Cologne and elsewhere are manifestations of the same 'old' phenomenon. It is now up to the Federal government not only to cleanse its ranks of the 'old guard', but also to educate and enlighten its younger citizens. Democracy requires effort, and the economic miracle has made the democrats content and tired (*satt und müde*). This Galinski views with alarm.[146]

A brief recollection by the sociology professor Max Horkheimer on his reasons for returning to Germany is followed by the final recording of the series, a remarkable, shouted plea by Father Roth, resident Catholic priest at the former Dachau concentration camp near Munich, which, at the time of the interview, still housed more than 2000 refugees from the East:

> Fr. Roth: It is more than ugly, I think, that the barrack in which the sick were gathered to be gassed, up until last year was a restaurant complete with dance floor. It is equally ugly that in the place where the cold water and malaria experiments took place accommodated a butcher's shop, that the pathology laboratory was a delicatessen and that barrack 26, where many priests met a terrible end, now has been converted into flats, that little children now play on the main road of the camp, where hundreds and thousands died, were hanged, beaten. That civilized people should be forced to live in such barracks![147]

At the end of the programme, the moderators appear baffled, 'pretty clueless in front of the facts' (*Wir sitzen ziemlich ratlos vor den Tatsachen*), and this, perhaps, is the programme's great strength: it shows a picture of West German society in the late 1950s, totally unable to come to terms with its past, held together by economic wealth and selective amnesia. At the same time the programme itself is an example of an attempted reconciliation, exposing a disparate and fragmented society, not only concerning its past, but also its future with real or imagined threats from the East. Surprisingly, it had been Thilo Koch in particular, as one of the few commentators in this debate outside the left-liberal consensus, who had voiced grave concerns about 'a radio-avalanche from the East', subverting the Federal Republic's young democracy with broadcasts from the clandestine (East German) stations such as the *Freiheitssender 904* and the *Bundeswehr*-orientated *Deutscher Soldatensender*.[148] But radio in the fledgling television age had a more normalising influence, with listeners being more critical of the broadcasters, and programmes such as *Hinter der Mauer des Schweigens* would have had the desired effect of encouraging personal reflection and some public debate.

Eichmann

To use a present-day term the Eichmann Trial was perhaps the first international 'media event'. The material surrounding the trial – and biographies of Eichmann himself – is enormous and still growing, but for the sake of brevity the media coverage of the 1961 event will be dealt with only briefly.

Not only had the capture of Eichmann provided the world with spectacular headlines, but the trial in Jerusalem had also provided the ideologically divided world with ample material to promote respective worldviews. 'Eichmann' not only became a conceptualised term of abuse but also an effective tool in Cold War propaganda. By October 1961 the West Berlin Senate had erected loudspeakers adjacent to the newly built Berlin Wall to broadcast news from the trial with intermittent announcements such as:

> Think of Eichmann! Shooting a person travelling from Germany to Germany is murder! One day you will be called to account. Act according to your conscience... Murder remains murder, even when ordered. Think of Eichmann![149]

Broadcasters and press agencies used the time from Eichmann's abduction in Argentina to the start of the trial as an opportunity to secure the most favourable reporting positions and negotiations were conducted at the highest levels.[150] West German broadcasters (television and radio) had secured access to the proceedings, as well as a number of GDR reporters, who had been under the instruction to 'prime the Eichmann case against Bonn with maximum effect'.[151]

The numbers of surviving programmes in the radio archives are evidence that the Eichmann issue was seen as a journalistic undertaking without precedent. For the 21-month period from July 1960 to April 1962 a total of 84 programmes are listed. Of these, 73 (87 per cent) of them dealt with the Eichmann Trial – 8 from East Berlin and 65 from West German stations. The numbers again do not give the whole story: most of the Western broadcasts are between three and 15 minutes in length, whereas the programmes from East Berlin range between 30 and 125 minutes and this even includes an 860-minute audio tape covering the third to the eleventh day of proceedings. These full-length recordings were often made by the GDR radio stations so that they could later be used in edited form for a variety of programmes.[152] The majority of reports for West German radio stations were dispatched by Wolf Posselt and Klaus Bölling, and have survived in the archives of the *Westdeutscher Rundfunk* in Cologne, *Radio Bremen* and the *Saarländischer Rundfunk* in Saarbrücken. Among the weekly and monthly reportage from Jerusalem only a few recordings, such as Posselt's summary of 15 August 1961[153] or the WDR's summary in the same month, are longer than five or six minutes.[154] The brevity of the surviving reports is somewhat surprising as reportage from later trials certainly centred on longer, in-depth programmes lasting 30 minutes or more. These were not, it appears, broadcast separately but remained part of general news bulletins. One 133-minute programme, however, made by Peter Schier-Gribowsky for the NDR in Hamburg, features a long and detailed interview with Joel Brand.[155]

The authors of the surviving radio transmissions of East German radio had the difficult task of proving the link between Eichmann and Chancellor Adenauer's private secretary, Dr Hans Maria Globke, their task set out in their titles, which had included 'There is Still Room for Dr Globke'[156] among others.

The Globke issue

For the East German regime, the 'campaign against Bonn' had not focussed exclusively on the Eichmann Trial for various reasons. First, whether Kaul would be able to appear as adjunct prosecutor in Jerusalem was far from clear and in the end was not possible. Second, the GDR's efforts in exposing former Nazis in the 're-Nazified' Federal Republic had taken a different turn. Economic difficulties, including 'potato riots' as a result of serious food shortages,[157] large parts of the population emigrating westwards and general discontent meant that the overall policy of the SED leadership concentrated on their anti-fascist campaign from an earlier date. The first efforts in this line of attack came in May 1957, when Norden issued a press statement entitled 'Yesterday Hitler's Blood Judges – Today's Judicial Elite in Bonn', listing 118 judges and prosecutors who were still holding office in the FRG.[158] This was followed by substantial evidence and new accusations, culminating in 1959 with the exposure of the Nazi past of the Minister for Expellees in the Adenauer government, Prof. Theodor Oberländer. According to the *Braunbuch*, the files on Oberländer were extensive: he had been a participant in the 1923 Munich 'Beer Hall' putsch, and an organiser of the raid on the *Gleiwitz* radio station in 1939. After 1941, he became an officer in charge of the *'Nachtigall'* battalion, responsible for the massacres in Lvov (Lemberg) and other towns in the Soviet Union. Following this, in 1942 he was placed in charge of the 'special troop' *'Bergmann'* which dealt with 'civilian unrest' in the occupied Soviet territories and also participated in the liquidation of the Warsaw Ghetto.[159] This extensive list of a very active Nazi past was too much even for Adenauer (and international opinion, more to the point) to overlook and in 1960 Oberländer resigned. In the GDR Oberländer was sentenced in absentia to life imprisonment as part of a series of show trials directed at undermining the government of the Federal Republic.

But the biggest coup in this campaign was undoubtedly the efforts against Dr Hans Maria Globke, director of Chancellor Adenauer's office, who wrote the legal commentaries for the 1935 Nuremberg Race Laws. As Jeffrey Herf puts it, 'Had Norden tried to create a figure to suit his purposes, or had Adenauer been seeking ways to give the Communists a tempting target, neither could have done much better than Globke.'[160] The *Braunbuch*, under the heading 'Intellectual murderer of the Jews', lists Globke's activities as a senior civil servant in the Reich's Ministry of the Interior from 1933 to 1945. In 1933, he had formulated parts of the 'Enabling Law' (*Ermächtigungsgesetz*), which gave Hitler dictatorial powers, as well as the law which dissolved the Prussian parliament as part of the *Gleichschaltung*. In 1937 he is credited, again according to the *Braunbuch,* as co-author of the Nuremberg Race Laws, particularly the law requiring persons of Jewish origin to have the additional first name of 'Sara' or 'Israel'. The legal framework for the deportation of Jews and Gypsies from the occupied Western territories, as well as the degrading or relinquishing of citizenship and laws regarding the 'Germanising' of occupied territories were said to be his work.[161]

This, of course, was an opportunity for Norden to point to the continuity of officials in high office – from high Nazi official to director of the Chancellor's office. The Globke issue was central to the work of the Committee of German Unity (*Auschuss für Deutsche Einheit*) and also dominated the output of radio programmes. The Globke question kept its topicality even after the Auschwitz Trial, as again and again the matter of finding the 'real' culprits, the high officials and industrialists, remained the target of the GDR's campaign. Every opportunity was taken to establish the links in this continuity.

In 1959 the desecration of the synagogue in Cologne and other West German cities gave Norden the opportunity to publish a pamphlet in a number of languages, distributed worldwide with the title '*An Appeal to the Conscience to the World*'[162] in which he writes:

> There is a great deal of disquiet about these anti-Semitic vandals in West Germany and West Berlin. Young people need human heroes. And what does Bonn offer them to worship? Speidel, unmasked as a murderer of hostages; Heusinger, a master of Hitler's military campaigns and a traitor to his fellow officers;[163] Globke and Oberländer, theoreticians and practitioners of racial murder; Franz-Josef Strauss, the whipper-up of the spirit of revenge, of which anti-Semitism is a part, and let us not forget Adenauer, the new Führer, an arch-reactionary throughout two generations, whose greatness consists in his greed and his opposition to the Nazis was confined to his acceptance – which can be proved – of hundreds of thousands of marks from them.
>
> There is therefore no cause for surprise when a muddled younger generation commits on a small scale the same kind of crimes which the ministers, generals, big business chiefs, judges and diplomats – in power today and yesterday – formerly committed on a large scale. It is clear that these young criminals are encouraged by the fact that this anti-Semitic, fascist gang now controls West Germany, politically, militarily and economically.[164]

In an article from 14 December 1991 entitled 'A Mass Murderer Makes Policy. Adolf Eichmann Was Sentenced to Death 30 Years Ago', Michael Wolffsohn and Ulrich Brochhagen claimed to have found evidence that the desecration actions were initiated and guided by the Stasi and the KGB. Hans-Peter Schwartz has also acknowledged this in his biography of Adenauer, in which he claims that Adenauer had been informed by the West German secret service of the Stasi's involvement in the defilement of the synagogues,[165] although Heinz Galinski's comments above would point to a long continuity of homegrown, West German anti-Semitism.

In Spring 1961, after prolonged and fruitless attempts by the SED leadership to 'sharpen the class antagonisms' in the FRG, Norden and Ulbricht decided that renewed action had to be taken on matters of ideology. Norden suggested to Ulbricht new measures, including increased leafleting and an increased use of agitational material on the radio. The state radio committee complained bitterly about this, as it felt unable to compete technically with the West. Norden's reaction to this was to re-establish a special department of the Central Committee responsible for counter-propaganda, capable of 'reacting immediately to the latest enemy arguments and to advise radio and press accordingly'.[166]

A good example of how these technical and ideological struggles manifested themselves is a programme of the *Deutschlandsender*, broadcasting to the FRG, in January 1963, entitled 'The Children of Zamość, or, How the White Colour of Innocence turned Black'.[167]

This programme, one hour in length, and written and recorded on location in Poland by the journalist Horst Grothe, dealt in part with the fate of 30,000 children of Zamość, a town in Poland which had been destined by the Nazis to be 'Germanised', evacuated in other words, and re-populated according to the Nuremberg Race Laws. Accordingly, Globke is heavily implicated in the murder of 15,000 of the 30,000 children, who were deported to the Majdanek death camp near Lublin. Listening to this programme is grim, at times unbearable, as every opportunity is taken to press home the unspeakable cruelty and inhumanity of the methods used in this 'resettlement'. But there are several features of the programme, which, to our ears today, sound overdramatic. These produce immediate and strong emotional responses in the listener, as sounds are disproportionally amplified and sequences surprisingly edited. The highly emotive use of language, music and editing appear to be interfering with the ability of judgement on a subliminal level, and this is used to very great effect in this programme.

A rendition of a Yiddish song *'Unzer Shtetl brent'* and a recording of Globke denying any knowledge of the real extent of the 'final solution' frame the programme. This is followed by a series of questions:

> Narrator 1: Saw nothing, heard nothing, knew nothing. This gentleman is enviable. Where was he living when the rivers of blood were flowing? When humans were being burnt, were rotting away, decaying. When six and a half million humans of flesh and blood were annihilated. Because a law said so. How did he manage to see, hear and to know nothing? Robinson on his island of ignorance.

Narrator 2: These questions are wrong (Pause)... All of them. (Pause)...

Narrator 1: You can't ask like this. (Pause)... Because someone, who led the department I/10 in the Hitler's ministry of the interior, the Jewish department, did see, did hear, did know. Therefore you have to ask:

Narrator 2: Why does this man lie so cold-bloodedly?

Narrator 1: There are two reasons for this:

Narrator 2: Firstly, the gentleman is, today, state secretary to a chancellor who openly accepts his lies as the truth, despite knowing all the facts. Secondly, the gentleman does not wish, – for career reasons and not for reasons of conscience – to burden himself with new blame.

Narrator 1: To date, there are six and a half million lives on the debit side of his account of guilt, snuffed out, trodden and suffocated lives. Six and a half million. That's quite a number. The statistic of death. The person in charge of it was in Berlin, in Hitler's ministry of the interior, a bureaucrat of death. (Pause)...

Narrator 1: (Loud, pronounced) Dr. Hans Josef Maria Globke! (Loud minor seventh chord for 6 seconds, then fade)

Narrator 2: A train rattles through the night...[168]

This very dramatic effect of the musical chord is repeated several times during the programme, used with less build-up, and slightly losing its desired effect. A hushed-voice commentary from the crematoria of Majdanek by Horst Grothe describes the hill of human ash outside, and the overseer's bathtub and WC inside, overlooking the burning process. The reason for the choice of Majdanek then becomes clear as the evacuation of the children of Zamość is mentioned, Globke being responsible for this. 'Responsible... (loud chord)'[169] An astonishing witness account of Globke's activities in the east is read out by a female narrator, claiming that he had been aware (if not in charge) of the shooting of the Polish intelligentsia. The following narrative about the evacuation of the town of Zamość and surrounding villages, which totalled (according to this programme) 110,000 persons, including 30,000 children carries a very moving account by a survivor of the children's transport, Maria Pieczynska, who was eight years old at the time. She describes the process of 'Racial and Psychological Selection', in which children with 'Aryan' features were sent on to orphanages, the parents and other children to the camps of Majdanek and Auschwitz. The legal framework for this process was the 'German People's List' (*Deutsche Volksliste*), which had four categories of citizenship, the last two subjecting its holders to the racial and psychological selection procedure. If deemed unsuitable for citizenship, they were destined for 'relocation' (*Umsiedlung*), which meant almost certain death. This the programme calls the 'Perpetuum Mobile of Death'. Its inventor, 'Dr. Hans Josef Maria Globke, Bonn, Federal Chancellor's Office, Koblenzer Strasse 139... (loud chord)'.[170]

From its emphasis on the children of Zamość, the programme shifts to the murder of children from the Warsaw Ghetto, as 'there is no difference; here as well as there governed the laws of the chief of the Jewish Department [referring to Globke]; here as well as there the children marched in the same direction: Majdanek, Sobibor, Treblinka.'[171] The emerging tale of the closure of Dr Janusz Korczak's Jewish orphanage in the Ghetto and deportation of the children to Treblinka, told by the narrator and Colonel Alev Bolkoviak,[172] a former commander of the 'people's guard' in Warsaw, is harrowing as well as interesting.

Colonel Bolkoviak recalls the forced assembly of children in the Ghetto's Szelesna Street, at the *Umschlagsplatz*, where they were herded into the cattle carts of trains to Treblinka. An incident in which a German soldier helps a child left for dead by the SS is remembered by the colonel as 'just as shattering as the cruelty of the SS' and pointed out by the programme with a dramatic 'but wait!' as a small proof that 'not all humanitarianism had died.'[173] Bolkoviak then proceeds to tell of Korczak's march with the children to the trains, the children enduring the whips, dogs and shooting of the SS.

Listening becomes difficult when the theme of the murder of children continues through various examples, such as children's shoes found among human remains in a field near Treblinka:

> They died with their blankets and toys, with their teddy bears, their dummies, rocking horses, balls and spinning tops. Next to the gas chambers in Majdanek stood an SS man. Next to him was a sack. From this sack he took sweets. Each child got a sweet before crossing the threshold to the house of death.[174]

But the programme returns to its emphasis on the children of Zamość and the Globke legislation:

> Narrator 1: 15,000 from Zamość went on the road of no return. They went because it said so in paragraph one of Globke's *Volksliste*.
> Narrator 2: For inclusion to the list married couples will be assessed independently. The same applies for children over 18 and children

without parents under 18. Otherwise children will be in the same category as their parents. Signed: Dr Globke, Minister of State.

Narrator 1: Parents to Auschwitz, Children to Majdanek, the same category. Do we have to continue proving the murderous guilt of this Dr Globke? Majdanek, or camp Lublin, as it was called officially, the last station of only 15,000 of his victims, here the white colour of innocence turned black.[175]

After another rendition of *'Unzer Shtedl brent'* the programme ends with the following sequence:

Dr Globke: I never heard of a 'Final Solution of the Jewish Question', in the sense that all Jews should be killed. The full extent of this horror I only found out after the war... It was possible, in a series of cases, to help the discriminated persons, meaning it was possible with people of mixed blood (*Mischlinge*) to calculate the fraction of the blood of the *Mischling* to their advantage.

Narrator 1: The bureaucrat of death calculated the fractions of parts of blood. He distinguished between three-quarters, five-eighths, seven-sixteenth. He tracked down Jewish blood to the 4th, 5th, 6th degree, like a bloodhound. He didn't extenuate, he didn't help, he clamped down...

You stand accused anew, (Mr Globke), as the bureaucrat of death, as the intellectual initiator of all we have described here. There are a thousand pages to this book, this has only been one: the murder of innocent, defenceless children.

We want to know, Mr Globke, how you told this to your own three children.

Fade in of accusation of murder read by female Polish schoolteacher (in Polish):

Overdub of translation of schoolteacher:

Because of the things we have heard here and elsewhere, our children, the children of Zamość and the children of all Poland accuse you of these crimes; because, as the proverb goes, the children, that's white, the colour of innocence, and the colour black, that is the colour of mourning and misery.

Narrator 1: A schoolteacher from Bilgoraj near Zamość accuses the murderer on behalf of the murdered.

Slow drumbeats and fade.[176]

As harrowing as it is listening to a programme such as this, there are several things that have to be borne in mind. The producers skilfully used the material – if somewhat heavy-handedly – to evoke emotional responses in the listener. The exaggerations of numbers, the muddling of places and the plurality of events could all be kept together by the overarching theme of Globke's part in formulating the anti-Semitic legislation. Furthermore, the theme of the murder of children and the symbols surrounding it – the shoes, the sweets, the toys – were used to link any conceptual gaps that could have appeared. Ideologically, 'The Children of Zamość' did not necessarily press home its in-built advantage. The accusations against Globke could have re-appeared in the form of stressing his present position and its implications – the 're-Nazified' Federal Republic, as well as the role played by the Soviet Union in defeating Hitler.

This was done in a programme aired three months later on the twentieth anniversary of the Warsaw Ghetto uprising entitled 'Collection Point Szelesna Street' (*Sammelpunkt Shelesnastrasse*), on 21 April 1963. The presenter and author of the programme is Horst Grothe again, and several witness statements reappear in the course of this 48-minute feature. It begins, just like the Zamość programme, with a song in Yiddish, a powerful rendition of *'As du gejst dem letzten Weg'*, then leading into the narrative of 'the last act of a terrible tragedy' of the Nazis and the 'first act of a heroic resistance of the defenders of the Warsaw Ghetto', with the order of 2 October 1940 establishing the Ghetto because of 'the risk of disease' (*Seuchengefahr*).

The following interview with Colonel Alev Bolkoviak shows the signs of ideological advantages that could be gained by tackling the topic of resistance:

> Narrator: The resistance was organised from the start. Colonel Gustav Alev Bolkoviak was at the time the commander of the people's guard in the Warsaw Ghetto.
> A.B.: Ah yes, this battle did not begin in April 1943 but it was in January 1942, when the Polish Workers' Party called upon the population to take up armed resistance against the occupiers; this appeal also penetrated into the Ghetto. Liaison people from the Polish Workers' Party forged the Anti-Fascist Block with the various youth organisations of the Warsaw Ghetto, and their armed associations, the fighter groups...
> Horst Grothe: Which associations belonged to these fighter groups?
> A.B.: The members of the people's guard, the Polish Workers' Party and the democratic groups of the Zionist youth organisations, Socialists, Zionists, Hechaluz and Ha-Shomer ha-Tsa'ir under the political leadership of the Polish Workers' Party.

H.G.: So they were the leading force...?

A.B.: The Polish Workers' Party was the leading force and the head of the fighting organisations of the Anti-Fascist block at the time was a communist, a Spanish civil war veteran and executive of the people's guard. And he came into the Ghetto and organised the fighters of the Anti-Fascist block. This was not only the people's guard but also the Zionist organisations.

H.G.: All together...

A.B.: Yes, all together. At this time I became the leader of the Anti-Fascist block.

H.G.: But you yourself were not in the Ghetto?

A.B.: Yes, I was in the Ghetto.

H.G.: But Anje Schmitt(?) came into the Ghetto from the outside?

A.B.: Yes, but I also came into the Ghetto from the outside.

H.G.: This is interesting.

A.B.: Yes, I came into the Ghetto at the end of 1941 and so did Anje Schmitt. Yes, Anje Schmitt came from the Soviet Union.

H.G.: Yes, this is an interesting side of this struggle, that it came from outside...

A.B.: Yes, from the outside.

H.G.: Yes, I think that this was the first significant sign that this was not an isolated battle.

A.B.: Well yes, of course, a sign that it was not an isolated battle was the understanding with the Polish Workers' Party, and in the Ghetto, too, was a Polish Workers' organisation, a Jewish organisation in the Ghetto and the people's guard, all part of the whole organisation, wholly Polish organisation.

H.G.: You could say then that it was not a spontaneous...

A.B.: No, no, not spontaneous, that is not so. It's a lie if you call it a spontaneous rising. No, it was part of the struggle, a part of the Polish struggle of the Polish people. It was no coincidence that during the uprising the Polish flags and the Zionist blue-white flags were painted on the walls, the red flag, blue-white flag and blue-red flag. This was a symbol that this struggle in the Ghetto was a part of the struggle of the Polish people, of international democratic elements, as well, against fascism.[177]

The claims contained within this sequence, the organising of the uprising under the leadership of the Polish People's Party, outside agents and the minimising of the Jewish organisations are unusual (but not surprising), to say the least, and are not found elsewhere in the literature of the Warsaw Ghetto uprising. The ideological narrative continues in the broadcast, augmented by detailed gruesome descriptions: the account of witness Noemi Schatz-Weinkranz – read by a female narrator – is almost unbearable to listen to:

> Sesha was a little girl, the daughter of a doctor. During an 'action' a German noticed her beautiful black eyes, which shone like diamonds. 'I could make two rings out of these, for me and my wife!' His mate got hold of the girl. 'We shall see how pretty they are. Best look at them in our hands.' There was general amusement in the crowd. Some joker suggested gauging the girl's eyes out. A piercing cry and a loud ringing of laughter ripped through the air. In the next moment the girl lay on the floor, unconscious, and instead of eyes there were two bloody wounds. A group of women held the mother, nearly insane with grief, by her hands.[178]

The theme of children is continued by a repetition from the Zamość programme of Colonel Bolkowiak's testimony of the rounding up of children in the Ghetto, in a slightly different edit. This programme, it appears, had benefited from a slightly more sophisticated technology, edits and overdubs are smoother and the blending of music and words, for instance, produces the desired amplification of emotional responses with a rendition – in stereo – of the Yom Kippur chant and an overdubbed witness account of the first Soviet air attack on occupied Warsaw.[179]

The combination of the twentieth anniversary and the continued attack on Globke found its expression in the links drawn out between the continuing deportations to Treblinka and the Jewish slave labour needed for German-owned factories in Warsaw. The owner of the factory mentioned (Schulz & Többins, manufacturers of household goods) is apparently alive and well in Bremen, as are Anton Brand ('the little Eichmann of Warsaw'), Dr Ludwig Hahn, Heinz Auerswald and others implicated in the running and the liquidation of the Warsaw Ghetto.[180] After the mention of each name there follows a sound of a hammer hitting an anvil twice, sometimes preceded with additional expert statement. Globke is mentioned in the context of being Brand's superior in Berlin:

> Narrator 1: The head of the Jewish – Historical Institute, Professor Bernard Mark, explained:
> Bernard Mark: In general Globke took part in the discrimination, isolation, deprivation and inhuman oppression of the Jews. In

this manner Globke exposed himself as a top racist and Nazi. He belonged to those fascist functionaries who paved the way for the *Einsatzgruppen*.
Narrator 1: Globke today is secretary of state in the Chancellor's office.
(Hammer on anvil sound)[181]

The interview with Alev Bolkoviak moves the programme along, describing the preparations for the uprising and the months of battle which ended with the complete destruction of the Ghetto. Bolkowiak continues to stress the involvement of the Polish Workers' Party and the Anti-Fascist block in and outside the Ghetto, the preparation for the armed insurrection and the first shot being fired to settle scores with a collaborator. At the end of the programme the slogan of the Ghetto fighters 'To overcome death in battle' (*Im Kampf überwinden sie den Tod*)[182] is repeated several times in various connections and Horst Grothe asks Colonel Bolkoviak:

> H.G.: Was this fight in vain? Did it have success?
> A.B.: I think it had great success. The Warsaw Ghetto showed the Polish people and all of humanity that you may (*daß man darf*), that you could fight the fascists, even if you were not strong. It was the first bigger revolt against the fascist occupation.
> H.G.: And it was also an example...
> A.B.: It was an example that a small group of armed people, who know that they are a part of a bigger struggle for humanity, can fight a mightier opponent for a long time.
> H.G.: And history has shown...?
> A.B.: And history has shown that they were right. The slogan 'in battle we overcome death' was the right slogan, in battle they did overcome death.[183]

This didactic end to *Sammelpunkt Shelesnastrasse* contained all the elements of effective propaganda: notions of heroism, the struggle of all humanity, the lessons of history and death. The programme was first broadcast on a Sunday (21 April 1963) at 11 a.m. on the *Deutschlandsender*, the station aimed at listeners in the West, at the time when Western radio stations would have carried religious services. It was followed by a selection of Yiddish songs, which also highlights the ambivalent attitude of the SED's propaganda attempts: the fact that it was mostly Jews that perished in the Holocaust is never forgotten but, as is evident from the radio programmes, the struggle against fascism was always under the leadership of the communist party.

Whereas the West German broadcasters were well on the way to turning the upcoming Auschwitz Trial into a media event, the GDR broadcasters continued with the Globke issue. In July 1963 a show trial against the West German Secretary of State was conducted. This material, comprising more than 76 hours (4,600 minutes) of material, survives in the audio archives. There is no evidence that any of it was used for broadcast. But one of the witnesses in the trial, the East German writer Peter Edel, was the subject of a 30-minute programme on the more culturally and educationally-orientated station DDR II. It consisted of Edel's witness statement and his suffering during the Nazi dictatorship. The programme was first broadcast on 20 July 1963 in the series *Radio-DDR- Hörbericht* under the title 'Fate under Globke's stars. Witness statement of the "Jewish *Mischling*" Peter Edel.'[184] The programme contains one section which is worth mentioning here:

Peter Edel: In Gross-Gehren I experienced for the first time how the SS practiced the Nuremberg Race Laws. The *Hauptscharführer* took me and several others in, threw the old (prison) uniforms at our heads and said: 'Now we'll have a Nuremberg Law control.' This happened like this: He asked me 'What are you?' and I said: 'A Jew'. He kicked me in the stomach and I fell to the floor and he said:' What are you? A Jew? You are a legal Jew (*Geltungsjude*)!' This was on his tick-list. 'What are you?' 'A legal Jew' 'What you bastard, a legal Jew? You are a criminal!! What are you?' 'A criminal' 'What a criminal? You are a pig of a Jew (*Saujude*), understand?' I stood up, another kick in the stomach, and this was repeated about ten times. 'What is your nationality?' 'German' 'German? You are not a German!' and when I said I was not German he said: 'Are you ashamed of being German?' and this went on and on until in the end, after the last kick to the stomach and getting up, and I don't know what prompted this feeling, when he again said 'What are you?' I said, 'A communist'.

Narrator: It was at this moment that this 22-year-old ceased to be alone. This strange initiation, in which a bull-necked SS man attempted to beat Globke's racial wisdom into or out of him, was the last he had to endure alone. He still had a long hard road to travel, but never again was he alone.[185]

It is interesting to note in this context that at a performance of Peter Weiss' play about the Auschwitz Trial, *Die Ermittlung*, in 1965, Peter Edel read the part of the Auschwitz torturer Willhelm Boger to great public acclaim.[186]

But the Globke issue had the desired effect. At first the Chancellor's secretary offered to resign, but Adenauer did not accept the resignation. Globke retired 'on health grounds' in late 1963 amongst claims from the GDR that it was their initiatives which led to the retirement.[187] Now Norden was hopeful. Both the Oberländer and the Globke affairs had raised the international awareness of former Nazi officials in the service of the Federal government. The decision to use the upcoming Auschwitz trial to strengthen this advantage was not a surprising one.

Consequently, there was hardly any need to alter the format and style of East German radio programmes; their efforts in the battle against the 're-Nazified' Federal Republic were highly valued. For West German broadcasters, however, issues such as the resignations of Oberländer and particularly Globke could not be overlooked. From approximately 1963 onwards, newer programmes dealing with the Nazi Past became longer, more analytical and critical, and they even dealt, belatedly, with the Eichmann Trial.[188]

4
Radio and the Auschwitz Trial

Preparations

To most West German radio listeners, the author included, East German broadcasts sounded alien, absurd and nearly incomprehensible. Everyday life in the GDR, as portrayed on air, appeared to consist of a strange mixture of committee meetings in 'agricultural production collectives' (*Landwirtschaftliche Produktionsgenossenschaft* or LPGs) and friendship treaties with the Soviet Union. Equally Western broadcasts appeared strange to most East Germans, although possibly more were listening. In a sketch by Alexander Kluge entitled 'Commentary of a radio-programme listener of the GDR', the young man, whose job it is to listen and record broadcasts from the West, reassures his girlfriend, who is also listening, not to take the prediction of the end of the universe in a billion years' time too seriously, as this was West German radio:

> It is also not true, what this Western astronomy is saying, replies the GDR programme listener. It is the scientific superstructure of desperation, which represents the downfall of capitalism. This is the capitalist sky, not ours.[1]

But the mass media nevertheless produces a certain amount of conceptual confusion, where clear distinctions are rare and everything appears to resemble itself.[2] Its power surpasses the ideological confines of any superstructure, as conformity carries with it the social reward of enjoyment.[3] This is also not lost on the couple in the above sketch, who decide, in case Western capitalist science should hold true, that as good socialists they should make contingency plans to 'relight the stars' when the time comes.[4]

In the late 1950s and early 1960s there must have been profound conceptual confusion among GDR listeners around the topic of the Holocaust and the Third Reich. The anti-fascist stance of the SED leadership appeared to conjure up and celebrate eight million resistance fighters where there had been perhaps 10,000,[5] rationalising the Nazi terror into a clear formula of the 'excesses of monopoly capitalism', whereas the broadcasts from the West painted the picture of the age of totalitarianism, where the banality of evil is carried out under the guidance of the master criminal. 'The banalising of evil goes hand in hand with the trivialising of the Enlightenment.'[6] For those who had lived through the war this led to an understanding of the 'lessons of fascism' in East and West Germany, which, in 1950, Max Horkheimer formulated as follows:

> What lessons for the future has the average European learnt from the post-war conditions in occupied Germany? He must have reached the conclusion that, in times of totalitarianism, it would have been unwise to be at the top, but prudent, if not advantageous, to be among the sympathisers; that it could have been risky to have actively participated in the worst atrocities, but committing lesser crimes was devoid of danger. He is being taught that the war's ideological elements were nothing but pretence, obscuring the true and final motives.[7]

In the light of the Cold War, this lesson was welcomed by the governments in Germany, easily disseminated by the mass media and convenient for troubled consciences. It also served the purposes of the GDR's campaign against Bonn.

Prof. Dr Friedrich Karl Kaul, who was later to be the adjunct prosecutor in the Auschwitz Trial, was a SED party member and on first name terms with both Ulbricht and Norden. He saw the worldwide interest in the prosecution of Nazi criminals as his opportunity to pursue the ideological battle on a 'judicial level'. In a letter Kaul suggested to Norden that he should be allowed to go to Jerusalem as an adjunct prosecutor, representing East German Jewish (communist) victims and their families from the GDR.[8] The wider argumentation on this matter was to be centrally coordinated, especially after Kaul's failure to be admitted to the court in Jerusalem. But a model had been worked out which remained relatively static throughout the 1960s, and was transferred into the arguments used at the Auschwitz Trial with ease. An article in the GDR judicial magazine *Neue Justiz* from 1964 offers a perfect summary:

> It is not the investigation and punishment of individual crimes of individual persons which is at stake here at the Auschwitz Trial. The crimes

committed by the accused were the final barbaric deeds of a systematically planned machinery of annihilation, carried out with satanic perfection... [What is] required is the uncovering of the roots of the crimes committed at Auschwitz, and to expose the main culprits...These are people of whom a few are again at the levers of power in West Germany. The Auschwitz Trial must help the West German population to understand that only the defeat of the might of German monopoly capitalism, and only with the complete relinquishing of anti-democratic and anti-humanitarian ideologies will there be a true guarantee that these kinds of crimes will not once again sully the good German name worldwide.[9]

The ideological battle had one added aspect when it came to the inter-German dialogue: Germans, from both the East and the West, did not want to be associated with a past which made them equally culpable for the Nazi crimes. As was already evident in the broadcasts from Nuremberg, the desire of Germany to be accepted once again as an 'honourable' nation was one theme all broadcast journalists could comment upon.

As already mentioned by Helmut Krausnick above, culpability was a matter of personal examination – it required reflection as well as political engagement. But precisely the political aspect begged the question of who was really guilty and how this could be established. At the heart of the 'broadcasting war' was the way in which these notions of objectivity were open to interpretation and subversion. Would the historians, the judges, the politicians or the individual listener make the decisions about the culpability of an individual? Could the efforts of the broadcasters change 'hearts and minds' to such an extent that it would lead to an overthrow of the system?

The broadcasts from the GDR were certainly hoping that state authority could be undermined if only the individual listener, the 'good' German, could be convinced that the 'bad' (Nazi) Germans were still in key positions in government and industry, whereas the moral appeal of the West relied on the listener to reject any form of totalitarian government.

The East German broadcaster Karl Eduard von Schnitzler, who after 1967 established a following in both East and West Germany through his weekly TV commentary programme 'The Black Channel' (*Der Schwarze Kanal*),[10] gives an interesting insight into the reasons as to why the Auschwitz Trial was held at all in a broadcast on the *Deutschlandsender* of 6 February 1964:

> Actually, do you know how it came to this trial? A birthday of an assessor was being celebrated at the 'Restitution Authority' (*Wiedergutmachungsbehörde*) in Wiesbaden in 1958. This is the

authority which has the task of offering restitution to the victims of the crimes of the Nazi regime. Which didn't stop the [staff at the] restitution authority in Wiesbaden from roaring out the most blood-curdling Nazi song: 'Crooked Jews, they wander here and there, through the Red Sea. The waves crash on them, the world is at peace.'[11] A Frankfurt newspaper reported this, and a West German of Jewish origin, Emil Wulkan, whose application to this infamous authority had been rejected, read it. Now he knew why. This occasioned him to remember that, in April 1945, he found a bundle of files in front of the burning SS courthouse in the then city of Breslau. Now he gave his forgotten find to the prosecutor-general of Hesse, Dr. Bauer, who identified the singed documents as 'shot-while-trying-to-escape' files from the concentration camp Auschwitz. This led the prosecutor-general to start inquiries and in five years they found 22 of the murderers: One a civil servant, others as well-respected and practicing doctors, one a chief cashier at a building society, one working as a civil administrator in the *Bundeswehr* – in short, they were upright citizens, mostly CDU voters, well satisfied with what Bonn calls the 'liberal-democratic order'.[12]

This account is as interesting as it is inaccurate. Fritz Bauer started proceedings against 24 men, initially, and only after one died and one was excused on medical grounds did the number become 22. What prompted Emil Wulkan to hand over the papers is not reported elsewhere, but in a sworn statement by Wulkan, reproduced in Herrmann Langbein's account of the Auschwitz Trial, he states that he did not find the files himself; rather, they were uncovered by one of his friends. Furthermore, it was only when a visiting journalist, Thomas Gnielka, of the *Frankfurter Rundschau* newspaper, asked him about them that he handed them over, initially not to the authorities but to Mr Gnielka. Only on the journalist's insistence were the authorities notified, and that was in April 1959.[13]

The discrepancies served two related aims: (a) to discredit the other; and (b) to subvert. And while this can definitely be said about some of the East German broadcasts, it is relatively rare to detect these aims in West German broadcasts. But all the selection criteria Luhmann mentions are there: surprise (by reporting a differing or novel story), numbers (how many killed, how few prosecuted), names (the main culprits), norm violations (their horrendous torture and murder), evaluation of norm violation (lack of prosecutions, etc.). All this could be listened to with relative ease, almost inconsequentially, providing the programme was not out of the ordinary, providing it remained a commentary (of approximately

5–10 minutes in length). Since 1945 there had been numerous NS trials and the attention of the listening public was not guaranteed. So in order for a radio programme to have enough of a surprise element to capture the listener for any length of time, the selection criteria had to be 'strengthened', that is to say it had to divulge new and startling information, the norm violations described in gruesome detail by concentrating on a few identifiable names having committed countless murders.

On air

One programme paving the way, or 'preparing the public' for the upcoming Auschwitz Trial, was written by Thomas Gnielka himself for the West German regional broadcasters for the *Land* of Hesse, *Hessischer Rundfunk*, after the preliminary inquiries had finished and a trial date had been set. Under the title *Konzentrationslager Auschwitz* in the *Zeitfunk* series, it was billed as a special broadcast (*Sondersendung*) to coincide with a commemorative 'Auschwitz Day'[14] and the setting of a trial date. At a length of 64 minutes, it appeared as the main feature on the *Hessischer Rundfunk's* 2nd programme (a station of more cultural and intellectual output), at 8:45 p.m. It was preceded by a programme focussing on the theme of Orpheus in the music of Gluck and Stravinsky and was followed by an additional Auschwitz remembrance broadcast.[15]

The programme's format is straightforward: Two narrators, Hans Korte and Alwin Rüffer, present the programme, which is alternated with witness interviews (interviewed by Thomas Gnielka) and witness statements spoken by the narrators. It plots the history of the concentration camp from its planning stages to the partial destruction and evacuation at the end of the Second World War. The emphasis lies on the main (known) culprits such as Boger, Klehr and Kaduk, and main witnesses Dr C. Glowacki, Dr Tadeusz Paczula, Dr Klodzinski and Kazimierz Smolen, as well as words from the prosecutor-general of Hesse, Dr Fritz Bauer.[16] Most of the issues are addressed in this programme: The lateness of the prosecutions, the obstacles to possible earlier prosecutions, the unrelenting views of most of the accused, the hell of Auschwitz. Many of the witnesses' statements make compelling listening and, in comparison to the dramatic tone of the narrators, are sometimes told with chilling matter-of-factness, sometimes continued by a translator as the witness fails to continue in German:

Narrator 1: The witness Dr Glowacki saw Klehr daily at work.
C.G.: Klehr was the one I knew best out of all the SS people. I saw him at the injections, how he did this, I saw this... [slow fade]

Narrator 1: Dr Glowacki is a doctor; he is used to dealing with unusual things. But when talking about Klehr he got too upset to continue in German. A translator had to continue with his statement.

Translator: Well, Dr Glowacki has drawn a plan of block 20, on this piece of paper. So here were the stairs and there was the entrance to the block, here was a corridor, there was as a divide, a blanket, so the room was divided into two parts. Here, on the right was a washroom and over there, on the right side of the block was a medicine cabinet. And there in this room Klehr carried out the injections. So the sick were brought here, down the stairs from the first floor, and queued, and one after the other were taken to the other side of the blanket. In this room, where Klehr had prepared the injections there was a chair and a table, on which the hypodermics lay. So one after the other they came into this room and had to hold their arm like so..., so Klehr could inject the hypodermic with phenol straight into the heart. And here were the corpse-carriers, they carried these people, the already dead people, into the washroom. Dr Glowacki thinks that Klehr is a degenerate, carrying out the killings gave him satisfaction, he did it with pleasure. He was satisfied when he had more candidates for those phenol injections. Well you see, Dr Glowacki saw him day in day out, and he could tell that this man loved his job.

Narrator 1: The former prison scribe of the hospital block, Dr Tadeusz Paczula – today he lives as a surgeon in Katowice – completes Klehr's profile.

T.P.: As far as I know Klehr had been in the KZ Auschwitz since 1941, he was known to me as SS-Unterscharführer at the time. He twitched with his eye-lashes, well, it was a nervous symptom, I am sure he has it still, allegedly a carpenter by profession. I had the impression that Klehr was a psychopath, an illiterate... The reason I say this: I know of occasions when Klehr, after having injected many prisoners, came into the hospital office and called for a scribe, and dictated a, well, a bill for 'special treatment' (*Sonderbehandlung*), well, eh, there has been, well I cannot recall the exact wording, but it was something like: For special treatment, on such and such a day, on however many prisoners, so many cigarettes, schnapps, food stamps...

T.G.: [interrupting]... So this means that those SS people who were carrying out the 'special treatment' received premiums...

T.P.: ...Yes, received premiums. In my estimate there were between 12 and 13,000...

T.G.: [interrupting]... who were murdered by Klehr alone?
T.P.: By Klehr alone.
T.G.: Over what period of time?
T.P.: From Autumn 1942 to the end of 1943.[17]

The witnesses' statements, on the whole, correspond to the transcripts and reportage of the trial.[18] What is notable in this programme, however, is the absence of any mention of the GDR adjunct prosecution. This omission is not deliberate: the politburo in East Berlin only made the decision, prompted by Norden, 'to turn the Auschwitz Trial into a tribunal against the I.G. Farben conglomerate'[19] on 19 November 1963. Correspondingly, the only reference to the GDR in Gnielka's programme appears during an explanation regarding the lateness of the prosecutions, referring to the Nazi files the Allies had taken from Germany after 1945: 'Later the Russians made theirs available to East Berlin, where these documents found their way to the public in the form of well aimed propaganda material against the Federal Republic.'[20]

Consequently, the *Konzentrationslager Auschwitz* programme of March 1963 achieved its aim of preparing the public for what was to come in a relatively moderate and considered manner. It becomes clear that Gnielka had engaged himself with the topic extensively and meaningfully. The programme ends with the following passage:

Narrator 1: Other voices, voices of West Germans, are of the opinion that it is about time to cease these trials. But they are mistaken, as in these trials the prosecution is able to deal with a complexity of crimes which has never existed in Germany. The Auschwitz Trial is the first.

Narrator 2: As can be gathered by the state prosecutors nationwide, other trials are on their way. Formal proceedings against members of the *Einsatzgruppen SS* and Gestapo in the then occupied Scandinavian countries are on their way.

Narrator 1: And it is worth remembering, that trials which deal with this part of the German past through criminal law investigations will always bring new proceedings in their wake. This, at least, is the opinion of the leading criminal lawyers in our country.

Narrator 2: That is why lately voices have been heard which call for a general amnesty for crimes committed during the Third Reich.

Narrator 1: But could there be such an amnesty without shaking the foundations of our criminal law? The prosecutor-general of Hesse, Dr. Bauer, has a different opinion about the meaning of trials like these; an opinion which is worth the closing statement of this programme.

Fritz Bauer: The aim of these proceedings is not just one of looking back (at the past). It is the task of these criminal proceedings to establish new values. Out of the ash and ruins of Germany grew a new state and a new economy. And a new human understanding is needed. This has to rise, like Phoenix, from the hell of Auschwitz and has to emerge from our Auschwitz Trial. What we mean is equality, lack of prejudice and tolerance towards everybody. I am here not to hate with but to love with, says the poet. This should be the lesson of this trial.[21]

The radio broadcaster for Frankfurt (and also the *Bundesland* Hesse), the *Hessischer Rundfunk,* prepared its listeners slowly over a period of months. In May 1963 in an hour-long programme entitled 'We Saw It' ('*Wir haben es gesehen*'),[22] the radio journalist Gerhard Schönberger brought together a number of statements from witnesses, victims, bystanders and perpetrators, read out by actors. The result is a very moving account of the (mainly) citizens of Frankfurt, seemingly caught up in a process they abhorred but could do little about. What is surprising about this (West German) programme is the mention of the industrial giants of Siemens, Krupp and I.G. Farben as the power behind the National Socialists. The overall impression is marred by the slightly condescending tone of the narrator, giving the broadcast a slightly imposed and 'top down' quality.

In an attempt to find a voice for the murdered and the survivors, shortly before the beginning of the Trial, in November 1963, the literary critic Roland H. Wiegenstein wrote and broadcast a 58-minute programme on the *Hessischer Rundfunk*'s second station, HR II, under the title 'Auschwitz and Literature – Three Attempts to Convey the Horrendous' (*Auschwitz und die Literatur – Drei Versuche, das Entsetzliche zu überliefern*). The format is familiar, but perhaps not to West German ears: a statement, or rather, in this case, two statements are repeated throughout the programme in a very dramatic fashion. Adorno's incomplete dictum 'It is barbaric to write poetry after Auschwitz' is juxtaposed with the statement 'Whoever was in Auschwitz can write poetry about it' at the beginning and the end of each of the discussed novels, most notable among them Tadeusz Borowski's 'The World of Stone' (*Die steinerne Welt*) where Borowski seems to concur with Adorno: 'there is no place for poetry in the gas chambers.'[23] In the light of the 'complete cultural void' which was Auschwitz

Wiegenstein asks the pertinent question whether this seeming capitulation of literature has nullified, or even broken the medium of language, but comes to the conclusion that language, and language alone, can commemorate, make visible and give hope. This 'metaphysical truth' of literature emerges even after the most horrendous destruction of mankind.[24]

Even before the trial broadcasts began, East German radio attempted to strengthen its agenda. A commentary, broadcast on the *Deutschlandsender* (broadcasting to the FRG) on 13 November 1963 at 19:42 by Wolfgang Dost, started with the following:

> Good evening, dear listeners.
>
> It was hard to believe, but now there is no doubt. The person in charge of the trial against the 23 SS torturers will be the director of the state court (*Landgerichtsdirektor*) Hofmeyer. The chairman of the Frankfurt third penal senate, Dr Forester, who prepared the trial, and had originally been named as the person in charge, Dr Forester, has been rejected on the charge of bias. So who is Dr Forester, who is Hofmeyer? First Dr Forester. A first class lawyer, a man with many years of experience of criminal proceedings. Is this not enough? Not by far. For instance, Dr Forester was not a Nazi. On the contrary. He was in a concentration camp, he and his relatives. This man is out of the question: 'biased'. Persons who were not, are not Nazis, are not allowed to be in charge of a trial against Nazis. Does this not call to mind a parallel from the Eichmann trial in Jerusalem? Did not (defence lawyer) Dr Servatius reject the court's judges in Jerusalem with the reason that they had been persecuted by the Nazis and therefore deemed 'biased'?...
>
> Who is Hofmeyer?... A man who, as is well known, had a complete Belgian family executed, 70-year-old grandfather and baby included, because they had aided a downed English pilot. Today he signs arrest warrants, nay, kidnap orders, like the one for Günther Hofe, chief of our *Verlag der Nation* (publishers) in Berlin. This is Hofmeyer. Nazi judge. He will be in charge of the Auschwitz Trial. He is the right one. He is not 'biased' – in plain German: With him there is no danger that the prosecutions will extend to the superiors of the 23 accused of Auschwitz; because, the 23 SS murderers are guilty by themselves, but others are as well, no less. And asked carefully: who are the others? As we know today, Dr Forester was deemed 'biased' when he went after three gentlemen: Mr Fritz ter Meer, Dr Walter Dürrfeld and Dr Otto Ambroß.[25]

The political undermining of the trial proceedings could not have been more blatant. Ter Meer, Dürrfeld and Ambroß were executives of the I.G. Farben conglomerate during the war and were now holders of prominent positions in the FRG's petrochemical industry.[26]

The accusations against judge Hofmeyer are not substantiated in any further GDR publications. Dr Forester had been appointed to lead the trial on 8 October 1963, but the following day he personally applied to be relieved from this position as he had doubts about his own impartiality, being half-Jewish, having been racially persecuted, and having lost members of his family in the camps at Majdanek and Theresienstadt. He was duly excused on 14 October 1963.[27] But, of course, these allegations did not need any corroboration. The rumour mill had been set in motion and left to run its course.

A programme on a somewhat more personal note, counteracting the claims of a 're-Nazified' Federal Republic, came, rather surprisingly, from the BBC, in one of their regular broadcasts to the GDR, on 28 November 1963. It is not documented whether this was an active attempt at 'very dynamic political warfare' or whether it was just a coincidence that this programme was considered to be an interesting take on the FRG. But the number of scribbles and various checks on the typescript manuscript give the impression that it passed through many departments and censors before it was recorded and aired. Entitled 'A German Jewess Returns Home' (*Eine deutsche Jüdin kehrt heim*), this nine-minute broadcast was a short account of the experiences of Karen Gershon on her return to West Germany after 25 years spent in exile in Britain.[28] At the age of 15 she had left Germany in 1938, as part of the *Kindertransporte*, and her parents were murdered in Auschwitz in 1941. With understandable apprehension she returned to her native Bielefeld, but to her surprise encountered only kindness and hospitality:

> I do know that they were not representatives of the German people. These were only a few individuals who thought it important enough, who made the effort – a few, who wanted to keep a few Jews in kind remembrance. But they are Germans, citizens of Bielefeld, they invited me into their homes, gave me food and drink, talked to me, just as you do with friends. Then, there I understood the difference it makes when someone has known you as a child, knew who your parents were – I had the feeling nowhere else could I be known so well as here in Bielefeld, where I was born.
>
> As a child I was convinced that it was impossible to be German and Jewish. I had always denied that I was German – the fact that

I had been expelled was ample proof that I was not. It took 25 years and this trip to instruct me to who I really am: A German Jewess. I wanted to make this trip by myself and I understand why: for my husband and my children Bielefeld would have been a foreign place, but for me it is still my home.[29]

Whereas it would not have been surprising for this (seemingly innocuous) broadcast to reach West German audiences, it is worth considering why it was broadcast to the 'Soviet Zone', and particularly at this time. As mentioned earlier, the BBC's East German service was highly politicised and very much embroiled in the propaganda wrangling. Norden's accusations that the BBC was a tool of the Adenauer government are firmly rebuffed in a letter dated 12 February 1963 from the Assistant Head of the German Service at the time, Richard O'Rourke, to the Labour MP Richard Crossman, in which he writes:

He implies we are tools of Adenauer. Evidently he has not been listening to our recent broadcasts about the Spiegel case and the Common Market in which we have tried to reflect that feeling in this country is hardly more friendly to the Federal Chancellor than it is to Herr Ulbricht.'[30]

Yet despite these reassurances the broadcast of this particular programme to East Germany is still something of a mystery, given the overtly political output of the BBC to the GDR at the time.

Broadcasts during the Trial

Evidence of a 'media event' on the scale of the Eichmann Trial have not survived in the radio archives at the beginning of the Auschwitz Trial, and even newspapers and magazines such as *Der Spiegel* carried only a limited coverage. However, the international interest was substantial, and undoubtedly broadcasters wanted at least to be seen to be tackling the important issues of the trial. One such programme, recorded on 13 December 1963 but not broadcast until 22 December, was the *Hessischer Rundfunk*'s 'Frankfurt Conversation' (*Frankfurter Gespräch*) with the theme of the Auschwitz Trial.[31] The conversation revolves around the most burning question of the foreign press, namely why it has taken so long for these proceedings to come before a court. The journalist Werner Ernenputsch interviews chief state prosecutor Dr Grossmann, who takes great care in explaining the legal complexities in dealing with doubtful evidence, interviewing witnesses abroad, securing amnesties for certain witnesses and the multilayered prosecution claims against the accused. It fails to quell doubts for critical ears, as Dr Grossmann's explanations never sound convincing and the difference between 'legal' public speaking and speaking on radio (into a microphone) appear in stark contrast.

A lack of 'microphone awareness' can also be detected in the programme dealing with the opening of the trial. This remnant of a (possibly) much longer recording – it lasts only for nine and a half minutes – has the reporter Horst Kickhefel describing the scene in hushed and reverential tones, commenting that the accused look 'like us, they could be our neighbours', while Judge Hofmeyer rather brashly and unceremoniously is more concerned with the correct swearing in of the jury.[32]

But by the end of the first day's proceedings the political aspects of this trial had spilled over into the radio commentaries. The following seven-minute report is transcribed in its entirety to highlight (and exemplify) the tone and form of most of the various radio stations' reports from the Auschwitz Trial. The *Hessischer Rundfunk's* chief political editor, Werner Ernenputsch, filed this dispatch at 18:05 on 20 December 1963:

> Today, ladies and gentlemen, in the Römer in Frankfurt, began the Auschwitz Trial. Many people, and not just in our country, ask themselves what good it will do again and again to conjure up the terrible past and to stir new resentment. What is the point of this trial? Is it vengeance which has led to this investigation and finally to this trial? I believe that the Old Testament adage of 'an eye for an eye and a tooth for a tooth' has lost its validity in the light of the millions of victims of Auschwitz. So should the accused atone? Now for what has happened at Auschwitz, there cannot be any atonement nor any restitution. Then should the present proceedings, one could continue to ask, act as a deterrent? The way things are here today, I believe, deterrence from killing children with phenol injections to the heart and the gassing of random men and women, regardless of religion, race or origin, such a deterrent, it seems to me, is in our time not needed anymore.
>
> What is needed, however, is that the law, which enables, and not regulates, our living together, that this law is respected, and that anyone who violates it, will be held accountable by this very law. Hopefully, nobody will entertain the thought that through this trial, by blaming the accused, our much cited past can be mastered.

Everyone who consciously experienced this past has to come to terms with it themselves. Nor is it the meaning of this trial to appear as an otherwise missed history lesson. What this Frankfurt Auschwitz Trial is about is to prosecute plain murder, if proven; and murder as well under the Nazi legislation. Because there can be no justice in a (nation) state where the law, based on human rights, is not respected.

But now to the proceedings themselves. Today were the first examinations of the accused persons. First off there was the export tradesman from Hamburg, Mulka; released from remand on a bail of DM50,000, looked the picture of a Prussian officer. If you take him by his word, then he joined the SS almost against his will. This former First World War officer and fighter in the Baltic states (*Baltikumskämpfer*), sentenced in the 1920s, justly or unjustly, for fraud, was, during the Nazi period, expelled from the corps of officer reservists, and during the war joined the SS, as the regular army would only have him as a private. Thus he became the adjutant to the first camp commander, Höß.

The other accused former Auschwitz adjutant, Hoecker, who, not only by profession but also by appearance, is a bookkeeper, joined the SS in 1933. He joined, so he says, because he feared for his position. For him too, Auschwitz was his last stop.

The bench was presented with a completely different picture with defendant Boger, who is accused of unimaginable cruelties, and has been in remand prison for the last five years. Boger, an SS member long before 1933, appeared for proceedings in highly polished shoes, answered the examination questions in the broadest Swabian dialect, lapsing self-consciously into blustering and bobbed up and down, bending his knees as if he was on the parade ground. Boger's last position was that of SS Oberscharführer and he belonged to the feared and infamous Political Section in Auschwitz. But enough of these descriptions.

As expected, the first day also brought with it the reprimands of the defence. Raised as precautions in anticipation of future intricacies. A totally legitimate concern, not an unusual procedure, especially when it comes to capital crimes. And as could be expected, the barrister Prof. Dr Kaul from East Berlin took the first possible opportunity to use the court for political agitation. Kaul wanted to be admitted as adjunct prosecutor, on behalf of nine inhabitants of the (Soviet) zone, who lost relatives in Auschwitz.

The court at first refused this request as Kaul had insufficient documentation. The explanation of one of the defence lawyers, that Kaul could not appear in a court of the Federal Republic because he had been barred by the Allied commissioners from entering West Berlin, and furthermore as a barrister and a prominent member of the SED he could not act freely and independently, gave Kaul the longed-for opportunity for propaganda. He believes, he explained, that as a member of the SED, as a German and as a citizen of the GDR, and as a former concentration camp inmate he possessed sufficient independence to withstand such accusations. And with this the SED barrister had delivered the first long anticipated headlines for the attending journalists from the East. There is no doubt that Kaul will be admitted as adjunct prosecutor once the formalities have been met. In this case it might be a good idea to ask Mr. Kaul to do something for Heinz Brandt, who had been imprisoned by the Nazis for eleven years in jails and concentration camps. Heinz Brandt, a West German trade union editor appears to have been abducted to East Berlin and in 1962 was sentenced by the Supreme Court of the Eastern Zone, on the grounds of alleged espionage, to 13 years hard labour. As is apparent, inhumanity wasn't only at home with the Nazis.[33]

Heinz Brandt, in the 1920s a member of the KPD, who had been interned in the concentration camps Sachsenhausen, Auschwitz and Buchenwald, and from 1945 to 1953 a leading SED member, had criticised Ulbricht's handling of the events of 17 June 1953. He fled to West Germany in 1958. He became an editor working for the metalworkers' union (IG Metall) and from this prominent position he had intended to publish 'his account' of the June 1953 uprising. To prevent this from happening, he was drugged and kidnapped by Stasi agents in 1961. He was released in 1964 after intensive lobbying by Amnesty International and the British philosopher Bertrand Russell. But at the time of the Auschwitz Trial, Brandt, having spent over a year in solitary confinement, had just been sentenced and the international outcry against it was at its most vocal.[34]

The East German programmes, as part of news bulletins as well as commentaries, continued to stress the role played by industry and commerce. One of the earliest surviving broadcasts in the GDR Auschwitz Trial reportage, the initial questioning of the main defendant Robert Mulka, is introduced by a harrowing description of the selection procedure at the ramp in Auschwitz by the (then) general secretary of the International Auschwitz Committee, Tadeusz Holuj. The narrator continues:

> Teeth, hair [and] bones for industry. The defendant Robert Mulka conducted the correspondence with the customers. A gruesome exchange

of letters. His [business] partners were I.G. Farben and their general directors Dr. Otto Ambroß, Dr. ter Meer and Dr. Strass. Ambroß wrote to Mulka: 'Regarding a new experiment with a new sleeping drug we would be grateful if you could acquire a number of women for us.' Mulka agreed. But Ambroß replied a little later: 'We received your answer but find the price of RM 200 per woman a little steep. We suggest a maximum price of RM 170 per woman. Providing you agree [to this] we will receive the women. We need about 150.' Mulka selected the candidates of death and sent them to Ambroß, who replied with thanks: 'Have received the ordered 150 women. Experiments carried out. Experiment objects have died. Will shortly be in contact regarding order of new consignment.' Ambroß is not in court today. Ambroß has better things to do than to defend himself against the charge of these beastly murders. He is busy as chief executive of the Scholven-Chemie AG and other I.G. Farben subsidiaries. Ter Meer and Strass have similar posts. The recipients of Mulka's wares of death and the producers of the poison Zyklon B convinced themselves of the effectiveness of their produce. The executed commander of Auschwitz, Rudolf Höß, explained: 'Dr. Otto Ambroß, he visited the camp two or three times during my time [there]. I can safely assume that he, as well as all other visitors, were aware of the destruction of humans in Auschwitz-Birkenau.' The now accused Robert Mulka was responsible for the gas-chamber-complex (*Vergasungsanlage*) and the provision of Zyklon B. But now in court he says:' I don't know, I can't say.' Even some of the 22 co-defendants shake their heads when Mulka proclaims:' I did not know that Auschwitz was a death camp. I have never seen [any] gas-chambers. [The fact that] humans were being gassed I only found out in due course.' Höß's second in command can't remember anything. Even Eichmann says that he was horrified by his deeds when visiting Auschwitz.[35]

The programme continues with a recording of Eichmann's statement on visiting Auschwitz from the Jerusalem Trial, but the recording is of such poor quality that it is overdubbed. The narrator concludes with the stipulation that Mulka, as well as the listeners, know that the main culprits are not present at the trial in Frankfurt today.

Other GDR broadcasts manage to pinpoint occurrences at the Trial which were not picked up by many Western commentators, such as the activities of the mysterious Mr Eisler, who visited witnesses on behalf of the defendant Capesius, the real or imagined solidarity between the defendants and their lawyers, and the work of the organisations of former SS members such as HIAG and *Stille Hilfe* (Silent Help).³⁶

Other aspects were also addressed by the East German radio journalists. In January 1964, in a series of three broadcasts, the editor-in-chief of the *Deutschlandsender*, Kurt Goldstein, himself a former inmate of Auschwitz, talked to the journalist Horst Grothe about his experiences and about his impressions of the trial proceedings in Frankfurt. Considerable effort went into the making of these programmes, as in addition to the interviews there are scripted sections with alternating narrators and audio tape footage to fit the interview. Goldstein's views come across as being less bitter than those of the commentators (this seems to be the case in all programmes), but the agenda of topics remains the same: the real culprits are not on trial here, the defendants were living quite openly in the Federal Republic, the present West German government was complicit in the crimes of the Nazi era. Other typical features, such as using West German newspaper readers' letters to stress a point, feature in this, the first of the three broadcasts – in this case the newspaper is not the often-cited right-wing *Die Welt*, but the more liberal *Frankfurter Rundschau*. In the following transcript Kurt Goldstein raises an interesting point from a financial report, but fails to follow it through with any meaningful or ideologically effective conclusion:

> K.G.: See here, I have an interesting report here. But it is from 1957. At the time a trial against I.G. Farben took place for the compensation claims for the many thousands of prisoners who were the slave labourers for I.G. Farben, who worked mostly in Buna (*Auschwitz-Monowitz or Auschwitz III*). And at the end of the trial IG Farben decided that it would be willing to pay out DM 30 million to the survivors of the I.G. Farben slave labourers.
>
> H.G.: This appears to be a noble gesture.
>
> K.G.: Yes, it looks that way. But, so the report continues, this allocating of the compensation has led to a rise in the share-price of I.G. Farben on the West German stock exchange, so shareholders can now expect a large dividend, which had been blocked for the course of the trial. This means, that I.G. Farben can retrospectively activate profits from the time of the Second World War, which they had to extract from the living and dead prisoners. And these criminals, who can all be named, today sit on the boards of directors of the companies which have emerged from I.G. Farben: the Bayer factories, the Badische Anillin und Soda Fabrik (BASF) in Ludwigshafen, the Hoechst factory, people like Mr. Ambroß.

H.G.: He was the founder of the factory in Auschwitz.
K.G.: Yes, the founder of the Auschwitz factory, those are the main culprits. These are the ones who were responsible. And they are not in court today.
H.G.: And who profited from those crimes in 1957.
K.G.: Yes.[37]

GDR radio continued to air provocative commentaries, particularly on the frequencies of the *Deutschlandsender*. The themes became familiar: The involvement of Krupps, Siemens and especially I.G. Farben in the NSDAP's rise to power (a theme, incidentally, which had been pursued since the late 1940s, most notably in the 1950 film *Der Rat der Götter*), the establishment of Auschwitz as a primarily industrial centre – hence the stress on the subsidiary camps of Auschwitz-Monowitz and others – and the continuity between Fascism and the 'monopoly capitalism' of the Federal Republic. Additionally, asking rather simplistic questions in emotional contexts and broadcasting the defendants' addresses were all part of GDR radio propaganda – as observed in this commentary by Alfred Fleischhacker, broadcast on the *Berliner Rundfunk* on 9 February 1964:

Only once did Capesius lose his cool in front of the jury in Frankfurt when he was asked: Where did he get the resources from to establish his pharmacy and beauty salon in Reutingen? The question remained unanswered. But survivors of Auschwitz know that SS-*Sturmbannführer* Capesius had a special interest in the personal medicaments of the ones who were about to be gassed: He had said that often valuable jewellery was hidden in the tubes and pill boxes. And today, dozens of people, young and old, and especially the infirm, will go to the Market Pharmacy in Göttingen, getting their prescriptions and medicines, hoping for a cure from their illnesses. Do they know that they are hoping for a cure from a murderer? Every day women visit the gynaecological department of the Elmshorn city hospital. Do these women, who are being treated by the consultant Dr. Franz Lukas, these women, who may be in labour, do they know that their child is being brought into the world by the hands of a murderer? Twenty-two, twenty-three years ago this Dr Lukas, dressed in a well-fitting SS uniform, stood on the ramp at Auschwitz and decided with a movement of the thumb who of the new arrivals should be gassed straight away and who should be worked to death in the I.G. Farben factory. Do the patients of the dentist Dr. Schatz, of Wichernstrasse 23, Hannover, know that they are expecting pain relief from a man who violated corpses in the most horrendous way ever to have occurred?[38]

What comes across in the programmes of the Auschwitz Trial so far, and an experience echoed by chief prosecutor Dr Fritz Bauer at the time, is the unwillingness to engage with the Nazi past that would genuinely attempt to embrace a 'new humanity' and repentance.[39] Instead the ideological priorities of the Cold War were shaping the arguments. Key in the SED's attempt to turn the Auschwitz Trial into 'a tribunal against the I.G. Farben conglomerate' was the expert report of the economics professor from the Humboldt University in (East) Berlin, Prof. Dr Jürgen Kuczynski.

A report about the involvement of commerce and industry had been asked for by Fritz Bauer for pre-trial hearings in 1962, and the prosecution had intended to present this along with the expert statements from the historians Dr Hans Buchheim, Dr Helmut Krausnick and Dr Martin Broszat in the first few weeks of the trial. Documents relating to this issue were available from the Nuremberg Trial against I.G. Farben in 1947, but in the atmosphere of economic miracle and Cold War any implication of complicity of West German industry was a taboo subject, and no such expert report from a West German academic was presented to the court.[40]

It was therefore Kuczynski's report, entitled 'The Interconnections Between the Interests of Economy and Security Police in the Establishment and the Running of the Concentration Camp Auschwitz and its Subsidiary Camps' (*Die Verflechtung von sicherheitspolizeilichen und wirtschaftlichen interessen bei der Einrichtung und dem Betrieb des KZ Auschwitz und seine Nebenlager*), which was presented, at the behest of the adjunct prosecutor Kaul, on 19 March 1964, in the middle of the cross-examinations of witnesses. After a lengthy questioning of Prof. Kuczynski by the defence the expert statement was rejected by the court, on the grounds that it was biased, as it had overlooked later amendments of various statements.

A couple of days earlier the West German president, Heinrich Lübke, had awarded the *Bundesverdienstkreuz* (equivalent to an OBE) to Dr Heinrich Bütefisch, a prominent industrialist who was on various boards of directors in the petrochemical industry. But what emerged from Kuczynski's report was Bütefisch's deep involvement with establishing the Buna plant at Auschwitz-Monowitz and the acquisition of slave labour. During the Third Reich Bütefisch had been on the board of I.G.

Farben and a member of the SS, and he had been awarded the *Ritterkreuz* ('Knight's Cross', a military honour; its British civil equivalent would be a KBE) by Adolf Hitler. So the connection between the rejection of Kuczynski's assessment and the awarding of the *Bundesverdienstkreuz* to Bütefisch was seen, not just by the GDR, as the often-remarked continuity between the Nazi past and the present-day situation found in the Federal Republic. In the evening commentary programme of the *Deutschlandsender* on 20 March 1964 the journalist Martin Radman pointed out that usually, in any trial, a statement which would exonerate the defendants would be welcomed by the defence lawyers. But in Frankfurt today, he argued, the defence reject the expert's statement not because it is from the GDR, but because the lawyers are protecting the real culprits and are in the pay of the government. This travesty of justice is evident in the honouring of Dr Bütefisch, who, among others, should be among the accused. By mentioning several other NS trials, which have occurred in the FRG as a result of tip-offs from the GDR, he implies that there is more to come:

> It is understandable, therefore, when the *Mannheimer Allgemeine Zeiting* writes in its editorial: 'There are, most probably, a multitude of such files in the archives in the East. They will not stay there forever. Again and again these drawers will open, and their mere squeaking will pale many a well-known man. It is lucky that these drawers exist.' Well, lucky for you, my dear listeners in West Germany. But these drawers do not excuse you from responsibility. On the contrary: nobody can say they didn't know. Just as Prof. Kuczynski yesterday, we will continue to call a criminal a criminal and the guilty one guilty, because with murderers there is no bias and no statute of limitations (*Verjährung*).[41]

The exposé from the east about Bütefisch's past could hardly have been more embarrassing for the Adenauer government and for the first time in the FRG's history a civil honour had to be recalled. The chancellor's office attempted to excuse itself with the explanation that the files about Bütefisch's past (and conviction to six years imprisonment by an Allied military court at Nuremberg in 1947) had been inaccessible as they were in the USA.[42]

Perhaps the most bizarre and intriguing radio programme about the Auschwitz Trial by the *Deutschlandsender* was broadcast shortly after the Bütefisch scandal, on 18 January 1965 – while the trial was still in progress. Entitled 'Men of Honour' (*Ehrenmänner*) and presented as a 'radio feature', it has as its central theme a courtroom confrontation between a survivor witness and the accused Dr Victor Capesius, interwoven into several narratives about the prosecution of Nazi crimes in the FRG, flashbacks to Auschwitz, recordings from prominent politicians and perpetrator statements. The Auschwitz survivor and witness mentioned in the programme is a certain Anna Silberstein, now residing in the GDR. No witness under this name appeared in the Auschwitz Trial. In the course of the programme the actress playing 'Anna Silberstein' even mentions her prisoner number – 7103, a number which, according to the Auschwitz Museum in Oswięćim, does not correspond with the name Silberstein.[43]

The programme begins with a yell of 'This is the truth!' (*Das ist die Wahrheit!*) and proceeds with the familiar claims of the missing real culprits and the complicity of industry in the running of the concentration camp system. This is followed by Chancellor Adenauer's comment on the Auschwitz Trial from 1962:

> Konrad Adenauer: I deem the Auschwitz Trial necessary, but on the other hand one must not succumb to the mistake to orchestrate some kind of witch-hunt. And those who have, in the past, done nothing but to err, those we should forgive and forget.[44]

The focus moves to the Frankfurt courtroom and to the 'thoughts' of Dr Capesius. This form of expressing 'internal dialogue' works well on radio. By getting the speaker close to the microphone and reducing all reverb and echo, this method can invoke the idea of a 'conversation in the head', an internally verbalised 'thought process', independent of the invariably private content (which, in this case are Capesius's thoughts of: 'She's alive, that's her, she survived!').[45]

The programme, which, incidentally, was again written by Horst Grothe, uses audio tape footage from his previous programmes, such as 'The Children from Zamość' and '*Sammelpunkt Shelesnastrasse*'. The relationship between Anna Silberstein and Dr Capesius is highlighted through these topics as it becomes clear, through the use of a 'flashback', that the Auschwitz prisoner Silberstein had attempted to save some of the children from Zamość from a terrible experiment by offering herself (sexually) to Dr Capesius. Capesius, having taken advantage of this, nevertheless submits the children to the experiments, which had been asked for by 'an industrialist to test phosphorous materials.' They suffer and die, and the surviving ones are gassed. 'This is the thanks for your whoring', Capesius tells Silberstein.[46]

But the general tone of this production differs through the very deliberate and continuous mixing of fact and fiction, and using sources which cannot be corroborated, as the following sequence demonstrates:

> Narrator 2: Non olet, or, blood does not stick to money. Money is just money. Valuables are just valuables. Gold is just gold. Capesius worked for I.G. Farben, and they, didn't they do just that? But this time, at this trial, it was hardly mentioned.
> Narrator 1: This time? Has there already been an Auschwitz Trial? Are those who critically commented that heels had been dragged for 20 years, are they wrong?
> Narrator 2: There has already been an Auschwitz Trial, or two to be precise. Maybe even three. But not here. It took place in Cracow. 1947. Höß's successor, commandant Liebehänschel, and 24 others were sentenced to death. The present accused Arthur Johann Breitwieser among them. Seven of the accused were sentenced to 15 years hard labour, among them the present accused Hans Hoffmann.
> Narrator 1: And this was the first Auschwitz Trial.
> Narrator 2: The second. The first one against Rudolf Höß took place a few months earlier. He was hanged in the place of his crimes.
> Narrator 1: And the third trial?
> Narrator 2: Took place in the Soviet Union. There, among others, the SS doctor Karl Klauberg and the *Rapportführer* Oswald Kaduk were sentenced to 25 years hard labour.
> Narrator 1: So why are Breitwieser, Hoffmann and Kaduk on trial again? Here in Frankfurt?
> Narrator 2: They were extradited to the Federal Republic.
> Narrator 1: Extradited?
> Narrator 2: To serve their sentences.
> Narrator 1: And did they?
> Narrator 2: On the contrary. They were released immediately and lived free for years.
> Narrator 1: Maybe they changed their names?
> Narrator 2: They lived under their own, rightful names, like Kaduk, Oswald Kaduk.
> Narrator 1: How can a man like that be released?
> Narrator 2: Why? Maybe because of this:
> (Fictional) Oswald Kaduk (at the pre-trial hearing): Yes Sir,... I did beat the prisoner Cyrankiewicz. The (now) Polish prime minister. I knew him from Poland. He was a communist. I really hate communists. If I'd had the chance, I would have killed him.[47]

Narrator 1: You are exaggerating. Because of this?
Narrator 2: I said *maybe* because of this.[48]

The programme continues by mentioning an article from a West German soldier's magazine, denying the existence of Auschwitz itself, which further stresses this implication of a rabid anti-communism in the FRG. 'A small German industrial accident. Whoever views Auschwitz like that will tolerate it again'.[49]

But central to the programme's argument is not just the atmosphere of anti-communism prevailing in the FRG, but also the point that as a result of it victims of the Nazi past, now living in the GDR, were further victimised through the West German judiciary by having their testimony rejected. This is played out in the following scene:

Anna Silberstein: I still have to report what happened to the children who remained after the experiments.
Judge: Weren't they gassed?
A.S.: All of them. But before they went on this road of no return, before they crossed the threshold into the house of death, they fell into the hands of him, over there!
Narrator 1: Again Anna Silberstein points at Boger. She knows now that her testimony will find no resonance here. But she takes up the fight. Just as then. But for her there is one big difference. Today her voice will travel further than this courtroom. Despite the lies and twists and turns the truth will find its way.
A.S.: Boger shouted: 'I will get you to know the devil' as he drove the children to the gassing block, where an SS man stood at the ready with a sack full of sweets. Because every child got a sweet before it stepped from life to death.
[Military band playing Eduard Künnecke's *'Glückliche Reise'* (happy journey) – the tune most played by the parade ground orchestra at Auschwitz – for 8 bars, then same tune played by a small dance band with strings to imply a more sedate setting, the boardroom of the I.G. Farben in 1942.][50]

On closer examination this section is remarkable. Not only does a non-existent witness interact with a real defendant, but the wording of her statements does not correspond even remotely with the court transcripts and comes from a radio programme broadcast two years earlier. The central theme of the feature, the alleged sexual misconduct of the accused with the survivor victim, is held together by a number of testimonies from other concentration camps as well as Auschwitz. Although billed as a 'feature' and not as a documentary programme, the claims of authenticity and truth occur time and time again throughout. How is this possible?

The theoretical foundation to present this as a relatively coherent continuity is the Marxist-Leninist distinction between 'objectivity' (*Objektivität*) and 'objectivism' (*Objektivismus*). The journalists of the GDR possess objectivity as they are aware that partiality (adhering to the party line) and objectivity 'form an inseparable unity' in Marxism-Leninism,[51] and that the so-called 'objectivity' of the Western capitalist media is merely a deception and a cover-up of bourgeois values, a false 'neutrality' which is termed 'objectivism'.

Consequently, the deviations from the known narrative of the court proceedings in the above sequence are possible by the virtue of the very argument it is trying to present. Any denial of the story by the West can be seen as further proof of continuity between the Third Reich and the FRG, further conspiracy against the true anti-fascist, cleansed German Democratic Republic. Second, by adopting the moral high ground, a GDR radio programme can intimidate the (West) German population into a shamed complicity with the murderers of Auschwitz. Therefore critical listening is diminished. And third, radio listening can be inconsequential. Whether 'Anna Silberstein' existed or not is unimportant to the listener, and, as the portrayed incident was perfectly within the realm of the possible, it could be argued, acceptable as a 'reality of an unimaginable occurrence'.[52] Furthermore, if the listening becomes too uncomfortable, the radio can be switched off or the station changed.

East German radio deemed it sufficient to give *Ehrenmänner* another airing on 15 December 1965, but the liberties taken with the portrayal of the victims must have given the broadcasting authorities cause for concern. Found in the reel casing there was a note for the programme's announcers:

Announcement before the programme:
   Good evening, ladies and gentlemen
   Yesterday, as you might have gathered from our news services, the second Auschwitz Trial began in Frankfurt/Main. For this reason we are repeating the feature *Ehrenmänner* by Horst Grothe – a programme, based on observations and documentary detail of the first Auschwitz Trial, which concluded in August this year with outrageously lenient sentences, and which, despite its distance to the past, has lost none of its burning actuality.

Run................Reel 1................
................Reel 2...........End
Announcement after the programme:
Ladies and gentlemen
We would like to point out to you that this feature dealt with true events. Even the names of the accused of first Auschwitz Trial, on which this [feature] was based, were not invented. In the witnesses' statements, though, events are concentrated – therefore the witnesses [here] are representative of all witnesses, just as some of the accused [here] stand for all others.[53]

Ehrenmänner remains one of the most curious programmes under discussion here.

Apart from the trial reportage West German stations started a more systematic engagement with the issues arising from the Auschwitz Trial. Historian Joseph Wulf made a number of programmes for the *Südwestfunk* in Baden-Baden, dealing with issues such as the language of SS euphemisms,[54] the diary of the Warsaw Ghetto archivist Emmanuel Ringelblum,[55] as well as a critical look at Hitler's Foreign Ministry, the *Auswärtiges Amt*, as it increasingly became the executor of racial policy, which Wulf recorded for the North German broadcaster *Radio Bremen*.[56]

Other programmes courted controversy, including debates around Hannah Arendt's Eichmann book[57] and Rolf Hochhuth's play on the complicity of the Vatican, *Der Stellvertreter*,[58] as well as the broadcasts of discussion evenings with prominent commentators.[59] But one programme above all others attracted attention, not just among journalists and specialised audiences, but nation-wide, in the press, on television and among the wider public. This was the transmission of Horst Krüger's lengthy radio essay 'In the Labyrinth of Guilt' (*Im Labyrinth der Schuld*) on 29 April 1964 by the *Südwestfunk*, Baden-Baden.[60] Horst Krüger had been the editor of the *Südwestfunk*'s nighttime programming (*Nachtstudio*) since 1952 and a prominent cultural critic in the newspapers. Having grown up and studied in Berlin, he was briefly arrested and imprisoned in 1940 for his contact with the communist Ernst Niekisch, then saw military service at the Russian front and Monte Cassino, where he was injured and deserted to the Americans.[61]

The 68-minute programme, broadcast relatively late at night – at 22:15hrs – came to the attention of the influential critic Marcel Reich-Ranicki after its first airing and subsequently appeared in the journal *Der Monat*, before being printed by the newspapers, including *Die Zeit*, the paper which carried Reich-Ranicki's column.[62] The essay came into being after Krüger had been urged by his friend Fritz Bauer to attend the proceedings in Frankfurt.

The programme itself is very simple: the actor Herbert Fleischmann reads the text calmly, without any embellishments. It starts with Krüger on his way to the twentieth day of proceedings of the Frankfurt trial, pondering over the previous night's dream about his military days, a corporal shouting at him, a nightmare. But the dream fails to make any sense; clothes, surroundings and, particularly, the language are alien and false.

His preconceptions of the trial are common: for months the newspapers have been reporting the preparations, which took five years; the document with the charges contains over 7,000 pages; who will be able to understand it all, have an overview, follow it? Who will be interested?

> Obligatory reporting for the broadsheets, obligatory lectures for no-one, not material for the tabloids; BILD [tabloid] was not present, not a topic for parties, for a moment an embarrassed and dismayed silence occurred among the evening's guests when I casually mentioned: 'I am going to the Auschwitz Trial'. 'God, yes, how terrible', someone said in the background. 'You poor thing!' added a lady, and the host poured more whisky and tried to change the topic. I remained silent; these people here weren't Nazis. I just used an inappropriate word at a dinner party: in our country using the word 'Auschwitz' after work is unpopular, it is a scorned word, just like the word 'GDR' in the office.[63]

Auschwitz, Krüger contemplates, is like a spectre, the word has turned into a metaphor of evil, horror, blood and fear, burning bodies, smoking chimneys, German bookkeepers administering the modern death: gas. Auschwitz is the myth of modernity, the dance of death of the industrial age, the new myth of the administered death, Rosenberg's vision, the myth of the twentieth century.

His aim is to de-mystify this preconception. This is, he feels, the last chance to witness, to come face to face with victims and perpetrators before it all disappears as 'history', passed over to historians and material for students.

On his initial arrival at the *Römer* he feels unease with the police and court officials, remembering his own encounter with German justice during the Third Reich, but he is politely shown to his seat. On the witness stand is Dr Otto Wolken, the first witness in the Auschwitz Trial. Although he does not yet know the identity of the witness, he is startled by the calm and composed recounting of the most horrendous experiences. For the inmates of Auschwitz survival appeared almost as complicity: In the city of death all are collaborating, whether you distribute gas or bread, you are part of it. 'Only he who takes his place in the mechanism of death has hope of survival.'[64] Survive in order to bear witness, one day, twenty years later, here in Frankfurt, on 27 February 1964, now in this hour of truth. Krüger finds himself strangely agitated. Yes, he knows this language, yes, the word *'Sanka'* (*Sanitätskraftwagen*) means ambulance, he drove one of them in Russia during the war. 'Most were immediately injected with carbolic acid (*Phenol*) in the *Sanka*', the voice in the courtroom says. Would he have driven the truck if the destination had not been Smolensk, but Auschwitz? Would he, if he had known, refused the order? Would he have been a hero?

> I believe I would not have murdered, along with the others. I couldn't have murdered, burned, selected. This is a different dimension. But wouldn't I have tried to distance myself from the whole affair, with the usual little soldier's tricks? Work in the depot, or office, or hospital? Surely I would not have been a hero. I would have distanced myself and kept my mouth shut. But who can tell how long I could have distanced myself? Even killing can become routine. Everything is routine. If 10,000 people are killed every day, who says I could not have become used to it after two years?[65]

Krüger's thoughts are interrupted sharply by Dr Wolken's continuing statement, recounting children being thrown into fires alive, because of a shortage of gas. Amid rising fear and horror, he realises that here, in the courtroom, although he only came to observe, no-one can remain impartial, no-one can just observe.

In a short recess he meets a colleague (very obviously the NDR journalist Axel Eggebrecht), who fills him in on the detail of the defendants, who they are, where they are sitting, the crimes they are accused of. He realises that many of the well dressed, upright citizens he had been sitting alongside are, in fact, the defendants. He recalls the title of Wolfgang Staude's 1946 film *'The Murderers are Amongst Us'*.

> But here are the modern, up to now unknown, murderers, the administrators and functionaries of the mass-death, the bookkeepers and button-pushers and writers of the machine: technocrats,

who operate without hate or feeling, the small functionaries of Eichmann's big empire. Here a new style of crime becomes evident: death in the technocratic age as an act of administration. The murderers are pleasant and correct civil servants, administrators like in one of Kafka's novels.[66]

As the court reconvenes, Krüger looks at the materials he has been given by his colleague. The majority of these former SS men are now employed as businessmen, pharmacists, nurses and (the largest category) bookkeepers. He pores over Boger's file: bookkeeper in a sales department in Stuttgart. If it had not been for Fritz Bauer's fastidiousness and resolve, Boger would still be bookkeeping, adding and subtracting in red, blue and green, not losing a minute's sleep. And Mulka, a seemingly upright democrat of the 'occidental' persuasion, who thinks of communism when he hears the word 'inhumanity', of Bautzen (prison in the GDR), of Waldheim (trials) and of Hilde Benjamin.

Dr Wolken continues among an embarrassed silence and – finally – dismay, a German dismay, Krüger calls it, from the spectators. He examines them and finds hope in the hopeful, young faces of the students, who, with unbelieving expressions, try to imagine the crimes of their parents. Their parents? Surely not, someone else's. Older faces as well, pensioners, bitter and broken. But no one in their forties and fifties, the ones who participated, who should concern themselves with this. They are too busy working, keeping the economic miracle going. Only losers look back.

The court rises for lunch and Krüger walks behind Breitwieser, the bookkeeper with *Zyklon B* experience. Where would he go for lunch?

> For a second I have the crazy idea to follow him, to see which car he gets into and with whom he will spend his lunch break. But I realise that this would not be very interesting. In this country people with *Zyklon B* experience eat and sleep and love like anyone else: they are contemporaries (*Kameraden*) of this sick and crazy time.[67]

Out in the midday traffic of Frankfurt there is no time to think about Auschwitz. Here, in the hustle and bustle of the free Germany, the men in their cars, all around 40 or so, seem out to kill you, right here on the zebra crossing in front of the *Paulskirche*. In a quieter back street Krüger finds time to reflect. Here, in Goethe's Frankfurt, the people believe that the poet's birthplace, which has been rebuilt, is an old building, and 90 per cent of the people reject the Auschwitz Trial, so the prosecutor said.

Later, in a restaurant, he goes over his notes: scribbled words like: go to the ramp, take away, make sport, shoot, *Zyklon B*, inject Muslims (*Muselmänner*), stand to attention, rabbit hunt, dog commando, and many more.

> As I scan these words I suddenly understand last night's dream. It is the language of the old [army] uniform, it is the word 'Sanka', which you couldn't remember. This language is still alive, it still exists, here in Frankfurt it comes alive, no matter how many new uniforms or golden garments we have. The corporal who screamed at me... was Hitler of course: he also still exists in us. He still rules in the dark, in the underground; he taught us all to jump. Some run after the money, others go to the Auschwitz Trial, some hide it and others uncover it – the two sides of the German coin. This Hitler, I think, will stay with us forever, until death.[68]

Reich-Ranicki challenged other German writers to attend the proceedings, to write about it, to engage with the Auschwitz Trial, and many, such as Günther Grass, Martin Walser and others, took up the challenge. Hubert Fichte, author of the novel *Aufbruch nach Turku*, was the first to respond and to warn of complacency, but he also expressed fear (with reference to the defendant Kaduk, who was a hospital porter), 'I do not want to be looked after by a mass murderer.'[69] But the appeal also had its critics, one of whom might be worth mentioning here: The WDR radio journalist Johannes F. Großmann, who had been reporting from other trials, commented from 8 June 1964 on the station *WDR I*:

> I fear a great proportion of the public has started, with more sophistication and anew, to nullify the [murder] victims as persons; and when they glance at Auschwitz through their opera glasses they recognise the pitiful existences of Kaduk, Boger, Bednarek and the like, but they only look with one eye when it comes to the mass murderers of Bialystok or Slonim or Mauthausen or Lemberg or Chelmno or Hadamar or other places, which appear, compared to Auschwitz, as pre-industrial places of human contempt.[70]

The extensive focus on Auschwitz itself is not the only problem that arises from the broadcast. Many issues in Krüger's essay appear marginalised, or even avoided. Nazi racial policy, anti-Semitism, is not mentioned at all, the references to Jews occur only in the context of other topics, such as a speculation on the accused Breitwieser's thoughts on the charges against him which include the gassing of 850 Russian POWs ('they were only Russian, not Jews'[71]), or expressing an understanding for Jews not wanting to return to Germany today.[72] The day of Krüger's visit, when Dr Wolken gave testimony, was filled with exclusive references to the treatment of Jews in Auschwitz and how the NSDAP's anti-Semitism was put into practice through the camp system. Dr Wolken himself gave a perfect explanation of the parameters of racial policy ('Auschwitz was not an [exclusively] Jewish affair'[73]), which could have exonerated Krüger's approach. But the omission of a mention of anti-Semitic policies all together in this context is somewhat startling. It is, however, not unusual; it appears that the hints given by Krüger are enough, particularly for the age-group he wants to address the most, the generation who consciously lived through the period of the Third Reich, the few references point to the assumption of a vague memory of a deeply engrained German anti-Semitism.

Most problematic, however, is the section of the essay which contains the sentence of the title – 'In the Labyrinth of Guilt'. The reference is taken up when he considers the defendant Emil Bednarek, who was a Kapo at Auschwitz and the only one of the accused who was also a camp inmate, a 'victim of Hitler who himself murdered' (*Ein Hitleropfer, das selber mordete*), as he terms it, 'this is the labyrinth of Auschwitz'.[74] From this he concludes that these prosecutions are not 'a new wave of de-Nazification, a late revenge on the SS, a witch-hunt of the little Nazis', but these are murder trials. Whereas this is undoubtedly true – and Krüger lingers on this point by recalling the Jewish police and *Judenräte* in the Ghettoes – the 'labyrinth of guilt' in his contemplation is clearly, and referred to in later texts,[75] the real or imagined complicity of the average German during the Hitler dictatorship; a fact which Krüger addresses well elsewhere, but not in the context of his 'labyrinth'.

Another noteworthy aspect of the programme is its specificity to the German context. Whereas most of the reportage and accounting of the Auschwitz Trial are clearly victim-orientated (or in one case perpetrator-orientated[76]), internationalised, and relatively clear-cut,[77] Krüger's contemplation reflects the confusion and shame evident in the Federal Republic of the 1960s, the absurdity of the contrast of living in the opulence of the *Wirtschaftswunder* and the horrors of Auschwitz.

After the success of his radio essay Horst Krüger left the SWF, devoted his time to writing and became a successful and popular travel writer. Certainly the importance and influence of 'In the Labyrinth of Guilt' in Germany cannot be understated. It is a prime example of 'working through the past' on the airwaves.

Axel Eggebrecht

The majority of the surviving reportage materials from the Auschwitz Trial are reports of the NDR reporter Axel Eggebrecht (1899–1991). A total of 24 monthly dispatches of varying length (between 45 and 90 minutes) from Frankfurt are to be found in the archives of the North German state broadcaster, as well as discussion programmes and additional commentaries. Eggebrecht's seemingly limitless energy and commitment are even more astounding when considering that he not only covered the Auschwitz Trial, but also, simultaneously, the trials of the Eichmann deputies Hermann Krumey and Otto Hunsche (also in Frankfurt) and the euthanasia trial against Gerhard Bohne and Hans Hefelmann in Limburg. Additionally, he wrote and broadcast a weekly programme under the title 'The Past in Court' (*Die Vergangenheit vor Gericht*) as well as his daily dispatches for the newsroom of the NDR 'The Daily Echo' (*Echo des Tages*).[78]

Eggebrecht's chequered career can only offer a partial explanation of his dedication. Born in Leipzig as the son of a physician in 1899, he volunteered in 1917 and was seriously injured in Flanders in April 1918. After his recovery he studied literature and philosophy, became involved in the Freikorps and participated in the failed Kapp Putsch in 1920. Later the same year he joined the communist party (KPD) and became a regional organiser. After the failure of the 1923 rising he sought refuge in Berlin, where he became acquainted with the satirist George Grosz and worked (as a packer) at the progressive Malik publishing house. As a party member he wrote occasionally for the party newspaper *Die Rote Fahne*, and after meeting Willi Münzenberg, was employed by the International Workers Aid (*Internationale Arbeiterhilfe, IAH*) to promote Soviet films in Germany, which involved lengthy stays in Moscow. Disillusioned with the Soviet Union and the KPD, Eggebrecht, with the help of Kurt Tucholsky, joined the writing staff of the independent left-wing literary journal *Die Weltbühne* in 1925. In March 1933 he was arrested and interned in the concentration camp Hainewalde (Saxony) and released three weeks later, and after 1934 gained permission to work as 'script-writer of apolitical films' at UFA film studios in Berlin. His countless efforts to help racially and politically persecuted persons did not go unnoticed by British Intelligence, and in July 1945 he was asked by the British military authorities to become part of the newly established radio station for north-western Germany, the NWDR. There he became responsible for the 'Re-education' programme on the radio, which included reporting from the Bergen-Belsen trial in Lüneburg in 1945.[79] Thereafter he remained at the NWDR (later NDR) as chief political commentator until his retirement.

Eggebrecht's tireless engagement with the Nazi past continued throughout his broadcasting (and publishing) career,[80] alongside his enthusiasm for young people, and for the training of young radio journalists.[81] But it is also his dedication to the medium of radio which comes across in his reporting. 'Radio became my profession' he declared, 'because it is the ideal instrument for the writer (*Literat*) who wants to have a direct influence on his environment.' The technology of the radio, he believes, can be mastered by the journalist and used, which is not the case in television, where the technical aspects dominate. 'The ear receives what is on offer in a concentrated manner, whether it is a report, a play or commentary. This is why the radio, so often declared as dead, is longer lasting that the flickering screen.'[82]

Here we will consider three of Eggebrecht's reports from the Auschwitz Trial, alongside one discussion programme. It is perhaps surprising to note that his friend and fellow journalist at the time, the German-Israeli writer Inge Deutschkron, writing for an Israeli newspaper, recalls how much Eggebrecht had to restrain himself to make his monthly broadcasts acceptable for an 'unrepentant' public.[83] Yet out of the (over) 36 hours of broadcast material it seemed apt to select these four programmes, which, when looked at consecutively, will not only present Eggebrecht's sharp insights and analysis, but also show how through the medium of radio the journalist and the listener can become seriously involved in a contemplation on politics and morality.

The first of Axel Eggebrecht's reports from the Frankfurt Auschwitz Trial begins with an introduction by Ernst Schnabel, on behalf of the editor, reflecting on the difficulties faced when planning these series of broadcasts. The editorial office assumes that the listeners are in agreement about the necessity of these trials and that a serious engagement with this topic will be in the mutual interest of all. The question which seemed difficult to answer was rather 'How should the Third Programme report from these trials?' and 'Who should speak?'[84]

The choice of Axel Eggebrecht was obvious:

> As you might remember, shortly after the war, a British military tribunal convened in Lüneburg to pass sentence over the SS corps of the concentration camp Bergen-Belsen. If ever there has been a thoroughly successful, correct, enlightening, ruthless and at the same time helpful radio reportage of contemporary events which stretched over months and involved us not only as witnesses but also as subjects,

it has been this one. We have asked Axel Eggebrecht to report from the Auschwitz Trial for the Third Programme because of his impeccable expertise and experience. He would probably refute this, and we would not want to burden him with such a dubious reputation. [But] we have asked him to travel to Frankfurt for us, for you, because we are of the opinion that these trials are even more important than the one in Lüneburg. Surely the material has remained the same. The victims seeking retribution are the same. The misery of the perpetrators is the same. But the continuing post-war legal processes have become something else; a historical instance, in the best possible case, an attempt to fill the gaps in history, in the historical consciousness of a nation, which cannot have a future as long as it is content with such a partial (*lückenhaft*) past. The reporting from the Auschwitz Trial, which promises to be *the* trial of the coming year, can only be complete, conscientiously complete, if it connects to the Lüneburg one, the first post war trial, because the gaps in our [historical] consciousness I mentioned, have dangerously widened in the past 18 years. Axel Eggebrecht will attempt to fill them with the truth. He reports.[85]

The editorial introduction is highly unusual in terms of format (the fact that the editor should express a direct opinion, addressing the listener) and in terms of content. Whereas other reporters might have mentioned the fact that 'the defendants look like our neighbours' or this was an issue concerning the German nation, here it is clearly stated that the listener is not only witness but also subject. It asks the listener to engage consciously with his or her past.

Eggebrecht starts with the suggestion that over the coming months he will take the listener on a journey into the past, the recent past. He stresses, quite vehemently, that he will not engage in debates about whether there has been an insufficient 'coming-to-terms-with' the past, nor will he decide what needs coming to terms with. He rejects the term, as it implies (in German) an over-powering, taming, a submission. This he distinctly wants to avoid. He wants to, the listeners want to, 'work through the past'.[86] The Auschwitz Trial represents such an opportunity, publicly to hear and see the victims and perpetrators and to understand how the system of terror worked.

He speculates that the listeners will demand that the reporting be impartial and objective; unfortunately, he says, this is not possible. He has an opinion and is quite sure that there will be convictions. The SS was declared a criminal organisation at Nuremberg and is considered as such by public opinion. Therefore it is impossible to achieve a total impartiality towards the defendants. He will, however, attempt always to indicate his personal opinions, as far as it is possible.[87]

At the outset of the trial, or a week after the first day's proceedings, when this programme was recorded, Eggebrecht estimated that the court would sit for about six months; but even before he launches into the details of the accused and their misdeeds, he reflects on a 1963 publication of the Federal government on the prosecution of National Socialist crimes,[88] which is a clear indication that, should this trial be conducted thoroughly, it would take a considerably longer time. He quotes from this publication, somewhat sarcastically, which claims that up to 1955 the law restricted German prosecutions, and that many of the documents needed were in foreign archives, unavailable. Eggebrecht's tone of voice suggests that he is fully aware that this is not so, as stated by Dr Fritz Bauer in the radio interview quoted above. But the publication is startlingly frank, and this much he is willing to admit, particularly the comments from the protestant minister Erwin Wilkins, who, in his article 'Drawing a line under Nazi Crimes?' (*Schlußstrich unter die NS-Verbrechen?*), writes that these trials force the German judiciary to instigate a clarification of its moral and ethical principles.[89]

Eggbrecht then reports from the first day's proceedings, giving his impression of the defendants, their claims of innocence and their seemingly good spirits. What strikes him is the apparent ill health of most of the defendants: Dylewski is suffering from 'brain cramps', Mulka has ulcers, Boger can't stand up. The SS appears to have consisted of a bunch of invalids, Eggebrecht comments.[90]

On the train home he reads Joachim C. Fest's *The Face of the Third Reich*,[91] and contemplates Fest's claim that the effects of National Socialism are longer-lasting than its political system and that in the Federal Republic at least, the postwar years have been a period of grace, where a different, new consciousness was not needed, as reasonable circumstances have prevailed:

> Many say that the accused are not dangerous anymore. This is correct, and is due to the reasonable circumstances Joachim Fest speaks of in his book. In this case we are dealing not with born criminals but with petit bourgeois gone wild (*wildgewordene Spießbürger*). Hannah Arendt, the German-American sociologist, has identified the unbound petit bourgeois as the true criminal of our century. And the question remains under which circumstances this hidden tendency surfaces. I think the environment is decisive here, the moral, political

and economic environment. And even more decisive is the reaction to the unleashing of the criminal petit bourgeois. But these reactions have not occurred here too often. We reassure ourselves, the 'Hitler in us' is dead, and forget all, forever. But is there any evidence for this? I do not know. But this trial could become a piece of this evidence, a useful test on how all Germans will follow, understand and work through it. Let's hope that this chance will not be missed.[92]

Around six months later Eggebrecht featured in an additional programme to the monthly reports from Frankfurt, this was the transmission of a 142-minute recording of a public discussion with the title 'Auschwitz – Singular Occurrence or Symptom?' (*Auschwitz – Einzelfall oder Symptom?*).[93] This night-time programme appears hastily arranged and certainly not intended for prime-time transmission, with its inefficient microphone positioning and unedited 'dead air' (broadcast time with no speakers or identifiable sounds). It was recorded at a discussion evening in Bonn on or a little earlier than the broadcast date, and the chairman and the speakers, with the exception of Eggebrecht, are credited neither on the audiotape nor on the accompanying papers from the archive.

After being introduced, Eggebrecht begins a lengthy monologue on the importance of the current trials taking place in Frankfurt and elsewhere, stating that he views the Auschwitz Trial as important, but the trial against the two Eichmann deputies Hermann Krumey and Otto Hunsche as the one that carries more weight.[94] Charges that these trials are being held too late he deems wrong. Rather he sees the interest these trials evoke in young people and that they can and will become a political affair with a moral aspect (*ein Politikum mit moralischem Akzent*).[95] He reflects on the Auschwitz Trial, commends Judge Hofmeyer for his astute grasp of the facts and expresses pity for the deluded and indignant accused. This he sees as an expression of the petit bourgeois hunger for self-assertion, the international phenomenon of mass-man, who will happily sit at home, profession: mass murderer.[96]

Astonishing remarks come not only from the witnesses – and here he mentions the now 80-year-old former SS doctor Johann Kremer, who, after having served his sentence, now quite freely and jovially admits to his murderous activities[97] – but also from defendants such as the accused Pery Broad's assertion in his 1947 report that 'Auschwitz was the biggest crime in all human history'.[98] In the light of such conflicting and paradoxical circumstances, he feels that the criminal law and the courts are inadequately equipped, and hopes that through these trials new categories of jurisdiction will emerge. Eggebrecht's introduction ends on a cautious note about the adjunct prosecutor from the GDR, Dr Friedrich Kaul. As much as he regrets the ideological wrangling in court, he feels that often Kaul has a point when he points to greater conspiracies and charges of collective crimes (*Bandenverbrechen*), which have no place in West German jurisdiction, but in a case like the Auschwitz Trial thinks that a change in law should be considered.[99]

In the discussion that follows the first question concerns the recent call for a general amnesty. Is this, according to the questioner, a sign of a judicial system that cannot cope? Eggebrecht is unsure. But he certainly rejects any call for a general amnesty. He would rather see a tightening of the law so that not only actual murderers but also the instigators and administrators feel the full force of the law, that civic duties and citizenship become more pronounced and Germans emerge from their insular self-interest. Further questions reveal an audience not necessarily in agreement with Eggebrecht over the timing of the trials or on the activities of the *Zentrale Stelle*'s activities.

For future reference, in order to make it certain that something like Auschwitz will never happen again, could he, so a questioner wants to know, point to a specific point in time when the German people should have realised, should have risen up against the Nazi terror? Here Eggebrecht comes into his own. With reference to another panellist, the historian Dr Peter Jacobsohn, he replies that it was not Stalingrad, but January 1933; though he himself would answer this differently:

> If you ask me, this matter dates back further; I am touching on a favourite topic of mine, one that has occupied me, I wouldn't say my whole life, but at least since the first time I was arrested in 1933 ... yes I think it dates back many decades, possibly centuries, the source of this, because something is missing in our history. (long pause) You asked me earlier why did these trials did not happen in 1945. Well, because we were not able to do so, we did not make a revolution; others had to liberate us from this system. We lack the ability to conduct rapid – and viewed historically as sometimes unjust – but essential reckonings, or if you wish to use the unpopular wording, we lack the ability to revolt against whatever oppresses us. Since 1519? When was the peasants' revolt? '21? I'm sorry, I don't know the precise date just now, we did not have a revolution, and it was crushed by the highest authority, and Luther, with Luther's help. All other, all other (heckling from the audience) ... no, that was not a revolution ... all other nations have founded their modern nation-state on successful

revolutions. The English, the French, the Americans. I find it extremely interesting how things become part of an organic development; that the conservative De Gaulle stands to military attention to the same tune with which the French aristocracy went to the guillotine. It has ceased to matter. It has been incorporated into history; the revolution is an organic component of all nations, apart from us, unfortunately. And if you realise this, a very pessimistic realisation, then you understand the quotation I read out earlier 'Let us beware the belief that this was a purely German affair', no, the petit bourgeois of all nations is in danger of becoming the criminal of the century, like *Herr* Boger, Kaduk, Klehr or Schlage, that we do not doubt, but [they] are contained by certain democratic virtues, which arise out of certain events, which have never happened with us. This would be my answer ...[100]

Whereas this type of German *Sonderweg* interpretation is by no means unusual, it is interesting to see how Eggebrecht incorporates it into his wider argumentation. Other questions from the audience, regarding the harnessing of racial and political prejudices, euthanasia and the psychology of the perpetrators, receive similar answers from the veteran journalist. The relationship between the modern citizen and the state has to be clarified, understood and incorporated into daily life, including in the conduct of criminal trials. Wider implications of this are that charges of crimes against humanity and genocide have to be made admissible in (German) national jurisdiction.

In his summary of the evening's discussion Eggebrecht states that it is far from his mind (and abilities) to propose coherent legal changes. He agrees with previous speakers in the statement that language itself seems to fail when it comes to dealing with crimes on the scale of Auschwitz. But he returns to the topic of 'democratic virtues', and in this context he mentions the American CARE parcels for Germany after the war, and the fact that, during his numerous visits to London in the 1950s, he noticed that buying things on the black market in Britain was viewed as something dishonourable, in contrast to the situation in Germany:

> And if you think a little about these things, then you come to [the conclusion that] private fate, which for us takes such a central place, to which we always retreat in case of catastrophe, is the source of great danger. If we were to think about the famed 'neighbour', the next person, a little more often and more actively and were more willing to act, then soon we would see where the first possible roots

of a similar misfortune lie. That it will not be identical is very clear; especially not regarding Jews, as there are too few here now, which reflects so sadly on our intellectual climate. But who knows what kind of fearsome black devils will be painted on our walls, and then we will not remain quiet, like perhaps we did in '33. Once it turns into law, the German will have difficulty to object. He will have to object before. This is perhaps the only lesson we can draw from all this.[101]

And Eggebrecht's programmes were listened to, despite his own doubts. His partner Inge Stolten wrote to him in June 1964 of a mutual friend, who noted, whilst at a lido, that 'everywhere around him there was Eggebrecht on the transistor radios, and people were listening to you!'[102] The programmes were received favourably nationally and internationally, particularly by the Israeli press.[103]

But as public interest waned, Eggebrecht's doubts about his own effectiveness increased. After eleven monthly reports, in November 1964, he delivered a provisional appraisal (*Zwischenbilanz*), a 90-minute programme of acute observations and comment,[104] but all was not so clear cut anymore. Whereas on the whole he sees the accused, and he singles out Mulka, Boger, Klehr and Kaduk, as guilty, he has doubts about some of the testimony given by some of the witnesses, and on the court's ability to come to any meaningful verdict at the end of it all. He appears unusually sombre in this broadcast, not only on the occasion of the 'Day of Prayer and Atonement' (*Bet – und Bußtag*, a West German public holiday), but also in his general demeanour, remembering the victims, particularly the women and children, and ends, unusually for the avowed agnostic, on a religious note, citing a letter he received from a vicar in Brandenburg (GDR) with a photograph of the church memorial plaque, which reads:

> Lord, you have afflicted us in 1933, 1939 and 1945. The ones killed in battle, through bombs, extinguished as unworthy of life, sacrificed in the resistance, murdered Jews, blood-witnesses of faith, the ones still missing, displaced and desperate persons. All blood cries up to you. Lord, have mercy on our misery and guilt. Turn us into messengers of your peace.[105]

Seven weeks after the verdict in the Auschwitz Trial, on 7 October 1965, Axel Eggebrecht delivered his summary over the airwaves of the NDR.[106] The listener very quickly notices that this 93-minute analysis of the greatest and most complex trial in postwar West German history has been arduous and soul-searching work for Eggebrecht. His doubts expressed in previous programmes have now taken on a resigned, bitter tone, but lack none of the sharp and intelligent insights of the earlier broadcasts. The structure of the summary is laid out clearly. Starting with the Trial's pre-history, it moves to the strategies of the prosecution and the defence, the convicted and acquitted, ending with a reflection on the witnesses and the judges. There are several points worth noting here, particularly but not exclusively, his more general observations.

In his introduction Eggebrecht comments that the potential significance of this trial could be enormous, 'if we want it to'. 'But do we?'[107] The dual task of the trial, to seek justice and to establish historical fact, makes it unlike any other in the history of Germany. Through one of the first postwar trials held in 1945, the Bergen-Belsen trial in Lüneburg, the term 'Auschwitz' became well known, as many of the SS had come from there, but it was not until nearly 20 years later that any kind of proceedings were possible. On the reasons why this took so long he does not wish to speculate, nor on the verdicts, which already have aroused enough attention, and are still to undergo the appeals procedure. But it is the court's opinion, the reasons for the verdicts, on which he expands. The resignation and frustration of the court in not being able to pass sentence on some of the most heinous crimes is often mentioned in the judge's summary, as well as the psychological strain of the witnesses, jury and court. Nevertheless wherever possible, it was the court's task to establish when and where a murder had been committed, and this, Eggebrecht feels, Judge Hofmeyer did thoroughly and with great skill.[108] Also the prosecution performed with subtlety and proficiency; state prosecutor Christian Raabe and adjunct prosecutor Henry Ormond were particularly noteworthy. But special attention, throughout the trial, was reserved for the adjunct prosecutor from the GDR, Dr Friedrich Kaul, whose presence often turned the trial into an arena of Cold War political argumentation, but, according to Eggebrecht, it was the near-hysterical objections from the defence counsels Dr Laternser and Dr Hermann Stolting II, which gave Kaul the upper hand.

The defence lawyers, of whom there were plenty (two for each of the 22 accused), he divides into three groups: one unconcerned for the fate of their clients; another attempting to find the best possible outcome for the defendants; and the last, which includes the two above named Laternser and Stolting II, as well as Dr Hans Fertig and Dr Wolfgang Zarnuck, as outright SS apologists, with a possible Nazi agenda. Their argumentation – that Jews should be inadmissible as witnesses because of their bias, that selection meant saving lives, and that the whole trial was a criminal undertaking (*frevelhaft*) – Eggebrecht considers to be beyond belief.[109] An additional question remains about the remuneration of these lawyers, as most defendants had to rely on assigned counsels, but these gentlemen were kept on by unknown funds and sources. 'It is strange', he comments.[110]

With regard to the sentences of the defendants he makes little comment, except to say that of all of the defendants only Boger struck him as an outright sadistic psychopath, and that the life sentence for the Kapo Bednarek was inappropriate, as he was the only one of the defendants who had no choice. Whereas the acquittals of Schobert, Breitwieser and Schatz were possible on technical grounds, he has grave doubts on the sentence passed on Dr Capesius – nine years, which appears extraordinary given the evidence heard in court, but perhaps, Eggebrecht speculates, it had something to do with the mysterious Mr Eisler, who had been visiting witnesses on Capesius' behalf during the trial.[111]

The witnesses, again, occupy Eggebrecht thoroughly, for the prosecution as well as the defendants. Former members of the SS were particularly untrustworthy but also, and this is somewhat surprising, one often-cited statement from the prosecution witness Dounia Wasserstrom regarding Wilhelm Boger.[112] The court and jury believed the incident Wasserstrom referred to, but Eggebrecht doubts it, although he fails to give reasons. Children, or witnesses who were children at the time, had the greatest impact on the veteran reporter and he comments that their relatively unbroken spirit today gives hope to all.[113]

In a somewhat long-winded conclusion Eggebrecht's doubts and disappointments remain, despite his efforts to talk up the merits of the Auschwitz Trial. In terms of justice the verdict appears as just as was possible under the circumstances. As for the matter of establishing historical fact and its political consequence, the 'historical-political search for the truth',[114] as he terms it, there remain serious doubts:

> Were we to apply the strict confines of ethics, then this trial should cause us to have serious concerns, but even during its course there was precious little of that, and even as little as there was has disappeared now. The Tübingen lawyer Jürgen Baumann once said (spoken by narrator): 'Too often one hears about the grass, which should grow over these things. No grass will grow over the Nazi mass graves and crematoria. The wound inflicted on the Germans and the world by these criminals is too deep. Should we forget, the world will remind us.' And the world did not forget Auschwitz, they observed the Auschwitz Trial much closer than we did. Although there have

been some notable exceptions in the broadsheets and also we in the radio stations are worth a mention. But: the usual vigorous public debate, which surrounds every murder trial, hardly occurred. Why? Let us not kid ourselves, many people were not just indifferent towards the Auschwitz Trial, but it was a nuisance; not just the facts, which came to light month after month, but the fact that the trial happened at all. It is not surprising when former fellow travellers say, 'let sleeping dogs lie', but what is much more disconcerting is the lax indifference of the uninvolved...[115]

And this, despite further elaborations on what lessons could be drawn from the trial, appears to be Eggebrecht's conclusion. He even mentions that he does not wish to end the report on a negative note,[116] thus ending with a quote from Hannah Arendt, but his overwhelming disappointment at the pubic response to the trial is the overall impression left with the listener.

Eggebrecht's contribution to the process of 'working through the past' has been enormous. His tireless efforts did not abate after the Auschwitz Trial; if anything he became more active politically, campaigning against a statute of limitations for Nazi crimes in 1969 and again in 1979.[117] His commitment to justice and his fiercely critical comments on political life in the Federal Republic were given a platform in his 1979 publication 'The Angry Old Men' (*Die zornigen alten Männer*),[118] a collection of essays by Eggebrecht, Jean Améry, Ossip Flechtheim, Eugen Kogon and others. In its introduction he is still baffled by the political lethargy and seemingly unrepentant wartime generation in West Germany, even expressing an understanding for the radicalisation of the student movement in the form of the RAF (Red Army Faction or Baader-Meinhof), although he clearly distances himself from their methods.[119] His enthusiasm for the student movement was matched by his thirst for new theory: 'Repressive tolerance and consumer-terror were indeed elements of this new un-freedom, which we all felt.'[120] He remained pessimistic about the new Germany, stating that in comparison to other European nations, 'here, the Enlightenment only happened in homeopathic doses.'[121] Axel Eggebrecht died in 1991.

The end of the Auschwitz Trial did not merit much airtime. The archives of the *Hessischer Rundfunk* contain a mere 2 minutes and 26 seconds from when the verdict was announced.[122] Subsequent reports of the court's reasoning for the verdicts (six life sentences, ten other jail sentences, three acquittals) were given some time by the *Südwestfunk* in Baden-Baden the day after the verdicts, and in some detail (53 minutes) by Werner Ernenputsch, broadcast, however, on the more specialised second programme of the SWF, at the unpopular time of 15:00.[123]

The aftermath

The widespread popularising of the Auschwitz Trial came, not through reporting on radio and television, but from the performances of Peter Weiss' play 'The Inquiry' (*Die Ermittlung*)[124] in October 1965, on stage, radio and television. This 'Oratorio in 11 Cantos' is based on the Auschwitz Trial, using witness and perpetrator statements, set in the Frankfurt courtroom. This unprecedented theatrical and media event – the play opened in 16 theatres throughout East and West Germany (and was performed by the RSC in London), as well as being broadcast on radio and television – caused a huge amount of controversy, dividing the Germanys not only ideologically but also by generation.[125] Facts and details about the Trial, and, more importantly, about Auschwitz were revealed to a new generation of Germans.

This event provoked a response everywhere, and Weiss' play was widely discussed on all radio stations, East and West. In an unprecedented move the East German *Deutschlandsender* devoted an hour-long programme to listeners' letters, which included a letter from the schoolmaster of St Joseph's College in Dumfries.[126] The Cologne-based WDR carried a programme by former inmate and political journalist Eugen Kogon, in which he recommends the play as set reading for A-level students, as well as to study the judicial reasoning of the sentences in the Auschwitz Trial.[127] But perhaps the most accurate, critical and least partisan comment on Peter Weiss' play comes (unsurprisingly) in a broadcast of 31 October 1965 from Axel Eggebrecht, veteran of the Auschwitz Trial. He notes that Weiss's recent public 'conversion' to Marxism does not bother him at all. If anything, he claims, the lack of political analysis in the play is one of its major faults. He comments:

> It is very likely, ladies and gentlemen, that you have heard or read the name Peter Weiss recently. The play 'The Inquiry' has had its premiere at several West German theatres simultaneously, and at least twenty others in both parts of Germany will follow. A radio version was broadcast last Wednesday; by November all radio stations will have broadcast it, and soon we will be able to view these versed, composed scenes of the Frankfurt Auschwitz Trial on television. The author calls it an 'oratorio', which he has divided into eleven 'cantos'; these bear subtitles such as 'the Canto of the Ramp', 'the Canto

of the Possibility of Survival', 'the Canto of Phenol', and 'the Canto of the Burning Ovens'. Weiss himself explains in the preface that he didn't want to re-create the courtroom on stage, as this would have been just as impossible as re-creating the (concentration) camp. What remains, and I quote, could only be a 'concentrated statement'. And: 'the personal experiences and confrontations will have to succumb to anonymity, so that the witnesses lose their names and are turned into mere mouthpieces (*Spachrohre*)'. However, Weiss deals differently with the accused: 'They carry their names, taken from the Trial' he says. 'This is significant, as during the time in question they had their names, whereas the prisoners had lost theirs.' With these words Peter Weiss points us to the problematic of his undertaking... When he explains in a Swedish newspaper that he had intended to denounce a capitalism that deals with gas chambers, then this is plainly not true. To him, the background appears very secondary. As he does not name witnesses, we do not find out the names of the I.G. Farben directors Ambroß and Bütefisch, who appeared as witnesses just as some of the NS-leaders, who hold prominent positions today. But for Weiss they are all anonymous puppets. Set against this, the detailed statements about torture and death do not stand up. This monotony does not heighten the effect, it lessens it. First reviews from the play's opening talk of a visible tiring of the audience.[128]

This very well-observed commentary on Weiss' play holds an interesting parallel to the abovementioned note found in the reel casing of *Ehrenmänner* and Weiss' comment concerning the names of the witnesses. Whereas Weiss claims that through concentrating statements of the witnesses their experiences will succumb to anonymity, the makers of *Ehrenmänner* claim that in their invented witnesses' statements, 'events are concentrated – therefore the witnesses [here] are representative of all witnesses'. This artistic liberty sits well neither with audiences nor with any serious engagement with the topic. A precise, unambiguous and clear approach is needed and expected from the audiences, be it in the theatre or on the radio. This slowly started to happen on West German radio in the period after the Auschwitz Trial.

A programme aired by the *Hessischer Rundfunk* in Frankfurt from a somewhat later date – 22 November 1967 – is worth mentioning here. Former Auschwitz inmate and trial witness Hermann Langbein wrote and chaired this discussion programme entitled 'Discussion on the Meaning and Justification of the NS Trials with Victims, Lawyers and Young People'. The format is relatively simple: a narrator links the (tightly edited) segments of discussions through the various issues arising from the Nazi trials. But to set the scene the programme opens with quotes from two (unidentified) female students:

> Many young people today join in with the adults to say: 'Lay off going on about the past, it was not our fault, we don't want to hear about it, we have already heard too much about it.

And:

> I would say that the reason why there is no interest in the Auschwitz Trials today is because one doesn't want to confront the past, as it concerns the past of all, and not just a part of the German people.[129]

There then follows a list of current (1967) NS trials: three in Frankfurt, others in Hagen, Bochum, Wuppertal, Hamburg, Cologne, one in Mainz where the main accused greeted the judge with a Hitler salute, commenting that he understood that this trial was necessary to stop the defamation of Germany, and the Babi Yar trial of Sonderkommando 4A in Darmstadt. This 'gruesome monotony' of listing mass murder trials leads to Langbein's first conversations with the lawyers, Professor Herbert Jäger[130] and the Frankfurt county judge Dr Heinz Düx, who are prompted by one of the students' questions: Why did it take so long to prosecute? Dr Düx sees no reasons for this other than a general reluctance to do so, after all, some of the 'Euthanasia' trials happened as early as 1947 in German courts and there was no reason then to stop the prosecutions.[131] Could it be, Langbein asks, that 'having to obey orders' (*Befehlsnotstand*) in a totalitarian society could be used, or even considered as an excuse, at least for the members of the SS? Düx and Jäger agree on this matter: it was not the case that one had to obey orders in situations of mass killings. In all his pre-trial investigations Judge Düx never came across one incident where the defendant had not acted out of his own volition. Prof. Jäger gives an overall figure of 10–15 per cent of all cases where the refusal to obey an order to kill would have had serious consequences.

In the opinion of Dieter Lau, Auschwitz Trial correspondent for the *Süddeutsche Zeitung*, this makes the completely unrepentant attitude of most defendants even more repulsive. Dr H.G. Adler, former inmate, agrees and points to treatment witnesses experienced in the courtrooms – such as being insulted by defence lawyers and harassed by judges. The judges' position is debated further. Due to a law passed in

1955, renewed prosecution of the higher echelons of the NSDAP, once tried in Nuremberg and elsewhere, was not possible. Therefore trials like the Auschwitz Trial in Frankfurt and the Sonderkommando one in Darmstadt concentrated on the ranks, the 'actual' killers rather than the commanding officers. The press' (and the courts') preoccupation with such persons – the likes of Boger, Klehr and Kaduk – limited the investigations and the trials to dealing with the symptoms rather than the causes. Furthermore, the judges' position was at times not very clear, as often accused officers were able to appeal to the 'bad conscience' of some judges, many former NSDAP members. Hermann Langbein puts this to Judge Düx:

> Langbein: What survivors criticise, especially after the first Auschwitz Trial, and the second, and the third, is that only the 'little people' are in the dock. Lower SS ranks, as well as prisoner-functionaries, who are undoubtedly guilty, but when you know that there were dozens of SS leaders active in Auschwitz, proven to have been active there, and their addresses are known, and that there are witnesses and materials against them, and they are not prosecuted, then this causes disquiet.
> Düx: I have been wondering about this myself, but I have to rely on what the state prosecutor presents to me. And when a 'lesser' culprit is presented, for instance a lorry driver who drove prisoners from the ramp to the gas chambers, then, as a preliminary hearing judge I have to take action against him, as he without doubt was an accessory to the overall murders in Auschwitz. But one has to start from the assumption that all of Auschwitz was a criminal institution.
> Narrator: The journalist [Dieter] Lau sums up his impressions.
> Lau: In my understanding what can be noticed is a certain tiredness of the judiciary, of the prosecutor's office, of the prosecutors, who were employed specifically to investigate and clear up NS crimes, already exhausted by the routine.
> Narrator: It is understandable that former concentration camp inmates follow the reactions to the NS trials with interest.
> Langbein: What is your opinion of what can be heard often in Germany today, that of 'put an end to these trials, how long do you want to go on with these trials?'
> H.G. Adler: Well, I think that is catastrophically wrong. These trials absolutely have to take place, if Germany is to recover. It's an ignominy (*Schmach*) to have any emotional or factual objections

against them, because the German people will never recover if there is no clarity about this abyss, and especially the German administration, the German judicial system will not be trusted abroad for a long time to come. It's not about revenge; it's not even about punishment as these terms have become meaningless with these unimaginable crimes. But it is, as far as humanly possible, about clearing things up and pronouncing guilt. For us old Auschwitzers and old camp people punishment is something that has little interest.[132]

That the sentences seem relatively unimportant to the former inmates is surprising to the younger participants in the discussion. The relationship of the crime committed to the sentences passed seemed so out of proportion to the students that it was felt that this leniency with mass murderers lessened the level of interest in the trials. Others thought that educators were trying to pamper young people by not letting them hear the full horror of Auschwitz. Is this a failure of the pedagogues?

> Narrator: The experiences of a Frankfurt sixth former do not sound encouraging.
> Female student: I would really say that the majority of people my age are indifferent to it. But when we were 14–15 [years old], during the first Auschwitz Trial, there were a few progressive teachers who took their classes to the proceedings, which showed people who could talk about these things in a cool, unemotional manner. But after that there was nothing.
> Narrator: Professor Jäger has more encouraging reports from the University of Giessen.
> Professor Jäger: I found a lot of interest among the students, although to varying degrees, some more, the majority less, but there is an engagement, more with the literature than with the on-going trials.
> Langbein: Perhaps because there are hardly any reports about the on-going trials anymore?
> Professor Jäger: Yes, this is really noticeable that since the end of the Auschwitz Trial the reportage has diminished drastically.
> Langbein: Do you see this as a drawback, in your professional view?
> Professor Jäger: Yes, I do see it as a drawback, but one has to admit that for those who do not particularly deal with this material, these reports can have a bit of a deadening (*abstumpfenden*) effect.
> Narrator: Dieter Lau is an expert.

Langbein: I read your reports with great interest and I could tell that they were written not only with the routine of a journalist but with the heart of a young person who wanted to learn, still wanting to learn. This is why I ask you: How do you see yourself continuing effectively in this direction?

Lau: Only through precise information about the events which happened in Auschwitz and other death camps. Though I doubt how possible this is, as even during and especially after the Auschwitz Trial there emerged a certain tiredness in the press in reporting these events to their readers.

Narrator: School is of course not the only source of information for young people.

Student 1: There is not enough information on offer, and in the end it comes down to the personal conflict between father and son or daughter. To the old question, how did you act back then? And it is easy for the parents today to say, 'well yes we were party members, but we didn't have anything to do with that. That was a thing some people did, who overstepped the boundaries, not the fault of the system. And those people, they are being prosecuted today.' And in this way I see a dangerous function in these trials, in the way they are being conducted at the moment. They ease the bad conscience of the others. By shifting the blame from the system to a few select ones who were close to the objects of death (*Tötungsobjekte*). And when one asks the fathers, they can point to this very well.' Well, Globke, for instance, wasn't he heavily involved, wasn't he rehabilitated in his post at the chancellor's office? And there are many of them.' And so every father can talk himself out of it.

Narrator: Is it possible to imagine how difficult it is for young people to learn about the recent past in which their parents have failed?

Student 1: You just give up, you resign, because the fathers evade the responsibility.

Langbein: And would you describe this as the norm?

Student 1: Yes. And because you see that the fathers, despite their incriminating past, are doing very well and are thus rehabilitated.

Narrator: The problems arising from the NS-trials are taken seriously by many students.

Student 2: Well, it's a question of this crazy ideology which is being preached today. Agree, agree, agree, that's our communal ideology and that is lovely. And life is lovely. Only life is not lovely.

> Today you have Vietnam, today you have the Emergency Laws (*Notstandsgesetze*), you have the black ghettoes in the US and there also exists the past, which has not yet been come to terms with. This needs to be worked on.
> Narrator: It would be surprising if this bitter knowledge did not lead to action. Student Hartmut Holzapfel adds:
> Holzapfel: This is very clearly a result which can be viewed as a direct analogy: the influence of the *Springer* (Press) organisation is reminiscent of the role Hugenberg played in the Weimar Republic.[133]

This 'certain tiredness', a recurring theme in the reportage of NS trials, is noteworthy, as it seems to evoke similar responses with many – resignation and anger. For this reason some fears of a resurgent German nationalism are expressed: through resignation on one hand and anger on the other an actual 'coming-to-terms-with' the past is avoided. Dieter Lau comments that the 'silent majority', harbouring feelings of 'wanting to be someone', talk behind cupped hands about an imaginary past. But, and there seems to be agreement from all, this would not stretch as far as voting for neo-Nazi parties, such as the NPD. Langbein agrees with this verdict. He sees the postwar (West) German democracy as a success and is heartened by an upsurge of democratic feeling (*ein Anleben des demokratischen Gefühls*). But the last words of this remarkable programme belong to Hermann Langbein and Dr Hans-Günther Adler, the Auschwitz survivors, about hope and the young Germans of today:

> Narrator: Finally Langbein asks his friend Dr Adler about his impressions.
> Langbein: What is your impression when you come to Germany these days, especially of young people, meaning those who belong to the generation who had not consciously experienced National Socialism, what are your impressions there?
> H.G. Adler: The impression with the youngest generation is not so favourable. I find they appear all very tired. Maybe they see different problems today and think they should be left in peace about [all] this. Of course I find this extremely unhealthy.
> Langbein: And why do you think it unhealthy?
> H.G. Adler: Because it buries the truth. And any burying of the truth, any displacing of truth is always – in my study of history, in my study of sociology – a mistake.
> Langbein: So how, do you think, can you tell the young people in Germany about the truth so that they will take it to heart?

H.G. Adler: I'm afraid that's beyond my expertise! (laughs)...The only thing I believe in is a calm reporting of the facts, no elaborating, no evoking of false sympathy, maybe no evoking of sympathy at all, but to look inhumanity in the eye and because the inhumane is not really a part of us, to be able to avoid it.

Langbein: Will you agree with me, I have always had the experience, when giving lectures, when talking to young people, that I instinctively hold back from telling the extremes of the cruelties.

H.G. Adler: This I think is absolutely correct. Because the extreme cruelties are, luckily, incomprehensible to the normal person. Comprehension can only exist where fantasy can follow. That is why, and whether the details were right or wrong is another matter, there was the unbelievable moral success of the Anne Frank story, because it could be imagined. It is not imaginable when I say 100,000 or four million people died in Auschwitz. It is unimaginable.

Langbein: So much from the quotes of my friends, of German lawyers and of representatives from the younger generation. The NS trials are continuing in German courts and will continue to do so for a long time to come. The crimes were just too many. The problems arising from these trials, the recent past that presents itself undisguised and not made up, will be there tomorrow, too. Should the young people be left alone with these problems? The young people who have to deal with such a troublesome inheritance? An inheritance passed on from our generation?[134]

Programmes like those discussed above became regular features on West German radio. Documentaries, discussions and features now engaged fully with the topic, aware of potentially younger audiences and also the changing attitudes of some of the older listeners. The NDR remained the broadcaster with the most dedicated editorial commitment, but others began to follow suit. One final programme is worth a short mention here, the NDR's February 1968 programme 'A Nation plays Blind Man's Buff or: the Search for Nazi Criminals',[135] in which a more positive sounding, but nevertheless wary Simon Wiesenthal states that the only winners in the Cold War are the Nazi war criminals that had avoided prosecution – a comment which would have been unthinkable in the early 1960s.

In the 'other universe' of GDR radio, the topic of the National Socialist era almost completely disappeared from the airwaves after the Auschwitz Trial. The archival listing from the German Radio Archive (DRA) contains only three short programmes from East Berlin for the period 1966–73, a sign, perhaps, that the attempt to use the Nazi past for ideological purposes had run its course. When the topic did surface, it was within the expected confines of Marxist-Leninist ideology, as seen, for example, one programme from April 1973, billed as 'Living History' (*Lebendige Geschichte*) with the title 'The German Grand-Bourgeoisie and the Beginnings of the Fascist Persecution of the Jews' by the historian Kurt Pätzold. Pätzold attempts, with the aid of documents, to prove a link between German capital and the Hitler regime, which is – in his opinion – interchangeable with the business dealings West German industry has with Israel:

> For a long time now there has existed a close political, economic and military alignment between the monopoly-capitalists of the Federal Republic and Israel. Their common ground is their anti-communism, specifically their anti-Sovietism, their hostility towards the anti-imperialist national liberation movements in Asia and Africa, and finally the profit arising from the permanent armed conflict in Israel and the Middle East. The reactionary core of this agreement is veiled by a slanderous campaign, which attempts to convey that the upper echelons of German Industry are concerned for the Jews of Israel, and their protection. The history of capitalism knows of such examples, which attach ideological and humanistic argumentation to highly odious businesses, to give it a 'higher' meaning. This is precisely what we have here: It is good for business today to be a philo-Semite and friend of the Zionists. If it was more convenient to be an anti-Semite back then, there was no hesitation. To prove this, we will study some documents, which will bear witness to the German grand-bourgeois attitude toward the fascist anti-Semitism and the emerging persecution of the Jews in the year 1933.[136]

Prof. Pätzold is still a prominent historian in Germany today, although it is doubtful whether he will want to be reminded of this radio escapade of his early career.

The programmes presented here represent a good cross-section of the archival material available. Overall, it can be said that a significant change occurred in the handling of the topic of the Nazi past during the 1960s, and that often the initiative came from radio journalists and through the output of radio stations, daring to confront the public with a wider dissemination of this topic. But what of the listeners? How did audiences deal with such a confrontation with their 'un-mastered past? This will be considered in the following chapter.

5
Radio and Memory

Memory makers and memory users

What listeners remember from radio broadcasts, and, more to the point, how this can be investigated, has been a problematic issue, not only for this study, but for radio research in general. The relationship between radio and memory is an unclear and contradictory one, remembering content not necessarily the primary focus and sourcing it to the radio often uncertain. Not only is it uncertain what listeners remember, but also finding concrete evidence of the programmes listened to, and, furthermore, remembered, appears to a near-impossible task, and has been attempted on only a few occasions. Nevertheless, programmes are listened to, and remembered, and do form, in one way or another, a kind of collective memory and with it, historical consciousness.

On the whole, listener figures, which are calculated in various ways, do not concentrate on specific programmes. They might be collected by individual radio stations, and will have sub-classifications such as genres of *music, entertainment, news and current affairs* and *sport*, or enquire about when and for how long the radio had been listened to, but individual programmes (with very few exceptions) are not part of listener surveys.

Additionally, the few attempts that have been made, such as the Lutz/Wodak study on the comprehension of news programmes,[1] have shown that listeners do not recall details correctly (if they remember them at all) and comprehend relatively little, despite considering themselves to be well informed. What complicates the issue still further is the fact that news items or programmes dealing with an issue, which carry little or no interest for the majority of the population, or are actively unwelcome, would be unlikely to be remembered. So how can the reception of these radio programmes be assessed?

Most studies on 'media effect' contradict the popular belief in the overwhelming power of modern mass media. The earliest attempts at measuring the influence of mass media, in this case radio, were conducted in the USA by Paul Lazarsfeld at Colombia University in the 1940s.[2] These early studies – and subsequent ones – cast doubt on the claim that radio can set opinions, or even influence them. In so far as any 'effect' is measurable, it lies rather in the realm of the social environment in which the medium is 'consumed', the family, workplace, educational background and personal communications.[3] The medium gains its relevance from non-mediated, direct social interaction, the content playing a secondary, but closely related role to the actual media consumption, the medium itself being 'more than the sum of its contents'.[4] This in turn can be seen as influencing, or forming the debate and opinion around the content, which reflect back into the social environment. The 'effect' of these radio programmes therefore must be seen within the wider debate of the German postwar 'coming-to-terms-with the past' (*Vergangenheitsbewältigung*), but nevertheless it can be assumed that, judging by the vehemence employed by broadcasters East and West in these programmes, the debate they created was part of the daily social interaction in the Germanies of the 1960s.

Because of the topic the relationship of media content to social environment should be of particular interest here, rather than the medium itself. Certainly the topic was never far from public debate, but one cannot speak of an identifiable public sphere which reflected the listeners. Did the broadcasts in any way reflect an already existing public opinion? Were these programmes moulding the public debate or were they tools in a wider ideological campaign? The programme makers certainly appear, by today's standard, a little heavy-handed. Wolfgang Mühl-Benninghaus points out that not only the SED leadership assumed an individually weak media consumer and the inferiority of the masses, using models of mass psychology of late nineteenth-century models like LeBon and others,[5] but also both Eastern and Western broadcasters did not trust their listeners to form their own judgements and viewed the listening public as easily malleable masses.[6]

This leads to an interesting and paradoxical scenario: radio programme producers, or their editors, set an agenda which is more or less ignored by their listeners in terms of content and the medium itself, radio, becomes the driving force; form becomes content, or, in the words of Marshall McLuhan, 'the medium is the message'.

But this broad sweep of a generalised assumption does not really stand up to detailed examination. Over a period of time, it becomes evident that programmes were listened to, reflecting and influencing public opinion through journalists as part of the public or able to capture popular opinion, expressing the thoughts of a 'collective memory' of the Nazi past.

In order to arrive at any meaningful interpretation of the possible listeners' reaction to the programmes outlined in previous chapters, some further clarifications and differentiations will have to be introduced. What has to be stressed here is that, apart from trying to assess whether these programmes were remembered, or formed a part of a 'collective memory' in the Halbwachsian sense, the programmes themselves dealt with something that had to be remembered, namely the time of the Third Reich and more precisely, the Holocaust.

Here the problematic nature of this undertaking becomes evident: In the postwar Germanies of the late 1950s and early 1960s remembering was more like forgetting. The initial trials at Nuremberg of the late 1940s had, for many, dealt with the past and the re-emergence of this topic in the shape of the Frankfurt Auschwitz Trial was very unwelcome indeed.

In recent years there has been an explosion of theoretical texts dealing with issues such as *Collective Memory,* or *Memory Discourse* Writers such as Pierre Nora and Kerwin Lee Klein have argued that the re-emergence of interest in Halbwachs' sociological study on 'Collective Memory', written in the 1930s,[7] is due to a crisis in traditional, modernist historiography.[8] Positioning memory and history as opposing terms, Nora comments that 'we speak so much of memory because there is so little of it left'.[9] This is explained by the distinction between the real environments of memory, *milieux de mémoire,* which in his opinion have disappeared with modernity, and the 'sites of memory', *lieux de mémoire,* of the present. Whereas Nora's study deals with topics such as the disappearance of peasant culture, 'that quintessential repository of collective memory', blaming the global movement towards democratisation and mass culture for this 'fundamental collapse of memory'[10] is questionable when considering this distinction. Could it not be possible that what we remember has changed, in accordance with global mass culture and democratisation, and that the collective nature of this memory is shaped by the users and makers of this memory? The 'acceleration of historical time' discussed by Koselleck (and also – for that matter – by Nora) certainly means that more (memory) can be discarded, but also that more is remembered.

This becomes evident in the recent wealth of 'memory' material concerning the Holocaust. Testimonies, diaries, film and sound recordings, memoirs, days of remembrance, monuments and museums all form part of an increasing volume of a collective memory in which one event in history, the Holocaust, is remembered. This, to affirm Nora, might be the result of an increasing urban (and literate) culture, and it could also be seen as a confirmation of Koselleck's assertion (cited earlier) that the condition of modernity is the ignorance or uncertainty of the future and therefore remembrance has to be practiced more actively and consciously, but above all Holocaust remembrance is practiced out of moral reasoning.

While a moral prerogative might cause problems with traditional historiography – as has been noted – the wealth of material presented through modern mass media throws up new and different problems. The 'real' environment of collective memory is formed though accessing 'sites' of memory which require not only a critical literacy but also a willingness to engage. Linda Reisch asserts that 'the further distant (in time) we are from Auschwitz, the closer we come to remembering this criminal event',[11] and certainly the culture of Holocaust remembrance is very pronounced in Germany today, which experienced a shift in collective memory from an initial relative lack of individual sense of guilt to the later generation's stronger and more defined, even 'conspicuous' public chest-beating.[12]

To separate memory from its apparent antithetical pole of history and historiography is further complicated by the fact that despite the unreliable nature of 'subjective' memory, history has to resound, or to correspond, or at least to relate, to memory. Popular misconceptions of historical facts might be plenty, but Halbwachs' assertion that 'history begins where memory ends' would cast doubt on any historiographical work of contemporary history, above all the Holocaust.[13]

The apparent unreliability of witness or survivor testimony is often startling, but hardly surprising as Dan Diner comments:

> Given Auschwitz's *un*narratability, the vacuum fills with surrogate tales possessing an epic structure. This epic form evokes a reversal to what seem familiar, historical images and recollections, those pointing to an antecedent remembrance. Thus the history of the Warsaw ghetto uprising, although peripheral in its importance when measured against the atrociousness and scope of the administrative and industrial mass murder, takes on the meaning of a narrative that substitutes for what cannot be properly recounted. In view of the

statistical vacuum that Auschwitz creates for posterity, the uprising provides a compensatory tale.[14]

Another often-quoted example dealing with Holocaust witness testimony and historical truth is the remarks made at a conference of a female (Auschwitz) survivor, recounting the uprising in crematorium IV in October 1944, where, according to this witness, 'four chimneys exploded, going up in flames'.[15] This testimony was doubted by historians at the conference, pointing to the fact that in the 1944 uprising only one chimney was destroyed by explosives. But Laub stresses that what the witness described was not the number of the destroyed chimneys, but the fact that the testimony described the exploding of the oppressive frame of the reality of Auschwitz. And this constituted the historical truth of the witness' testimony.[16] There, of course, lies the difference between psychoanalysis and history; the analyst will attempt to listen with empathy, whereas the historian will confront fact with other facts.[17]

Dominick LaCapra, who also comments on this case, extends this debate further when he uses terminology such as 'perpetrator trauma',[18] but the problem of trying to ascertain how a 'collective' and in this case 'perpetrator' or 'bystander' memory might be constructed, is not addressed. So is it possible at all to find this 'site of memory', or 'counter-history that challenges the false generalisations of exclusionary History' (Werner Sollors),[19] and if so how would it be recognisable? Would, as Klein claims, 'in such constructions, memory's notorious vagaries become its strengths', as 'therapeutic potential'?[20]

Klein's quote from the historian Amos Funkenstein provides a useful hint: 'Collective awareness presumes collective memory',[21] but the fact is that it is still individuals who remember and that an accumulation of individual memories do not equate with the term 'collective memory'. Rather, Funkenstein argues, the relationship between collective and individual memory appears more like the difference between (the Saussurean) *langue* and *parole*:

> Collective memory..., like 'language', can be characterised as a system of signs, symbols and practices: memorial dates, names of places, monuments and victory arches, museums and texts, stereotype images (incorporated, for instance, in manners of expression) and even language itself (in Saussurean terms).The individual memory – that is, the act of remembering – is the instantiation of these symbols, analogous to 'speech'; no act of remembering is like any other.[22]

This, of course, is where the problem lies: when the symbol is the (banned) swastika, the memorial date the lost war and the placename Auschwitz. Wulf Kansteiner notes that, when it comes to the Holocaust, 'there is no simple access to the truth'.[23] The collective memory is represented by reminders of the most unspeakable horrors, of perhaps personal involvement or just indifference which can only, and perhaps most adequately, be addressed through the mediated form of the radio broadcast,[24] to invoke a personal act of remembering, individual memory.

On the other hand, this personal act is also a public one, in as much as it is mediated through the radio: a public service, with public processes which are not individually crafted to suit individuals, but made collectively and aimed at an anonymous, imagined public. The imagined collective has a presumed collective memory, and the ambiguity felt by most Germans towards the Nazi past made the production of programmes about it a difficult and rather unclear task. How should the listener be approached? Even in the ideologically crass terms of the GDR broadcasters this topic could only rely on the smallest common denominator: anti-fascism.

And here the relationship between memory and (individual or collective) identity becomes apparent. Whatever the listener's personal ability to remember certain events of a shared past, they will be intricately interwoven with the programme's content, which is attempting to shape this memory. Therefore the relationship between any collective or individual memory and radio listeners is ambiguous: on the one hand it might recall a memory which will contradict the broadcasters' intentions, or it will produce – and this is the most likely outcome – a conforming adaptation or even acceptance of the programme listened to, be it though on subjective, personal terms. This, of course, makes it almost impossible to measure 'effect', as Kansteiner notes:

> In addition, reception-conscious students of collective memories encounter another serious problem in their quest for reliable data. The media of representation tend to disappear from the consciousness of the audience in the process of consumption. Radio listeners, for instance, regularly forget the source of their memories of historical events; they can recall the stories but have no conscious recollection of listening to them on the radio and often attach them to other sources, including television, textbooks, and relatives. As a result, consumers might wholeheartedly subscribe to certain historical interpretations,

but they would not be able to identify their origins even if one undertakes the cumbersome task of asking them directly.[25]

Interestingly enough, the affirmative and habitual (and perhaps regional) nature of broadcasts seems to have been more important to the listeners than any 'searching' for a missing truth: A 1952 study by the *Allensbacher Institut für Demoskopie* noted that about half of the West German population could receive the Eastern radio stations (and frequently did so) but did not like the content.[26] Conversely, over 80 per cent of East-Berliners continued to listen habitually to the (East German) *Berliner Rundfunk* and *DDR I* in preference to other stations well into the mid-1980s.[27]

For the state broadcasters in the Federal Republic an active involvement of the radio audience in a 'coming-to-terms-with-the-past' could initially be carried out, tucked away on the second or third programme, only by small groups of engaged, committed journalists and intellectuals, and even then they often enraged the public. As the FRG grew in international stature, the economic miracle and reconstruction were not enough to restore a balanced national identity. Despite the tension of the Cold War and the seeming unwillingness of the Allies and the West German government to pursue Nazi perpetrators, the past remained 'un-mastered'. But regardless of where the impetus came from to engage with the topic, caution and care were always needed. The careful approach of the spoken word programme, a 'talking cure', could, with the mediation of the radio, become a 'listening cure', a role reversal of the standard psychoanalytical process.

Many psychoanalytical key terms are involved in the literature around memory and the Holocaust: *trauma, transference, melancholia, mourning* and *working through*. While this is not surprising for the surviving Holocaust victims, this terminology was also used in the Mitscherlichs' *Inability to Mourn*,[28] first published in 1967, trying to deal with the West German population's attitude to the recent past. Another such study is the 1955 *Gruppenexperiment*, Friedrich Pollock's qualitative interviews with a large cross-section of the West German population, which first gave rise to the term 'non-public opinion'.[29] This term – which to some extent could be equated with Foucault's 'counter-memory' – best describes the ambiguous relationship many Germans had with their past and suggests that the 'quietism' of the Adenauer years offered, at least publicly, the path of least resistance.

Whether the memory is 'repressed' or 'dormant', radio offered a way of working through the past which other media could not: the private, almost accidental catalyst which changed the mind. The accessing of 'collective' memory through the process of listening to the radio – a process in which the collective memory is not only continuously negotiated between available historical records and current social and political agendas,[30] but consciously manipulated, and still manages to give the listener the feeling of 'empowerment' (through various levels of attentiveness and being able to switch the radio set off) – establishes a unique relationship between the programmes' producers and listeners. The broadcaster has the authority of the transmission, yet is ignorant about the number of recipients and reception of content, whereas the listener can only receive but by making reception a matter of choice, feels authoritative. Any interaction between broadcaster and listener has a time lapse, in which the broadcaster's authority can be restored while the listener's memory fades.

Broadcasters, while aware of the use of the radio for propaganda purposes from the wartime experiences, did not see themselves primarily as in this role of the analyst, in charge of 'the talking cure'. But the influence, or 'effect' of radio programmes dealing with the Nazi past in Germany during the 1960s is perhaps best looked at in this psychoanalytical model, with the broadcasters being (what Kansteiner calls) 'the memory makers'[31] and the listeners, 'the memory users', in an analyst–patient relationship, accessing the 'sites of memory' for the retrieval and re-evaluation of traumatic past experiences.

So the model proposed here to analyse the reception of radio broadcasts on the topic of the NS past in East and West Germany is, in the absence of precise polling data of radio audiences on specific programmes, structured in the following manner:

- The radio stations are portrayed here in their role as *memory makers* (East and West), their programme policies and realms of influence, translated into programmes and programme structure.
- The listeners are the *memory users*, their responses are measured in (general) audience research figures, and attitudes on the topic of the Third Reich and the Holocaust through a number of opinion polls.

While this method might appear inadequate for obtaining precise conclusions about the reception of specific programmes, it does, in the absence of such information, present a *possible* (if somewhat diverse and fractured) picture of the producers' intentions and how the programmes in question might have been received and of the debates they might have created.

Memory makers (East)

One of the features of radio broadcasting in the Third Reich was that for every hour of news, talks and features there were approximately seven hours of music and light entertainment.[32] This was, at the time, seen as a feature of propaganda, and different from the public service broadcast ethos of the European Allies, and was a departure from the cultural-didactic approach of the Weimar broadcasters.[33] That this talk/music ratio should become commonplace again by the late twentieth century could not have been imagined when the broadcasters in Germany were considering their function in the postwar society.

But the relationship between broadcaster and listener differed distinctly between the FRG and the GDR. Because of its pluralist set-up, the Western radio stations felt bound to the listener through the various control mechanisms and constitutional arrangements. In the monolithic media system of the GDR the broadcasters, well aware that up to 80 per cent of their listeners were able to listen to 'enemy' broadcasts, could not assume uncritical consumption of their output.[34] The 'totalitarianism' of the GDR State Radio Committee (*Staatliches Rundfunkkomittee* or StRK) had to consider this, just as they had to take into account the steep learning curve that radio audiences world wide had undergone through their wartime experiences, which had started to shift the radio from being the 'voice of authority' to the secondary and seemingly powerless 'background entertainment'.

When it came to the recent past and the National Socialist dictatorship, however, the GDR state media believed that it had the upper hand: 'anti-fascism', as one of the founding principles of the GDR, as a recurring theme in broadcasts dealing with this matter, not only glorified the KPD-led resistance during the Hitler dictatorship – and thereby legitimised the SED regime – but also managed, with little effort, to portray the Federal Republic as the continuation of the Third Reich, and therefore as the enemy.[35]

The Marxist-Leninist distinction between 'objectivity' (*Objektivität*) and 'objectivism' (*Objektivismus*) was deployed, which made an adherence to the party line easy, whatever the circumstances.[36] Gerhart Eisler, the chairman of the *Staatliches Rundfunkkomittee*, extrapolated on this even further in a speech at a conference on news-broadcasting to the committee on 22 January 1961:

> Briefly: Even when the facts are uncomfortable, we do not deny them. This is also another way in which we distinguish ourselves from

bourgeois journalism, with their falsified and denied reproduction of facts, their half- and quarter truths. Only by our being objective and establishing facts, and at the same time commenting on their societal significance and direction, are we revolutionary journalists the vanguard of the truth; we strengthen the trust of our readers and listeners of what we say, and we strengthen the authority of the radio, newspapers and television. The basic condition of our news broadcasting policy is that the news presents a real picture of the social conditions and of the concrete political movements. And these should be as multi-faceted and colourful as the facts which make up this picture of reality.[37]

Examples of such interpretative 'objectivity' extended to the incorporation of commemorative dates and anniversaries, such as the 7th anniversary of the capitulation of Field Marshall Paulus' 6th Army at Stalingrad. Stalingrad became the communists' victory over 'the 100-headed Hydra of fascism and her imperialist master', it symbolised a new epoch of history, which was the 'foundation of a new German path which had found its expression in the founding of the German Democratic Republic.'[38] This, according to a broadcast from February 1950, was the 'wonderful encouragement' of Stalingrad, which, at that point in time, 'dawned on the totally demoralised German soldiers on their way to being POWs in the Soviet Union and on a way to a new life', and that this released a 'winning and encouraging new energy' which would bring forth 'a true national front' to liberate West Germany.[39] The Stalingrad commemoration served as a central tenet in the founding myth of the GDR and as proof of the 'military, political and moral superiority of the Soviet peoples.'[40]

And, as Classen points out, this 'anti-fascist' rhetoric worked well, not only because it dignified the resistance and honoured the victims of National Socialism, but also because it created little or no resentment within the general population, occupying the moral high ground and ensuring continued support for the government.[41] Other examples of this are mentioned above such as blaming Lord Home for 'the destruction of Coventry' or the mingling of fact and fiction in various 'documentary features'.

The continuing policy of 'agitation through facts' was not exclusively the domain of news and current affairs, as outlined by the SED radio chronicler Alfred Duchrow:

> As there is no such thing as 'apolitical' broadcasting, 'apolitical' information, entertainment or instruction – a natural law, it is not

the relation of the genres to each other, but the partiality [to the party – *Parteilichkeit*] within all genres, which is decisive whether our broadcasting has understood all aspects of party and government.[42]

In other words, all of the radio output in the GDR was politicised. The comprehensive planning structure meant that apart from broadcasters being closely monitored – even in their personal lives – the output had to correspond to the needs and expectations of the listeners (as defined by the SED). Broadcasting 'past' (*vorbeisenden*) the listeners was not permitted.[43]

The existence of press freedom in the GDR could be deduced from the constitutional article on 'free expression of opinion' (*freie Meinungsäußerung*) which states that 'The right to free expression of opinion is guaranteed to each citizen according to the principles of the constitution, e.g. in accordance with Marxism-Leninism.' So it follows that 'misuse of the right to free expression against the interests of the workers and their government is prohibited.' Therefore 'the socialist press cannot be considered free to disorient socialist consciousness.'[44]

This left little room for any private ambitions of individual broadcasters. Despite this some journalists managed to become high-profile radio personalities, such as Herbert Geßner, Manfred Klein, Manfred Fleischhacker, Egbert von Frankenberg und Proschlitz, and, most prominently, Karl-Eduard von Schnitzler, all in the role of political commentators.[45]

And these journalists were on the whole ideologically committed. Many had experienced the war years in exile or in concentration camps and the ideal of a better, socialist future seemed something worth fighting for; some, like von Schnitzler, Max Burghardt and Karl Gass, had come from the Western zone to help establish the new, anti-fascist – democratic – society.[46] During the early years of the GDR the idealism of these journalists was practically unwavering, even after the events of 17 June 1953.[47] The period up to the 11th SED Central Committee plenum in December 1965 was, according to former GDR journalists, a time of committed, relatively critical and investigative journalism, which exercised self-censorship, and which strengthened itself after the erection of the Berlin Wall in two distinct ways: firstly the 'bulwark against fascism' militarised GDR society thoroughly, so that a style of 'wartime reporting' established itself. Secondly, the Wall made the GDR 'feasible'; a new generation was growing up in a socialist state, concerned with matters relating entirely to their own experiences and initially did not want to be drawn into comparisons with the 1920s or 1930s or with the West.⁴⁸ In time this produced its own problems, particularly with oppositional thought from the left (such as Wolf Biermann).⁴⁹

The over-wordiness of the earlier broadcasting in the late 1940s and 50s – up to 45 per cent of all programmes – gave way slowly to a more mixed programming of spoken word, culture and entertainment. On the first programme – *Radio DDR I* – for the years 1955 to 1957, during the evening schedule between 19:00hrs and 22:00hrs, spoken word programmes occupied 33 per cent of all broadcast time, and of this more than 80 per cent were political commentaries.⁵⁰ Apart from the daily comment on current affairs, which was usually broadcast immediately after the news, weekly political commentaries with titles like 'One Sixth of the Planet' (a programme about the Soviet Union), 'The Truth about America', 'We Speak for West Germany' were commonplace.⁵¹ While these programmes, at least in title, disappeared in the 1950s, the topics chosen for news broadcasts continued with these themes which more often than not dealt with international, rather than national issues. The siege mentality of the SED leadership was reflected in the fact that out of 983 news items only 82 were about GDR matters but 275 concerned the Federal Republic.⁵²

Fearing that the monotonous drone of political commentaries would make the listeners switch off – or, worse, re-tune to a western station – and, following extensive audience research in 1956, Albert Norden launched an attack on the news and political programme makers, accusing them of forgetting the primary task of the political journalists – that is, 'agitation through facts' and the mobilising of the masses. He saw 'ideological causes' for this 'wrong news policy' which showed the alarmingly false bourgeois attitude that 'a news service should primarily have an informative role'.⁵³

The purge which followed these criticisms led to a complete restructuring of the GDR radio service. From now on the emphasis shifted towards entertainment, socialist humour and more light music, alongside spoken word programmes such as 'From Working Life' (*Aus dem Arbeiterleben*). Daily political commentaries, however, continued to 'agitate through facts'.

Bearing in mind that a constant, albeit unacknowledged, competition with western broadcasters was taking place, the aims of the *Staatliches Rundfunkkomitee* had to be revised repeatedly. Continued attacks on the broadcasting committee from Norden in the wake of the crisis of 1961 meant that by 1963 contingency plans had been drawn up for a more dynamic and internationally compatible broadcasting service, entitled 'A General Line in the Development of the German Democratic

Broadcasting Service up to 1980' (*Generallinie der Entwicklung für den Deutschen Demokratischen Rundfunk bis 1980*). It states:

> Radio constitutes, among other media, an effective information and propaganda instrument in the hands of the party of the working class, the government of the German Democratic Republic and the German Democratic National Front. Now, in the period of the extensive construction of Socialism and the establishing of conditions for the transformation to Communism in the GDR, the tasks facing broadcasting are even more wide-ranging and even more definite. It must help to speedily develop the socialist consciousness of the workforce; it must help to reach a high level of education and culture for all the population. It must, as a collective organiser, with all possible assistance of all available political, artistic and technical opportunities, further the socialist society of the GDR; it must with all its inherent possibilities have a mobilising effect on the productive forces and be responsible to meet the needs of the working population in their needs for extensive information, education and entertainment.
>
> Therefore the radio (service) of the GDR has to concentrate its entire activity upon these aims and has to use all its means and possibilities actively and operatively to engage in the realisation of the political, economic and cultural tasks as decided at the VI. Party Congress of the SED.[54]

In real terms this meant a reorganisation of the radio broadcasting service, modelled on the BBC (and Radio Moscow, which in turn was modelled on the BBC), with emphasis on an effective and fast dissemination of news and a wide choice in entertainment and cultural output:

> The broadcasting needs of the population of the German Democratic Republic must therefore be met with programmes of the following character:
>
> 1. An operative mass programme (similar to the present programmes of DDR I and the Berliner Rundfunk although of a more operational character);
> 2. A programme (station) for musical-aesthetic education and culture (for this no example as yet, but first signs of this is the new II. programme of Radio DDR);
> 3. A programme (station) of political information and entertainment (especially for transistor-radio listeners, listeners in cars, and

listeners who might only be listening for short periods, conscripts etc.);
4. A programme for the capital of the GDR, Berlin;
5. A programme for West Germany;
6. A programme for West Berlin;
7. A foreign service.

These characteristics identify only the main emphasis of the respective programmes, and it is understood that each will have elements of the other, particularly political information.[55]

With the exception of the specific station for West Berlin, all the others were realised (which included regional stations), with the foreign service, *Radio Berlin International*, broadcasting on shortwave around the world in several different languages. Each station had an editor-in-chief, akin to a director-general, *(Intendant)* directly responsible to the state broadcasting committee. Programme topics remained under close (if not closer) scrutiny of the StRK with its close links to the Ministry of State Security (MfS).

But the programme structure shifted away from ideological commentaries to a broad and populist mêlée of light entertainment, as Table 5.1 indicates.

Programmes on the Nazi past, if part of a topical debate, would have been part of the information service (news and current affairs), or in documentary form appearing as radio plays and features in the cultural category. Despite this shift, the steady stream of news, commentaries, interviews and transmissions from political events was much more pronounced in the radio landscape of the GDR than the FRG, as most of the programmes in the cultural or information categories would have been highly politicised within the context of the daily ideological confrontation with the Bonn government.[56] This emphasis was particularly pronounced was this emphasis when the political debate in the Federal Republic coincided with the anti-fascist

Table 5.1 Dimensions of programme development

	FRG	GDR
Information	28	31
Culture	37	25
Entertainment	35	44

Source: Based on Konrad Dussel, *Hörfunk in Deutschland*, p. 383.

agenda in East Berlin, as in the case of the Auschwitz Trial.[57] The East German programme makers were 'censored without censor',[58] broadcasting being 'a different form of the class struggle',[59] with the aim of exposing the conspiracy of 'imperialists and monopoly capitalists' who want to inflict their campaign of 'greed and unbounded megalomania' with their 'Nazi helpers' for the seamless continuation of 'fascist German imperialism'.[60] Unfortunately, much of this archival material and additional evidence in these categories has, as Dussel comments, 'virtually vanished into thin air'.[61]

Memory makers (West)

When the Allies gradually relinquished control of the radio stations in the late 1940s, the focus of the proposed future broadcasting was on the areas of culture and education. A genuine public service was to be established, a new cultural institution that was to be in the service of the listener with a new democratic consciousness. Perhaps the best (and most often-quoted) example of this new work ethic came in the form of the inaugural speech of the director-general (*Intendant*) of the NWDR (*Nordwestdeutscher Rundfunk*), Adolf Grimme, in November 1948:

> He who makes use of this (new) broadcasting service will find more than entertainment. He will find it a helper for a rediscovery of meaning in life. And with this it will give us the ultimate Why? Of broadcasting: to overcome our intellectual poverty. Our descent into faithlessness, caused by our blindness to the world of values and their hierarchy is the greatest source of our suffering. We lived in a vacuum and became directionless. By providing us with renewed access to real values, the radio will become the compass in our intellectual wanderings and a guide for a new picture of humanity and their programmes for the world. Thus working for radio means working for a new humanitarianism, not the humanitarianism of the academics, but a humanitarianism for the people (*Volkshumanismus*),which shall make all the people aware of what it means to be human.[62]

Grimme was not the only one to espouse such high-sounding ideals. Most of the new *Intendanten* had to show a clear break with the past and a definite commitment to Allied policies. Culture and education had also dominated the immediate postwar re-education/de-Nazification/vospitanie v kulturu programmes (which had included the Nuremburg Trial broadcasts) and at least initially, in the late 1940s, dealing with the Nazi past seemed a regular part of the new radio stations' output.

But the attitudes of the military authorities in respect of radio broadcasting varied greatly in their approach to the listener. Contrary to what came later, the friendly and familiar approach of the *Berliner Rundfunk*, under the control of the Soviet Military Administration in Germany (SMAD), proved to be the most popular (regional) station, up to 1948.[63] Whereas the American and Soviet military administrations were both concerned about using the radio for re-education purposes, differences such as using German personnel to represent the Military authority – and not the Military authority itself – gave the Soviet-controlled radio stations an advantage. Other populist measures employed by the *Berliner Rundfunk* included the use of 'vox pop' techniques – letting Berliners speak on air, and extensive agitation on the causes of the fascist dictatorship (where the blame lay firmly with the excesses of monopoly capitalism, not the wider population). In comparison the output of RIAS (*Radio im Amerikanischen Sektor*) sounded distant and heavy-handed, and the question of guilt, combined with the de-Nazification programme, loomed uneasily on the listeners.[64]

But the building of a democratic consensus in the Western zones was encouraged by the military authorities and a number of German public figures (such as the philosopher Karl Jaspers) engaged with the question of guilt and the building of a liberal democracy. In the radio community it was the abovementioned Adolf Grimme, in a broadcast of the popular BBC to Germany, who commented on his experiences on his visit to Britain in 1946, carefully circumventing the concepts of 'collective responsibility' and instead concentrating on 'democracy':

> I have always known that the respect of individual liberty was the cornerstone of Anglo-Saxon society. But never before have I had such living proof of this fact as in recent weeks. While National Socialism had complete disregard for people and humanity, here the respect for people and the individual is a way of life. In other words: Here one experiences that democracy is not just a term in political power play, but a self-evident atmosphere of soul and intellect. Here it is more than just a way of government; here democracy is not debated, here democracy is lived!
>
> This respect for differing opinions, even when totally opposed to it, what is it if not the respect of anyone who is human? Here people still have faith in humanity, while we had lost ours...

> Dear compatriots, the fact that I can speak these words freely from a country we are not at peace with yet is perhaps the best sign that in this country democracy is more than a system of government. Democracy is a way of life here, where the respect for the other's opinion is common currency. This, I would like to tell you, is my strongest impression here.[65]

In the initial postwar period, this type of public declaration from persons in positions of authority remained commonplace and indeed was more popular than the self-critical examinations around the issue of guilt Jaspers engaged in. Debate among returnees and leading intellectuals took place primarily in the newspapers (then also still under Allied control) with the *Neue Zeitung* – printed in the former *Völkischer Beobachter* printing works in Munich – establishing itself as the publication with the greatest readership – 1.5 million.[66] What is interesting to note here is that one of the NZ's leading contributors, the author Thomas Mann, was shunned by the radio stations and by the public. Mann had, in the early Weimar years, clearly disassociated himself from German politics with his 1919 publication 'Reflections of a non-political Man' (*Beobachtungen eines Unpolitischen*),[67] but, during the war years indicted the German population for their lack of interest in politics (which, according to him, led to the rise of the NSDAP) with his hard-hitting wartime BBC broadcasts from his exile in California. This meant that Mann, despite the success and popularity of *The Magic Mountain*, was an unwelcome voice. Inge Marßolek comments on this:

> The returning emigrants were, generally speaking, not welcomed with open arms, and this was also the case at the radio stations. As with other professions, it was felt that the returnees held up a mirror to their colleagues as living reminders of the crimes of National Socialism. The debate around Thomas Mann, evoked by Frank Thiess, was symptomatic of this sentiment. Hans Bedrow, radio pioneer and (former Weimar) secretary of state, adopted these resentments when he commented to the board of Radio Munich that 'it would be more effective if the German people learned the truth about the last twelve years from Germans who lived through them. What Thomas Mann has to say on this matter would not impress.[68]

Readings of his novels, however, such as *The Magic Mountain* and *Buddenbrooks*, tended to be broadcast more often on East German radio than in the West.[69]

The NWDR, the largest postwar radio station, which was transmitted to the whole of north-western Germany from Hamburg via Cologne to Berlin, had initially been set up by the British Military Authority and worked in conjunction with the BBC. When it started to broadcast formally it defined its function partly as follows:

2A. To retain its audience and to build effectively a new tradition in German broadcasting, NWDR must not be too obviously concerned with the re-education of the audience or even with the raising of cultural standards. Entertainment will not be too obviously edifying and information not too obviously instructional. Excessive attention by the NWDR to the political and historical re-education of Germans will destroy its credibility, and it follows that 'world' and 'British' views of current and past events should be conveyed to the Germans by other means.

2B. The re-education of the German people is the direct concern of the BBC German Service. The projection of Britain, in the widest sense of the term, must be one of the main tasks of any BBC service in Europe and will directly contribute to the end of re-education.

3. To function efficiently even as an instrument of Military Government, and much more as a long-term means of influencing the German mind, NWDR must not unduly increase the proportion of British official announcements and relays from outside Germany to programmes originated by Germans on the spot. Control Commission policy, for instance, should be explained by Germans; and regular relays, as opposed to occasional relays of special programmes, should generally be avoided.[70]

In the initial postwar period manifestations of a liberal public service broadcasting ethic were most evident at the NWDR, where the influence of the BBC had been dominant. A group of broadcasters which included Axel Eggebrecht, Ernst Schnabel, Peter von Zahn and Peter Bamm, based in Hamburg, all had impeccable credentials and their ability to engage critically with the complexities of the immediate postwar political landscape was not lost on Sir Hugh Carleton Greene, then controller of the BBC German Service and later (from 1961) director-general of the BBC, who commented on them in the NWDR annual of 1949/50:

In those early months the traditions of freedom were established, drawing men from all parts of Germany to Hamburg, because they knew that they could speak their minds [there], even when it meant criticising the Military Government.[71]

And criticise they did. Whereas Axel Eggebrecht made no qualms about his opposition to the death penalty during his reporting from the Bergen-Belsen trial and in his comments on Nuremberg, Peter von Zahn's 1946 broadcast 'Dealing with the Victors' (*Über den Umgang mit den Siegern*) is exemplary in its insight into the difficult situation that faced Germans and Allies alike:

> The relationship between victors and the losers has already often been worked through. But what becomes evident from this is that very few useful methods have come to mind so far. And victors are human beings, too. And when dealing with human beings a number of useful experiences are available to us...
>
> The intention is not to blame the overwhelming and still increasing misery of our days on misunderstandings. This misery is the inevitable result of the substantial mistakes, by the greatest part, of the national socialists, by the smaller part of the conquerors of the Nazis. When the victors got hold of the reigns to pull the cart out of the dirt, they often mistook them with the brake. This is common knowledge. Just as the mistake promising the Germans improvements which could not be fulfilled... However, these mistakes must not lead to us disengaging from the victors. We can never get out of our embarrassing situation (!) if we set ourselves against them, only if we co-operate. And on all fours. And not a single word against any of them. If we set the victors against each other for tactical advantage, within a short time they will be convinced that our concern is not the fate of 74 million unhappy people, but that our motivation is driven by nationalist hatred.[72]

Von Zahn's broadcast was indicative not only of the relationship between the military authorities and the German population, but also of the wider aspect of press freedom in an occupied country. The authorities – in this case the British military – were aware that editorial autonomy of the radio stations was an important policy to maintain the support of the population (although 'Pre-Broadcast-Scrutiny' remained in place until the stations were handed over to German control between 1947 and 1949).[73]

The initial five West German regional broadcasters, *Nordwestdeutscher Rundfunk (NWDR), Süddeutscher Rundfunk (SDR), Bayerischer Rundfunk*

(BR), Südwestfunk (SWF) and, after 1948, the *Hessischer Rundfunk (HR),* were bound not only by the constitution (*Grundgesetz*) but, until 1955, when the status of occupation was lifted, by the Allied High Commission.[74] The position of the *Radio im Amerikanischen Sektor* (RIAS) in Berlin was somewhat different, as this station was funded partly by the US Military. The director-generals of the regional broadcasting stations were, in many cases, well-known public figures and had open political affiliations, such as Erich Rossmann, *Intendant* of the SDR, who had been an SPD member of the Weimar Reichstag.[75] Rossmann saw the task of (radio) broadcasting as primarily an educational one, although

> ...not in a narrow, pedagogic or even school-masterly fashion, but a free, easy, unobtrusive and constant one, always seeking the voluntary agreement of the listener. This is why radio cannot be politically biased, nor be a medium of shallow, superficial, not to mention lewd or offensive, entertainment. The spirit of this educational task has to weave like a red thread through all the output, light and serious.[76]

And the director-general of the SWF Friedrich Bischoff wanted radio to 'fulfil the task of therapy for the soul' (*eine seelentherapeutische Aufgabe zu erfüllen*) when it came to the spoken word, and to positively avoid the 'trend of diversion' in music. Radio programming at the SWF would not be for the 'convenience of the individual' but would set out to 'earn their work with the listeners'.[77]

Both Grimme and Bischoff had a very optimistic understanding of – or even demands on – the listening public. Even by the late 1940s, it was becoming clear that the picture of the family seated around the radio set, and listening attentively, was increasingly outdated. Trying to avoid the tendency of the radio becoming 'a lulling opiate of diversion' was commendable, but it was not necessarily possible and it was certainly not popular.[78]

In the early 1950s debates arose around the political commentary programmes, which, similar to the output from East Germany, had become a feature following the main evening news programmes.[79] The intention had been to popularise politics and to present critical opinion, to offer a way through the diversity of political opinion the average German encountered, which consisted of a mixture of 'an incomprehensible gobbledygook of scientific concepts and adages, ideologically or party-politically distorted,[80] by presenting the listener with a 'middle way' and a 'translation', which would lead to the creation of responsible citizens. But the commentaries were, for many, too critical. Peter von

Zahn at the NWDR and Reinhard Gerdes and Klaus-Peter Schulz at the SWF were regularly criticised for their outspokenness by political parties and media watchdogs alike.[81] The vitriolic exchanges and accusations in the press frequently called for the removal of such commentators, as in the case of one of von Zahn's broadcasts in November 1951, which led the press office of the CDU/CSU to issue a statement under the heading 'Switch off – Peter von Zahn!', calling it 'one of the worst cases of political well-poisoning we have ever encountered'.[82] All von Zahn had commented on was pointing to the fact that the unions had the option to press for their demands through organising a demonstration.[83]

Increasingly throughout the 1950s the Federal and *Länder* governments attempted to influence the broadcast policies, although it was individual broadcasts, not the stations as a whole which often caused the offence.[84] But the undoubtedly political nature of everyday life in the divided Germany meant that the radio stations could not, and would not avoid politics, and, as in the case of their GDR counterparts, talk about the 'other' Germany, which, of course, was always politically sensitive. The NWDR, which in 1956 split into the NDR (for the Hamburg region), WDR (Cologne and Ruhr) and Sender Freies Berlin (SFB – Berlin), carried the most programmes concerning their East German neighbours, but others, such as the SWF and HR, also aired commentaries and information programmes, aimed at the GDR audience (broadcast on MW) with titles such as 'The Home not Forgotten' (*Unvergessene Heimat*), 'The View from the West' (*So sieht es der Westen*) and 'In Common Care' (*In gemeinsamer Sorge*), whereas the NWDR – and later the WDR and SFB – had less euphemistic titles, such as 'Germany Indivisible' (*Unteilbares Deutschland*) and 'Greetings to the Zone' (*Gruß an die Zone*).[85]

Direct governmental, political influence on any of the West German broadcasters was prohibited by Article 5 of the *Grundgesetz* (constitution), and the federal structure ensured that (especially) the emerging television broadcasters were an amalgamation of the regional broadcasters (ARD – *Arbeitsgemeinschaft der öffentlich-rechtlichen Rundfunkanstalten Deutschlands*). But the growth of television saw calls for a second channel which led to fears that the centrally controlled (and state owned) *Deutsches Fernsehen GmbH,* which was to start broadcasting the second TV channel in early 1961, would turn into the 'Adenauer' channel and contravene the principles of press freedom as enshrined by the constitution. The case was rushed through the Constitutional Court (*Bundesverfassungsgericht*) which ruled in favour of the regional broadcasters on 28 February 1961.[86]

This judgement also had clear implications for the radio stations. It meant that even the station which was broadcasting both nationwide and internationally, *Deutsche Welle*, would be controlled by the ARD and would carry programmes selected from the regional stations' output, free from central government interference.

The topic of the Nazi past, however, had remained troublesome for radio in West Germany throughout the 1950s: even though a few memorial dates were observed and some reporting from war crimes trials made the headlines, radio plays in particular were not considered to be a place for dealing with this topic. Heinz Schwitzke, head of radio plays at the NWDR, insisted on absolute authority on all manuscripts, as he viewed the function of broadcasting as a means of leadership, which would give concrete values to 'that amorphous mass, which stands helpless before the phenomena of our time and the world'.[87] His control was such that any mention of the persecution of the Jews, the NS state or rearmament of the FRG would be struck off the manuscripts, even if only mentioned incidentally.[88] In other aspects as well, such as dealing with requests for more popular music on the radio, public service broadcasters explored 'the possibilities of an unnoticeable and cautious steering, that is to say, influencing of the audience', in order to overcome 'the tyranny of public taste'.[89] This relative position of authority nevertheless gave some journalists and public figures the opportunity to dictate the agenda.

With the court ruling of February 1961 and the international interest in the Eichmann Trial in Jerusalem, a newer generation of journalists and broadcasters and renewed public interest started to produce bolder programming, although this was often tucked away in the newly created second and third programme frequencies. At the beginning of the television age radio was attempting to offer something that the visual medium could not. Finding this new balance was, in the early 1960s, often 'hit-and-miss'. Only in the latter half of the decade, when it had become evident that radio would coexist easily with television, did the radio stations of the FRG dare to engage freely with the topic of 'the difficult past'.

Memory users (East)

The curiosity of the SED leadership and the *StRK* (State Broadcasting Committee) about their listeners only developed slowly in the GDR. Before 1956/57 there had been no audience research to speak of.[90] In the late 1940s and early 1950s occasional distributions of questionnaires in factories and households did not have the desired results. The picture that emerged was that the radio listener in the GDR wanted to hear light entertainment, occasional news and weather, but not political commentaries. A percentage would be listening to RIAS and did not show signs of being committed socialists.[91] As unwanted as this information might have seemed to the StRK, it was not ignored. In order to be the 'broadcaster of the people' (*Rundfunk des Volkes*) it had to show its closeness and attachment to the masses (*Massenverbundenheit*).[92] But the 'new type of press' (which included broadcasting), as Ulbricht had imagined, did not foresee the troubles of 17 June 1953 nor the influence (if not direction) of the western radio stations in the actual demonstrations (especially RIAS).[93] Detailed profiles of the radio-listening public were not compiled, although after June 1953 the Central Committee urged broadcasters to take listeners' letters seriously, and to make them 'the first and foremost concern of all editors.'[94]

Just how seriously the editors took the listeners' comments, and whether the views aired on programmes like '...and what does the listener say?' (*...und was sagt der Hörer?*) actually reflected received letters is impossible to ascertain.[95]

Serious investigation into audience research only became possible after the SED had stopped denouncing sociological research methods as 'bourgeois non-science', sometime in the late 1950s.[96] Figures for radio listeners in the GDR are also uncommonly vague. The figure of 86 out of 100 households possessing (or listening to) a radio set seems to be the standard for the late 1950s and early 1960s, both for the GDR and the FRG,[97] whereas the actual number of listeners rose in the GDR from 3.5 million in 1950 to about 5.6 million in 1960.[98] By the end of the 1980s there were 279 radio sets per 100 households.[99] The numbers of listeners tuning to the second or third stations carrying the programmes discussed here are also roughly the same for East and West for the 1960s: one-eighth of the total audience.[100] This figure diminished during the 1970s and 1980s as there was a growth in the number of listeners to Western stations.[101]

Where the GDR radio listeners differed from their western counterparts was in terms of the time (of day) and the choice of radio station: Whereas listeners in the FRG increasingly listened to the radio only in the morning (mainly to accommodate evening television), East Germans maintained the habit of listening to the radio in the evening, listening to more than one station, most likely one from the West.[102] As 'listening to the enemy' could be a cause for denunciation – but only in exceptional circumstances leading to imprisonment – official statistics of 'listening to the West' were never compiled by the GDR authorities. It was, however, an over-optimistic 'West-German common sense' which assumed the wide-ranging desire of East Germans to listen to the West, but empirically this assumption is not sustainable.[103] Only the American High Commission continued to assess (and hope for an increase in) these figures, but the increasing quality of the GDR output meant that even as early as 1954 only a third of refugees coming over to the West stated that they had been listening to Western stations regularly.[104] Without overstating the case, it can be assumed that by 1960 about a quarter of the GDR radio listening public were listening to the West[105] (as opposed to only about 9 per cent of the West German listeners who were listening to the East[106]) at some point during a 24-hour period.

One 1957 study of 'listener satisfaction' revealed that political commentaries and current affairs features, although not as popular as the music and entertainment programmes which preceded and followed them, received a 73.3 per cent approval rating among listeners in the GDR, who stated that they were satisfied with the range of political information on offer.[107]

Once research institutes had been established in 1965, the efforts of the media researchers in the GDR remained under the strictest scrutiny, not only from the StRK but also from the party leadership.[108] Any unauthorised attempts to incorporate some of the findings into policy proposals frequently ended in immediate dismissals.[109] When finally, in 1969, media research became part of a wider sociological investigation, the researchers at the first GDR Sociology Congress set themselves the following parameters for their research:

- How does radio influence and stimulate socialist ideology, motivations for behaviour and actions of personality, and the development of the socialist community (collective)?
- What importance, in respect of reception, does radio have in the system of ideology producing and disseminating means of communication?[110]

This very narrow remit, of course, was not only a continuation of the ongoing self-censorship, but also did not allow incorporation of any 'deviant' findings. A slight change occurred after Honnecker became First Secretary in 1971, when the tasks of the media researchers were outlined as:

>...to publish the experiences, wishes and aspirations of the working population and to integrate these into social consciousness.

This is made possible by the working population using the radio and expressing this themselves. Radio in a socialist society means a careful consideration of expectations and to satisfy the needs of the listeners. This is the present task of GDR audience research. Its duty is to investigate the social circumstances and subjective conditions, as well as listening habits and needs of the population of the GDR.[111]

The findings of the GDR media researchers – even if they were ever made public – never had any influence on the programme output.[112] Throughout the 1960s and 1970s no questions were asked about who listened to Western broadcasts and the research results appeared to be constant. When it was possible – through anonymous polling – to record the number of listeners to 'other stations' in the 1980s, it is noticeable that the GDR listener was catered for in terms of light entertainment and popular music, which ensured that until the late 1980s the populist radio station DDR I managed to maintain relatively high percentage of the listeners, never exceeding the number of listeners to Western broadcasts (indicated by 'other stations' in the table below), while stations more akin to the West German broadcasters (the pop-music youth radio DT64 and regional stations) gained in audience numbers (see Table 5.2).[113]

It is much more difficult, however, to assess the attitude of the East German population towards the Nazi past during the 1950s and 1960s. The initial KPD/SED line did not exonerate the public from responsibility, as Alexander Abusch's 1946 'The Error of the Germans' (*Der Irrweg der Deutschen*), a popular publication in the GDR, states:

Table 5.2 GDR radio listeners

Station	Percentage of listeners			
	1985	1986	1987	1988
DDR I	30	27	24	20
DDR II	1	1	1	1
Berliner Rundfunk	17	15	14	11
Stimme der DDR	9	10	9	9
Jugendsender DT64	2	6	9	12
Regional stations	10	14	16	16
Other stations	15	16	20	20

Source: Liselotte Mühlberg, 'Hörerforschung des DDR-Rundfunks', in Heide Riedel (ed.), *Mit uns zieht die neue Zeit... 40 Jahre DDR Medien*, p. 177.

The German people cannot deny responsibility for the fact that Germany, in the middle of the high civilisation of the twentieth century, became the stronghold of Hitler's inhuman theory and practice. Even when the Germans were murderously oppressed by the Nazi dictatorship, in 1933 they were not helpless victims, jumped on in their sleep. Some former politicians of the Weimar Republic abroad are trying to portray the German people simply as Hitler's victims. This is historically wrong and an ill-thought out service to the German people, if they are ever to think and act as a mature and democratically responsible nation again.[114]

But in order to accommodate reconstruction and a new, socialist future, the SED turned into the 'big friend of the little Nazi' (*der große Freund des kleinen Nazis*) by integrating many of the former fellow travellers after 1949 back into their former professions,[115] and the politically correct coming-to-terms with the past was centrally co-ordinated by the SED through a combination of 'anti-fascism' and the heroic portrayal of the KPD resistance during the Third Reich. There was no particular emphasis on Nazi racial policy, as this was seen as an interchangeable variant of 'monopoly capitalism'. In the GDR 'militarism, Nazism and Fascism had been annihilated by its roots' and therefore there was no reason to pay any reparation to the Jewish victims of National Socialism residing in the GDR.[116] The first publication dealing with the destruction of the European Jews appeared in 1966, as all previous accounts of the Third Reich had been portrayed as the 'excesses of monopoly capitalism' and its concomitant ideology, fascism.[117]

So, of course, the programmes dealing with this question could not – and did not – stray from the prescribed line, but they might have (although no empirical evidence exists for this) touched on a few raw nerves, or kindled some memories. What does exist, however, are a number of studies, conducted after 1990, which deal with the attitudes of East Germans to the subject of National Socialism and recent German history: the ones selected here are the by now famous 2002 Welzer/Moller/Tschuggnall book 'Grandpa was no Nazi' (*Opa war kein Nazi*) and two opinion polls from 1995 conducted by the *Institut für Demoskopie Allensbach*, 'The Divided Sky – Historical Consciousness in East and West Germany' (*Der geteilte Himmel – Geschichtsbewußtsein in West- und Ostdeutschland*) and 'Peace, not liberation – what the war generation thinks of 8 May today' (*Frieden, nicht Befreiung – wie die Kriegsgeneration heute über den 8.Mai denkt*).

In the absence of polling data from the 1960s, the choice offered here is by no means extensive, but it is a representative selection of the qualitative aspect of the 2002 publication and the quantitative one of the 1995 opinion polls. What is also slightly problematic here is that the lapse of time and current events might be (or is most certainly) reflected in the opinions and attitudes of the interviewees, and therefore will not present an accurate picture of the time it is trying to investigate. However, it will point to the differences in historical awareness and interpretation and will therefore also include some of the figures from the contrasting West.

The opinion poll 'Peace, not liberation...' was commissioned by the *Frankfurter Allgemeine Zeitung* (FAZ) and the results were published in a weekday edition of 25 April 1995. The questioning took place throughout March 1995 on samples varying in size from 188 to 999 throughout Germany, divided into the old 'Western' and new 'Eastern' *Länder*.

What is striking at first glance is that in many cases the answers show little variation between East and West, the predominant association with the term '8 May 1945 End of the War' being 'ruins' (67 East, 68 West). A 'new beginning' also scored similar figures (63 East, 64 West). 'Peace', however, scored relatively higher in the East than in the West (72 East, 62 West), as did 'liberation' (43 East, 33 West), while 'fear' was equally present (29) for East and West. Further noticeable discrepancies show up in the associated words of 'relief' (49 East, 65 West), 'capitulation' (16 East, 21 West), 'humiliation' (11 East, 14 West), 'uncertainty' (24 East, 34 West) and 'liberty' (20 East, 29 West).[118]

When asked (of persons born before 1933): 'What were your feelings on the 8 May 1945, do you remember? Was it more a feeling of liberation or one of capitulation?', the difference in the answers between the Eastern and Western *Bundesländer* also reveals an interesting rift: 32 per cent of the interviewed East Germans answered 'capitulation' (56 per cent said 'liberation'), whereas only 17 per cent of the West Germans had a feeling of 'capitulation' (and 67 per cent one of 'liberation').[119] But, it has to be added here, this question had been asked previously, albeit only in the former West Germany, ten years earlier (in 1985), when 32 per cent had expressed feelings of 'capitulation' and only 44 per cent had expressed feelings of 'liberation'.[120]

The second in the series of opinion polls for the FAZ, published on 3 May 1995 and carried out by the *IfD Allensbach*, paints an even more diverse picture than the earlier one. East and West Germans, when asked what attributes distinguished German history from the history of other countries, gave a variety of answers (see Table 5.3).

Table 5.3 IfD Allensbach Opinion Poll: 'What distinguishes German History?' (May 1995)

	West				East			
	Jan 1989	Aug 1992	March 1993	April 1995	Dec 1990	Aug 1992	March 1993	April 1995
3rd Reich	52	52	49	49	4	11	16	19
thereof: the Nazi crimes/ the destruction of the Jews	(13)	(17)	(16)	(21)	(1)	(4)	(6)	(8)
Divided Country/ Reunification	11	11	15	10	36	30	22	26
Many Wars	23	22	22	26	36	36	39	41

Source: Institut für Demoskopie Allensbach, Archive no. 5514, IfD Umfrage 6014, Tabelle 3.

The same 1995 study also asked the question: 'Sometimes one hears the comment that the German population followed Hitler blindly, without offering any resistance. How do you view this: Do you think there were opportunities to resist, or did they not exist?' 43 per cent of East Germans thought that there were practically no opportunities to resist, while 36 per cent thought that there were (21 per cent expressed themselves as 'Don't knows'). The interesting figures here come again from the West German interviewees, where this question had been asked in 1969, 1988 and 1995. In 1969 only 19 per cent thought that there had been opportunities to resist, a figure that increased to 24 per cent in 1988 and to 32 per cent in 1995 (the corresponding figures for 'No opportunities to resist' were as follows: 1968 – 63 per cent, 1988 – 60 per cent, 1995 – 54 per cent).[121]

Another aspect of this poll is generational. About half of those younger people asked stated that they had talked to the older generation about the Hitler dictatorship. Only 4 per cent of the East German younger generation thought that their elders had something to hide, while an overwhelming 83 per cent believed them to be accurate historical witnesses. Young West Germans were more suspicious; 12 per cent distrusted the accounts of the war generation, while 77 per cent believed them.[122] Further questioning revealed similar answers: Asked whether they believed the often-repeated statement that the older generation had little or no knowledge of the Nazi crimes at the time, 77 per cent of East Germans wanted to believe this to be true, while 12 per cent doubted it (the corresponding figures for the West were as follows: believe 67 per cent, doubt 21 per cent).[123]

The authors of *'Opa war kein Nazi'*, Harold Welzer, Sabine Moller and Karoline Tschuggnall explain these last sets of figures with the simple fact that the young East Germans, in their turn, did not resist the SED dictatorship themselves, and therefore had little reason to distrust their elders.[124] What also becomes evident from the interviews in this publication is that the comparison between the NSDAP and SED regimes surfaces regularly, the memory being 'layered', as the authors call it.

Within the setting of the family, where these interviews took place, there existed a 'subversive', non-public sphere, where opinions could be freely expressed during the GDR era, as one of the respondents explains:

> That one spoke completely differently within the family, with your friends, than officially,... Well there was watching West-TV, that was taboo. Even though everyone knew that everyone else, or nearly everyone else was doing it. And then it was accepted, with a wink. And so there existed one, and the another world.[125]

This awareness of 'the one, and another world' runs through most of the interviews, but it becomes quite evident that the older generation, having lived through the period of the Nazi dictatorship, were not so willing to submit to more of the same after 1945, although some reminiscences appear distinctly 'post-1989' in their portrayed attitude towards authority.[126] Others, however, describe it vividly:

> The first campaign I had to follow was in 1961, I was living in Köpenick, and there were TV sets in the shop windows. And there were signs saying 'Watching West TV is watching the capitalist enemy' or something like it. And two people were sent to me, and then they came to my flat and said why wasn't I joining the campaign (against the West-TV) and I said : 'You know, what I saw in that shop reminds me of my childhood. "The enemy is listening" was plastered all over the walls of the city. And people were denounced, who were listening to the English radio station, the BBC, yes, and now this again, do you think that it is right that people can't watch West-TV?' I remember that, that was my first/that was really like in Nazi times.[127]

In other places the memory (particularly of the older persons interviewed) gets muddled, so that the terms 'Nazis', 'Russians' and 'communists' are used interchangeably.[128]

And the generational aspect prevails through some of the interviews. In the following, a mother and her (adult) daughter recall an incident when the family had discussed the NS past:

> Mother: You and your brother were here, and others, I don't remember who. And then you asked us: 'Tell, us, we really can't believe that you didn't know what was happening in the concentration camps!' And then dad gave a very clever answer, because at the time the Stasi had their building just to the south of here, in the Brandenburger Straße, just over there. And dad said: 'Do you know what happens there, in the Stasi building?' And that was right here in the city!
> Daughter: Well, yes, I believe this, now, retrospectively. But at the time I did not, and it was the question which concerned us the most. 'Why did they not look?'
> M: Well, we couldn't know it!
> D: How can they glorify those days, after so many terrible things have been discovered! But we really didn't know what happened in Bautzen and other prisons during GDR times. That only became public knowledge much later. And that's why we have to be quiet now, when our children ask us 'Why were you quiet then?' And we also have to say: 'We didn't know. We didn't even guess!' This is what I believe today.[129]

The tensions that remain between the family members here are quite evident. Any (positive) reminiscing (by the mother) could be misconstrued (by the daughter) as glorification, whilst (partially) admitting her own inaction and ignorance. But the identification of 'the murderers amongst us' had never been as easy as in Staudte's film of the same name. The past, as taught in schools, looked different, as another (younger) respondent remembers:

> The anti-fascists were always really quite celebrated, naturally, in school, or that is to say, they were always the goodies. And then there were the baddies. Who were completely undefined and somehow this topic of 'willing executioners' and the like, that was, well it was just an (undefined) mass, it was somehow excluded... And you always felt a GDR school kid, because we were the goodies, and that, on the whole, went for all of the republic.[130]

The picture that emerges from the above of the average GDR radio listener's attitude to the NS past – in as much as it is possible to sense this at all – is that of a privately critical and outwardly regime-sympathetic person, in both instances undoubtedly honest, particularly as the anti-fascist rhetoric occasionally made up morally for the lack of consumer goods materially. Particularly in the early 1960s, when the competition for material goods and living standards with the FRG was still an issue, the apparent 're-Nazification' of the West, and the leniency of the courts against known perpetrators, much commented on and reported in the state-controlled media, gave East Germans the moral high ground.

Memory users (West)

Compared to the East German data on radio listeners and their opinion in relation to National Socialism, there is a comparative wealth of information concerning the West German 'memory user'. Not only were the radio stations keen to find out the likes and dislikes of their listeners, but public opinion polls were conducted by many research establishments and published widely in the media.

However, no one particular poll was conducted about the Auschwitz Trial coverage on the radio, but several – which will be examined below – did deal with the wider issues of the Nazi past in the media, and some used the 'vox pop' method to air random opinion polls on documentaries or news and current affairs programmes.

The area coverage of the initial West German regional broadcasters all overlapped at certain points and, although it was unlikely that a listener in Hamburg would be able to receive the Munich station on his or her radio set, it was very likely that a listener in Wiesbaden was able to pick up the NWDR, SDR and SWF without too much interference on the FM (VHF) frequencies. An early sample of the choice on hand for the West German listener is published in a much referred-to and often-mentioned 1962 study by Prof. Fritz Eberhard of the Free University Berlin, which examines the listeners of the SDR.[131] The table below refers to a sample from 1950, when the above stations were still broadcasting only one programme (stations) on medium wave (MW) and reception was rather 'hit and miss', but, as MW can transmit over far wider areas than FM, the choice was extensive and the listeners in the SDR region (Baden-Württemberg and Rheinland-Pfalz) made use of it (see Table 5.4).

According to the resolution of the Copenhagen Conference of 1948, the Allies re-distributed radio frequencies for Germany, as part of a

Table 5.4 Radio listeners in West Germany, 1950

Radio station	Listeners
Only SDR	17
SDR and other stations	82
thereof:	
Munich	46
Frankfurt	23
Leipzig (DDR I)	21
SWF	20
NWDR	17
American Forces Network	17
Beromünster	15
Berlin (East)	13
RIAS Berlin	10
Deutschlandsender (GDR)	8
Vorarlberg (Austria)	6
BBC	5
Moscow	2

Source: Fritz Eberhard, *Der Rundfunkhörer und sein Programm*, p. 31.

wider postwar settlement, stating that all long wave (LW) transmissions had to cease in Germany, and that transmissions on MW (from mid-1950 onwards) could only transmit the same programmes as their FM broadcasts. A complete switchover to FM of all German broadcasters was actively encouraged. Two MW frequencies were allocated to each of the occupation authorities, whose frequencies could also be used by other European stations.[132]

This was, in a way, designed to 'neutralise' the power of the German broadcasters, and to make way for the increasingly intense efforts of the Cold War broadcasters Voice of America, Radio Free Europe and Radio Moscow.[133]

The importance attached to audience research by the West German radio stations was waning throughout the 1950s, perhaps because of the growing popularity of television. Dussel comments that after the split-up of the NWDR into NDR, WDR and SFB in 1956, none of these broadcasters carried out their own research, but commissioned it to the *Infratest* or to the *Allensbacher* Institutes.[134] The above mentioned 1962 study is one of the increasingly rare academic studies into the listening habits of the radio listener, and holds a wealth of information on a subject which appeared doomed at the time of its publication. But the examples given and dates (1950–1958) mean that Eberhard's investigation is slightly problematic, as this was a time of rapidly changing listening habits and broadcasting policies.[135] The switchover to majority FM listening occurred not only as the result of the Copenhagen Conference, but also as a clear preference of the listeners to be able to have the clearer and better-quality broadcasts of the VHF transmission, albeit slowly. Accompanying this change was also the increasing use of radio in cars, availability of cheap, portable transistor radios and the increasing importance of local news and reports. Nevertheless, as late as 1960 the majority of radio listeners in West Germany still listened to the radio on MW and one of the few *Infratest* surveys into nationwide radio listening habits (commissioned by the ARD) revealed the following:

1. 95 per cent of all households have at least one radio set
2. 85 per cent of these have FM reception
3. Between 28 per cent (weekday, Summer 1960) and 36 per cent (weekend, Winter 1961) of respondents stated that they have a television set at home.
4. Respondents listening to the radio at least once a day (%) (see Table 5.5).

And here another interesting aspect of radio listening becomes apparent: not only do the figures vary by frequency, but they are also seasonal in nature: in the colder Winter months people listen to the radio for

Table 5.5 Respondents listening to the radio at least once a day and average daily listening time per listener

Weekday Summer	69	Saturday Summer	59
Weekday Winter	68	Saturday Winter	68
Friday Summer	65	Sunday Summer	58
Friday Winter	70	Sunday Winter	64

	MW (AM)	FM (VHF)	Other	Total
Weekday Summer	1hr 18mins	36mins		1hr 54mins
Weekday Winter	1hr	39mins	2mins	1hr 41mins
Friday Summer	59mins	35mins	3mins	1hr 37mins
Friday Winter	1hr 20mins	53mins	4mins	2hrs 17mins
Saturday Summer	1hr 2mins	35mins	1min	1hr 38mins
Saturday Winter	1hr 19mins	52mins	4mins	2hrs 15mins
Sunday Summer	1hr 3mins	31mins	2mins	1hr 36mins
Sunday Winter	1hr 17mins	58mins	3mins	2hrs 18mins

Source: Bessler, *Hörer- und Zuschauerforschung* p. 135.

substantially longer periods of time. And this points to the increasing changes in radio use. While at home, particularly in the Winter, listeners still might have been focussed attentively on the radio, while at other times, especially during the week, radio listening occurred at the workplace, in the car, outdoors or just in snatched moments.

In West Germany the prime time for listening to the radio was also changing, from the evening to the mornings, or, to be more precise, listeners increasingly stopped listening to the radio in the evening – preferring to watch the television instead. In 1951 the majority of listeners to the SDR had their radio sets switched on between 19:00 and 22:00 hrs (weekdays) with 47 per cent of all potential listeners, a figure that rose to 64 per cent on Saturdays.[136] Just two year later, in 1953, the weekday figure remained the same but the Saturday audience had decreased by 8 per cent. Ten years later, in 1963, the same target audience had changed their listening habits completely: only 28 per cent of the potential radio audience were listening during the same evening hours on a weekday – even fewer on a Saturday (18 per cent). In 1968 the number of evening listeners had become even smaller (13 per cent weekdays and 8 per cent Saturdays). By 1971 the evening radio audience had virtually disappeared (9 per cent weekdays and 7 per cent Saturdays). At the same time, morning listening increased slightly during the week, from 27 per cent in 1953 to nearly 30 per cent in 1971.[137]

The first ever broadcast on German radio had occurred in the evening, in Autumn 1923 between 20:00 and 21:00 hrs. This had been the prime time of the radio and it held this position until the mid- to late 1950s. Second and third programmes of broadcasting organisations, now broadcast exclusively on the FM band, catered for an ever smaller, but attentive audience. Their input, in terms of listeners' letters, comments in the press or participation in (broadcast) discussion programmes was substantial. But specialist 'minority tastes', if they were catered for at all, were moved to programme times which did not interfere with other, more popular interests, as the case of jazz on West German radio illustrates. While it was possible to listen to jazz on the radio, it did not come from the West German stations. 25 per cent of all jazz on the radio in the FRG was transmitted by the British Forces Network (BFN).[138] The approximately 1 per cent of programming output of each station which could be called a jazz programme was usually broadcast somewhere after 23:00, sometimes as late as 2 a.m.[139] More adventurous were the attempts in the late 1950s, when the SWF dared to engage the station's own big band in a mid-evening spot, fortnightly on Saturdays (*Jazz mit dem Orchester Kurt Edelhagen*).[140] Of course, as was the case everywhere, jazz had its aficionados, but, predominantly, it had opponents. When listeners of the NWDR were asked, in 1952, which were their favourite programmes, only 1 per cent mentioned jazz, whereas in the same poll, the programme which irritated the listeners the most was very same jazz programme with 11.1 per cent. In Bavaria, in a similar questionnaire by the BR in 1957, these figures were, respectively, 3 per cent and 30 per cent.[141]

But the development of a defined minority audience for the second and third programmes was important in terms of overall output. Most of the director-generals and upper management still had the ideals of (somewhat high-brow) Weimar broadcasting standards and did not want to submit to the 'tyranny of public taste'.[142] By catering to the 'high culture' and minority audiences, public service broadcasting in West Germany managed to distinguish itself from the private populist broadcasters like Radio Luxemburg. Writers, intellectuals, academics and newspaper editors all regularly became contributors to radio programmes.[143]

In 1962 the broadcaster with potentially the largest audience was the NDR in Hamburg. It could reach an estimated seven million listeners.[144] What becomes evident from their audience research is that radio audiences had become more sophisticated and independent. Over one quarter of listeners (26 per cent) were quite prepared to change stations during a broadcast, to listen either to Radio Bremen, Deutschlandfunk, Radio Luxembourg or GDR stations, while only 48 per cent did not change station (26 per cent did not listen to the radio at the time).[145]

Generally, the 1962 NDR listeners were interested in politics (73 per cent),[146] the radio being the second most important source of information (36 per cent) after newspapers (40 per cent), more sceptical of television (23 per cent).[147] The most popular time to listen to the news was 7 a.m. (39 per cent) and 7 p.m. (55 per cent), while a third of all listeners listen to the news more than once a day.[148] Out of the 73 per cent of politically interested listeners more than half (58 per cent) also enjoyed the political commentary after the evening news, while 42 per cent did not.[149] Listeners interested in politics are, according to the result of this survey, predominantly male (63 per cent),[150] listen to the radio 15 minutes longer than the average listener,[151] are well educated, of middle-class origin and look for additional information in the spoken word programmes, in addition to newspapers, although some of more frequent radio users are also the very poor and pensioners.[152]

The marginal output of the second and third programmes continued throughout the 1960s. Another audience research paper, this time from April 1970 and carried out by the EMNID Institute, Bielefeld, showed that over one-third of all NDR listeners had no idea what kind of programmes were being transmitted on the third programme and could not find the station on the radio dial.[153] But the small audience listening to the (mostly spoken word) third programme knew what it used the station for, although their preferences for programmes were, interestingly, not confined to the programmes of the NDR output, as Table 5.6 indicates.

Whereas the radio listeners invariably make their choice from what is on offer, ultimately supplied by the broadcasters, the scope of opinions offered by the general public (and reflected in opinion polls) is always more varied and diverse. In articular, qualitative assessments of 'public opinion' generate such a wealth of diffuse material that often a quantitative analysis fails to capture it.

In order to capture public attitudes towards the Nazi past and the ongoing prosecutions against the perpetrators in West Germany in the 1950s and 1960s, several publications, polls and radio programmes will be used here. There are the two above polls from the *Allensbach Institut für Demoskopie*. In addition, Friedrich Pollock's 1955 *Gruppenexperiment* is probably the most extensive early research project on this theme, combining qualitative interviews with quantitative analysis. Also published by the *Institut für Sozialforschung* in Frankfurt is the 1967 Regina Schmidt/Egon Becker book *'Reactions to Political Events'* (*Reaktionen auf politische Vorgänge*), which carries a specific section on the Eichmann and Auschwitz Trials. Further insights are offered by Margarete and Alexander Mitscherlich's controversial *'The Inability to Mourn'* (*Die Unfähigkeit*

Table 5.6 NDR radio listeners, 1970

Type of programme	Regularly listened to	Specifically NDR
News	53	43
Interviews and reportage	11	5
Commentary and reports	11	4
Practical advice and tips	5	3
Series, documentaries, discussions	4	2
Radio plays	5	3
Dialect (Plattdeutsch)	10	5
Traffic	14	4
Education (School radio)	6	5

Source: Staatsarchiv Hamburg, EMNID Institut, Bielefeld Umfrage, Hörgewohnheiten im Sendegebiet des NDR 1970; Band 3: Kommentar der Verhaltens- und Meinungsbefragung April 1970; Akte 621-1(NDR) Signatur 848, p. 43.

zu trauern), first published in 1967. Despite the many criticisms this book has received, some of the interviews in it are, even when not used in the psychoanalytic context, remarkably insightful. The Welzer/Moller/Tschuggnall study *Opa war kein Nazi* will also be used to track changes of opinion within families. Some newspaper and magazine articles and their responses at the time will allow further reflection on a wider 'public opinion', while an excerpt from the 1960 NDR radio programme 'Behind the Wall of Silence' (*Hinter der Mauer des Schweigens*) uses the 'vox pop' method to sample a random selection of the public.

While this cross-section cannot lay claim to a specific, accurate public opinion – in as much as public opinion can be considered accurate – it is hoped that by a chronological arrangement the differences (and similarities) over a period of time will become apparent and that a clearer picture of the West German public's attitude to the NS past will emerge.

The problem of assessing 'public opinion' is dealt with impressively in Pollock's *Gruppenexperiment*. In the introductory section he points out that the statistical data arrived at through opinion polls bears no resemblance to the truth of its content, so that the opinion of respondents who believe that $2 \times 2 = 5$ is just as valid as the opinion of those who believe that $2 \times 2 = 4$.[154] He further raises the points which Lazarsfeld already noted in his radio studies of the 1940s: who forms and influences this public in their opinions is not taken into account. Each opinion is one data entry, producing an unrepresentative, egalitarian picture, not allowing for uneven distribution of power and influence.[155] The 'opinion of all' and 'public opinion' Pollock equates to Rousseau's distinction between *volonté de tous* and *volonté générale*, two different entities, which in the broader public translate to a multiplicity of contradictory opinions versus the most publicised opinion.[156] The instability of individual opinion,[157] as well as the unfamiliarity[158] of the interview situation[159] are further variables which make this seeking of a 'public opinion' highly volatile. In order to minimise or to circumvent these variables, the institute's researchers decided on a group discussion format in short sessions lasting 45 minutes to an hour, modelled on (possible conversations in) a railway compartment in size and number of participants, with only very occasional interceptions from the discussion chair (*Versuchsleiter*).[160]

The examples selected here are only a very small fraction of the 600-page study, which was in turn a selection from the hundreds of hours of recordings from the approximately 1,500 participants in the Winter of 1950/51. At this particular point in time, in West Germany, the majority of the population would have had some experience of the Nazi era and the war, and thus the comments voiced can be seen as being reasonably representative. Discussion participants are only identified by a letter (presumably of their surname) and are, on the whole, only interrupted by other participants. The following appears under the heading of 'National Socialism and War', subsection 'Guilt of All':

> N.: That's all nonsense, what they're trying to blame us for, because: it is not only us who are to blame.
>
> I.: ...and I would like to say that (in reference to the recognition of the Hitler regime by the Allies) this was the encouragement, and that is why we cannot be seen as the sole instigators of the catastrophe, but just a drop of responsibility is more important to us, as somebody said so nicely, than an ocean of sympathy.[161]

Subsection 'Recognition of the social achievements of the National Socialist regime':

> B.: You had work and you had money again. Everybody was satisfied, everyone could live.
>
> U.: And apart from the war coming, a lot of good was done, wasn't it. (I) would just mention that streets were being built etc. And I have to add, everybody lived well.
>
> R.: The big majority, the big block, how we used to cheer then, and we did, I'm not denying that, and there were reasons to cheer, only the smallest part, only very few didn't have it that good. And during that time the only ones having a bad time were the ones who opposed the dictatorship, National Socialism from the start. They were having a bad time.[162]

Section 'Concentration Camps and War Crimes', subsection 'Admission':

> Z.: But all Germans knew that something was amiss there, and something had to be done about it, but nobody did. And that is what us Germans are to blame for, that I will admit.
>
> A.: In my opinion we firstly paid for this dearly but also on the whole we have managed an inner reconciliation that most of us now will admit that the German people are burdened with a guilt which will not disappear from history.

Subsection 'Conditional Calculations':

> S.: And they are guilty, they also didn't ask, they also killed women and children, didn't they?

W.: ...and besides we can prove that the Americans sanctioned the whole resettlement of the refugees from the East, from the Sudetenland, East Prussia, Pomerania. They agreed to it therefore are to be blamed for it as well. I really do not wish to know how many millions of Germans died there. They shouldn't all come with all their moralising and moaning, because they're no better themselves.

U.: He (the American) found Frankfurt, he found every house in Frankfurt, he found the children's hospital, from which I personally retrieved 146 bodies. But he didn't find the IG Hoechst (Farben). I think only one bomb fell on IG Hoechst, and that hit the casino (canteen). And the IG skyscraper he didn't find either.

S.: Well I think there is, firstly it is an exaggeration when there is talk of millions of Jews, and secondly history has already taken its revenge on the existing millions of Germans, what already has happened to them, hasn't it? Well there is – I mean, there is no need to, – there is no need to stir it up.

Subsection 'Hints at the Impossibility of Resistance'

H.: Today the Americans know for sure that we couldn't resist, once it was all set up, we couldn't resist, or open our mouths. We all know that, don't we? It was too late then, we would have been for it.

D.: You just couldn't express your opinion, because there was always the danger that the same fate would befall you.

Subsection 'Calculations'

O.: Well one was avenged with the other and what happened with the Czechs and everywhere, well that was shocking, surely that was worse than any German concentration camp; what happened in Bromberg?

P.: Why guilt? What is it with guilt? If we, on the one hand, were guilty of those concentration camps, where is the guilt of the other side, or to be more precise, what does the American tell himself, that he is to blame for all that went on here in Germany after the war, that they wanted to educate, or like the English call it democracy from below, they should eat democracy, but on the other hand they let 15 million be expelled from the East, chucked out disregarding any losses, and letting them partially starve to death;...

Z.: In my opinion there is no difference between passing an anti-communist law, depriving people of their livelihood, and virtually sentencing them to starvation, like they do in all Western democracies, or if you chase them into crematoria.

D.: Does the American have any feelings of guilt, about the damage he caused to the Germans? German cities, which he completely destroyed. No feelings of guilt about it?

Subsection 'Not Knowing':

A.: What happened there, we all didn't know.

U.: And regarding concentration camps, it is an indisputable fact that nobody in Germany knew what went on there. This cannot be ignored.

L.: The propaganda was such that we hardly knew what went on the concentration camps. We did read newspapers, but that wasn't in them.

B.: Us little people did not know about a lot of things. I did not know of concentration camps, I can say this with honesty. So nowadays you can't hold me...

G.: Yes, why were they locked up? Why were they sent to the concentration camps? Especially in the countryside less than 10 % knew about them. I believe that particularly the Germans did not know that the Jews were being killed.[163]

These initial sessions do not give the whole picture of the *Gruppenexperiment*. They do, however, show the diversity of opinion and confusion of the issues of a wide cross-section of the population, who experienced the war, recalling many of their own difficult and ambiguous feelings. The authors of the study stress that it was far from their intentions to pre-empt any results or to direct results by introducing specific themes, such as collective guilt,[164] and the above sections appear to have a logical sequence of conversation. The study also reveals, particularly in the later interviews – which take place with a greater input, or probing, from the discussion chair – a much wider knowledge of, for instance, what went on in the concentration camps, or personal experiences (witnessing) of the persecution of Jews, from inhabitants of the countryside:

Sch.: Once our neighbour had this Ukrainian and his friend staying. And he was such a good guy, truly. I worked with him a lot, in

> the field. And then he had to leave, and went somewhere else, and then he came back and said: 'oh missus, you so good, where I am now is no good, much work, little food', he says, and cold. A pair of gloves, he said. Well I gave him this and that, and a loaf of bread and off he went again. And later his friend heard about it and told me, oh my friend in Auschwitz, he said, he went through the chimney long time ago. This much I know.[165]

Or in the west end of Frankfurt:

> B.: A fine Jewish woman, she lived in – street, on the corner of – , on the first floor, she was a lawyer, and she was crying for help, from the first floor, and there were two young men, they threw her out of the window. They were dangling her by the legs and then let her go. I saw that, how she cried for help.[166]

Many of the opinions expressed, particularly in the first five or six subsections, would be considered a 'non-public opinion'; opinions which would not be considered as acceptable among the wider public, in the 'public sphere' of journalism and politics, and certainly not by any international standards. But the proximity to the war experience meant that these expressions remained commonplace.

Eight years after the *Gruppenexperiment* interviews, the journalist and TV documentary film-maker Peter Schier-Gribowsky (who, incidentally, was the ZDF television reporter at the 1961 Eichmann trial in Jerusalem) set out to sample public opinion in West Germany on the issue of the NS past. The resulting film, '*...Als wär's ein Stück von Dir*' (*As if it was a part of you*),[167] was shown at the time of the anti-Semitic attacks in Cologne and elsewhere in Autumn 1959. The NDR ran a weekly four part accompanying radio series on the making of this documentary, which featured Schier-Gribowsky in conversation with the writer Thilo Koch, entitled '*Hinter der Mauer des Schweigens*' (Behind the Wall of Silence), the first programme being broadcast on 20 February 1960, in weekly instalments. The following is a four-minute sequence in the first (and repeated in the last) programme, which features questions asked of random passers-by in a Frankfurt street, sometime in the Summer of 1959:

> Interviewer: Did you live in Germany during the Nazi times?
> Male respondent 1: Yes
> I.: What do you think, should this (time) be forgotten or should we talk about it?

M.R.1: One should talk about it, obviously, but not too much, but the young people should know about it.

I.: Thank you very much. – What do you think, should we talk about it or should we forget it?

M.R.2: No, my point of view is that we should forget it at last, so that the young people don't hear about it.

M.R.3: We should finally have the courage to forget about it.

I.: In school, did you learn something about what happened in the Nazi era?

M.R.4: Yes.

I.: Do you think one should talk about it or forget it?

M.R.4: Certainly talk about it.

I.: I thank you. And what do you think about this?

M.R.5: I am a special case, I am a Jew from Israel, visiting. I lived in Germany until 38...

I.: ...and what do you think, from your point of view, should these things be forgotten or...

M.R.5: You don't have to talk about it all the time, but it mustn't be forgotten...

Female respondent: ...I think, especially what Hitler did to the Jews, that is something, God knows, that should not be forgotten.

I.: What do you think of when you hear the word *Kristallnacht*?

M.R.6: *Kristallnacht*? A variety show.

I.: *Kristallnacht*, are you familiar with this term?

M.R.7: Yes, persecution of the Jews.

I.: Did you live in Germany during the Nazi times?

M.R.8: Yes, as a matter of fact, yes.

I.: And did you know then, did you have an idea that Jews were being killed during that time?

M.R.8: Yes, one knew. That seeped through. I lived about six kilometres from Auschwitz, much seeped through there, and we also knew – [inaudible] that it was six millions. Even if only half of that was true, I mean half of that [figure] not true, it is still terrible.

I.: In school, did you hear something about the Nazi times?

M.R.9: Yes, of course.

I.: And do you know, approximately, how many Jews were killed, back then?

M.R.9: Yes, six millions.

I.: Do you know what anti-Semitism is?

M.R.10: What's it called?

I.: Anti-Semitism.

M.R.10: Yes, I know it.
I.: And what is it, please?
M.R.10: That is one, I mean, it is against a question of race.
I.: What do you think, are there too few or too many Jews in Germany today?
M.R.11: There are too few, I would say, the Jews were always good for the economy, this impetus (?) is now lacking.
I.: Some war criminals are still imprisoned today, in Spandau. Should they be released or serve their sentence?
F.R.2: No, they should be released.
I.: War criminals who might still be at large today. Should they be persecuted or not?
F.R.2: Oh no, love thy enemy, so it says in the Bible.
I.: Thank you, I thank you.
F.R.3: You should, I mean the ones who really committed terrible atrocities, they should be punished.
I.: Do you know the name Alfred Rosenberg?
M.R.12: Yes, a Jew.
I.: Do you know the name Ludwig Zint?
F.R.4: Ludwig Zint, that's some (kind of) politician.
I.: A politician.
F.R.4: A minister – president of a *Land*.
I.: Do you know the name Alfred Rosenberg?
F.R.5: Yes, he is a well known personality. He was a big chief [*ein großes Tier*] with the Nazis.
I.: Do you perhaps know the name Ludwig Zint?
M.R.13: No, not known to me.
I.: ...and Romy Schneider? Anne Frank?
M.R.13: Yes, I know them.
I.: I thank you very much. – Could I just ask you, would it be better if Jews living in Germany stayed here or if they emigrated to Israel?
M.R.14: (They) should stay here
I.: ...and what do you think?
M.R.15: They should earn their keep here.
(Another respondent talking over/in between/ only partially audible/ sounds like 'It was stupid to have fought them' (*War'n ja auf der Pelle daß wir die bekämpft haben*))
I.: Did you learn anything about the Nazis in school?
M.R.16: I couldn't say.
I.: You haven't heard anything about it at school?
M.R.16: No, not yet.

I.: Not yet. And from parents or elsewhere?
M.R.16: No, neither.
I.: Thank you. – Would you marry a Jew?
F.R.6.: No, I wouldn't.
I.: You wouldn't. I thank you. – Would you, under certain circumstances, marry a Jew?
F.R.7.: Yes, I would.
I.: You would. – And you?
F.R.8: I would as well.
I.: Thank you. – What do you think, would it be possible today, in Germany, for a man like Hitler to come to power again?
M.R.17: Yes.
M.R.18: I think it's impossible.
I.: And you think it's possible?
M.R.17: Yes.
M.R.19: No.
I.: And you?
M.R.20: No.
I.: (You) don't think so either.
M.R.20: There is a reaction(ary force), but I don't think it is strong enough to make something like that possible.[168]

Whereas these random samples can avoid the problem of peer pressure of group discussion situations, the volatility and instability of the expressed opinions is still very much in evidence. But perhaps the difference between the 1951 and 1959 polls in opinions expressed could be described thus: The bitterness of the direct war experience has waned through economic prosperity and a seeming indifference has taken its place, although the prosecution of war criminals had, seemingly unbeknown to the above respondents, increased after the setting up of the *Zentrale Stelle* in 1958.

While the investigation for prosecutions in West Germany – and in particular the preparation for the complexities of the Auschwitz Trial – were ongoing, international attention focussed on the kidnapping, prosecution and trial in Jerusalem of Adolf Eichmann, the RSHA man who had been in charge of the transportation of Jews to the death camps. Apart from the spectacular capture and abduction of Eichmann in Argentina by the Israeli secret service MOSSAD, the newsworthiness and public debate of the Eichmann Trial really lay elsewhere, particularly in (West) Germany: on trial here were not the actual murderers, the ones who pulled the triggers or operated the gas chambers, nor the top ideologues or decision makers, but a fastidious bureaucrat. A person concerned with complying with the set quotas of deliveries, paperwork, and train timetables; the type of person who lay at the heart of the postwar West German *Wirtschaftswunder* (economic miracle). This opened up a whole set of uncomfortable questions, as is illustrated by this extract written by Robert Pendorf and published in the weekly newspaper *Die Zeit* on 21July 1961:

> All those thousands of simple policemen, soldiers, *SS – Sturm* men or whatever they were called, who had the finger on the trigger, their machine guns pointing at defenceless humans, they were, before [the war] just normal people, and astonishingly, are so again today. Some are even policemen again. [This is] Unsettling...
> Eichmann: 'Yes, Mr. President, I will give you a clear answer, as you wish. I have to admit that I view the murder of the Jews, the annihilation of the Jews as one of the most terrible crimes in human history.'
> Judge Halevi: 'This is what you think now. What did you think then?'
> Eichmann, after a few introductory sentences: '....even then I saw something unlawful, something terrible and despicable in the violent solution of the Jewish problem'. 'But', and even this long awaited confession is followed with an excuse, 'unfortunately what I did I had to – because I had been sworn to loyalty and obedience...'
> And then, triggered by another question by Judge Halevi, came the evil ending: In his innermost, admitted Eichmann, he had managed to put the blame for these crimes he recognised on his superiors, and thus found inner peace.
> This is what makes this much more terrible than a sadist here and a brutal butcher there: the uncanny human ability to degrade themselves to robots of even the most horrific things, to rid themselves of what makes them human, namely to take responsibility for their own actions. And this can happen to us anywhere and any day. This is the bitter lesson of this trial.[169]

The Düsseldorfer *Rheinische Post* warned, in its editorial of 29 July 1961, of this shirking of responsibility. Urging 'the big organisations of the state, the economy and of political parties' to abandon the search for the most loyal employees and instead to look for 'the functionary with heart and education' (*Funktionär mit Herz und Bildung*), it comments:

No, it was not 'his responsibility': not the march of death in Hungary, not the persecution of the children of Lidice, not the 'Final Solution'. The fact that he was 'unable' to order the genocide has become clear now, after his cross-examination. But here before the court stood a man who had become a criminal through standing to attention, through saying 'yes', a militarist of the worst kind, who would get barked at by his superiors, a man without civil courage, bowing and scraping to all he deemed responsible, even when their crimes were obvious. Just like Eichmann, he would relinquish responsibility by shrugging his shoulders and tell himself: An order is an order...

The Eichmann case has, as shocking as this might sound, already reached a verdict for the German people, even before sentence has been passed. Because there are many Eichmanns among us. This trial in Jerusalem has been an eye-opener for many citizens, to expose this type of human. It showed, how insignificant and feeble-minded these [types of] people are, but also how huge and catastrophic their actions can be. [We] all are responsible for setting them limits, for teaching them civil courage, as well as being responsible for alleviating the unimaginable suffering caused to the Jewish people.[170]

Many other publications at the time engaged, not only with the topic of the Nazi past, but also with the problematic of the 'desk-perpetrators' (*Schreibtischtäter*). Particularly the *Frankfurter Allgemeine Zeitung* urged its readers to exercise resolution and clarity towards the younger generation in order to 'find hope in the sins and misfortunes of their fathers', so that history could not repeat the horrors of the past.[171]

But much of the Eichmann Trial coverage, as extensive as it was at the time, owed its volume and ferocity to outside, that is to say international news reporting and pressure. It is quite possible that the newspaper editors and press agencies had their eye on international responses, aware that other nations were curious to see how his trial reflected itself in the West German media. International opinion polls, carried out during this time by the Gallup group of pollsters in the UK, US, Switzerland and the FRG seem to confirm this (see Table 5.7).

And a broader question, asked by the EMNID Institute in Bielefeld on 17 June 1961, to respondents in the same countries, yielded the answers seen in Table 5.8.

Again it was left to the *Institut für Sozialforschung* in Frankfurt under the direction of Theodor W. Adorno to deal with the more complicated and difficult issues surrounding the West German public. At

Table 5.7 'Which of the following do you consider the correct action by the government of Israel?'

	UK (%)	USA (%)	Switzerland (%)	FRG (%)
Trial in Israel	44	44	53	28
Trial in Germany	3	6	3	25
International Court	32	31	36	32
Acquittal	4	1	2	4
No opinion	17	18*	6	11

* 13% have never heard of the Eichmann Trial.
Source: 'Deutsche und Weltmeinung über den Eichmann Prozess' in: Hans Lamm (ed.), Der Eichmann Prozess, p. 71.

Table 5.8 'In your opinion, do you think it is a good thing or a bad thing that the world is reminded of the horrors of the National Socialist concentration camps?'

	UK (%)	USA (%)	Switzerland (%)	FRG (%)
Good	56	62	70	34
Bad	29	18	19	45
No opinion	15	20*	11	21

* 13 % have never heard of the Eichmann Trial.
Source: Hans Lamm (ed.), Der Eichmann Prozess, p. 72.

the time of the Eichmann Trial interest in the issue of prosecuting Nazi war criminals was relatively high. The Institute's 1966 publication 'Reactions to Political Events' (*Reaktionen auf politische Vorgänge*), which carries a section on the Eichmann Trial, puts the public interest in the court's proceedings at the beginning of the trial in 1961 at around 90 per cent,[172] a figure which was only equalled (in terms of public interest) by the launching of the first satellite *Sputnik* in 1958. The authors claim that an actual engaging with the issues, nevertheless, did not take place. Only about 15 per cent of the population (respondents) kept up with the proceedings in Jerusalem,[173] while at the same time about 75 per cent claimed to have read two or three articles in the newspapers. The issues at stake, however, were far from being understood, and a selective processing of the topics arising took place among West Germans. Schmidt and Becker point to the fact that when asked (in an IfD poll), a number of respondents – around one in 12 – agreed with the statement that Eichmann had been just a 'minor recipient of orders' (*ein kleiner Befehlsempfänger*), whereas the majority said it could not comment on this issue. Only 25 per cent disagreed with the statement.[174] This is taken as evidence that most West Germans viewed Eichmann's – and their own – actions during the Nazi dictatorship in terms of having acted under orders, and that resistance was impossible, the argument put forward by Eichmann's defence counsel, Dr Servatius.

When viewed in the context of Adorno's 1959 essay 'What Does Working Through the Past Mean?', in which he sees the postwar German public as possessing a 'damaged collective narcissism, which is waiting to be repaired, which grasps at anything that will bring the knowledge of the past into agreement with the (individual) narcissistic wishes',[175] then, so the authors argue, whether Eichmann was just obeying orders or was personally responsible became interchangeable in the opinion of the respondents.[176]

The study also points out that, unlike the Auschwitz Trial, where there were numerous accused, the Eichmann Trial benefited from the fact that only one person was in the dock, that one person was sentenced and executed, and thereby the matter was closed. This is evidenced by the much lower percentage of public interest in the Auschwitz Trial, three years later. At the beginning of the Eichmann Trial, in 1961, 95 per cent of persons questioned knew of it occurring, at the beginning of the Auschwitz Trial, in December 1963, only 60 per cent of respondents had heard of it. After six months of proceedings in Frankfurt, in 1964, only 40 per cent of respondents were still aware that the trial was taking place.[177]

While there was still a clear majority in favour of prosecutions in 1961,[178] this looked very different during the Auschwitz Trial. The frequently mentioned 'certain tiredness' with NS trials is reflected in the poll from 1964 (carried out by the DIVO *Pressedienst*) (see Table 5.9).

The report further questions the often-repeated argument that the Auschwitz Trial lost the interest of the public because of its length and the waning of press reporting. The authors rather view the lack of interest as a (unconscious) response to the nature of the details emerging from the court proceedings and not wanting to identify with them:

> The fact that the lack of interest in the prosecution of national socialist crimes in the courts has increased in the German population, must have specific causes: unlike the court proceedings in Jerusalem, the Auschwitz Trial did not take place a long distance away; no foreign nation made someone responsible for the murder of its inhabitants.

Table 5.9 Persons who have heard of the Auschwitz Trial (1159)

Are of the opinion	%
I think it is right to have these trials of mass murderers from the NS times today, so that the German public can learn about horrors and suffering committed by Germans.	17
I think it is right that these trials are happening today, so the ones guilty of mass murder in Auschwitz will be sentenced and punished.	36
I think it would be better to do without these trials, after so many years, it's better not to stir things up.	39
Other opinion	5
Don't know	3

Source: Schmidt and Becker, *Reaktionen auf Politische Vorgänge*, p. 116.

Former National Socialists were being sentenced for their crimes, here in Germany, in front of a German court. This made the realising of the wish of not wanting to identify with horrors that had occurred difficult. 'This wish displaces the read, heard or watched information about the Auschwitz Trial into the unconscious – after a while it ceases to exist and appears never to have existed.'[179]

The 'conscious' effort to displace information of NS prosecutions came in the form of calls for a statute of limitations (*Verjährung*) to be introduced for wartime manslaughter and murder, or just to 'draw a line under it all' (*Schlußstrich*) from many. The reasons given from this last group are also quite astonishing. 196 persons who professed to the *Schlußstrich* attitude were asked why they wanted to draw a line under the issue (see Table 5.10).

In the light of such findings it is not difficult to understand the reasons for the psychoanalytical approach adopted by the Mitscherlichs in their 1967 publication *The Inability to Mourn* (*Die Unfähigkeit zu trauern*). By concentrating on the so-called 'HJ' (Hitler Youth) generation, Margarete and Alexander Mitscherlich identified a part of the population who were not only deeply affected by their experience of the dictatorship in their pubescent teens, but were now, in the 1960s, in positions of authority and influence.

Through tearing the child out of traditional identification models, National Socialist ideology devalued the authority of the father and family, by an oath of loyalty to the *Führer*, disturbing the development with

Table 5.10 'Why do you want to draw a line under it all? Please indicate with this list' (multiple answers possible)

Because the others have also committed war crimes, and they are not being prosecuted	66
Because we Germans have to stop fouling our nest	57
Because too much time has passed and it is impossible for the courts to establish guilt without reasonable doubt	54
Because the law sets the statute of limitations at 20 years and you cannot deviate from this	40
Because you should have pity for the Nazi criminals	6
Other or no answer	2

Source: Schmidt and Becker, *Reaktionen auf Politische Vorgänge*, p. 118.

the standard oedipal conflict of the pubescent child.[180] In a traditional family setting, the growing child would switch from seeing the parent of the opposite sex as a (sexual) rival to a greater identification with the parent of the same sex. But particularly this last development is disturbed by a totalitarian dictatorship, where the identification with the leader, the infallible leader, will make identification with the parent of the same sex impossible. This pushes the development of the teenager back into the phase of oedipal conflict, arousing strong feelings of envy and particularly jealousy.[181] These feelings were (unknowingly) utilised by the National Socialists by presenting the 'single man' Hitler, exclusively there for his people, for his children, his brother, his sister, projecting the envy and aggression towards the parental part of the family. A further bond was created through party organisations:

> Identification with peer groups corresponded with the genuine desire of the adolescent for mutual identification in the formation of groups associated with the *Führerkult*, like the HJ, BDM etc. This interchangeable identification strengthened the young people's rejection of, or at least confrontation with, traditional ideals. During this time it (even) met with the blind agreement of the parents. A strong stimulus for group identification was created though a mass idol like Hitler, who put the world values of the parents in the shade to dictate his own. The possibilities to influence the young were cleverly manipulated in the Third Reich. The stabilising of national socialist world values was simultaneously achieved by idealising the person of Hitler: If you adore the *Führer*, you are a good person. If you are a good person, you too can be adored as part of the group, in which all are equally good.[182]

After the end of the war this generation in particular had difficulties adjusting, managing only through *infantile self-idealisation* and repression to cope with the loss of their values.[183] This generation, along with the one born towards the end of the Nazi dictatorship and the war, subsequently had a very different attitude towards their elders and parents. The 'sins of the fathers' were so colossal that it seemed impossible to make any return to a traditional model of family authority.[184] Instead, the younger generation rebelled against 'unworthy' opponents (fathers) who could not present meaningful values to them, only material prosperity, the fears of the Cold War, and a government representing values of the previous century (as expressed in some of the programmes mentioned above). This turned the majority of young West Germans into a type, referred to by the Mitscherlichs, as 'identity-shy' (*Identifikationsscheu*), an opposite of the traditional youth, not searching for new models of identification, with a prolonged pubescent phase and an eternal conflict with authority. This type of person is not looking for new experiences, only trying to amass material security and never really breaking the bond with the (very little respected) parents.[185]

The (abovementioned) reactions of the public to the Auschwitz Trial confirm this picture. The resulting indifference towards a meaningful engagement with the Nazi past is also reflected in later opinion polls, such as the *IfD Allensbach* report from April 1995. 'Progressive indifference' seems to sum up the opinion towards the soldiers of the Second World War (see Table 5.11).

Also historical details appear to be fading with only 40 per cent of respondents (in May 1985) knowing that large number of Germans voted for Hitler, 28 per cent disagreeing and 32 per cent indifferent/not knowing. In 1990 this last figure had risen to 34 per cent.[186]

And this brings the survey of opinion polls and public opinion to an interesting phenomenon, namely the slowly changing memory, particularly the family memory, in favour of a more 'bearable' past, as

Table 5.11 How do you view the German soldiers in the Second World War?

	16–34 yrs	35–59 yrs	60 and older
With admiration	28	40	58
Indifference	43	31	18
Negatively	20	18	16
No answer	9	11	8

Source: Institut für Demoskopie Allensbach, Allensbach, Archive no. 5514, IfD Umfrage 6014, Tabelle 13.

exemplified in the abovementioned study *Opa war kein Nazi* (*Grandpa was no Nazi*), the very title already expressing the continuation of an active repression of the realities of the Hitler dictatorship. The authors continuously manage, by constant and clever probing, to uncover such stories within the family setting, where, through the passing of time, the 'identity-shy' family members, now more reconciled with their parents, are starting to believe their parents' claim that they had not been 'Nazis', or that conditions were such that they had to join the party or party organisations.

One such example is a certain Frau Brach (born 1912), who clearly distinguishes between 'the Nazis' and 'us', as well as 'the Jews', but insists that her husband was not 'a Nazi' despite having joined the SA (in order to get work).[187] Nor, apparently, was an acquaintance of her husband's, who, on home leave while serving as a soldier in Poland, brought with him some photographs:

> And there the Jews. Well he took snaps of it, the Jews had to dig their own graves. Completely, full. And then they were in it. And they shot them and [them] in it... But what could we have done, what could they have done, if they would have said anything, they would have hanged us immediately, the Nazis.[188]

But a stereotypical portrayal of the 'rich Jews', and, more importantly, a clear distinction between Germans and Jews, was transmitted through the generations unscathed, as told by Birgit Roth (born 1939):

> I don't know why they wanted to get rid of the Jews, Jews were actually the best business people, had the biggest part [of business] back then, didn't they. Big stores everywhere and the Germans worked in them.[189]

The younger generations are even less interested in the detail; Nina Jung, born in 1975, can only recall that her grandmother told her that during that time 'the Jewish girls were disappearing from school'.[190] Equally the younger generation tended to believe their parents' or grandparents' claims that nobody knew anything. Maria Schulze (born 1947) stated that her mother told her that the media was different. 'Today you have television, it didn't exist then'.[191] And Sylvia Hoffmann, born 1972, said:

> Well starting with Grandma, her line was 'I didn't hear of anything' and 'us here in the countryside didn't know' and the like. And I think that she is honest about it, because there was no media.[192]

This 'cumulative glorification' (*kumulative Heroisierung*),[193] as the authors term it, reaches quite astonishing proportions when viewed as quantitative data. Olaf Jensen, one of the contributors to the *Opa war kein Nazi* investigations, researched this issue further. In his sample of 40 family interviews he found that a significant majority of respondents born between 1964 and 1973 (65 to 71 percent, depending upon their educational background) was of the opinion that their parents or grandparents suffered under National Socialism, but were equally convinced (63 per cent) that their elders had enjoyed the NS community (*Volksgemeinschaft*).[194] Jensen adds:

> It is [therefore] surprising that 35 per cent of respondents ascribe a *distancing* from the regime to their relative ('If possible did not participate') – dominant here is the 'child generation' of the respondents aged between 40 and 60 (41–44 per cent) – even more surprising are the 26 per cent of respondents who believe that their parents or grandparents 'helped persecuted persons'. If calculated on the population of nearly 70 million 'national comrades' (*Volksgenossen*) at the time, one would arrive at a figure of close to 20 million people who assisted victims of National Socialism. With 40–49 year olds (1954–1963) this figure is as high as 33 percent, icompared with 25 per cent for the 30–39 year olds (1964–1973). This estimation also rises according to educational background. An oppositional stance ('always opened their mouths') is named by 17 per cent, and resistance ('did actively resist') by 13 per cent.[195]

While these kinds of impressions of relatives and family are perhaps not so surprising, precisely because they are expressed within the somewhat subversive and subjective family environment, some profound changes must have occurred in the narration of the Nazi dictatorship, as first encountered in the respondents of the *Gruppenexperiment*. This mediation of narrative structures and frames did most likely occur through the wider community, and most definitely through the media. How could this process have worked?

Radio: making memory usable

Kansteiner's distinction between 'memory makers' and 'memory users' is again very useful in this context. Whereas in the above examples the makers and users are within the same family, the distance between radio programme and listener is somewhat more pronounced and possibly involves a greater deference to the speaker. But while confrontations within a family are, on the whole, avoided (hence the favourable views), the radio journalist or commentator can challenge the listener relatively easily, pointing to norm violations in order to fulfil their function of 'the maintenance and reproduction of morality'.[196]

In the German case, however, the broadcaster's task was the establishment of a new morality, the memory maker asserting new ethical standards, in order to make the memory of the NS dictatorship usable. The effect this had within the private sphere of the family, as can be ascertained from the above, is that the stories changed according to the 'new' morality and degrees of family harmony. Within wider society, however, this process is far from simple and the media appears to have an almost paradoxical role. The above mentioned facts, such as the listener's inability to remember the radio news, or the 'cognitive slippage' occurring when attempting to recount a radio programme, are all essential parts within the system of the mass dissemination of information. Luhmann explains it as follows:

> The mass media may not have an exclusive claim on constructing reality. After all, every communication contributes to constructing reality in what it takes up and what it leaves to forgetting. However, the involvement of the mass media is indispensable when the point at issue is widespread dissemination and the possibility of anonymous and thus unpredictable uptake. As paradoxical as it may sound, this means not least, when it is a matter of generating *non-transparency* in reactions to this uptake. The effect if not the function of the mass media seems to lie, therefore, in the reproduction of *non-transparency of effects* through the *transparency of knowledge*.[197]

Anonymous and unpredictable uptake is particularly evident with the radio, as often listening is a 'secondary' or accidental activity, but, as Andrew Crissell points out, the effects might be more evident:

> It may be precisely because it is ignored that radio is capable of strong effects, that its content can infiltrate the listener just because [his or] her conscious faculties are primarily engaged elsewhere and her defences therefore down. This is a plausible challenge to the conventional view that the most influential media are the visual ones: there seem good reasons for arguing the opposite, that they are more resistible for being perceived consciously and being conceived 'out there', as separate from the events of our own lives.[198]

Therefore, attempts precisely to measure the 'effects' of radio programmes will remain an impossible task. But from the above studies of the efforts of the broadcasters – the memory makers – and their audiences – the memory users – of the 1960s divided Germany some conclusions can be drawn.

The prescribed party line of the East German radio stations' output did not necessarily challenge the listener. While there remained the task of setting new ethical standards and new ideological paradigms, agreement was all that was required from the listener; East Germany was a country of resistance fighters that had 'cleansed' itself of Nazis after the war. While the memory users had to adjust their reminiscences to the new order, no personal reflection was needed for this. Undoubtedly, there was a certain level of genuine engagement from journalists and audience, and through this anti-fascist stance, particularly in the 1960s, support for the regime. What also emerges from the family interviews above is that East Germans who had lived through the war readily, if somewhat sceptically, accepted this new reality. Challenges only came in the form of gruesome and emotional accounts of wartime atrocities, radio was at its most ineffective and outdated, but the listeners' wartime memory was usable again, because, to use Eggebrecht's distinction, the past had been 'tamed'.

For the West German broadcasters, this process of 'making memory usable' was far more complex and had very unpredictable results. At the time of the period of reportage from the Auschwitz Trial, as indicated through the opinion polls and interviews above, a precise recollection of events was distinctly unwelcome, an 'infantile self-idealism' and repression were preferred to critical self-examination.

The 'talking cure' of continuous critical engagement with the radio journalists and commentators (what Luhmann would refer to as 'a transparency of knowledge') produced a type of therapy the outcome of which was unknown (a non-transparency of effects). The known (and conscious) responses at the time were unfavourable. Eggebrecht's pessimism and the results of opinion polls are proof of a distinct resistance to this type of therapy. The process of 'working through the past' (rather than 'coming-to-terms-with' it, or 'taming' it) was aided by a younger generation's curiosity, which, however, often would not, and could not, comprehend their parents' deeds and experiences. Nowhere more so than in West Germany did the student unrest of the late 1960s produce such a clear and wide generation gap – at one of the extremes stood the terrorist action of the RAF (Baader-Meinhof) and at the other a resurgence of Nazism. But even when this process could have been deemed successful, that is to say, when the radio programmes achieved a meaningful working through the past, the picture which emerges in the newer studies still points to perpetrators for ever being 'the other' (as the title 'Grandpa was no Nazi' suggests) and a 'cumulative glorification'; or, and this has been noted since the 1950s, the 'infantile self-idealism' manifests itself through a 'conspicuous public chest-beating'. While both of these manifestations imply a clear acceptance of universal (liberal-democratic) ethical standards, doubts still remain.

6
Radio and History

A return to the *Deutsche Welle* programme

Tadeusz Paczula ends the *Deutsche Welle* programme *Das Lager* significantly with the sentence: 'It is the same but yet it is not the same'.[1] In this instance he is referring to the way the Auschwitz Memorial site appears to him today, but this is also a phrase that could be used in the context of the Auschwitz Trials and the various NS prosecutions which occurred in the 1960s. Yet another Nazi crimes trial, reported on the radio, but there is a distinct difference: In the early part of the decade, the radio programmes dealing with his topic had been, in the case of transmissions from the GDR, full of indignation and outrage, or, as was the case for the West German programmes, critical but somewhat stilted. Now, in 1968, *Das Lager* presents the trial from Frankfurt as something rather everyday in the Federal Republic, aired (internationally) on the *Deutsche Welle* as an example of a common occurrence in Germany: this is how we live today.

But is it? Has such a profound change taken place within such a brief period of time? If so, how? In order to answer these questions, the Third Auschwitz Trial, the trial against the Kapos Bonitz and Windeck needs to be looked at more closely.

The so-called 'Third Auschwitz Trial' took place from 30 August 1967 to 14 June 1968 in Frankfurt amid very little publicity and no public interest, and was a prosecution of two of the concentration camp inmates, Josef Windeck and Bernhard Bonitz, who were Kapos in Auschwitz. These two German small-time criminals had been moved to the concentration camp after the completion of their prison sentence, into 'protective custody' (*Schutzhaft*), and were given favoured positions, in charge of a group of prisoners or work detail, fulfilling some guard and/or

SS duties, in return for food, alcohol, cigarettes and other privileges. The precarious position of Kapo was just one of the many functions in the carefully worked-out hierarchy of the prisoner self-administration (*Häftlingsselbstverwaltung*), used by the SS to 'divide and rule' the concentration camp population. Heinrich Himmler, *Reichsführer SS*, offered this definition of the functions of the Kapos (from the view of the SS) to the generals of the Wehrmacht in Sonthofen, on 21 June 1944:

> Okay, so one man is the responsible supervisor, I mean to say chief, with power over 30, 40, over 100 other prisoners. Once he becomes Kapo, he no longer sleeps together with them. It's his responsibility to see that they reach the performance target, that there are no acts of sabotage, that the men are clean, and their beds made according to regulations... A fresh recruit in a military barracks can't be any neater and more thorough than what is expected here. And the Kapo has responsibility for this. So he has to push his men. The moment we're not satisfied with him, he's no longer a Kapo, and he goes back to sleep with his men. But he knows full well that he'll be murdered by them the first night. The Kapo receives certain advantages. I do not have to – and let me reiterate this point – establish a welfare state here, but I have to remove the subhuman from the German streets and harness him for victory. This is our mission, and it will be carried out.[2]

The highly complex 'prisoner self-administration' had been set up in the concentration camps to minimise resistance, to save on SS personnel and to ensure order. The chief (or camp) Kapo was usually responsible for Kapos in charge of the work details (*Kommandos*), themselves divided between head-Kapo and sub-Kapos. Within the camp the camp elder (*Lagerälteste*) held most power, within one barrack (or 'block') or living quarter it was the block elder (*Blockältester*). All these competing positions were appointed by the SS, but some other minor, but nevertheless important privileged position such as the room-scribe (*Stubenschreiber*) could be selected by the Kapo or *Blockältester*.[3] After 1936, with the introduction of 'protective custody' for prisoners who had served their sentence, prisoner-functionary roles were usually allocated to 'professional criminals' (*Berufsverbrecher* or *BV*), identifiable by their green triangle.[4] The power of the Kapos was enormous. Levi writes:

> But the power of which the functionaries of whom we are speaking disposed, even if they were low-ranking such as the *Kapos* of

work-squads, was, in substance, unlimited; or, more accurately put, a lower limit on their violence, in the sense that they were punished or deposed if they did not prove to be sufficiently harsh, but there was no upper limit. In other words, they were free to commit the worst atrocities on their subjects for any transgressions, or even without any motive whatsoever. Until the end of 1943 it was not unusual for a prisoner [in Auschwitz] to be beaten to death by a *Kapo*, without the latter having any fear of sanctions.[5]

During the initial postwar period trials of Kapos were common, and they were dealt with harshly. Many of the known Kapos in the camps of Dachau, Mauthausen and Flossenburg were sentenced to death,[6] as were some of the Jewish Kapos, later, at the time of the Eichmann Trial in Jerusalem.[7] During the liberation of the camps such as Auschwitz and Bergen-Belsen many Kapos were summarily executed or lynched. In many ways they were deemed beneath contempt, dangerous and 'untrustworthy by definition: they betrayed once and they can betray again'.[8] Nevertheless trials of Kapos in the immediate postwar era were rare. Niethammer cites 149 prominent Buchenwald inmates, among them 29 Kapos, of whom three were prosecuted.[9]

In Israel a series of Kapo trials occurred between 1951 and 1964, conducted under the Israeli *Nazi and Nazi Collaborators Punishment Law* (1950), with about 30–40 prosecutions.[10] Details of the trials are vague as the files have been sealed by a 1995 order for 70 years from the date the judgements were rendered.[11] From the little information that is available about these court proceedings, it can be gathered that sentences were lenient: in 26 (out of 38) trials there were 11 acquittals and 15 sentences of imprisonment.[12] The judges' uneasiness to use the law to its full extent (which includes the death sentence), indeed the judges' discomfort with, even dislike of and often alienation from these 'grey cases',[13] resulted in mild sentences and guarantees of anonymity. It appears that in Israel, at least, the Kapo issue, which poses 'an incredibly complicated internal structure and contains within itself enough to confuse our need to judge' (Levi), was dealt with using due care and consideration.

Ulrich-Dieter Oppitz comments on the West German verdicts and subsequent gaol terms of the 1950s: by 1958 the percentage of former concentration camp inmates among those convicted to life imprisonment is relatively high (4 out of 59 – 8 per cent); but higher still is the percentage of those still imprisoned in 1973 (2 out of 6 – 33 per cent).[14] 'The only remaining former inmate still incarcerated in 1976 had by this point spent 27 years in prison and as such was the longest serving prisoner of all Nazi criminals.'[15]

But not all Kapos had been collaborators and not all had been feared and hated by the rest of the concentration camp prisoners, as is shown by the astounding case of the Buchenwald camp (near Weimar). Here, in a camp with (initially) predominantly political prisoners, many of the inmates were KPD members who had managed to form clandestine committees and underground organisations. This led to the decision that party members should accept the positions of Kapo or block elder or other positions of influence, in order to alleviate the suffering of their comrades. Nevertheless, the role of Kapo in a concentration camp always involved violence and some mistreatment of others in the zero-sum set-up of absolute power of the SS terror. By the time the Americans arrived at Buchenwald, the camp was completely under the control of the prisoners, the SS had either fled or been overpowered. The initial report of the US investigation commission, led by Egon W. Fleck and Edward A. Tenenbaum, noted the following on 14 April 1945 – a week after liberation:

> This report is sensational in many ways. It tells of a concentration camp within a concentration camp, of a terror machine within a terror machine, of a Communist dictatorship in a Nazi extermination centre. It is, unfortunately, not the result of detailed investigation, since sufficient time was not available for the undersigned to check many important points. It should, therefore, perhaps be considered as an indictment rather than a sentence.[16]

Although this 'indictment' was later removed from the published version of the Buchenwald Report,[17] its sentiment became symptomatic not only of the discourse around the role of Kapos in concentration camps, but of the ideologically-laden interpretations of the Nazi dictatorship in general during the 1960s. The criminality of the Kapos' actions in Buchenwald had very little to do with the nature of the enquiries which were taking place in the GDR after the war. 'Doing away with' (*abfertigen*) was quite readily admitted by the members of the Buchenwald Central Committee (of former communist inmates), as well as influencing selections and phenol injections.[18] 'Discipline' was ruthlessly enforced by the 'red' Kapos and the 'camp police' (*Lagerschutz* – manned by inmates) in Buchenwald and most 'liquidations' carried out by *Kapos* were decisions reached by the clandestine 'Central Committee'. The charges which sent the *Kapos* Busse and Reschke to the Gulag were more concerned with their 'political reliability', the treatment of Soviet POWs in Buchenwald and visits to the camp brothel.[19] The subsequent rehabilitation of both men in 1956 (Busse died in 1952) can be viewed as evidence that their convictions were politically conditioned in the era of high Stalinism.

The Buchenwald Report, which was prepared by a special intelligence team of the US Psychological Warfare Division with the aid of prominent former inmates such as Eugen Kogon, found that after 1937 most Kapo positions in the camp were held by German communists, who managed, in a combination of iron discipline and cunning, to exploit the corruption and increasing complacency of the SS as the war progressed. This, in turn, led to a mythologizing of the communist Kapo leadership in later times in the GDR – the much-hailed self-liberation of the camp by inmates had actually been an ordered handing over of control by the camp commander to the chief Kapo.

For the GDR, at least officially, the continued and organised resistance of communists in the Buchenwald camp was at the heart of the doctrine of East German anti-fascism, but the struggle within the KPD (later SED) continued between the former inmates of Buchenwald (the so-called Buchenwald ZK) and the returnees from Moscow (Ulbricht Group). By the 1960s the Buchenwald memorial site had become a point of pilgrimage for all young East Germans and symbolised the anti-fascist credentials of the GDR.

Within this context the Committee of Anti-fascist Resistance Fighters in the GDR (*Komitee der antifaschistischen Widerstandskämpfer in der DDR*) and the National Council of the National Front for the democratic Germany (*Nationalrat der Nationalen Front des demokratischen Deutschland*) issued a pamphlet in 1968 entitled 'Auschwitz cautions' (*Auschwitz mahnt*) – with the subtitle 'Statement on the trial against Windeck and Bonitz in Frankfurt/Main by former political prisoners of the concentration camp Auschwitz in the GDR'.[20] This publication, aimed at a West German audience and published towards the end of the trial (possibly in May 1968), combines the standard GDR political propaganda argumentation of monopoly capitalism being the cause of fascism and the Nazi terror with fairly dubious Photostat copies of correspondence between industrialists and SS and explanations of the camp system. It nevertheless asks some pertinent, if not necessarily relevant questions surrounding this trial. When dealing with the function of the Kapo, it points heavily in the direction of the exceptional circumstances of Buchenwald:

> In as much as the prisoners were, on the whole, at the mercy of the SS camp leadership, within the form of these functions [of Kapos]

there nevertheless existed many an opportunity to alleviate the terror, by a just distribution of food rations, of footwear and clothing or by improving standards of hygiene. In some camps these positions were even used to organise escapes for some of the prisoners or even the liberation of the whole camp.[21]

The brochure does not detract from the crimes of the accused. The 189 cases of murder of which Bonitz and Windeck are accused are, in the view of the authors, an underestimation.[22] But it points to the problems of the legal restrictions the West German court had to operate under, namely that since the abandoning of *Kontrollratsgesetz Nr. 10* in 1955, a prosecution of the 'real' culprits, that is to say of organisations and corporate bodies which set up the concentration camp system and enabled it to function, were beyond the reach of the law. It states:

> In the reporting – particularly in the West German press, there is talk of the '3rd Auschwitz Trial'. We deem this description as misleading. It attempts to create the impression that this [trial] is the logical continuation of the two previous Auschwitz Trials which took place earlier, here in Frankfurt. We would like to point out that in the first two Auschwitz Trials the GDR resident and representative of the adjunct prosecution (*Nebenkläger*) Prof. Dr Kaul had presented proof that the accused did not break the law in the conventional way but were guilty of crimes against humanity. They belonged to an intricately networked gang of murderers and knowingly and willingly put themselves at the disposal of the Nazi extermination machine.
>
> Knowingly and willingly they took part in the mass murder of Soviet prisoners of war, of civilians of the occupied countries, in the industrial scale complete annihilation of whole sections of the population of various nations, especially Jews. Their actions contravened the most basic principles of human existence, they committed genocide.[23]

Windeck and Bonitz were, so the pamphlet states, only the last links in the chain of command which enabled this genocide, and the 'intellectual initiators and desk-murderers' (*Schreibtischmörder*) and particularly their accomplices in industry, the civil service and high society are back, unpunished, in their prominent positions in today's West Germany.[24]

The East German prosecutor Kaul had attempted to get the Court to accept evidence which could have pointed to a charge of 'corporate murder' or manslaughter, but under West German law this was inadmissible. Only Allied military courts could try charges of genocide and belonging to a criminal (state) organisation. In the GDR the USSR still upheld this right whereas in the Western zones, after 1955, this was considered a legal impossibility. The complicity of business conglomerates in the industrial complexes around Auschwitz had been highlighted in the '2nd Auschwitz Trial' (14 December 1965–16 September 1966) through the prosecution of camp personnel who had been in charge of obtaining the *Zyklon B* gas used in the gas chambers. Despite the obvious links to a greater collusion between the concentration camp and the I.G. Farben conglomerate, only prosecution of individuals could proceed.[25] A further trial against I.G. Farben, also held in Frankfurt, collapsed in 1966.[26]

The prosecution of the Kapos Windeck and Bonitz was, of course, a different matter. It could only go ahead on the premise of the individual acts of murder which could, with the aid of witnesses and other material, be ascribed directly to them, but nevertheless the GDR attempted to influence proceedings by pointing to the complicity of industry and 'monopoly capitalism'.

The judgement of the trial, a 180-page document, is extremely detailed, consisting of two categories, unequal in length, of eight sections each.[27] Category A deals with the general conditions of the camp, its history, background and the background of the accused, Section B – which is much more substantive – elaborates on the specific accusations, witness statements and the judicial reasoning which led to the convictions. Whereas some of the general remarks in section A are recognisable work from previous cases, and had been compiled by historians,[28] it is noticeable that many of the general findings concerning the camp are augmented by over a hundred witness (and the accused) statements.[29] The details which emerge from the judgement present a valuable insight into the changing attitudes within the West German judiciary, brought about, no doubt, by the continuing engagement of the media (and their international observers).

The details of the accused are as follows:

Heinrich Bernard Bonitz was born in 1907 in Chemnitz, where he attended school up to the age of 14. He became an apprentice baker, qualifying three years later and working in his profession and other jobs. In 1926 he moved to Berlin where he married in 1933. By 1936 he had been convicted 12 times for various crimes and misdemeanours ranging from theft to safe-cracking. In March 1937, whilst working on a building site, he was taken into 'protective custody' and taken to the concentration camp at Sachsenhausen (near Berlin), classified as a 'professional criminal' (*Berufsverbrecher*) and given a green triangle. There he was given responsibilities as block elder and barrack duty.[30]

In May 1940 Bonitz was transferred, together with an additional 29 prisoners, to Auschwitz, the first to arrive there as 'foremen', in charge of Jewish citizens of Oświęcim (Auschwitz), who were building the camp. As 'privileged prisoners' (*Vorzugshäftlinge*) these first thirty all had their own rooms and lacked little in the way of home comforts. He worked in various commandos in various locations in and around the camp, including as Kapo in the building commando of the Birkenau extermination camp and in the tannery and leather factory, where he was chief Kapo. During this time he served two short spells in solitary confinement (in the so-called 'Bunker'), once for obtaining toys for a Polish mother and on another occasion for smuggling out gold and currency. During his interrogations by the notorious SS-*Unterscharführer* Grabner of the camp Gestapo he was, so he stated, 'treated decently'.[31]

By June 1944 Bonitz had volunteered to join the infamous 'Dirlewanger' Waffen SS unit, a notorious and brutal unit made up of desperadoes, former camp inmates and lower SS ranks. Before the end of the war he left the unit and returned to Berlin, where he worked as a car mechanic and metal worker until his arrest in May 1966.[32]

The crimes Bonitz was accused of ranged from grievous bodily harm to murder. In 1965 a law had been passed in West Germany which limited the prosecution of crimes committed during the Third Reich with premeditated attempted or completed murder (or any crime which carried a life sentence) being the only ones which could still be prosecuted after a period of 20 years.[33] This 'statute of limitations' had to be considered in many of the cases of which Bonitz and Windeck were accused, and even if the court found them guilty, a sentence could not be passed.

Bonitz was accused of at least 72 counts of murder, for nine of which he was pronounced guilty of having inflicted grievous bodily harm, but could not be sentenced.[34] Only in one instance did the court heard convincing, multiple evidence of a particular killing and Bonitz was found guilty of murder and sentenced to life imprisonment.[35]

In the case against Windeck the following facts emerged:

Josef Joachim Windeck was born in 1903 in Rheydt /Rhineland as one of 17 children. As a child he suffered from TB but otherwise had average schooling. After the age of 14 he left school to accompany his father to work on a building site and from then on remained an unskilled labourer, often unemployed until about 1933. He married in 1927. He had been in and out of prison for various small offences since 1920 and in 1936 was interned in the concentration camp of Esterwegen-Papenhausen. He was released and re-arrested shortly thereafter for the theft, as well as for resisting arrest.[36] At the high court in Mönchen-Gladbach he was sentenced to two years hard labour, but when he was due to be released at the end of his sentence he was taken into police custody in Düsseldorf and transferred to the Sachsenhausen-Oranienburg concentration camp near Berlin. Windeck stayed there until he was transferred to Auschwitz, together with 99 other prisoners, in August 1940. There he was classified as an 'anti-social' (*Asozialer*) and received the black triangle. He was made Kapo of the digging commando and, after a short while, camp Kapo. He held this position until March 1941. Proud of his position, according to one witness, he paraded around 'as if the son of the camp-owner'.[37] The much-feared Windeck always carried a whip, with which he randomly beat fellow prisoners. Between periods of solitary confinement and other punishments he held positions as Kapo in Auschwitz-Monowitz where he enjoyed single room accommodation and his own servants (these were mostly children taken from the RSHA transports). Due to further accusations of theft in mid-1943 he was transferred to the Birkenau camp, where he again was installed as Kapo, in the men's camp B II d. He remained there until August 1944 when he was transferred to the concentration camp Ohrdruf, and from there to Buchenwald. He managed to escape but was captured by (German) military police, became a soldier in the closing months of the war and ended up as a Soviet POW in May 1945. A military court in the USSR sentenced him to 25 years hard labour in 1949 but he was released, along with thousands of other POWs, in 1955. After his return to (West) Germany he continued to work on building sites until his retirement in 1963. Although re-arrested the same year and held on remand, he was released in May 1964, on health grounds.[38]

Josef ('Jupp') Windeck was charged with 117 counts of murder, all of which he denied. He was found guilty of 105 cases of inflicting grievous bodily harm, but could not be sentenced. In three cases he was found guilty of attempted murder, receiving jail sentences of twice eleven years and one of ten years, running concurrently (which were commuted to a sentence of 15 years, with time spent in a Russian POW camp taken into account). He was acquitted of seven counts of murder but found guilty of only two, for which he received two life sentences.[39]

Whilst the court acknowledged that both defendants were prisoners themselves, the judicial reasoning of the sentencing measure cites several instances where witnesses stated that they, as fellow Kapos, admonished the accused for their brutality towards other prisoners.[40]

The complete denial of any misdoing by both defendants is remarkable. Windeck, in his utter conviction that he had done nothing wrong, even made appeals on West German television to find character witnesses; all he could remember was the pride of having been camp (chief) Kapo, and remained full of self-pity about having to appear in court now.[41] The judge explains this by referring to Windeck's egocentricity, which 'made him suppress and forget much he deemed unpleasant to him.'[42]

The true reason for their deeds was, so argues the court, the knowledge that the mistreatment of fellow prisoners would go unpunished because of their national or racial origin and that their actions were sanctioned by their masters, the SS. Acting out of this motivation is mean, contemptuous and morally despicable.[43]

Decisive for the court were the 'few guiding principles of humanity', which are the indispensable core of the law and are anchored in the general public knowledge of what is right and wrong. In the basic human understanding of justice the killing of innocents for reasons of racial hatred is deeply abhorrent. Despite the conditions in the National Socialist concentration camps and the circumstances which allowed the defendants to view racially motivated killing as an everyday occurrence, the court held that ethical judgement in such cases cannot be withheld by the murderer – it remains the moral foundation of all humanity, which forms part of the human conscience.[44]

Therefore both defendants have to be viewed as sole perpetrators, not acting as helpers or assistants as this was their 'inner attitude' to these deeds. They were not coerced to commit murder but acted out of their own impulse. For this they quietened their conscience so that no doubts, or moral wrangling or regrets accompanied their actions. On the contrary, they were proud of their accomplishments, which gained them a fearful power.[45]

What becomes apparent from the judgement above is that a certain simple logic could be applied to the prosecution of Bonitz and Windeck. At first glance nothing could really be considered problematic in this case: after all, two vicious murderers were judiciously sentenced, by a huge weight of evidence, to life imprisonment. The problem only arises in connection with other NS-trials and the wider considerations of this particular judgement.

There is no doubt that both Kapos in this case were murderous thugs who more than deserved their sentence. The court made numerous concessions to their deeds and the statute of limitations limited, at least in theory, the length of their prison sentence. But for the court to base their reasoning on the assumption that a moral 'categorical imperative' continued to exist within the concentration camp, even when not evident, and to view Bonitz and Windeck as 'sole perpetrators' it might be construed that the formulation of the charges were used to fit the law, a reversal of standard procedure in the absence of a charge of 'corporate' crimes against a wider circle of perpetrators.

At the time of the Third Auschwitz Trial the understanding of the role of the Kapos was based on the initial Allied reports such as the Buchenwald Report, the elaborations of Eugen Kogon and the historian Martin Broszat. A section of the trial judgement document entitled 'The living conditions of the prisoner-functionaries and their power'[46] states that 'from the standpoint of the ordinary prisoner, the power of the prisoner-functionaries was unlimited'.[47] The Kapo could spread fear and terror, but did not have to, and there was no general guideline that Kapos had to beat, torture or kill other prisoners. On the contrary, Windeck himself had stated that the survival chances of the Kapo did not depend on whether or not he beat fellow prisoners, and it was much more likely that he would get deposed or murdered if he was deemed too brutal.[48] Most Kapos in Auschwitz were, on the whole, concerned with not attracting too much attention and avoiding the wrath of the SS.[49] Others, however, keenly supported their camp masters and took every opportunity to conduct their 'games' with deadly outcomes. The two accused found themselves in this environment against their will,[50] so the court stated.

The prosecution and sentencing of these 'last links in the chain of terror' took place in the series of so-called 'complex' trials in Frankfurt which began in December 1963. It had been the intention of the prosecution, if not to circumnavigate then at least to point to corporate culpability and a greater complicity around the Auschwitz concentration and death camp. In the light of Cold War tensions much of the evidence offered in this direction was deemed inadmissible. It was also legally impossible since the abandoning of the statutes in 1955 which would have allowed for such charges. Even in the first and second Auschwitz Trials much of the sentencing appeared to be in inverse relationship to the accused's seniority and responsibility. Whereas it is indisputable that Windeck and Bonitz deserved their life sentences, other sentences, of senior SS personnel, in other cases, appear ludicrously light. In terms of a coherent prosecution and sentencing policy, West-German courts offered no consistency. A conviction for murder required proof of 'malicious' (*heimtückisch*) and cruel intentions which were often impossible to prove. Many senior Nazis were acquitted on the grounds that the real culprits were Hitler, Himmler or the RSHA.[51]

Much of the reasoning of various courts, including the *Bundesgerichtshof* (the highest appeal court), appears simply incomprehensible by today's standards, including the trials of the various euthanasia doctors, such as Dr Faltlhauser in 1949,[52] Dr Leu in 1951[53] and Dr Borm in 1970,[54] as well as the 1974 trial of former police chief inspector Heinz Gerhard Riedel in Kiel,[55] who were all acquitted. Only a very small percentage of the *Zentrale Stelle's* investigations ever came to trial, and an even smaller percentage managed to secure convictions.[56]

What hindered convictions and harsher sentencing was not just the generally unfavourable climate of NS prosecutions, but also the fact that the priorities of the Cold War often stood in conflict with an earnest quest for justice as is illustrated by the following case, which had set a precedent through the appeal court (*Bundesgerichtshof*): the 1962 defection of the Soviet agent Stachynskij after he had murdered two Ukrainian dissidents in Munich. This double murder, according to the German court, had to be viewed against the background of mitigating circumstances, as the accused man's actions could not be deemed his own as he had not enough courage to resist state-sanctioned criminal deeds and his 'inner attitude towards the deed' was not malicious. Therefore the culprit was the KGB chief Chelipyn and not Stachynskij. This case continued to be quoted by many defence councils in NS-trials throughout the years to come.[57] The incredible inconsistency of West German courts in the sentencing of Nazi criminals is difficult to comprehend. Müller argues that it was the judiciary's assumed obligation to state authority, rather than a search for justice, which hampered these trials.[58] But even when considering this, and the judges' perhaps 'tainted' past, the general political willingness and public opinion, many of the judgements simply remain not credible.

There was only minimal public interest in the case against Bonitz and Windeck. This was in contrast to the first 'great' Auschwitz Trial of 1963–65, which had still attracted over 20,000 visitors over the course of its 18-month duration. On the day of judgement in the second trial, only around 30 people were in the public gallery.[59] There are no reports on the numbers of spectators and reporters at the judgement in the Third Auschwitz Trial, but it can be safely assumed that the figure was even less.

So what made this trial important to the radio stations? Initially, there must have been an interest from the journalist or editor to attend the trial. There is ample proof that particular radio reporters, such as Siegurt Guthmann (in this case), Axel Eggebrecht and others, took a leading role in the reporting from NS trials. But considering the relative 'insignificance' of this Kapo trial, additional reasons must be sought. One fact that has been mentioned already was undoubtedly a response to international pressure for the Federal Republic to 'get its house in order', to portray the prosecutions as an ongoing process of coming to terms with the past. However, at the time there were a number of other trials which would have been better examples of *Vergangenheitsbewältigung*. What makes the recorded reporting from the Third Auschwitz Trial so remarkable is the intensity of the survivor statements and the above cited confrontation between Minz and Windeck, an opportunity provided by (radio) technology, which makes such compelling listening. There is little doubt that this was also the reason that the international broadcaster *Deutsche Welle* chose to repeat this programme in edited form and broadcast it around the world.

The content nevertheless points to a changing wider picture: the statute of limitations, which made it impossible to prosecute certain crimes committed during the Nazi dictatorship after 1965, was welcomed by a majority of West Germans. The debate around the statute of limitations (*Verjährungsdebatte*) had raged in the West German Bundestag since the early 1960s and there have been repeated attempts, especially but not exclusively by the conservative CDU/CSU party alliance, to introduce a statute of limitations for the prosecution of murder as well and calls for a general amnesty. To this day, this has not happened and the prosecutions for murders committed during the Third Reich are still occurring.

By 1968, at the time of the Third Auschwitz Trial, this limiting of prosecutions was frowned upon internationally. Instead, many West German courts meted out sentences as if a statute of limitations had already occurred, and despite reassurances their judgements were based on 'the moral foundation of all humanity' which reside in the conscience, very few judges dealt more harshly with Nazi crimes, and many Nazi criminals escaped prosecutions altogether. And this, unsurprisingly, had been, and continued to be, a focal point in the GDR's accusations of West Germany in the 1960s.

Radio as history

When writing about radio, its historical importance and its assessment within historical processes, a number of issues arise which distinguish from standard historiography: Above all the radio's direct influence is not necessarily an empirically measurable process, but nevertheless is very present. But also other factors come into play, such as exploring theoretical models, understanding broadcasting policies, the wider political and social context and – most importantly – the consumption of media products (listening or viewing).

And as more and more media products become sources of and reflections on history, it will be increasingly important for historians to find productive and effective ways of dealing with them. In addition to the content of the materials researchers are faced with many other aspects, including critical awareness of the production process and audience reception. Radio, as the first of the 'electric (or electronic)' mass media, still holds a remarkable sway; its output is considered important enough to remain subject to strict regulation and (self-)censorship and national public broadcast authorities remain in receipt of state funding.

In the divided Germany of the 1950s and 1960s the importance of the radio as a means of disseminating information was paramount, reaching a greater audience than any other medium, and as such played a crucial part in the confronting of the National Socialist past. Whereas the cinema and (increasingly) television were the visual, direct and conscious form of addressing this issue, the radio maintained a position of constant and indirect influence. Less restricted than the visual media, the radio programmes dealing with the Nazi past were able to operate on different levels, taking into account the varying degrees of concentration, presenting the past as either documentary evidence, critical discussions or entertainment (as radio plays). The overall audible impression as well as content was decisive; in some cases, as outlined above, they were not identical.

Historians dealing with this kind of material thus have to be aware of the differing 'modes' of listening that can exist, primarily 'away' from a purely textual, or content driven interpretation. The overall impressions gained from listening incidentally not only can introduce listeners to new, or unusual material, but has the ability to present this material in the familiar ideological context.

Therefore, when examining these programmes as historical sources, it can be noted that, for instance, in the GDR programmes, such as *Sammelpunkt Shelesnastrasse*, the impression the listener is left with is that the Warsaw Ghetto Uprising was the result of the organisational skills of the Polish Workers Party, whereas the precise wording only tentatively implies this. Programmes from West German stations equally can, at times, give misleading impressions outside the Cold War rhetoric: overtly critical of the FRG's (capitalist) judicial structures, they nevertheless cannot be mistaken for broadcasts from the East. Firmly lodged within their ideological foundations, these broadcasts represent the most (at the time) acceptable form of *Vergangenheitsbewältigung*, incorporating the Holocaust narrative through precise facts while at the same time upholding the correct ideological 'veneer' as well as maintaining the overall sentiment of horror and repulsion of the Nazi regime, both in East and West German radio programmes.

However, a note of caution has to be added: programme makers, particularly during the Cold War, were very aware of this ephemeral nature of their radio broadcasts. Therefore the overall impression possibly carried more significance than content and greater emphasis remained with ideological consistency. Consequently radio broadcasts, when used as historical sources, cannot be analysed from their textual content alone: they require a theoretical and interpretive context, which incorporates content with overall impression and audience with producers.

And, as demonstrated throughout this study, the interpretive concepts remain fluid: audiences as well as programme makers learn quickly, change attitudes, habits and production methods. The attention to detail required of the historian of audio sources, and particularly radio programmes remains paramount, for as long as familiarity to the broadcast format, in form and content, falls roughly within the confines of the expected and the usual, its assumed inconsequentiality could, at least in theory, have far-reaching effects.[60] If radio programmes – the shorthand of history – are to be used as historical sources, then their production processes and reception have to be evaluated as thoroughly as their content.

Conclusion

So where can radio programmes, such as those investigated in this book, and the medium of radio in general, be placed in the process of *Vergangenheitsbewältigung*, or even wider social processes? As this study has shown, radio as an agent of change developed and diversified itself, particularly in the postwar period, and therefore an assessment of its influence can easily be viewed as either speculative guesswork at worst, or inductive reasoning at best. I would like to argue, however, that there is concrete and convincing evidence that radio in Germany, and in particular radio programmes dealing with the issue of the Holocaust, made a profound and lasting impact on the German population, in both the GDR and the FRG. In order to do this I will briefly summarise some of the main points.

Viewed historically, radio can certainly be termed 'the agent of modernity'. As the first genuine mass medium radio had started to establish itself as a household item by the 1930s, and radio programming became a political issue. The domination of media products, as is identified by Peukert's definition of 'Classical Modernity', becomes almost total with the introduction of the radio. But the assumed 'triumph of Western rationality', also seen as a defining feature by Peukert, takes a somewhat different route when it comes to radio broadcasting. Here Brecht and Benjamin also err: the incorporation of the technological aspects fails to find attraction. Equally the assumption of the rational listener and responsive interplay does not materialise, and instead a monolithic 'voice of authority' establishes itself in most countries' developing broadcasting services.

Radio in Nazi Germany was undoubtedly the clearest expression of this 'reactionary modernism'. As was evidenced above, broadcasts inciting racial hatred were commonplace and as such created the precondition for genocide. Nazi ideology depended on the most widespread dissemination and radio was the means to achieve this. Again we see that Enlightenment rationality was abandoned in favour of myth and authority, with radio acting as a key agent in ideology formation and transmission. But also evident towards the end of the war and later, during the Cold War, was a certain ideology displacement: multiple transmissions, conflicting reports and statements, misinformation and agitation gave rise to the critical listener, the rational citizen. In theoretical terms neither a conspiratorial 'Culture Industry' nor a complete abandoning of reality through simulacra can fit the emerging picture of postwar radio in the divided Germany. In the midst of fierce ideological exchanges between governments, and the print media, East and West German radio managed to maintain a comparatively rational debate by focussing on the 'irrationality' of the Holocaust.

From the Nuremberg Trail transmission onwards it became increasingly evident that public service broadcasting fulfilled a desire of the listeners to be informed, and to be taken seriously. Broadcasters and audiences started to establish the interactive radio protocol – neither, as Brecht had imagined, as something similar to the telephone, nor as the later phone-in or technological extension of self-expression, but as a dialogue more akin to psychoanalysis. The relationship to 'the radio' became a personal matter, able to probe into private moments and memory, and, in the context of this study, an opportunity for the war and postwar generations to ask themselves, and their parents questions. And this 'working through the past' on the radio, which I had termed the 'listening cure' earlier, the efforts of the radio stations, East and West, were impressive, as well as the media awareness of the persons involved in the judicial and retributive processes (such as Fritz Bauer,

Hermann Langbein). At a time when these media were still commanding 'mass' audiences (as opposed to the now smaller, digital, niche and specific target audiences) in both the GDR and FRG, the level of critical engagement appears to have been relatively high, but in the absence of a 'measurement' of its effectiveness, and underlying policy decisions of the broadcasters, the findings presented here remain a little speculative. While the relatively high levels of interest might have been helped along by the media coverage of the Eichmann Trial on television and radio, the focus which emerged around the Frankfurt Auschwitz Trials was by no means surprising, as these prosecutions centred on Germans being tried in Germany on an unprecedented scale. Added evidence of the continuous interest in the Trial was, without doubt, the stage, radio and television performance of Peter Weiss' *Die Ermittlung*, which cemented the term 'Auschwitz' firmly into German consciousness. Aided, popularised and spurred on by the mass media, these events surrounding the Auschwitz Trial are clearly the pivotal point in German postwar history, when Adorno's new categorical imperative of 'Never Again' undoubtedly took hold.

In technical terms, or as far as a measurable reaction from the radio audiences is concerned, the proof, or evidence of a precise moment in time, for this change to have occurred can only be inferred. But from the available evidence from the radio stations and their policy makers, as well as a number of opinion polls over a period of time, we can deduce that the critical engagement and concerted effort of the *memory makers* (the radio stations) and the *memory users* (their audiences) helped to bring about this change sometime after the first Auschwitz Trial.[61] Listening to radio programmes dealing with the Nazi past became a form of therapy: the moral outrage at one's parents, grandparents or fellow Germans (or even at a former, now abandoned self) now yielded therapeutic satisfaction. Working through the past, as done with these 'mediated Holocaust products', enabled the start of a coherent collective memory formation in Germany, particularly in the West. Whereas some distinctions have to be made in this process between the GDR and the FRG – particularly in the light of Cold War aspects in which the Nazi past turned into an ideological tool – it has to be stressed that during the period in focus here, there was ample evidence that the wish to master this past was genuine from both German nations.

We can almost view this period as a readjustment of 'classical' modernity'; Peter Weiss' *Canto of the Fire Ovens* (from 'The Investigation) or Axel Eggebrecht's trial reportage as pivotal moments in this process, all disseminated by the medium of radio.

Towards the end of the 1960s, and in particular around the time of the Third Auschwitz Trial in 1968, the tone of the (West) German broadcast is almost conciliatory, as is evident in the *Deutsche Welle* broadcast mentioned above. Nationally and internationally, both Germanies appeared to be 'coming-to-terms-with' the past, and the public's willingness to engage with the topic was now firmly established. The complexities of the debates around the issues of the Holocaust were now starting to be a matter of broad pubic interest and were supported by the public service broadcasters.

The subsequent interplay between radio broadcasters and radio audiences, or memory makers and memory users, managed to start a process which has produced the most comprehensive understanding of the Holocaust and public expressions of atonement. This process, while aided from the 1960s onwards by the influence of television,[62] developed, minute by minute, hour by hour, on the airwaves of East and West German radio.

Notes

Introduction

1. 00'00"–00'35", *Das Lager. Gespräche mit Überlebenden des Konzentrationslagers Auschwitz*, Ton-und Wortdokumentation, Deutsche Welle, Cologne, Archive no. DW 4025830, first broadcast 20 November 1968.
2. Ibid., 00'58"–02'08".
3. Kapos, or prisoner-functionaries, were mostly German criminals moved to concentration camps after the completion of their prison sentence, into 'protective custody' (*Schutzhaft*), and were given favoured positions, in charge of a group of prisoners or work detail, fulfilling some guard and/or SS duties, in return for food, alcohol, cigarettes and other privileges. The word 'Kapo' originated not, as often commented, from the Italian (capo – sub-lieutenant in the Mafia), but was one of those euphemisms invented by the SS *Kameradschaftspolizei* or comrade-police. See Lutz Niethammer, *Der gesäuberte Antifaschismus.Die SED und die roten Kapos von Buchenwald* (Berlin: Akademie Verlag, 1994), p. 534.
4. *Das Lager*, 3'54"–4'38".
5. Ibid., 7'16"–7'33".
6. Ibid., 15'17".
7. *Das Lager*, 20'20"–22'09".
8. Ibid., 24'37"–24'44".
9. *So arbeitet das Lager – Unterricht im Deutschen; Beobachtungen beim Dritten Auschwitz Prozess in Frankfurt*. Ton und Wort Dokumentation, Hessischer Rundfunk, Frankfurt/Main, Archive no. 2990-00100, first broadcast 26 June 1968.
10. Andrew Crisell, *Understanding Radio*, 2nd edn (London: Routledge, 1994), p. 3.
11. Crisell, *Understanding Radio*, p. 59; see also Benedict Lutz and Ruth Wodak, *Information für Informierte – Linguistische Studien zur Verständlichkeit und Verstehens von Hörfunknachrichten* (Vienna: Verlag der Österreichischen Akademie der Wissenschaften – Philosophisch – Historische Klasse 488.Band, 1987), which deals entirely with the comprehension of radio (news) programmes.
12. Carin Åberg, 'Radio Analysis? Sure! But How?', in Andreas Stuhlmann (ed.), *Radio Kultur und Hör-Kunst – Zwischen Avantgarde und Populärkultur 1923–2001* (Würzburg: Königshausen & Neumann, 2001), p. 104.
13. Adelheit von Saldern and Inge Marßoleck use the concept of the *longue durée* to explore continuities against changing political systems in the context of *Mentalitätsgeschichte* (history of mentality). Attitudes towards objects, such as the radio set, evolve at their own pace regardless of political structures. Adelheit von Saldern and Inge Marßoleck (eds), *Zuhören und Gehörtwerden II: Radio in der DDR der 50er Jahre. Zwischen Lenkung und Ablenkung* (Tübingen: edition discord, 1998) pp. 16–17.
14. Kate Lacey, *Feminine Frequencies: Gender, German Radio and the Public Sphere* (Ann Arbor: University of Michigan Press, 1996). This study is set in the time

of the Weimar Republic, at the very beginning of the radio's existence, and subsequently there was a much wider, and public, discourse.
15. Bertolt Brecht, 'Radio – eine vorsintflutliche Erfindung?', in *Gesammelte Werke 18 – Schriften zur Literatur und Kunst I* (Frankfurt/Main: Suhrkamp, 1967), p. 119.
16. Walter Benjamin, 'Zweierlei Volkstümlichkeit', *Gesammelte Schriften IV.2* (Frankfurt/Main: Suhrkamp 1972), p. 671–2.
17. *'Ganz Deutschland hört den Führer mit dem Volksempfänger.'* This was the slogan on the posters advertising the radio sets. Helga Maria Wolf (ed.), *Auf Ätherwellen – Persönliche Radiogeschichte(n)* (Vienna: Böhlau Verlag, 2004), p. 31.
18. Konrad Dussel, *Hörfunk in Deutschland: Politik, Programm, Publikum (1923–1960)* (Potsdam: Verlag für Berlin-Brandenburg, 2002).
19. Lacey, *Feminine Frequencies*.
20. Walter Roller/Susanne Höschel (eds), *Judenverfolgung und jüdisches Leben unter den Bedingungen der nationalsozialistischen Gewaltherrschaft, Band 1: Tondokumente und Rundfunksendungen 1930–1946* (Potsdam: Verlag für Berlin-Brandenburg, 1996).
21. Adelheit von Saldern and Inge Marßoleck (eds), *Zuhören und Gehörtwerden I, Radio im Nationalsozialismus: Zwischen Lenkung und Ablenkung* (Tübingen: edition discord, 1998).
22. Wolf (ed.), *Auf Ätherwellen*; Mihail Sebastian, *Journal 1935–1944* (London: Heinemann, 2000).
23. Max Horkheimer and Theodor W. Adorno, *The Dialectic of Enlightenment (1947)* (Stanford: Stanford University Press, 2002).
24. Theodor W. Adorno, *Critical Models* (New York: Columbia University Press, 1998).
25. Marshall McLuhan, *Understanding Media* (London: Routledge, 2002).
26. *Time Magazine* said in a review of *Understanding Media* that it was 'fuzzy-minded, lacking in perspective, low in definition and data, redundant and contemptuous of logical sequence.' Phillip Marchand, *Marshall McLuhan: The Medium and the Messenger* (Cambridge, MA: MIT Press, 1998), p. 180.
27. Crisell, *Understanding Radio*.
28. Paddy Scannell, *Radio, Television and Modern Life: a Phenomenological Approach* (Oxford: Blackwell, 1996).
29. Denis McQuail (ed.), *A Reader in Mass Communication Theory* (London: Sage, 2001).
30. Niklas Luhmann, *The Reality of the Mass Media* (Stanford: Polity, 2000).
31. Lutz and Wodak, *Information für Informierte*.
32. Stefan Heym, *Wege und Umwege* (Munich: Wilhelm Goldmann Verlag, 1985).
33. Ansgar Diller and Wolfgang Mühl-Benninghaus (eds), *Berichterstattung über den Nürnberger Prozess gegen die Hauptkriegsverbrecher 1945/46–Edition und Dokumentation ausgewählter Rundfunkquellen* (Potsdam: Verlag für Berlin-Brandenburg, 1998).
34. Karl Jaspers, *Die Schuldfrage* (Zurich: Artemis Verlag, 1946).
35. Christoph Classen, *Faschismus und Antifaschismus: Die Nationalsozialistische Vergangenheit im ostdeutschen Rundfunk 1945–1953* (Cologne: Böhlau Verlag, 2004).
36. Axel Schildt, *Moderne Zeiten: Freizeit, Massenmedien und der 'Zeitgeist' der Bundesrepublik der 50er Jahre* (Hamburg: Christians Verlag, 1995).

37. Hans Bausch, *Rundfunk in Deutschland: Band 3 Rundfunkpolitik nach 1945; Erster Teil* (Munich: dtv, 1980). This is the third of dtv's *Rundfunk in Deutschland* series, which appears in two volumes.
38. The German Radio Archive has compiled their archival holdings on the theme of 'Persecution of the Jews and Jewish Life Under the Conditions of the National Socialist Dictatorship' in three volumes, which have been extremely helpful in finding individual programmes. Most (but not all) programmes mentioned in this study were found in this register. Felix Kresing-Wulf (ed.), *Judenverfolgung und jüdisches Leben unter den Bedingungen der nationalsozialistischen Gewaltherrschaft, Band 2/1 und 2/2: Tondokumente und Rundfunksendungen 1947–1990* (Potsdam: Verlag für Berlin-Brandenburg, 1997).
39. *Hinter der Mauer des Schweigens*, Schall- und Wortarchiv Norddeutscher Rundfunk, Hamburg, Archive no. DWR 11458, first broadcast 15 February 1960.
40. Norbert Frei, *Adenauer's Germany and the Nazi Past: The Politics of Amnesty and Integration* (New York: Columbia University Press, 2002).
41. Von Saldern and Marßoleck (eds), *Zuhören und Gehörtwerden II: Radio in der DDR der 50er Jahre*, also Heide Riedel (ed.), *Mit uns zieht die neue Zeit... 40 Jahre DDR Medien* (Berlin: Vistas Verlag, 1993).
42. These reached their high point with the publication of the *Braunbuch* ('brown book'), a list of prominent West Germans with Nazi pasts in public office. Norbert Podewin, *Braunbuch: Kriegs – und Naziverbrecher in der Bundesrepublik und Berlin (West). Reprint der 1968 Ausgabe* (Berlin: edition ost, 2002).
43. The standard reference for the Auschwitz Trial still remains Bernd Naumann's *Auschwitz: A Report on the Proceedings against Robert Karl Ludwig Mulka and others before the Court in Frankfurt* (London: Pall Mall, 1966); as well as Hermann Langbein's two-volume *Der Auschwitz Prozeß: Eine Dokumentation* (Frankfurt/Main: Verlag Neue Kritik, 1995).
44. Rebecca Wittmann, *Beyond Justice: The Auschwitz Trial* (Cambridge, MA: Harvard University Press, 2005); Devin O. Pendas, *The Frankfurt Auschwitz Trial 1963–1965* (Cambridge, MA: Cambridge University Press, 2005).
45. Fritz Bauer Institut, *Auschwitz Prozeß 4Ks 2/63 Frankfurt am Main* (Frankfurt/Main: Campus Verlag 2004).
46. Fritz Bauer Institut/Staatliches Museum Auschwitz Birkenau, *Der Auschwitz Prozeß – Tonbandmitschnitte, Protokolle, Dokumente*. DVD-ROM (Berlin: Digitale Bibliothek, 2005).
47. Ingo Müller, *Furchtbare Juristen: Die unbewältigte Vergangenheit unserer Justiz* (Munich: Kindler Verlag, 1987).
48. Jeffrey Herf, *Divided Memory: The Nazi Past in the Two Germanys* (London: Harvard University Press, 1997) and Pendas, *The Frankfurt Auschwitz Trial 1963–1965*.
49. An excellent collection of essays on these issues can be found in: Fritz Bauer, *Die Humanität der Rechtsordnung* (Frankfurt/Main: Campus Verlag, 1998), a more personal account in Axel Eggebrecht (ed.), *Die zornigen alten Männer: Gedanken über Deutschland seit 1945* (Hamburg, 1979) and Claudia Fröhlich and Michael Kohlstruck (eds), *Engagierte Demokraten: Vergangenheitspolitik in kritischer Absicht* (Münster: Westfälisches Dampfboot, 1999) recounts the lives of many critical commentators.
50. Peter Weiss, *The Investigation – Oratorio in 11 Cantos* (London: Calder and Boyars, 1965).

51. Reception of and reaction to Weiss' play can be found in: Christoph Weiß, *Auschwitz in der geteilten Welt – Peter Weiss und die 'Ermittlung' im Kalten Krieg* (St Ingbert: Röhrig Universitätsverlag, 2000).
52. Friedrich Pollock, *Gruppenexperiment: Ein Studienbericht* (Frankfurt/Main: Europäische Verlagsanstanstalt, 1955).
53. Regina Schmidt and Egon Becker, *Reaktionen auf politische Vorgänge – Drei Meinungsstudien aus der Bundesrepublik* (Frankfurt/Main: Europäische Verlagsanstanstalt, 1967).
54. Harold Welzer, Sabine Moller and Karoline Tschuggnall, *Opa war kein Nazi – Nationalsozialismus und Holocaust im Familiengedächtnis* (Frankfurt/Main: Fischer Taschenbuch Verlag, 2002).

2 Radio and Modernity

1. Detlef Peukert, *The Weimar Republic: The Crisis of Classical Modernity* (London: Penguin, 1991), p. 82.
2. Anthony Giddens, *The Consequences of Modernity* (Cambridge: Cambridge University Press, 1990), p. 18.
3. Reinhart Koselleck, *The Practice of Conceptual History* (Stanford: Stanford University Press, 2002), p. 111.
4. Ibid., p. 113.
5. E.P. Thompson, 'Time, Work-Discipline and Industrial Capitalism', *Past and Present*, 38 (1967), 56–97.
6. Sean Moores, 'The Box on the Dresser: Memories of Early Radio and Everyday Life' in: *Media, Culture and Society*, 10 (1988), 23–40.
7. The precise origins of radio are far from clear. While Hertz and Marconi can certainly lay claim to some of the technical developments, when it comes to the actual radio set and first broadcasts, many nations and individuals profess to have done this: see Crisell, *Understanding Radio*, pp. 17–20. Soviet claims in N. Izyumov and D. Linde, *Fundamentals of Radio* (Moscow: Mir Publishers, 1976), p. 20, Austrian claims in Wolf (ed.), *Auf Ätherwellen*, p. 11, and countless others.
8. A distinction has to be made here between crystal sets – listened to with headphones, which were considerably cheaper than the valve sets, which had a speaker. See Crisell, *Understanding Radio*, p. 19.
9. McLuhan, *Understanding Media*, pp. 332–3.
10. Lacey, *Feminine Frequencies*, p. 34.
11. von Saldern/Marßoleck (eds), *Zuhören und Gehörtwerden II*, p. 11.
12. Lacey, *Feminine Frequencies*, pp. 37–8.
13. Brecht, *Gesammelte Werke 18*, p. 120.
14. Ibid., p. 121.
15. Ibid., p. 130.
16. *Erläuterungen zum 'Ozeanflug'*, ibid., pp. 124–6.
17. '...den Rundfunk aus einem Distributionsapparat in einen Kommunikationsapparat zu verwandeln.' Brecht realised that in order for the radio to fulfil its potential, the incorporation of the listener into the broadcasting process was vital. Ibid., p. 129.
18. Ibid., p. 120.

19. Roger Behrens, 'Die Stimme als Gast empfangen – Walter Benjamins Überlegungen zur Radioarbeit' in: Andreas Stuhlmann (ed.), *Radio Kultur und Hör-Kunst*, p. 117.
20. Ibid., p. 124.
21. Ibid., p. 132.
22. Walter Benjamin, *Gesammelte Schriften IV.2*, pp. 639–72.
23. Sabine Schiller-Lerg, *Walter Benjamin und der Rundfunk: Programmarbeit zwischen Theorie und Praxis* (Munich: K. G. Saur, 1984).
24. Behrens, *Die Stimme*, p. 119.
25. Ibid., p. 121.
26. Ibid., p. 127.
27. Benjamin, *Gesammelte Schriften IV.2*, p. 672.
28. Walter Benjamin, *Illuminations* (London: Fontana Press, 1992), p. 218.
29. A precise translation for the concept of 'Bildungsbürger' is difficult. It could also be interpreted as 'educated bourgeoisie'. Dussel, *Rundfunk in Deutschland*, p. 137.
30. Ibid., p. 165.
31. Ibid., p. 39.
32. Ibid., p. 50.
33. Lutz and Wodak *Information für Informierte*, pp. 24–6.
34. Horkheimer and Adorno, *The Dialectic of Enlightenment*, p. 95.
35. Ibid., p. 100.
36. Ibid., p. 109.
37. Ibid., p. 118.
38. Dussel, *Rundfunk in Deutschland*, pp. 55–6.
39. Ibid. pp. 56–7.
40. E. Kurt Fischer, *Dokumente zur Geschichte des deutschen Rundfunks und Fernsehens* (Göttingen: Musterschmidt Verlag, 1957), p. 259.
41. Dussel, *Rundfunk in Deutschland*, p. 263.
42. Ibid., p. 57.
43. Julius Streicher, Rundfunkansprache anläßlich der Volksabstimmung am 12. November 1933 (broadcast 25 October 1933), Roller and Höschel (eds), *Judenverfolgung und jüdisches Leben unter den Bedingungen der nationalsozialistischen Gewaltherrschaft, Band 1: Tondokumente und Rundfunksendungen 1930–1946*, pp. 28–9.
44. Lacey, *Feminine Frequencies*, p. 102.
45. Fischer, *Dokumente*, p. 295.
46. Lacey, *Feminine Frequencies*, p. 103.
47. Ibid., p. 122.
48. Julius Streicher, 'Ansprache auf einer Großkundgebung im Berliner Sportpalast' (broadcast 25 January 1939), Roller and Höschel (eds), *Judenverfolgung*, p. 131.
49. Ibid., p. 9.
50. Robert Ley, 'Ansprache auf einer Kundgebung des Deutschen Handwerks in der Festhalle in Frankfurt am Main' (broadcast 21 May 1939), Ibid. pp. 151–2.
51. Theodor W Adorno, 'The Psychological Technique of Thomas' Radio Addresses', in *Gesammelte Schriften 9.1; Soziologische Schriften II* (Frankfurt/Main: Suhrkamp Verlag, 1975), pp. 140–1.

52. Ibid., p. 132.
53. Ibid., p. 133.
54. Robert Ley, Ansprache auf einer gemeinsamen Kundgebung der NSDAP und der NSB in Heerlen (Holland) (broadcast 11 May 1942), Roller and Höschel (eds), *Judenverfolgung*, p. 212.
55. This also holds true for later uses of the radio in genocide, such as in Rwanda 1990–1994. See: Article 19, *Broadcasting Genocide: Censorship, Propaganda and State-Sponsored Violence in Rwanda 1990–1994* (London: Article 19, 1996), p. 114.
56. Mihail Sebastian, *Journal 1935–1944* (London: W. Heinemann, 2000).
57. Wolf (ed.), *Auf Ätherwellen*.
58. Mary Kenny, *Germany Calling* and Nigel Farndale, *Lord Haw Haw* among many.
59. The 'Nazi Swing' big band of 'Charlie and his Orchestra' broadcast regularly to Britain with jazz standards with altered (anti-Semitic) lyrics. A CD 'Propaganda Swing: Charlie and His Orchestra' has recently been released; see also Horst J.P. Bergmeier and Rainer E. Lotz, *Hitler's Airwaves: The Inside Story of Nazi Radio Broadcasting and Propaganda Swing* (New Haven: Yale University Press, 1997).
60. Erich Kästner, *Notabene 45. Ein Tagebuch* (Munich: dtv, 1993), p. 99. The Munich station had been taken over by the US military.
61. Brecht seems to have understood and even anticipated this when he called it an 'antediluvian invention, rediscovered'.
62. McLuhan, *Understanding Media*, p. 17.
63. Ibid., pp. 24–5.
64. Ibid., p. 33.
65. Ibid., p. 324.
66. Horkheimer and Adorno, *Dialectic*, pp. 183–4.
67. McLuhan, *Understanding Media*, p. 327.
68. Ibid., p. 328.
69. Ibid., p. 330.
70. Ibid., p. 333.
71. Jean Baudrillard, *Selected Writings* (Stanford: Stanford University Press, 1988).
72. Ibid., p. 170.
73. Luhmann, *The Reality of the Mass Media*, p. 2.
74. Horkheimer and Adorno, *Dialectic*, p. 115, also Herbert Marcuse, 'The Affirmative Character of Culture', in *Negations: Essays in Critical Theory* (London: Free Association, 1988), pp. 88–131.
75. Luhmann, *Reality*, p. 25.
76. Ibid., pp. 28–35.
77. Ibid., p. 40.
78. Slavoj Žižek, *Did Somebody Say Totalitarianism?* (London: Verso, 2001), p. 150.
79. Lutz and Wodak *Information für Informierte*, p. 26.
80. Luhmann, *Reality*, p. 1.
81. This position is maintained particularly by Ernesto Laclau and Chantal Mouffe, *Hegemony and Socialist Strategy: towards a Radical Democratic Politics*, 2nd edn (London, Polity, 2001).

82. 'Durch Ökulei zu Pispilei !' = Durch ökonomisch-kulturellen Leistungsvergleich zu Pionier- und Spitzenleistungen! Through economic and cultural exchange towards pioneer- and top achievements!, see Martin Ahrends, *Klirrende Wörter. Kleiner Sprachführer in ein dahingehendes Deutsch* (Frankfurt/Main: Fischer, 1990).
83. Lutz and Wodak *Information für Informierte*, p. 28.
84. Luhmann, *Reality*, pp. 39–40.
85. Heym, *Wege und Umwege*, p. 406.
86. Ibid., pp. 409–10.
87. Slavoj Žižek, 'The Spectre of Ideology', in Slavoj Žižek (ed.), *Mapping Ideology* (London: Verso, 1994), p. 12.
88. Martin Jay, *The Dialectical Imagination* (Berkeley: University of California Press, 1996), Preface to the 1996 edition, p. xvii.
89. Theodor W. Adorno, 'Prologue to Television', in *Critical Models* (New York: Columbia University Press, 1998), p. 55.
90. David Bathrick, 'Making a National Family on the Radio: The Nazi Wunschkonzert', *Modernism/Modernity*, 4(1) (1997), 116.
91. Alexander and Margarete Mitscherlich, *Die Unfähigkeit zu trauern: Grundlagen kollektiven Verhaltens* (Munich: Piper, 1977).
92. Bertolt Brecht, 'Der Rundfunk als Kommunikationsapparat', *GW 18*, p. 129.
93. Adorno, 'The Meaning of Working through the Past', in *Critical Models*, p. 89.
94. Norbert Frei, *Adenauer's Germany and the Nazi Past: The Politics of Amnesty and Integration* (New York: Columbia University Press, 2002).
95. Robert G. Moeller, *War Stories: The Search for a Usable Past in the Federal Republic of Germany* (Berkeley: University of California Press, 2001).
96. Adorno, 'Prologue to Television', in *Critical Models*, p. 56.
97. 'Interfering in social reality' is seen as the task of the artistic avant-garde by Peter Bürger, *Theory of the Avant-garde*, translated by Jochen Schutte-Sasse (Manchester: Manchester University Press, 1984).

3 Radio and the Holocaust

1. Christof Schneider, *Nationalsozialismus als Thema im Programm des Nordwestdeutschen Rundfunks 1945–1948* (Potsdam: Verlag für Berlin Brandenburg, 1999), p. 161.
2. Diller and Mühl-Benninghaus (eds), *Berichterstattung über den Nürnberger Prozess*, p. 9.
3. Schneider, p. 33.
4. For a brief period the British authorities produced their own broadcasts. Ibid., p. 36.
5. Ibid.
6. For map see Appendix at the end of the book.
7. Schneider, p. 43.
8. Diller and Mühl-Benninghaus, pp. 10–11.
9. Ibid.
10. Very little information is available about Oulmán. Originally from Vienna, he joined the NSDAP in 1933, from which he was expelled for fraud in 1937. After the war he claimed to be a Cuban Jew, and was known to have used his position to acquire (de-Nazification) clearing certificates (*Persilscheine*)

for prominent Nazis in exchange for cash and valuables. A semi-fictional account exists in: Maximillian Alexander, *Das Chamaeleon: Der Mann, der sich Gaston Oulmán nannte* (Hamburg: Glöß Verlag, 1978).
11. Schneider, p. 43.
12. Ibid., p. 164.
13. Diller and Mühl-Benninghaus, pp. 12–13. The majority of transcriptions in this publication are Schütz's radio reports.
14. Ibid., p. 12.
15. Diller and Mühl-Benninghaus, p. 11.
16. Fritz Ermarth, *Volk und Staat: Zehn ausgewählte Rundfunkvorträge* (Karlsruhe: unknown publisher, 1947) cited in: Edgar Lersch, 'Die Thematisierung des Nationalsozialismus im Rundfunk der Nachkriegszeit' in: *Rundfunk und Geschichte*, Vol. 29, No. 1/2 (January/April 2003). pp. 5–19.
17. Schneider, pp. 47–9.
18. Ibid., pp. 274–80.
19. Ibid., pp. 280–4. Von Schitzler's outspoken and at times confrontational 'anti-fascist' stance clashed later with von Zahn's 'softer' approach to the listeners, leading to his resignation from the NWDR and move to the East German *Berliner Rundfunk* in 1947. Ibid., p. 69.
20. Diller and Mühl-Benninghaus, p. 12.
21. Ibid.
22. Ibid., p. 13.
23. Ibid., p. 15.
24. Ibid., p. 54.
25. Ibid., pp. 202–3.
26. Schneider, p. 67.
27. Ibid., pp. 68–9.
28. Hans Otto Gericke, 'Die Presseberichterstattung über den Nürnberger Prozeß und die Überwindung des faschistischen Geschichtsbildes', *Zeitschrift für Geschichtswissenschaft*, Vol. 33, No. 10 (1985), 917.
29. Donald Bloxham, *Genocide on Trial* (Oxford: Oxford University Press, 2001), p. 148.
30. Peter Steinbach, 'Nationalsozialistische Gewaltverbrechen in der deutschen Öffentlichkeit nach 1945', in Jürgen Weber and Peter Steinbach (eds), *Vergangenheitsbewältigung durch Strafverfahren? NS-Prozesse in der BRD* (Munich: Olzog Verlag, 1984), p. 18.
31. Diller and Mühl-Benninghaus, pp. 90–1.
32. Annette Weinke, *Die Verfolgung von NS-Tätern im geteilten Deutschland* (Paderborn: Ferdinand Schöningh, 2002), p. 24.
33. Ibid., p. 25.
34. Ibid., p. 26.
35. Diller and Mühl-Benninghaus, p. 187.
36. Ibid., p. 188.
37. Ibid., p. 190.
38. Ibid., pp. 194–5.
39. Schneider, p. 169.
40. Ibid., p. 168.
41. Margot Berghaus, 'Wie Massenmedien wirken', *Rundfunk und Fernsehen*, 47(2) (1999), 181–99.

42. Ibid., p. 181.
43. Ibid., p. 183.
44. Ibid., p. 190.
45. This is a term which emerged from the Friedrich Pollock/Theodor W. Adorno study conducted in 1955, denoting an 'underhand' or purely verbal public opinion. See Friedrich Pollock, *Gruppenexperiment: Ein Studienbericht* (Frankfurt/Main: Europäische Verlagsanstalt, 1955).
46. Markus Wolf, *Memoirs of a Spymaster* (London: Pimlico, 1997), pp. 41–2.
47. Schneider, p. 59.
48. Hannah Arendt, 'Organisierte Schuld', in: *Die Wandlung*, 1, 1945/46, No. 4, p. 337, cited in Jürgen Danyel, 'Vom schwierigen Umgang mit der Schuld: Die Deutschen in der DDR und der Nationalsozialismus', *Zeitschrift für Geschichtswissenschaft*, 40(10) (1992), 918–19.
49. Bausch, *Rundfunk in Deutschland*, p. 22.
50. Ibid., p. 23.
51. A Radio Scrutiny Report: One Year of Cultural Radio, July 1949–June 1950. Radio Branch. Information Services Division Office of the U.S. High Commissioner for Germany. In Fischer, *Dokumente*, pp. 216–17.
52. Von Saldern and Marßolek (eds), *Zuhören und Gehörtwerden II*, p. 261.
53. Ibid., p. 260.
54. Jürgen Danyel, *Vom schwierigen Umgang mit der Schuld*, p. 923.
55. Cited from Ingrid Pietrzynski, 'Die Gegenwart zwingt zur Besinnung: Die Thematisierung von Kriegsschuld in Kommentaren und Betrachtungen des DDR-Rundfunks der 50er Jahre' in: *Rundfunk und Geschichte*, Vol. 26, No.1/2 (2000), online version: http://www.medienrezeption.de/zeitschriften/rundfunk/RuG1+2_00/miszellen/piet.html (accessed 5 October 2005).
56. Naumann, *Auschwitz*, p. xxii.
57. Jaspers had anticipated these problems by giving his publication the subtitle 'There is no statute of limitations for genocide' (*Für Völkermord gibt es keine Verjährung*).
58. Jaspers, *Die Schuldfrage*, p. 11.
59. Hannah Arendt/Karl Jaspers, *Briefwechsel 1926–1969* (Munich: Piper, 1985).
60. Karl Jaspers, *Wohin treibt die Bundesrepublik? Tatsachen, Gefahren, Chancen* (Munich: Piper, 1966).
61. Alfred Streim, 'Die Verfolgung von NS-Gewaltverbrechen in der Bundesrepublik Deutschland', in: agenda: *Nationalsozialismus und Justiz: Die Aufarbeitung von Gewaltverbrechen damals und heute* (Münster: Agenda Verlag, 1993), p. 18.
62. Ibid.
63. Kurt Pätzold, 'NS-Prozesse in der DDR', in agenda: *Nationalsozialismus und Justiz*, p. 40.
64. The death penalty is prohibited in the Federal Republic by the constitution (*Grundgesetz*) of 1949, but was still in use by Allied Military courts until 1951.
65. Steinbach, *Nationalsozialistische Gewaltverbrechen*, p. 19.
66. Ibid.
67. Rebecca Wittmann, 'The Wheels of Justice Turn Slowly: The Pretrial Investigations of the Frankfurt Auschwitz Trial 1963–65', *Central European History*, 35(3) (2002), 346.

68. Marc von Miquel, 'Wir müssen mit den Mördern zusammenleben! NS-Prozesse und politische Öffentlichkeit in den sechziger Jahren', in Fritz Bauer Institute (ed.), *'Gerichtstag halten über uns selbst' – Geschichte und Wirkung des ersten Frankfurter Auschwitz Prozesses* (Frankfurt/Main: Campus Verlag, 2001), p. 98.
69. Ibid.
70. Fritz Bauer, *Die Humanität der Rechtsordnung* (Frankfurt/Main: Campus Verlag, 1998), p. 103.
71. Ibid.
72. Ibid., p. 105. This claim seems very unlikely, but coming from an authority such as Dr Bauer it must have some validity.
73. Heiner Lichtenstein, 'NS-Prozesse und Öffentlichkeit' in *Juristische Zeitgeschichte*, Vol. 4 (Cologne: Justizministerium des Landes Nordrhein-Westfalen, 1996), p. 228. Simultaneously McCloy had also been very active in securing the early release of Nazi war criminals.
74. Streim, *Nationalsozialismus und Justiz*, p. 19.
75. Pätzold, *Nationalsozialismus und Justiz*, p. 41.
76. Gerald Reitlinger, *Die Endlösung: Hitlers Versuch der Ausrottung der Juden Europas 1939–1945* (Berlin: Colloquium Verlag, 1956), first published 1953, English edition *The Final Solution: The Attempt to Exterminate the Jews of Europe 1939–1945* (London: Valentine Mitchell, 1953).
77. Bauer, *Die Humanität der Rechtsordnung*, p. 107.
78. Michael Greve, 'Von Auschwitz nach Ludwigsburg: Zu den Ermittlungen der 'Zentralen Stelle der Landesjustizverwaltungen zur Aufklärung nationalsozialistescher Gewaltverbrechen' in Ludwigsburg', in: Fritz Bauer Institut (ed.), *Im Labyrinth der Schuld* (Frankfurt/Main: Campus Verlag, 2003), p. 44.
79. Von Miquel, p. 101.
80. Ibid.
81. Ibid., p. 102.
82. Pätzold, *Nationalsozialismus und Justiz*, pp. 38–9.
83. Ibid., pp. 42–5.
84. Ibid., p. 47.
85. Lichtenstein, *NS-Prozesse und Öffentlichkeit*, p. 227.
86. Annette Rosskopf, 'Anwalt antifaschistischen Offensiven – Der DDR Nebenklagevertreter Friedrich Karl Kaul' in: Fritz Bauer Institute (Ed.) *'Gerichtstag halten über uns selbst'*, p. 145.
87. Norbert Podewin (ed.), *Braunbuch –Kriegs und Naziverbrecher in der Bundesrepublik und Berlin(West). Reprint der 1968 Ausgabe* (Berlin: Edition Ost, 2002) and D. Unverhan, *Das 'NS- Archiv' des Ministeriums für Staatssicherheit* (Berlin: LIT Verlag, 1998).
88. Hermann Langbein, *Der Auschwitz Prozess: Eine Dokumentation*, 2 Vols. (Frankfurt/Main: Verlag Neue Kritik, 1995), Vol. 1, p. 22.
89. Ibid., p. 25.
90. Ibid., pp. 32–4.
91. Rosskopf, pp. 143–4.
92. Ibid., p. 145.
93. Podewin, *Braunbuch*, p. 141.
94. Ibid.
95. Weinke, p. 239.
96. Rosskopf, p. 146.

97. Ibid., p. 147.
98. Felix Kresing-Wulf (ed.), *Judenverfolgung und jüdisches Leben unter den Bedingungen der nationalsozialistischen Gewaltherrschaft, II: Tondokumente und Rundfunksendungen 1947–1990*, 2 Vols (Potsdam: Verlag für Berlin-Brandenburg, 1997).
99. Walter Roller and Susanne Höschel (eds), *Judenverfolgung und jüdisches Leben unter den Bedingungen der nationalsozialistischen Gewaltherrschaft, 1: Tondokumente und Rundfunksendungen 1930–1946* (Potsdam: Verlag für Berlin-Brandenburg, 1996).
100. Diller and Mühl-Benninghaus (eds), *Berichterstattung über den Nürnberger Prozess*.
101. This information courtesy of Susanne Höschel at the DRA in Potsdam and Walter Roller at the DRA in Frankfurt (now in Wiesbaden) in conversation with the author in June 2003.
102. *Prozeß gegen den ehemaligen stellvertretenden Standortarzt im KZ Auschwitz-Monowitz, Horst Fischer, vor dem Ersten Strafsenat des Obersten Gerichts der DDR*. DRA Potsdam-Babelsberg, Archive No.: DRA Berlin 2014746X00.
103. This information courtesy of Susanne Höschel at the DRA in Potsdam, in conversation with the author in June 2003.
104. Oskar Groehler 'Verfolgten- und Opfergruppen in den politischen Auseinandersetzungen in der SBZ und DDR' in Jürgen Danyel (ed.), *Die geteilte Vergangenheit* (Berlin: Akademie Verlag, 1995), p. 18. What also stands to reason that the Hitler- Stalin pact is not mentioned in any of the GDR's resistance claims.
105. Ibid.
106. Ibid., p. 20.
107. Ibid., p. 21.
108. Ibid., p. 22.
109. *Der Schwur von Buchenwald*, DRA Potsdam-Babelsberg, Archive No. 2013603002, 2nd programme on montage reel DOK 1274. Unknown first broadcast date, but sometime in 1955.
110. There is extensive material on the issues surrounding Buchenwald: Lutz Niethammer, *Der gesäuberte Antifaschismus; Die SED und die roten Kapos von Buchenwald* (Berlin: Akademie Verlag, 1994), David A. Hackett (ed.) *The Buchenwald Report* (Boulder, CO: Westview Press, 1995) among many.
111. *Richard Kuchardzyk über die Selbstbefreiung des KZ Buchenwald unter der Führung der KPD*, DRA Potsdam-Babelsberg, Archive No. 2013603007, 10th programme on montage reel DOK 1274 Unknown first broadcast date, sometime in 1956.
112. Groehler, p. 20.
113. Jeffrey Herf, *Divided Memory: The Nazi Past in the Two Germanys* (London: Harvard University Press, 1997), p. 91.
114. Ibid. p. 99.
115. Ibid.
116. Ibid., p. 103.
117. Ibid., p. 174.
118. Ibid., p. 170.
119. *Lin Jaldati über das Schicksal der Anne Frank*, DRA Potsdam-Babelsberg, Archive No. DRA Berlin 2013625003, first broadcast 19 April 1957.

120. *Geheimblitz München: Funkdokumentation zum 20. Jahrestag der 'Kristallnacht'*, DRA Potsdam-Babelsberg, Archive No. DRA Berlin 2011989000,first broadcast 19 November 1958.
121. *'Der Ewige Jude' – Der Fall Eberhard Taubert. Funkdokumentation*, DRA Potsdam-Babelsberg, Archive No. DRA Berlin 2013250000, first broadcast 16 June 1959.
122. *Dokumentation über Nazi Verbrechen: Dokumentation über den Nazi Verbrecher Werner Ventzki, ehemaliger Bürgermeister der Stadt Lodz (Litzmannstadt)*, DRA Potsdam-Babelsberg, Archive No. DRA Berlin 2013704001, first broadcast 15 March 1960.
123. Schildt, *Moderne Zeiten*, p. 225.
124. *Auszug des Geistes*, Archive Nos. Radio Bremen, RBWO1715–RBWO 2100 (26 programmes).
125. *Nach Auschwitz – Lebensbericht des Kommandanten Rudolf Höß*, Südwestfunk, Baden-Baden, Archive No. SWF 5773019100/200, first broadcast 12 March 1959.
126. *Zur Woche der Brüderlichkeit: Der Aufstand im Warschauer Ghetto*, Archive No. SWF 5773793000, first broadcast 14 March 1960, and *Lodz, das erste und letzte geschlossene Ghetto Polens 20 Jahre nach seiner Gründung*, SWF 5773892000, first broadcast 12 April 1960, both Südwestfunk, Baden-Baden.
127. *Auschwitz*, Westdeutscher Rundfunk, Cologne, Archive No. WDR DOK 2163/2177, first broadcast 28 October 1961.
128. *Hinter der Mauer des Schweigens – Bilanz einer Reise. Ein Gespräch zwischen Peter Schier-Gribowsky und Thilo Koch mit dokumentierenden Interviews*. Norddeutscher Rundfunk, Hamburg, Archive No. NDR DWR 11458/1-4, first broadcast 20 February 1960.
129. *...als wär's ein Stück von Dir!* Germany (FR), 1959, Directed by Peter Schier-Gribowsky, production: NDR, Hamburg, 70 mins. First broadcast 14 September 1959, ARD.
130. A complete transcript of this sequence can be found in chapter 5, pp. 186–9.
131. *Hinter der Mauer des Schweigens*, 10'51". The timings in minutes and seconds for *Hinter der Mauer des Schweigens* are consecutive and not divided into separate programmes.
132. Ibid., 12'44"–14'50".
133. In particular: Nicolas Berg, *Der Holocaust und die westdeutschen Historiker* (Göttingen: Wallenstein Verlag, 2003). Berg accuses the historians of the IfZ of 'conducting research without remembering', excluding the work of Jewish or foreign historians (referring to Josef Wulf) p. 319. This is not supported by the findings of this research, which, in terms of their work for the radio, cannot fault the members of the IfZ.
134. *Hinter der Mauer des Schweigens*, 27'40".
135. As far as it is possible to ascertain, Mrs Israel's maiden name was Mosse, part of the Mosse publishing company.
136. Ibid., 32'20".
137. Ibid., 33'50"–34'28".
138. Ibid. 35'45".
139. Ibid.: 43'15–44'14".

140. Gitta Sereny, *Into that Darkness: from Mercy Killing to Mass Murder* (London: Pimlico, 1995).
141. *Hinter der Mauer des Schweigens*, 52'00"–56'57".
142. Ibid., 58'52"–59'51".
143. Ibid., 96'47".
144. Ibid., 106'08"–111'11". The Ludendorff movement was banned in 1961, but due to a technical mistake in the Constitutional Court's ruling, allowed again in 1996. Nowadays it publishes a journal (*Mut und Mass*) and has Internet presence – www.ludendorff.info (accessed 9 October 2005), a publishing house as well as a residential 'youth' hostel on the Starnberg lake in Bavaria.
145. Ibid., 119'17".
146. Ibid., 125'37"–130'40".
147. Ibid., 153'05"–154'59".
148. Schildt, *Moderne Zeiten*, p. 232. The *Freiheitssender 904* and *Deutscher Soldatensender* were short-lived East German stations pretending to be broadcasting from within the Federal Republic, mixing Western pop music with Marxist-Leninist indoctrination.
149. Peter Krause, *Der Eichmann-Prozeß in der deutschen Presse* (Frankfurt/Main: Campus Verlag, 2002), p. 78.
150. File E1/1961/Eichmann at the Written Archives Centre of BBC Monitoring, Caversham Park, Reading.
151. Krause, *Der Eichmann-Prozeß*, p. 211.
152. This information according to Susanne Höschel and Dr. Ingrid Pietrzynski at the DRA Potsdam, in conversation with the author, June 2003.
153. *Der Fall Eichmann. Zusammenfassung des bisherigen Prozeßverlaufs*, Radio Bremen, Archive No. RBAW 4004/210, first broadcast 15 August 1961.
154. *Prozeß gegen Adolf Eichmann vor dem Bezirksgericht in Jerusalem*, Westdeutscher Rundfunk, Cologne, Archive No. WDR1000698004, first broadcast 14 August 1961.
155. *Das Leben des Joel Brand. Gespräche zwischen Joel Brand und Peter Schier-Gribowsky über die Judenverfolgungen in Ungarn und Adolf Eichmann*. Norddeutscher Rundfunk, Hamburg, Archive No. NDR D ÜB 6678/1-5, first broadcast 11 July 1960.
156. *Radio-DDR-Hörbericht. Da ist noch Platz für Dr. Globke – Bericht und Abrechnung. Der Eichmann-Prozeß*, DRA Potsdam, Archive No. DRA Berlin 2013251000, first broadcast 30 June 1961.
157. Michael Lemke, 'Kampagnen gegen Bonn', in *Vierteljahrshefte für Zeitgeschichte*, 41 (April 1993), p. 154, footnote 4.
158. Herf, *Divided Memory*, p. 182.
159. *Braunbuch*, pp. 292–4.
160. Herf, *Divided Memory*, p. 184.
161. *Braunbuch*, pp. 326–7.
162. Albert Norden, *An Appeal to the Conscience to the World* (English; no date – date-stamped by Bodleian Library, Oxford: 7 April 1960).
163. Adolf Heusinger: Lieutenant-General, Chief of the Infantry of the Third Reich, co-plotter of the 20 July 1944 plot but reprieved by Hitler; sentenced at Nuremberg as a war-criminal, from 1955 chairman of the military council of the *Bundeswehr*, from 1961 to 1964 member of the standing committee of NATO in Washington, DC.

164. Norden, *An Appeal*, p. 5.
165. Lemke, p. 160, footnote 14.
166. Lemke, p. 159.
167. *Die Kinder von Zamość oder Wie die weisse Farbe der Unschuld schwarz wurde*, DRA Potsdam, Archive No. DRA Berlin 2013261000, first broadcast 24 January 1963.
168. *Kinder von Zamość*, 2'26"–4'26".
169. Ibid., 15'53".
170. Ibid., 37'20".
171. Ibid., 37'52".
172. The spelling of this name varies, according to the two available sources: phonetically, and on a recent website by the German state broadcaster ARD, this person's name is spelled 'Alev Bolkoviak', whereas in the archive listing of the DRA it is 'Alex Bolkowiak'.
173. Ibid., 40'55"–41'58".
174. Ibid., 47'53"–48'15".
175. Ibid., 49'54"–50'53".
176. Ibid., 55'40"–59'59".
177. *Sammelpunkt Shelesnastrasse. Dokumentation zum 20. Jahrestag des Aufstandes im Warschauer Ghetto*. DRA Potsdam, Archive No. 2013258000, 5'48"–9'34".
178. Ibid., 14'47"–15'40". Noemi Schatz-Weinkranz's memoir was widely available in the GDR, and was, in fact, one of the first Warsaw Ghetto memoirs to be published in 1947 – Noëmi Szac-Wajnkranc, *Przeminęło z ogniem – Pamiętnik pisany w Warszawie w okresie od założenia getta do jego likwidacji (Perished in the Fire – A Memoir written in Warsaw during the period of the Establishing the Ghetto until its Liquidation)*. In 1963 the Chr. Kaiser Verlag in Munich published a version of it in a collection entitled *Im Feuer vergangen*. Im Feuer vergangen – Tagebücher aus dem Ghetto (Munich: Chr. Kaiser Verlag, 1963)
179. Ibid., 21'00".
180. Ibid., 23'20"–28'00".
181. Ibid., 26'20"–26'50".
182. Ibid., 44'10".
183. Ibid., 44'52"–46'02'.'
184. *Radio DDR Hörbericht. Schicksal unter Globke's Sternen. Zeugenaussage des "jüdischen Mischlings" Peter Edel*. DRA Potsdam, Archive no. 2013529000.
185. Ibid., 13'56"–16'09".
186. Fritz Bauer Institut, *Auschwitz Prozeß 4Ks 2/63 Frankfurt am Main*, p. 677.
187. *Braunbuch*, p. 326.
188. *Die Banalität des Bösen. Der Eichmann-Prozeß in Jerusalem nach einer Analyse von Hannah Arendt*, Westdeutscher Rundfunk, Cologne, Archive No. WDR 3097485, 220 minutes in seven parts, first broadcast 16 May 1964.

4 Radio and the Auschwitz Trial

1. Alexander Kluge, 'Kommentar eines DDR-Programmabhorchers', in *Neue Geschichten: Hefte 1–18, 'Unheimlichkeit der Zeit'* (Frankfurt/Main: Suhrkamp Verlag, 1977), p. 268.

2. Detlev Claussen, 'Die Banalisierung des Bösen', in Michael Werz (ed.), *Antisemitismus und Gesellschaft: Zur Diskussion um Auschwitz, Kuturindustrie und Gewalt* (Frankfurt/Main: Verlag Neue Kritik, 1995), p. 14.
3. Ibid.
4. Kluge, *Kommentar*, p. 269.
5. Peter Krause, *Der Eichmann-Prozeß in der deutschen Presse*, p. 209.
6. Claussen, *Die Banalisierung*, p. 25.
7. Cited in Claussen, *Die Banalisierung*, p. 26; also Max Horkheimer, *Gesammelte Schriften 8* (Frankfurt/Main: Fischer Taschenbuch Verlag, 1985), p. 34.
8. Rosskopf, *Anwalt*, p. 157, footnote 8.
9. Ibid., pp. 157–8, footnote 17.
10. During the war von Schnitzler served in a propaganda section, then became a POW in Britain. Became part of the 'German Service' of the BBC before returning to the NWDR in Hamburg in late 1945. Left (or was dismissed) in 1947 and joined the East German *Berliner Rundfunk* and rose to the position of chief commentator for the state broadcasting committee. *Der Schwarze Kanal* continued until the autumn of 1989. See: Schneider, *Nationalsozialismus*, p. 261.
11. Orig.: *Krumme Juden ziehn dahin, daher, wohl durch das Rote Meer; die Wellen schlagen zu: die Welt hat Ruh!*
12. Deutsches Rundfunkarchiv Berlin, Potsdam-Babelsberg, Signatur: Kommentare 1963/64, File 207/01/02/06-9.
13. Langbein, *Der Auschwitz Prozess*, vol. 1, pp. 30–1.
14. The broadcast date of the programme was 16 March 1963, at a time when there was no standardised commemorative 'Auschwitz Day' (27 January).
15. Hessischer Rundfunk, Frankfurt/Main, Archiv Ton und Wort Dokumentation, Sendepläne 516.
16. The fact that so much incriminating 'evidence' was broadcast before the trial even began would certainly have been, in any other trial or circumstance, viewed as undue influencing of the jury. Werner Renz of the Fritz Bauer Institute in Frankfurt consulted the (now) retired lawyers of the Trial regarding this issue on behalf of the author in November 2004, who all confirmed that at the time there was no concern about this issue (see appendix). There are some broadcasters at the time, however, such as Axel Eggebrecht, who regularly mention their caution towards influencing the trial jury.
17. *Sondersendung 'Konzentrationslager Auschwitz' vor Beginn des Auschwitz Prozesses*, Hessischer Rundfunk, Frankfurt/Main, Archive No. HR 187043/187044, 12'14"–16'54".
18. See Langbein, also the audio recordings of trial proceedings on the DVD-ROM: Fritz Bauer Institut/Staatliches Museum Auschwitz Birkenau (eds), *Der Auschwitz Prozeß – Tonbandmitschnitte, Protokolle, Dokumente*.
19. Rosskopf, *Anwalt*, p. 141.
20. *Konzentrationslager Auschwitz*, 44'23".
21. Ibid., 61'33"–64'00".
22. *Wir haben es gesehen. Augenzeugenberichte über die Judenverfolgung im Dritten Reich*, Hessischer Rundfunk, Frankfurt/Main, Archive No: N/A.
23. The English edition of Borowski's short stories, which includes 'The World of Stone' are published under the title *This Way for the Gas, Ladies and Gentlemen* (London: Penguin, 1976).

24. *Auschwitz und die Literatur – Drei Versuche, das Entsetzliche zu überliefern*, Hessischer Rundfunk, Frankfurt/Main, Archive No: 11357/11357.
25. DRA Berlin, Potsdam-Babelsberg, Signatur: Kommentare 1963, File 207/01/02/06-7.
26. According to the *Braunbuch*, ter Meer was found guilty at Nuremberg and sentenced for I.G. Farben's involvement in the war effort (including the Buna plant at Auschwitz-Monowitz) and re-emerged as honorary chief executive of Bayer; Dürrfeld had been in charge of the Auschwitz plant, had been acquitted at Nuremberg and was on the board of directors of several industrial giants; Ambroß had been in Auschwitz before Dürrfeld, had been found guilty at Nuremberg and held equally as many, if not more directorships in various industries.
27. This information according to Werner Renz at the Fritz Bauer Institute, Frankfurt, in correspondence with the author in October 2003 (see Appendix).
28. Karen Gershon, *Eine deutsche Jüdin kehrt heim*, Written Archive Centre, BBC Monitoring, Caversham Park, Reading, File: German Scripts to East and Soviet Zone 1958–1976.
29. Ibid.
30. Written Archive Centre, BBC Monitoring, Caversham Park, Reading File: E1/1957/1 22 Germany, Norden, Albert (Prof.).
31. *Frankfurter Gespräch: Auschwitz-Prozeß in Frankfurt*. Hessischer Rundfunk, Frankfurt/Main Archive No. HR 3.261192, first broadcast 22 December 1963.
32. *Auschwitz Prozeß in Frankfurt – Erster Tag und Eröffnung*. Hessischer Rundfunk, Frankfurt/Main. Archive No. HR 4171978, first broadcast 20 December 1963.
33. *Erster Tag Auschwitz Prozeß*, Hessischer Rundfunk, Frankfurt/Main, Archive No. HR 4173737, first broadcast 20 December 1963.
34. See Herf, p. 428, footnote 56, also: Heinz Brandt, *Ein Traum, der nicht entführbar ist. Mein Weg zwischen Ost und West* (Frankfurt/Main: Fischer Taschenbuch Verlag, 1985).
35. *Auschwitz-Prozeß in Frankfurt am Main. Bericht über den Prozeß – Verhandlugen gegen den Angeklagten Robert Mulka, 1942/43 Adjutant des Lagerkommandanten Rudolf Höß und verantwortlich für die Vergasungsanlagen and die Beschaffung des Zyklon B.*, DRA Potsdam-Babelsberg, Archive No. DRA Berlin 2013722001, 2'35"–5'12".
36. One such programme is the five-minute-long *Auschwitz-Prozeß in Frankfurt am Main. VVN-Prozeßbeobachter Höhn über seine Eindrücke vom Auschwitz-Prozeß in Frankfurt am Main*, DRA Potsdam-Babelsberg, Archive No. DRA Berlin 2013724003.
37. *Der Auschwitz Prozeß von Frankfurt am Main. Kurt Goldstein über seine Häftlingszeit und seine Eindrücke vom Prozeß in Frankfurt am Main*. DRA Potsdam-Babelsberg, Archive No. DRA Berlin 2013723002, 8'25"–10'14".
38. DRA Potsdam-Babelsberg, Signatur: Kommentare 1963/1964, File 207/01/02/06-9.
39. Irmtrud Wojak, 'Im Labyrinth der Schuld: Fritz Bauer und die Aufarbeitung der NS-Verbrechen nach 1945', in Fritz Bauer Institut (ed.), *Im Labyrinth der Schuld Täter – Opfer – Ankläger. Jahrbuch 2003 zur Geschichte und Wirkung des Holocaust* (Frankfurt/Main: Campus Verlag, 2003), p. 33.

40. Florian Schmaltz, 'Das Historische Gutachten Jürgen Kuczynskis zur Rolle der I.G. Farben und des KZ Monowitz im ersten Frankfurter Auschwitz-Prozess', in: *Gerichtstag halten über uns selbst*, p. 119.
41. DRA Potsdam-Babelsberg, Signatur: Kommentare 1963/1964, File 207/01/02/06-9.
42. Schmaltz, *Das Historische Gutachten*, pp. 128–30.
43. The museum in Oswięćim wrote the following after the author's request for information on this matter:

    'Further to your letter of November 10, 2003, sent to the Museum via e-mail, we would like to inform you that we are not familiar with either the facts or documents pertaining to experiments with incendiary phosphorus, carried out by SS-Hauptsturmführer Dr Victor Capesius on Polish children from Zamosc region. Victor Capesius – head of SS pharmacy – from December 1943 carried out pharmacological experiments in KL Auschwitz. Together with other SS physicians he tried out on camp prisoners (males and females) tolerance andefficacy of new medicine on commission from German IG-Farbenindustrie, mainly Bayer company, belonging to this concern. By way of example, in 1944 he and SS physicians Weber and Rhode, tried out meskaline on Jewish prisoners – it was an unspecified drug, which was supposed to get military secrets from POWs.

    From prisoner staff, employed by him in the camp pharmacy, two women from Transylvania are known. They were deported to the Auschwitz Concentration Camp in 1944, in transports from Hungary: a woman called Pirozshka, chemist by profession, and Eva, a pharmacy student. Their family names, though, are unknown. In the Museum's archives, in the partly preserved camp documentation, there are two female prisoners, called Anna Silberstein. In both cases their Auschwitz serial numbers are not known. One was Anna Silberstein – Hungarian Jew –, b. September 15, 1923 in Halmosa, the other Anna Silberstein – Slovakian Jew –, b. August 12, 1927 in Bratislava. Both were transferred form Auschwitz to Hohenlebern, Germany, on September 12, 1944.

    Another female prisoner, called Silberstein, whose first name begins with 'A' letter, a French Jew, aged 36, and whose camp serial number was 50319, lived to be liberated in KL Auschwitz. We do not know, however, whether any of them had anything to do with Capesius in KL Auschwitz.'
44. *Ehrenmänner*, DRA Potsdam-Babelsberg, Archive No. DRA Berlin FEA 3, 6'24"–6'45".
45. Ibid., 7'18".
46. Ibid., 29'06".
47. This is also mentioned in Bernd Naumann's account of the Trial. Bernd Naumann, *Auschwitz*, p. 111.
48. *Ehrenmänner*, 22'14"–24'17".
49. Ibid., 36'29"–36'41".
50. Ibid., 37'04"–38'01".
51. John Sandford, 'What are the Media for? Philosophies of the Media in the Federal Republic and the GDR', *Contemporary German Studies Occasional Papers No.5* (Glasgow: University of Strathclyde, 1988), p. 14.
52. Shoshana Felman and Dori Laub, *Testimony: The Crisis of Witnessing in Literature, Psychoanalysis and History* (London: Routledge, 1992), p. 61.

53. Paper found by the author in the reel casing of *Ehrenmänner*, DRA Berlin, Potsdam-Babelsberg.
54. *Lexikon der Mörder, Sonderbehandlung: Exekution*, Südwestfunk, Baden-Baden, Archive No. SWF 5776503000, first broadcast 12 March 1964.
55. *Das Ringelblum-Archiv im Warschauer Ghetto*, Südwestfunk, Baden-Baden, Archive No. SWF 5776990000, first broadcast 11 March 1965.
56. *Das Auswärtige Amt und die 'Endlösung der Judenfrage': Das Auswärtige Amt und seine Mitarbeiter im Dritten Reich*, Radio Bremen, Archive No. RB AW4141, first broadcast 17 May 1965.
57. *Gespräch mit Karl Jaspers über Hannah Arendts Eichmann-Buch, den deutschen Widerstand im Dritten Reich und die Rolle der jüdischen Organisationen*, Westdeutscher Rundfunk, Cologne, Archive No. WDR 1005189004, unknown first broadcast date, sometime in 1965.
58. *Zur Diskussion steht das Theaterstück 'Der Stellvertreter' von Rolf Hochhuth*, Westdeutscher Rundfunk, Cologne, Archive No. WDR 10055404001, first broadcast 28 April 1964.
59. *Das Nürnberger Gespräch 1965. Auschnitte aus der Podiumsdiskussion (29. und 30. April 1965) 'Was hat Auschwitz mit dem deutschen Menschen zu tun?'*, Bayerischer Rundfunk, Munich, Archive No. BR Nürnberg Dok 1740N Dok 1741N, first broadcast May 1965. H.G. Adler chaired the discussion with the participation of Dr. Fritz Bauer, Dr. Ernst Weymar, Dietrich Strothmann and Horst Krüger.
60. *Im Labyrinth der Schuld. Ein Tag im Frankfurter Auschwitz-Prozeß*, Südwestfunk, Baden-Baden, Archive No. SWF 5776567100/200, first broadcast 29 April 1964.
61. Fritz Bauer Institut, *Auschwitz Prozeß 4Ks 2/63 Frankfurt am Main*, p. 760.
62. Ibid., p. 762.
63. *Im Labyrinth der Schuld*, 3'23"–4'15".
64. Ibid., 21'00"–21'20".
65. Ibid., 27'42"–28'25".
66. Ibid., 36'04"–36'33".
67. Ibid., 59'17"–59'39".
68. Ibid., 67'25"–68'30".
69. Fritz Bauer Institut, *Auschwitz Prozeß 4Ks 2/63 Frankfurt am Main*, p. 763.
70. Ibid.
71. *Im Labyrinth der Schuld*, 41'24".
72. Ibid., 45'03"–45'57".
73. Naumann, *Auschwitz*, p. 98.
74. *Im Labyrinth der Schuld*, 50'27".
75. For instance, Irmtrud Wojak, 'Im Labyrinth der Schuld: Fritz Bauer und die Aufarbeitung der NS-Verbrechen nach 1945', in Fritz Bauer Institut (ed.), *Im Labyrinth der Schuld Täter – Opfer – Ankläger*.
76. Hans Laternser, *Die andere Seite im Auschwitz-Prozeß 1963–65* (Stuttgart: Seewald Verlag, 1966).
77. Such as Langbein, Naumann and, more recently, Pendas and Wittmann.
78. Fritz Bauer Institut, *Auschwitz Prozeß 4Ks 2/63 Frankfurt am Main*, p. 747.
79. Axel Eggebrecht, *Der Halbe Weg: Zwischenbilanz einer Epoche* (Hamburg: Rowohlt Verlag ,1984), and Fritz Bauer Institut, *Auschwitz Prozeß 4Ks 2/63 Frankfurt am Main*, pp. 747–8.

80. Axel Eggebrecht (ed.), *Die zornigen alten Männer: Gedanken über Deutschland seit 1945* (Hamburg: Rowohlt Verlag, 1979).
81. Fritz Bauer Institut, *Auschwitz Prozeß 4Ks 2/63 Frankfurt am Main*, p. 749.
82. Eggebrecht, *Der Halbe Weg*, p. 342.
83. Letter from Inge Deutschkron to the author, 23 January 2005.
84. *Erster Bericht vom Auschwitz-Prozeß*, Norddeutscher Rundfunk, Hamburg, Archive no. WR14469/DWR14469, 0'00"–1'08", first broadcast 27 December 1963.
85. Ibid., 1'43"–3'46".
86. Ibid., 6'11".
87. Ibid., 10'52"–12'58".
88. Presse – und Informationsamt der Bundesregierung, *Die Verfolgung nationalsozialistischer Straftaten in der Bundesrepublik* (Bonn, 1963).
89. *Die Verfolgung nationalsozialistischer Straftaten*, p. 31.
90. *Erster Bericht vom Auschwitz-Prozeß*, 35'59".
91. Joachim C. Fest, *The Face of the Third Reich* (London: Weidenfeld and Nicolson, 1970).
92. *Erster Bericht vom Auschwitz-Prozeß*, 41'53"–43'10".
93. Mitschnitt der Diskussionsveranstaltung 'Auschwitz – Einzelfall oder Symptom?' Norddeutscher Rundfunk, Hamburg, Archive No. NDR D N996/1-4, first broadcast 13 July 1964.
94. Ibid., 5'15".
95. Ibid., 12'00".
96. Ibid., 29'10"–31'00".
97. Ibid., 42'10".
98. Ibid., 55'08".
99. Ibid., 60'18"–61'58".
100. Ibid., 95'01"–97'46".
101. *Auschwitz – Einzelfall oder Symptom?*, 141'31"–142'57".
102. *Auschwitz Prozeß 4Ks 2/63 Frankfurt am Main*, p. 748.
103. Ibid.
104. *Zwischenbilanz vom Auschwitz-Prozeß*, Norddeutscher Rundfunk, Hamburg, Archive No. NDR DWR 1519/1-2, first broadcast 17 November 1964.
105. Ibid., 89'24"–90'11".
106. *Abschlußbericht über den Auschwitz-Prozeß in Frankfurt/Main*, Norddeutscher Rundfunk, Hamburg, Archive No. NDR DWR 16072, first broadcast 7 October 1965.
107. Ibid., 0'25".
108. Ibid., 16'30"–17'05".
109. Ibid., 30'02".
110. Ibid., 33'55".
111. Ibid., 44'35".
112. According to Wasserstrom, Boger grabbed a young boy, who was eating an apple, by the legs and smashed his head against the wall until he was dead. He later calmly ate the apple. Ibid., 78'01"; also mentioned in Naumann, Langbein and others.
113. *Abschlußbericht*, 83'52".
114. Ibid., 86'56".
115. Ibid., 87'06"–88'51".

116. Ibid., 90'42".
117. *Auschwitz Prozeß 4Ks 2/63 Frankfurt am Main*, p. 751.
118. Axel Eggebrecht (ed.), *Die zornigen alten Männer: Gedanken über Deutschland seit 1945* (Hamburg: Rowohlt Verlag, 1979).
119. Ibid., p. 23.
120. Ibid., p. 24.
121. Ibid., p. 25.
122. *Urteilsverkündung im Frankfurter Auschwitz Prozess*, Hessischer Rundfunk, Frankfurt/Main, Archive No. 2945619/102, first broadcast 20 August 1965.
123. *Urteilsbegründung im Auschwitz-Prozess am 21. August 1965*, Südwestfunk, Baden-Baden, Archive No. 5951764100/200.
124. Peter Weiss, *The Investigation – Oratorio in 11 Cantos* (London: Calder and Boyars, 1965).
125. Christoph Weiß, *Auschwitz in der geteilten Welt – Peter Weiss und die 'Ermittlung' im Kalten Krieg* (St Ingbert: Röhrig Universitätsverlag, 2000) This two-volume, 1,400-page work deals with all aspects of the performances of Weiss's play, including comprehensive citations from newspapers and radio stations.
126. Ibid., vol. 2, p. 851.
127. Ibid., vol. 2, p. 304.
128. Ibid., vol 2, pp. 688–90.
129. *Diskussion über Sinn und Bedeutung der NS-Prozesse mit Opfern, Juristen und Jugendlichen*; Hessischer Rundfunk, Frankfurt/Main, Archive No. 42600/42601, 0'06"–0'41".
130. Herbert Jäger, *Verbrechen unter totalitärer Herrschaft: Studien zur nationalsozialistischen Gewaltkriminalität* (Frankfurt: Suhrkamp Verlag, 1967).
131. *Diskussion*, 7'50"–8'53".
132. Ibid., 29'19"–32'09".
133. Ibid., 38'43"–43'07".
134. Ibid., 55'14"–58'05".
135. *Ein Volk spielt Blinde Kuh' oder: Die Suche nach den NS-Verbrechern*, Norddeutscher Rundfunk, Hamburg, Archive No. DR DWR 18840/1, first broadcast 19 February 1968.
136. *Lebendige Geschichte: Die deutsche Großbourgeoisie und die Anfänge der faschistischen Judenverfolgung*, Radio DDR II, Berlin, Archive No. DRA Berlin 2012014000, first broadcast 29 April 1973.

5 Radio and Memory

1. Lutz and Wodak, *Information für Informierte*.
2. Paul Lazarsfeld, *Radio Listening in America: The People Look at Radio* (Chapel Hill: University of North Carolina Press, 1946).
3. Margot Berghaus, *Wie Massenmedien wirken*, p. 182.
4. Ibid., p. 183.
5. Wolfgang Mühl-Benninghaus, 'Medienpolitische Probleme in Deutschland zwischen 1945 und 1989', in: Heide Riedel (ed.), *Mit uns zieht die neue Zeit... 40 Jahre DDR Medien* (Berlin: Vistas Verlag, 1993), p. 9.

240 Notes

6. Ibid., p. 11.
7. Maurice Halbwachs, *On Collective Memory* (Chicago: University of Chicago Press, 1992).
8. Pierre Nora, 'Between Memory and History: Les Lieux de Mémoire', *Representations*, 26 (Spring 1989), p. 8; and Kerwin Lee Klein, 'On the Emergence of Memory in Historical Discourse', *Representations*, 69 (Winter 2000), p. 138.
9. Pierre Nora, *Between Memory and History*, p. 7.
10. Ibid.
11. Linda Reisch, 'Gleitwort' in: Hanno Loewy (ed.), *Holocaust: Die Grenzen des Verstehens. Eine Debatte über die Besetzung der Geschichte* (Hamburg: Rowohlt, 1992), p. 7.
12. Dan Diner, *Beyond the Conceivable: Studies on Germany, Nazism and the Holocaust* (Berkeley: University of California Press, 2000), p. 181.
13. Bernd Faulenbach, 'Erinnerungsarbeit und demokratische Kultur heute', in: Claudia Lenz, Jens Schmidt and Oliver von Wrochem (eds), *Erinnerungskulturen im Dialog – Europäische Perspektiven auf die NS-Vergangenheit* (Hamburg: Unrast Verlag, 2002), p. 86.
14. Diner, *Beyond the Conceivable*, p. 179.
15. Shoshana Felman and Dori Laub, *Testimony: The Crisis of Witnessing in Literature, Psychoanalysis and History* (London: Routledge, 1992), p. 59.
16. Ibid., p. 60.
17. Aleida Assmann, *Erinnerungsräume: Formen und Wandlungen des kulturellen Gedächtnisses* (Munich: C.H. Beck, 2003), p. 276.
18. Dominick LaCapra, *Representing the Holocaust: History, Theory, Trauma* (Ithaca, NY: Cornell University Press, 1994) and *History and Memory after Auschwitz* (Ithaca, NY: Cornell University Press, 1998).
19. Klein, *On the Emergence*, p. 137.
20. Ibid., pp. 137–8.
21. Ibid., p. 133, Klein citing Funkenstein.
22. Ibid.
23. Wulf Kansteiner, 'Finding Meaning in Memory: A Methodological Critique of Collective Memory Studies', *History and Theory*, 41 (May 2002), p. 187.
24. Ibid., p. 180.
25. Ibid., p. 194.
26. Axel Schildt, 'Zwei Staaten – eine Hörfunk – und Fernsehnation. Überlegungen zur Bedeutung der elektronischen Massenmedien in der Geschichte der Kommunikation zwischen der Bundesrepublik und der DDR', in Arndt Bauerkämper, Martin Sabrow and Bernd Stöver (eds), *Doppelte Zeitgeschichte. Deutsch-deutsche Beziehungen 1945–1990* (Bonn: Verlag J.H.W. Dietz Nachfolger, 1998), p. 60.
27. Konrad Dussel, 'Vom Radio- zum Fernsehalter. Medienumbrüche in sozialgeschichtlicher Perspektive', in: Axel Schildt, Detlef Siegfried and Christian Lammers (eds), *Dynamische Zeiten* (Hamburg: Hans Christians Verlag, 2003), p. 673.
28. Alexander and Margarete Mitscherlich, *Die Unfähigkeit zu trauern: Grundlagen kollektiven Verhaltens* (Munich: Piper, 1977).
29. Friedrich Pollock, *Gruppenexperiment: Ein Studienbericht* (Frankfurt/Main: Europäische Verlagsanstalt, 1955).

30. Kansteiner, *Finding Meaning in Memory*, p. 187, footnote 36.
31. Ibid., p. 197.
32. Konrad Dussel, *Hörfunk in Deutschland: Politik, Programm, Publikum (1923–1960)* (Potsdam: Verlag für Berlin- Brandenburg, 2002), p. 241.
33. Ibid.
34. Peter J. Humphreys, *Media and Media Policy in Germany: The Press and Broadcasting since 1945* (Oxford: Berg, 1994), p. 315.
35. Christoph Classen, '"Guten Abend und Auf Wiederhören". Faschismus und Antifaschismus in Hörfunkkommentaren der frühen DDR', in Martin Sabrow (ed.), *Die verwaltete Vergangenheit. Geschichtskultur und Herrschaftslegitimation in der DDR* (Leipzig: Akademische Verlagsanstalt, 1997), pp. 238–9.
36. Sandford, *What are the Media For?*, p. 14.
37. 'Unsere Nachrichten: objektiv und wahr', in: Konrad Dussel and Edgar Lersch, *Quellen zur Programmgeschichte des deutschen Hörfunks und Fernsehens* (Göttingen: Muster Schmidt Verlag, 1999), p. 185.
38. Classen, *'Guten Abend und Auf Wiederhören'*, p. 247.
39. Ibid., pp. 247–8.
40. Ibid., p. 248.
41. Ibid., pp. 252–3.
42. Dussel, *Hörfunk in Deutschland*, p. 296.
43. Inge Marßolek, 'Radio in Deutschland 1923–1960', in *Geschichte und Gesellschaft*, 27, 2 (2001), p. 224.
44. John Sandford, *What are the Media For?*, p. 8.
45. Dussel, *Hörfunk in Deutschland*, p. 303.
46. Hans Benzien, 'Wer besitzt das bessere System? – Zum Selbstverständnis des DDR Journalisten', in Heide Riedel (ed.), *Mit uns zieht die neue Zeit… 40 Jahre DDR Medien*, p. 33.
47. Ibid., p. 34.
48. Ibid., pp. 36–7.
49. Ibid., p. 37.
50. Dussel, *Hörfunk in Deutschland*, p. 297.
51. Ibid., p. 307.
52. Ibid., p. 301.
53. Ibid., p. 302.
54. Dussel and Lersch, *Quellen zur Programmgeschichte*, pp. 186–7.
55. Ibid., pp. 189–90.
56. Christoph Classen, 'Zum öffentlichen Umgang mit der NS-Vergangenheit in der DDR. Das Beispiel des Radios', in *Dynamische Zeiten*, p. 170.
57. Ibid., p. 171.
58. Ibid., p. 168, footnote 10.
59. Ibid., p. 169.
60. Ibid., pp. 179–80.
61. Dussel, *Hörfunk in Deutschland*, p. 382.
62. Dussel and Lersch, *Quellen zur Programmgeschichte*, p. 255, also in Dussel, *Hörfunk in Deutschland*, p. 315 and Fischer, *Dokumente*, p. 214.
63. Petra Galle, *RIAS Berlin und Berliner Rundfunk 1945–1949. Die Entwicklung ihrer Profile in Programm, Personal und Organisation vor dem hintergrund des beginnenden Kalten Krieges* (Münster: LIT Verlag, 2003), p. 241.
64. Ibid., p. 50.

65. Adolf Grimme, *Selbstbesinnung* (Braunschweig: Georg Westermann Verlag, 1947) pp. 221–6.
66. Humphreys, *Media and Media Policy in Germany*, p. 28.
67. Thomas Mann, *Beobachtungen eines Unpolitischen* (Frankfurt/Main: S. Fischer, 1919); trans. *Reflections of a Non-political Man* (New York: F. Unger, 1983).
68. Inge Marßolek, 'Vertraute Töne und Unerhörtes. Radio und Gedächtnis im Nachkriegsdeutschland', in: Elisabeth Domansky and Harald Welzer (eds), *Eine offene Geschichte. Zur kommunikativen Tradierung der nationalsozialistischen Vergangenheit* (Tübingen: edition discord, 1999), p. 157.
69. Ingrid Pietrzynski, 'Die Menschen und die Verhältnisse verbessern' Literaturvermittlung in Literatursendungen des DDR-Rundfunks', in Monika Estermann and Edgar Lersch (eds), *Buch, Buchhandel, Rundfunk 1950–1960* (Wiesbaden: Harrasowitz Verlag, 1999), p. 139.
70. Dussel and Lersch, *Quellen zur Programmgeschichte*, p. 242.
71. Hans Bausch, *Rundfunk in Deutschland. Band 3: Rundfunkpolitik nach 1945*, vol. 1, p. 153.
72. Ibid., p. 154.
73. Ibid., p. 155.
74. Ibid., p. 160.
75. Dussel, *Hörfunk in Deutschland*, p. 315.
76. Ibid., p. 316, also in Dussel and Lersch, *Quellen zur Programmgeschichte*, p. 257.
77. Dussel, *Hörfunk in Deutschland*, p. 316.
78. Ibid.
79. Ibid., p. 340.
80. Schildt, *Moderne Zeiten*, p. 241.
81. Dussel, *Hörfunk in Deutschland*, p. 340.
82. Schildt, p. 241, footnote 245.
83. Ibid.
84. Dussel, *Hörfunk in Deutschland*, p. 343.
85. Ibid., pp. 344–5.
86. Bausch, *Rundfunk*, pp. 430–8.
87. Dussel, *Hörfunk in Deutschland*, p. 351.
88. Ibid.
89. Schildt, *Moderne Zeiten*, p. 244.
90. Dussel, *Hörfunk in Deutschland*, p. 111.
91. Ibid., p. 112.
92. Ibid.
93. The level of the involvement of RIAS in the events of 17 June 1953 is still far from clear. Some explanations are offered in Wilfried Rogasch,'Kalter Krieg im Äther', in Katharina Klotz, Winfried Ranke and Wilfried Rogasch, *Deutschland im Kalten Krieg – Eine Ausstellung des Deutschen Historischen Museums* (Berlin: Argon, 1992), footnote 62.
94. Dussel, *Hörfunk in Deutschland*, p. 113.
95. Ibid., p. 114. Also the origin of this listener correspondence was unclear. Were they party functionaries or 'your average listener'?
96. Liselotte Mühlberg, 'Hörerforschung des DDR-Rundfunks', in Heide Riedel (ed.), *Mit uns zieht die neue Zeit... 40 Jahre DDR Medien*, p. 174.
97. Dussel, *Hörfunk in Deutschland*, p. 119.

98. Ibid., p. 120.
99. Mühlberg, *Hörerforschung des DDR-Rundfunks*, p. 177.
100. Schildt, *Moderne Zeiten*, p. 258.
101. Mühlberg, *Hörerforschung des DDR-Rundfunks*, p. 177.
102. Dussel, *Hörfunk in Deutschland*, pp. 121–3.
103. Ibid., p. 117.
104. Ibid., p. 118.
105. Ibid.
106. Ibid., p. 116.
107. Ibid., p. 310.
108. Mühlberg, *Hörerforschung des DDR-Rundfunks*, p. 175.
109. Ibid.
110. Ibid., p. 176.
111. Ibid.
112. Ibid., p. 180.
113. Ibid., p. 177.
114. Michael Kohlstruck, *Zwische Erinnerung und Geschichte – Der Nationalsozialismus und die jungen Deutschen* (Berlin: Metropol Verlag, 1997), p. 47.
115. Ibid., p. 47. The reintegration of former Nazis was not, however, as far reaching as in the FRG; professions such as teachers, judges, policemen and public service posts remained closed to ex-NSDAP members.
116. Ibid., p. 50.
117. Ibid., pp. 51–2.
118. Institut für Demoskopie Allensbach, Allensbach, Archive no. 5513, IfD Umfrage 6013, Tabelle 3a.
119. Institut für Demoskopie Allensbach, Allensbach, Archive no. 5513, IfD Umfrage 6013, Tabelle 2a.
120. Ibid., Tabelle 2b.
121. Ibid., Tabelle 9.
122. Ibid., Tabelle 11.
123. Ibid., Tabelle 12.
124. Harold Welzer, Sabine Moller and Karoline Tschuggnall, *Opa war kein Nazi – Nationalsozialismus und Holocaust im Familiengedächtnis* (Frankfurt: Fischer Taschenbuch, 2002), p. 16.
125. Ibid., p. 168.
126. Ibid., p. 173.
127. Ibid., p. 174.
128. Ibid., p. 176.
129. Ibid., pp. 183–4.
130. Ibid., p. 192.
131. Fritz Eberhard, *Der Rundfunkhörer und sein Programm – Ein Beitrag zur empirischen Sozialforschung* (Berlin: Colloquium Verlag, 1962).
132. Ibid., p. 29.
133. Ibid., pp. 29–30.
134. Dussel, *Hörfunk*, p. 110.
135. Hansjörg Bessler, *Hörer- und Zuschauerforschung: Rundfunk in Deutschland Band 5* (Munich: dtv, 1980) p. 120.
136. Eberhard, *Der Rundfunkhörer und sein Programm*, p. 287.
137. Bessler, *Hörer- und Zuschauerforschung*, pp. 116–17.

138. Ibid.
139. Dussel, *Hörfunk*, p. 380.
140. Ibid.
141. Ibid., p. 381.
142. Ibid.
143. Ibid., p. 348.
144. Ibid., p. 349.
145. Staatsarchiv Hamburg, NDR/Infratest Hörerbefragung, August/September 1962; Akte 621 – 1(NDR) Signatur 848, p. 7.
146. Ibid., pp. 4–5.
147. Ibid., pp. 95–6.
148. Ibid., p. 97.
149. Ibid., p. 99.
150. Ibid., p. 102.
151. Ibid., p. 104.
152. Ibid., p. 105.
153. Ibid., p. 106.
154. Staatsarchiv Hamburg, EMNID Institut, Bielefeld Umfrage, Hörgewohnheiten im Sendegebiet des NDR 1970; Band 3: Kommentar der Verhaltens- und Meinungsbefragung April 1970; Akte 621-1(NDR) Signatur 848, p. 4
155. Pollock, *Gruppenexperiment*, p. 18.
156. Ibid., p. 21.
157. Ibid., pp. 22–3.
158. Ibid., p. 27.
159. Ibid., p. 28.
160. Ibid., p. 29.
161. Ibid., pp. 33–7.
162. Ibid., pp. 155–6.
163. Ibid., p. 156
164. Ibid., pp. 157–9.
165. Ibid., p. 283.
166. Ibid., p. 297.
167. Ibid., p. 300.
168. '...*als wär's ein Stück von Dir!*', Germany (FR), 1959, Directed by Peter Schier-Gribowsky, production: NDR, Hamburg, 70 mins. First broadcast 14 September 1959, ARD.
169. *Hinter der Mauer des Schweigens*, 00'54"–04'58".
170. Hans Lamm (ed.), *Der Eichmann Prozess in der deutschen öffentlichen Meinung* (Frankfurt: Ner-Tamid-Verlag, 1961), pp. 44–5.
171. Ibid., pp. 50–1.
172. Ibid., p. 59.
173. Schmidt and Becker, *Reaktionen auf politische Vorgänge*, p. 108.
174. Ibid., p. 109.
175. Ibid., p. 110.
176. Ibid.
177. Ibid., p. 111.
178. Ibid.
179. Ibid., p. 113.
180. Ibid., p. 117.

181. Alexander and Margarete Mitscherlich, *Die Unfähigkeit zu trauern*, p. 250.
182. Ibid., p. 251.
183. Ibid.
184. Ibid., p. 253.
185. Ibid., p. 259.
186. Ibid., p. 262.
187. Institut für Demoskopie Allensbach, Allensbach, Archive no. 5514, IfD Umfrage 6014, Tabelle 10.
188. Welzer, Moller and Tschuggnall, *Opa war kein Nazi*, p. 150.
189. Ibid., p. 151.
190. Ibid., p. 148.
191. Ibid., p. 149.
192. Ibid., p. 161.
193. Ibid., p. 160.
194. Ibid., p. 54.
195. Olaf Jensen, *Geschichte machen: Strukturmerkmale des intergenerationellen Sprechens über die NS-Vergangenheit in deutschen Familien* (Tübingen: edition discord, 2004), p. 42.
196. Ibid., p. 43.
197. Luhmann, *The Reality of the Mass Media*, p. 31.
198. Ibid., p. 103.
199. Crissell, *Understanding Radio*, p. 220.

6 Radio and History

1. *Das Lager*, 24'37"–24'44".
2. Wolfgang Sofsky, *The Order of Terror: The Concentration Camp* (Princeton: Princeton University Press, 1993), p. 314, footnote 19.
3. Ibid., p. 131,
4. Ibid., p. 134.
5. Primo Levi, *The Drowned and the Saved* (London: Abacus, 1989), pp. 30–1.
6. Niethammer, *Der gesäuberte Antifaschismus*, p. 345.
7. Hanna Yablonka, 'The Development of Holocaust Conciousness in Israel: The Nuremberg, Kapos, Kastner and Eichmann Trials', *Israel Studies*, 8.3 (2003), p. 2.
8. Levi, p. 28.
9. Lutz Nietmammer, *Der gesäuberte Antifaschismus*, pp. 493–519. The three prosecuted *Kapos* were Ernst Busse, Arthur Dietsch and Erich Reschke. Busse and Reschke, after having occupied prominent political positions in the fledgling GDR, were both arrested by SMAD in 1950 and sentenced to life imprisonment in a Soviet Gulag, where Busse died. Reschke was rehabilitated in 1956. Dietsch was sentenced to 15 years imprisonment by an US military court in 1947 and released after appeals by Kogon and others in 1950.
10. Orna Ben-Naftali and Yogev Tuval, 'Punishing International Crimes Committed by the Persecuted: The Kapo Trials in Israel (1950s–1960s)', *Journal of International Criminal Justice*, 4 (2006), p. 150.
11. Ibid., p. 151.

12. Ibid., p. 150, citing Hanna Yablonka (in Hebrew), see also: Hanna Yablonka, 'The Development of Holocaust Consciousness in Israel: The Nuremberg, Kapos, Kastner and Eichmann Trials', in: *Israel Studies*, 8, 3 (Fall 2003), 1–24.
13. Ben-Naftali and Tuval, 'Punishing International Crimes', p. 162.
14. Ulrich-Dieter Oppitz, *Strafverfahren und Strafvollstreckung bei NS-Gewaltverbrechen* (Ulm, 1976), p. 308.
15. Ibid., p. 309.
16. Karin Hartewig, 'Wolf unter Wölfen? Die prekäre Macht der kommunistischen Kapos im Konzentrationslager Buchenwald', in: *Abgeleitete Macht – Funktionshäftlinge zwischen Widerstand und Kollaboration*, Beiträge zur Geschichte der nationalsozialistischen Verfolgung in Norddeutschland; Heft 4 (Bremen: Edition Temmen, 1998), p. 118.
17. David A Hackett (ed.), *The Buchenwald Report* (Boulder, CO: Westview Press, 1995).
18. Nietmammer, *Der gesäuberte Antifaschismus*, pp. 271–82.
19. Ibid.
20. Komitee der antifaschistischen Widerstandskämpfer in der DDR, *Auschwitz mahnt: Stellungnahme der ehemaligen politischen Gefangenen des Konzentrationslagers Auschwitz in der DDR zum Prozess gegen Windeck und Bonitz in Frankfurt am Main* (East Berlin: Komitee der antifaschistischen Widerstandskämpfer in der DDR, 1968).
21. *Auschwitz mahnt*, p. 8.
22. Ibid., p. 11.
23. Ibid.
24. Ibid.
25. Christian Dirks, 'Wie die DDR ihr eigenes Tribunal inzenierte', *Frankfurter Rundschau*, 4 October 2001.
26. Archiv Fritz-Bauer-Institut, Frankfurt/Main, File: IG Farben Prozeß.
27. Archiv Fritz-Bauer-Institut, Frankfurt/Main, File: Dritter Auschwitz Prozeß, Nachlass Henry Ormond (NHO 1 thereafter).
28. NHO 1, p. 50, reference to Martin Broszat.
29. Ibid., p. 49.
30. Ibid., p. 44.
31. Ibid., p. 45.
32. Ibid., p. 46.
33. Ibid., p. 135.
34. Ibid., pp. 130–50.
35. Ibid., pp. 54–71.
36. Ibid., p. 47.
37. Ibid., p. 47.
38. Ibid., pp. 48–9.
39. Ibid., pp. 89–178.
40. Ibid., p. 114.
41. Ibid., p. 115.
42. Ibid. 'In seiner Egozentrik und mit großem Selbstmitleid, die in der Hauptverhandlung deutlich erkennbar waren, hat er vieles ihm Unangenehme verdrängt und vergessen.'
43. Ibid., p. 109.

44. Ibid., pp. 109–10.
45. Ibid., p. 113.
46. NHO 1, p. 39.
47. Ibid., p. 40.
48. Ibid., p. 41.
49. Ibid., p. 42.
50. Ibid., p. 43.
51. Müller, *Furchtbare Juristen*, p. 251.
52. The regional court in Tübingen accepted that Faltlhauser did not act maliciously, as the murders committed at the euthanasia institute of Grafeneck had been carried out of 'pity, one of the noblest motivations in human activity.' Müller, *Furchtbare Juristen*, p. 256.
53. Leu was acquitted in October 1951 by a Cologne court, as he participated in the euthanasia programme 'out of idealism', the proof of which was, in the judge's opinion, the fact that he was concerned about the acquisition of coffins for the victim. Ibid.
54. SS-Obersturmführer Dr. Borm, who had personally pushed over 6,000 disabled persons into improvised gas chambers, where they were killed by carbon monoxide, was found not to have acted 'maliciously', as he viewed the victims' deaths as their 'salvation' and as 'mercy killing'. In 1974 the appeal court supported the original verdict and Borm remained a free man. Ibid. pp. 255–6.
55. Riedel had, on his own initiative and without orders, locked seven 'partisans' into a gassing van, where they died of monoxide poisoning. After hearing evidence from a medical expert, the court decided that Riedel was not guilty of murder, as this action was neither malicious not cruel, as death by carbon monoxide poisoning was not considered 'cruel', and the charge of maliciousness was eliminated on the grounds that the partisans knew full well that the Germans had such gassing vans. Ibid., p. 257.
56. The most comprehensive overview of all German legal proceedings against Nazi criminals from 1945 onwards is the University of Amsterdam's massive project *Justitz und NS-Verbrechen* under the guidance of Dr Dick W. de Mildt and Professor Christiaan Frederik Rüter. Their extensive published material is supplemented by an on-line database containing details thousands of trials in East and West Germany. It is accessible through: http://www1.jur.uva.nl/junsv/inhaltsverzeichnis.htm (accessed 9 October 2005).
57. As in a case against SS-Unterstrumfuehrer Alois Haeferle – who, in the Chelmno death camp, murdered 89,000 persons, but was only deemed an accomplice to murder as the deeds were not considered 'his own'. An appeal by the prosecution was rejected due to the above ruling and Haeferle was acquitted in 1964. Müller, *Furchtbare Juristen*, pp. 253–4.
58. Ibid., p. 299.
59. Christian Dirks, '*Wie die DDR ihr eigenes Tribunal inzenierte*', *Frankfurter Rundschau*, 4 October 2001.
60. Within the research for this study this could be highlighted by the muddling and misplacing of sources by various radio stations concerning the origins of the GDR broadcast *Sammelpunkt Shelesnasrtasse*. As mentioned above, a key witness in this broadcast, a certain Colonel Alex Bolkowiak, claims that, among other things, that the Warsaw Ghetto uprising had been directed by

agents from Moscow and the Polish People's Party, as well as another witnesses' statement. These two witness' statements are extraordinary in their content by themselves, but above all, they cannot be verified by any other source. In continuing attempts to find references to these names I came across them on a website of the German broadcaster ARD, entitled *60 Jahre Kriegsende*. (http://kriegsende.ard.de/pages_std_lib/0,3275,OID1303944,00.html accessed 9 October 2005, first accessed May 2005). There these two sources are attributed to the West German broadcaster NDR, and although the extracts for listening on the website and the ones cited here are not identical, they do stem from the GDR programme. I have been extremely cautious regarding the authenticity of these statements, but was told, in an enquiry to the ARD regarding this, that the web page represents a 'journalistic and not a scientific' undertaking, and have received no further explanations since. For correspondence see Appendix.

61. Certainly in most of the literature of the German '68er' generation the first point of politicisation/radicalisation occurred through becoming aware of the Auschwitz Trial. See: Gerd Koenen, *Das rote Jahrzehnt: Unsere kleine deutsche Kulturrevolution* (Cologne: Kiepenheuer & Witsch, 2001), Rudi Dutschke, *Die Revolte: Wurzeln und Spuren eines Aufbruchs* (Hamburg: Reibek, 1983), Peter Mosler, *Was wir wollten, was wir wurden* (Hamburg: Reibek, 1988) and others.

62. An excellent exposition of (West) German television of the issue of the Holocaust can be found in part 3 of Wulf Kansteiner's *In Pursuit of German Memory – History, Television and Politics after Auschwitz* (Athens, OH: Ohio University Press, 2006), pp. 109–83.

Appendix

Map 1 German broadcasters' areas after 1948.

Source: http://www.dhm.de/lemo/objekte/karten/Nachkriegsjahre_HungerNachKultur/index.html. Note that the NWDR also covered Berlin, where the Americans had set up the separate station RIAS (Radio im Amerikanischen Sektor).

Email correspondence between the author and Werner Renz of the Fritz Bauer Institute in Frankfurt (16 December 2003) regarding the last-minute appointment of Judge Hofmeyer

Lieber Herr Wolf,

> diese Frage kann ich Ihnen auf der Grundlage meiner Aktenkenntnis beantworten.
>
> Forester war als Vorsitzender des Schwurgerichts entsprechend des Geschäftsverteilungsplans vorgesehen.
>
> Er war jüdischer Herkunft und hat einen Antrag auf Selbstablehnung gestellt, weil er sich selbst als Betroffener für befangen hielt.
>
> Ich kopiere Ihnen aus meiner unveröffentlichten Arbeit die entsprechenden Angaben in den laufenden Text.

Mit besten Grüßen

Werner Renz

> Der Präsident des LG Frankfurt am Main bestimmte mit Verfügung vom 8.10.1963 "den Zusammentritt des Schwurgerichts zu seiner nächsten, der 3. Tagung, auf den 20. Dezember 1963".11 StA F, 4 Ks 2/63, HA, Bd. 89, Bl. 17596. Laut Geschäftsverteilungsplan für das Jahr 196322 StA F, 4 Ks 2/63, HA, Bd. 126, Bl. 20409-20410. war Senatspräsident Forester zum Vorsitzenden der 3. Schwurgerichts-Tagung bestellt.
> Forester machte aber am 9.10.196333 StA F, 4 Ks 2/63, HA, Bd. 91, Bl. 17823. gemäß § 30 StPO Anzeige von dem Verhältnis, selbst "rassisch Verfolgter" zu sein. Außerdem sei sein Bruder "in dem KZ Lublin/Majdanek umgebracht", seine Mutter in das "KZ Theresienstadt" deportiert worden. Foresters Selbstablehnungsantrag beschied die 3. Strafkammer b. LG Frankfurt am Main positiv. Mit Beschluss vom 14.10.196344 StA F, 4 Ks 2/63, HA, Bd. 91, Bl. 17824. wurde Forester "wegen Besorgnis der Befangenheit von der Mitwirkung als Richter entbunden".
> Auch der laut Geschäftsverteilungsplan für das Jahr 1963 als 2. Beisitzer der 3. Schwurgerichtsperiode zugeteilte Amtsgerichtsrat Johann Heinrich Niemöller zeigte am

11.11.196355 StA F, 4 Ks 2/63, HA, Bd. 88, Bl. 17309. an, Sohn von Martin Niemöller, der von 1938 bis 1945 in den Konzentrationslagern Sachsenhausen und Dachau inhaftiert gewesen war, zu sein. Obgleich Niemöller sich nicht für befangen hielt, rechtfertigte das angezeigte Verhältnis die Annahme, dass die Angeklagten dies anders beurteilen würden. Auch Niemöller wurde mit Beschluss vom 13.11.196366 Ebd., HA, Bd. 88, Bl. 17310. wegen Besorgnis der Befangenheit von der Mitwirkung als Richter an dem Verfahren entbunden.
Bereits am 1.10.1963 hatten die Rechtsanwälte Stolting II und Eggert namens ihrer Mandanten Höcker und Nierzwicki Landgerichtsrat Koch, Berichterstatter der 3. Strafkammer b. LG Frankfurt am Main, aus Besorgnis der Befangenheit77 Ebd., HA, Bd. 88, Bl. 17063.
abgelehnt. Laut Antrag der Verteidigung gehöre Koch "selbst zu dem Kreis der rassisch Verfolgten", weshalb die Annahme naheliege, Koch habe "Verwandte, sonstige Angehörige oder Freunde und Bekannte in den Massenvernichtungslagern des so genannten Dritten Reiches verloren".88 Ebd., HA, Bd. 88, Bl. 17064.
 Koch99 Ebd., HA, Bd. 88, Bl. 17066. hielt sich nicht für befangen, die Kammer erachtete die Ablehnung Kochs für unbegründet.110 Ebd., HA, Bd. 88, Bl. 17067.0

Werner Renz
(Abt. Dokumentation)

Fritz Bauer Institut
IG Farben-Haus
Grüneburgplatz 1
60323 Frankfurt am Main

Tel.: 069/798322-25
Fax: 069/798322-41
E-mail:
Internet: www.fritz-bauer-institut.de

Email correspondence between author and Werner Renz of the Fritz Bauer Institute in Frankfurt (4 February 2004) regarding undue press influence during the Auschwitz Trial

Lieber René Wolf,

lange hat es gedauert, bis ich den besagten OStA a. D. erreicht habe.

Er gab mir auf Ihre Anfrage den Hinweis, dass es nach deutschem Strafverfahrensrecht keine Schwierigkeiten mache, wenn Geschworenen vor dem Beginn der Hauptverhandlung durch die Medien bereits Informationen über das Tatgeschehen in Auschwitz zugänglich waren.

Auch die Tatsache, dass Zeugen vor dem Prozess sich in Medien bereits geäussert haben, stellt keine Beeinflussung dar.

Beste Grüße

Werner Renz

Email correspondence between author and the Auschwitz museum regarding the claims contained in the GDR programme *Ehrenmänner*

Oświęcim, December 16, 2003

ref. iv-bad./464/15066/03

Dear Rene Wolf,

Further to your letter of November 10, 2003, sent to the Museum via e-mail, we would like to inform you that we are not familiar with either the facts or documents pertaining to experiments with incendiary phosphorus, carried out by SS-Hauptsturmführer Dr Victor Capesius on Polish children from Zamosc region.

Victor Capesius – head of SS pharmacy – from December 1943 carried out pharmacological experiments in KL Auschwitz. Together with other SS hysicians he tried out on camp prisoners (males and females) tolerance and efficacy of new medicine on commission from German IG-Farbenindustrie, mainly Bayer company, belonging to this concern. By way of example, in 1944 he and SS physicians Weber and Rhode, they tried out meskaline on Jewish prisoners – it was unspecified drug, which was supposed to get military secrets from POWs.

From prisoner staff, employed by him in the camp pharmacy, two women from Transylvania are known. They were deported to the Auschwitz Concentration Camp in 1944, in transports from Hungary: a woman called Pirozshka, chemist by profession, and Eva, a pharmacy student. Their family names, though, are unknown.

In the Museum's archives, in the partly preserved camp documentation, there are two female prisoners, called Anna Silberstein. In both cases their Auschwitz serial numbers are not known. One was Anna Silberstein – Hungarian Jew –, b. September 15, 1923 in Halmosa, the other Anna Silberstein – Slovakian Jew –, b. August 12, 1927 in Bratislava. Both were transferred form Auschwitz to Hohenlebern, Germany, on September 12, 1944.

Another female prisoner, called Silberstein, whose first name begins with 'A' letter, a French Jew, aged 36, and whose camp serial number was 50319, lived to be liberated in KL Auschwitz. We do not know, however, whether any of them had anything to do with Capesius in KL Auschwitz.

Sincerely yours,
Jerzy Wróblewski

Director
Auschwitz-Birkenau State Museum

Email correspondence between the author and Dr Bogdan Musial at the German Historical Institute Warsaw (February 2004) regarding Colonel Bolkoviak's claims made in the GDR programme *Sammelpunkt Shelesnastrasse*

Date: Mon, 10. Feb 2004 20:08

From: "René Wolf

To:

Subject: eine Anfrage

Sehr geehrter Dr. Musial Ich bin ein PhD Student an der Royal Holloway University of London und mein Doktorvater ist Dr. Dan Stone, der mir ihren Namen vermittelte. Ich recherchiere die Rundfunkberichterstattung ueber den ersten Auschwitz Prozess im Ost und Westdeutschen Rundfunk und waehrend meinen Recherchen habe ich jetzt etwas einigermassend Merkwuerdiges gefunden, und es ist das folgende: In einer Sendung des Deutschlandsenders (DDR) vom April 1963 mit dem Titel "Sammelpunkt Shelesnastrasse" befindet sich ein Interview mit einem "Oberst" der Polnischen Volksgarde mit dem Namen Gustav Alex Wolkowiak (also die Buchstabierung ist phonetisch, da dies vom Tonband transkriptiert wurde). Oberst Wolkolwiak behauptet da in diesem Programm dass die Polnische Arbeiter Partei die Fuehrung des Ghetto Aufstandes "schon im Januar 1943 uebernahm", und dass ein "alter Spanienkaempfer" mit dem Namen Anje Schmitt von der Sovietunion in das Warschauer Ghetto ging um den Aufstand zu leiten. Er selbst (also Oberst Wolkowiak) sei auch selbst ins Ghetto gegangen um den "Anti-Faschistischen Block" (Zionistische Jugendorganisationen, Sozialisten, Zionisten, Hechaluz und Ha-Shomer ha Tsa-ir unter der Fuehrung der Polnischen Arbeiter Partei) zu fuehren. Waehre das moeglich gewesen? Fuer mich ist es das erste mal dass ich gehoert habe dass Leute von aussen ins Ghetto gingen um den Aufstand zu organisieren. Auch die Namen sind mir nicht bekannt, vor allem "Anje Schmitt". Wuessten Sie vielleicht etwas darueber? Es wuerde mich freuen wenn Sie antworten koennten Mit freundlichen Gruessen.

René Wolf

Lieber Herr Wolf,

Um ehrlich zu sein, war ich zunaechst genauso ueberrascht wie Sie. Ich habe nie davon gehoert, dass der Ghetto-Aufstand von Aussen (und noch dazu von der Polnische Arbeiter Partei (PPR)) vorbereitet worden sei. Auch habe ich noch nie von Oberst Wolkowiak und Anje Schnitt gehoert. Ich werde aber noch einen Bekannten fragen, der gerade zur Geschichte der PPR waehrend des Krieges promoviert hatte, nach diesen Namen. Vielleicht hat er von diesen Personen gehoert. Ich kann den Kollegen aber erst nach meiner Rueckkehr nach Warschau (in etwa 8 Tagen) fragen. Falls ich es vergessen sollte, schicken Sie mir eine kurze e-mail, denn ich bin zur Zeit beim Umzug von Warschau nach Deutschland und ich vergesse viele Sachen.

Auf den zweiten Blick erscheint jedoch das alles nicht so ueberraschend. Denn die PPR, die waehrend des Krieges eher bescheidene militaerische Erfolge vorzuweisen hatte, schrieb sich nach 1945 viele Aktionen zu, die von anderen Formationen durchgefuehrt worden waren. Viele Aktionen sind einfach erfunden worden, andere aufgebauscht usw. Die kommunistische Propaganda, die sich uebrigens bis heute auswirkt, machte aus der PPR die Haupttraegerin des Widerstandes gegen die deutsche Besatzung in Polen. Es ging um die Legitimation der eigenen Herrschaft nach 1945. So dass eigentlich nicht ueberrascht, dass sich die PPR auch den Ghetto-Aufstand zuschreiben versuchte. Wenn wir dazu noch bedenken, dass ab 1956 im kommunistischen Apparat antisemitische Tendenzen immer staerker wurden, was 1968 mit Vertreibung der meisten in Polen uebriggebliebenen Juden endete, erscheint dies alles irgendwie "logisch".

Kurzum: Ich halte es fuer ausgeschlossen, dass die PPR den Ghetto-Aufstand vorbereitete und leitete. Fuer durchaus wahrscheinlich halte ich jedoch den Versuch der kommunistischen Propaganda, nach 1945 die Verdienste um den Ghetto-Aufstand der PPR zuzuschreiben. Das von Ihnen gefundene Interview belegt das.

Mit herzlichen Gruessen
Bogdan Musial

Email correspondence regarding ARD website '60 Jahre Kriegsende' (May 2005)

Name: Wolf, René

Nachricht:
Sehr geehrtes ARD

Ich bin ein Doktorandenstudent and der Royal Holloway University of London und befasse mich mit der Rundfunkberichterstattung ueber den Holocaust im Ost- und Westdeutschen Rundfunk. In ihrem Beitrag (webpage) zum Warschauer Ghetto haben sie Auszuege von den Zeitzeugen Alef Bokoviak und Noemi Schatz-Weinkranz und bezeichnen den NDR als deren Quelle. Soviel mir jedoch bekannt ist, kommen diese Auszuege von einem DDR programm des Deuschlandssenders vom April 1963 mit dem Titel Sammelpunkt Shelesnastrasse (DRA Berlin Archivnummer 2013258000). Ich moechte sie daruf hinweisen dass diese Zeitzeugenaussagen – vor allem im weiteren Zusammenhang des Programmes – nicht bestaetigt werden koennen und wahrscheinlich nicht wahr sind, obwohl es moeglich gewesen waere. Gibt es diese Aufnahmen im NDR? Und wenn es diese gibt, gibt es noch mehr Information ueber diese Zeitzeugen?

Beste Gruesse
Ihr
René Wolf

Sehr geehrter Herr Wolf,

herzlichen Dank für Ihre Maiil und für Ihre Hinweise. Die von Ihnen genannten Zeitzeugen tragen deshalb die Quellenbezeichnung "NDR", weil sie in der Tat einem Beitrag aus dem NDR Archiv entnommen sind. Alle NDR Archivangaben können Sie dem angehängten PDF-Dokument entnehmen. Es ist sehr gut möglich, dass die Autorin des Beitrages, Christiane Glas, auf die von Ihnen genannten Quelle zurückgegriffen hat. Das kann ich aber nicht beantworten. Ich möchte Sie bitten, diese Frage direkt mit Frau Glas: c.glas.fm@ndr.de zu klären. Was den Wahrheitsgehalt der Aussagen betrifft: Bitte haben Sie Verständnis dafür, dass es sich bei www.kriegsende.ard.de um ein journalistisches und kein wissenschaftliches Projekt handelt. Ich bin selbst Historiker und weiß, wie zweifelhaft Projekte der "oral history" sind, weil sich natürlich Erinnerungen mit der Zeit verändern und Zeitzeugen möglicherweise überzeugt davon sind, Dinge erlebt zu haben, die sich in der Realität ganz anders abgepielt haben. Da aber die angesprochenen Aussagen, wie Sie selbst einräumen, möglicherweise wahr sind und zumindest die Vorfälle im Warschauer Ghetto nicht in ein gänzlich falsches Licht rücken, halte ich es für vertretbar, sie auch auf der Seite darzustellen. Es ist bei der Fülle der Themen nicht zu leisten, jede Erinnerung darauf zu überprüfen, ob sie sich tatsächlich so abgepielt hat. Dass deutsche Soldaten im Ghetto unfassbare Gräuel verübt haben, ist denke ich, völlig unstrittig, wie etwa auch die Autobiografie von Marcel Reich-Ranicki "Mein Leben" so schmerzlich wie eindrucksvoll dokumentiert.

Ich hoffe, sie kommen bei Ihrer Suche nach den Originalquellen weiter und verbleibe mit besten Grüßen

Thomas Luerweg

Norddeutscher Rundfunk

Programmdirektion Hörfunk
PB Programmbegleitende Dienste/Multimedia
Redaktion Internet & Intranet
Rothenbaumchaussee 132–134
20149 Hamburg

Bibliography

Sound archive sources of radio programmes listened to and transcribed

Deutsche Welle, Ton-und Wortdokumentation, Bonn

Das Lager; Gespräche mit Überlebenden des Konzentrationslagers Auschwitz; Deutsche Welle series Das Politische Feature, Archive No. DW 4025830.

Deutsches Rundfunkarchiv (DRA) Potsdam Babelsberg (GDR programmes)

Auschwitz-Prozeß in Frankfurt am Main. Bericht über den Prozeß – Verhandlugen gegen den Angeklagten Robert Mulka, 1942/43 Adjutant des Lagerkommandanten Rudolf Höß und verantwortlich für die Vergasungsanlagen und die Beschaffung des Zyklon B. Archive No. DRA Berlin 2013722001.

Auschwitz-Prozeß in Frankfurt am Main. VVN-Prozeßbeobachter Höhn über seine Eindrücke vom Auschwitz-Prozeß in Frankfurt am Main. Archive No. DRA Berlin 2013724003.

Der Auschwitz Prozeß von Frankfurt am Main. Kurt Goldstein über seine Häftlingszeit und seine Eindrücke vom Prozeß in Frankfurt am Main. Archive No. DRA Berlin 2013723002.

Der Schwur von Buchenwald, Archive No. DRA Berlin 2013603002.

Die Kinder von Zamość oder Wie die weisse Farbe der Unschuld schwarz wurde, Archive No. DRA Berlin 2013261000.

Lebendige Geschichte: Die deutsche Großbourgeoisie und die Anfänge der faschistischen Judenverfolgung. Archive No. DRA Berlin 2012014000.

Prozeß gegen den ehemaligen stellvertetenden Standortarzt im KZ Auschwitz-Monowitz, Horst Fischer, vor dem Ersten Strafsenat des Obersten Gerichts der DDR. Archive No. DRA Berlin 2014746X00.

Radio DDR Hörbericht. Schicksal unter Globke's Sternen. Zeugenaussage des 'jüdischen Mischlings' Peter Edel. Archive No. DRA Berlin 2013529000.

Richard Kuchardzyk über die Selbstbefreiung des KZ Buchenwald unter der Führung der KPD, Archive No. DRA Berlin 2013603007.

Sammelpunkt Shelesnastarsse. Dokumentation zum 20. Jahrestag des Aufstandes im Warschauer Ghetto. Archive No. DRA Berlin 2013258000.

Hessischer Rundfunk, Ton – und Wortdokumentation Frankfurt am Main

Auschwitz Prozeß in Frankfurt – Erster Tag und Eröffnung. Archive No. HR 4171978.

Auschwitz und die Literatur – Drei Versuche, das Entsetzliche zu überliefern. Archive No: HR 11357/11357.

Diskussion über Sinn und Bedeutung der NS-Prozesse mit Opfern, Juristen und Jugendlichen. Archive No. HR 42600/42601.
Erster Tag Auschwitz Prozeß. Archive No. HR 4173737.
Frankfurter Gespräch: Auschwitz-Prozeß in Frankfurt. Archive No. HR 3.261192.
So arbeitet das Lager – Unterricht im Deutschen; Beobachtungen beim Dritten Auschwitz Prozess in Frankfurt. Archive No. HR 2990-00100.
Sondersendung 'Konzentrationslager Auschwitz' vor Beginn des Auschwitz Prozesses. Archive No. HR 187043/187044.
Urteilsverkündung im Frankfurter Auschwitz Prozess. Archive No. HR 2945619/102.

Norddeutscher Rundfunk, Schall – und Wortarchiv, Hamburg

Abschlußbericht über den Auschwitz-Prozeß in Frankfurt/Main. Archive No. NDR DWR 16072.
Ein Volk spielt Blinde Kuh' oder: Die Suche nach den NS-Verbrechern. Archive No. DR DWR 18840/1.
Erster Bericht vom Auschwitz-Prozeß. Archive No. WR14469/DWR14469.
Hinter der Mauer des Schweigens, Archive No. NDR DWR 11458.
Mitschnitt der Diskussionsveranstaltung 'Auschwitz – Einzelfall oder Symptom?' Archive No. NDR D N996/1-4.
Zwischenbilanz vom Auschwitz-Prozeß. Archive No. NDR DWR 1519/1-2.

Südwestfunk, Ton – und Wortdokumentation, Baden-Baden

Im Labyrinth der Schuld. Ein Tag im Frankfurter Auschwitz-Prozeß. Archive No. SWF 5776567100/200.
Lexikon der Mörder, Sonderbehandlung: Exekution. Archive No. SWF 5776503000.
Urteilsbegründung im Auschwitz-Prozess am 21. August 1965. Archive No. SWF 5951764100/200.

Written word sources from radio archives

BBC Written Archive Centre, Caversham Park, Reading

E1/1957/1 22 Germany, Norden, Albert (Prof.).
E1/22 Germany, Richard O'Rourke Programmes/Scripts of commentaries to the GDR 1956–75.
E1/1961/Eichmann Trial.
Eine deutsche Jüdin kehrt heim by Karen Gershon. German Scripts to East and Soviet Zone 1958–76.

Sendemanuskripte DRA Potsdam-Babelsberg

13 November 1963, Wolfgang Dost. Signatur: Kommentare 1963, File 207/01/02/06-7.
6 February 1964, Karl Eduard von Schnitzler. Signatur: Kommentare 1963/64, File 207/01/02/06-9.
9 February 1964, Alfred Fleischhacker. Signatur: Kommentare 1963/64, File 207/01/02/06-9.
20 March 1964, Martin Radman. Signatur: Kommentare 1963/1964, File 207/01/02/06-9.

Hessischer Rundfunk, Ton – und Wortdokumentation Frankfurt am Main

Sendepläne 516 (1963–1965).

Other archives

Fritz Bauer Institut, Johann Wolfgang von Goethe Universität, Frankfurt am Main

Archiv Fritz-Bauer-Institut, File: IG Farben Prozeß.
Archiv Fritz-Bauer-Institut, Nachlass Henry Ormond File: Dritter Auschwitz Prozeß.

Institut für Demoskopie Allensbach, Allensbach

IfD Umfrage 6013 Archive no. 5513, Tabelle 2a.
IfD Umfrage 6013, Archive no. 5513, Tabelle 3a.
IfD Umfrage 6014 Archive no.5514 Tabelle 10.

Staatsarchiv Hamburg

EMNID Institut, Bielefeld Umfrage, Hörgewohnheiten im Sendegebiet des NDR 1970, Band 3: Kommentar der Verhaltens- und Meinungsbefragung April 1970. Akte 621-1(NDR) Signatur 848.
NDR/Infratest Hörerbefragung, August/September 1962; Akte 621 – 1(NDR) Signatur 848.

Internet resources referred to (all last accessed 9 October 2005)

http://www1.jur.uva.nl/junsv/inhaltsverzeichnis.htm
http://www.bbc.co.uk/radio4/history/sceptred_isle/index.shtml
http://kriegsende.ard.de/pages_std_lib/0,3275,OID1303944,00.html
http://www.ludendorff.info
http://www.medienrezeption.de/zeitschriften/rundfunk/RuG1+2_00/miszellen/piet.html

Journals and newspapers

Arendt, Hannah, 'Organisierte Schuld', *Die Wandlung*, 1(4) (1945/46).
Bathrick, David, 'Making a National Family on the Radio: The Nazi "Wunschkonzert"' in: *Modernism/Modernity*, 4(1) (1997).
Berghaus, Margot, 'Wie Massenmedien wirken', in: *Rundfunk und Fernsehen*, 47(2) (1999).
Danyel, Jürgen, 'Vom schwierigen Umgang mit der Schuld: Die Deutschen in der DDR und der Nationalsozialismus' in: *Zeitschrift für Geschichtswissenschaft*, 40(10) (1992).
Dirks, Christian, 'Wie die DDR ihr eigenes Tribunal inzenierte', *Frankfurter Rundschau*, 4 October 2001.

Gericke, Hans Otto, 'Die Presseberichterstattung über den Nürnberger Prozeß und die Überwindung des faschistischen Geschichtsbildes', *Zeitschrift für Geschichtswissenschaft*, 33(10) (1985).
Kansteiner, Wulf, 'Finding Meaning in Memory: A Methodological Critique of Collective Memory Studies', *History and Theory*, 41 (2002).
Klein, Kerwin Lee, 'On the Emergence of Memory in Historical Discourse', *Representations*, 69 (2000).
Lemke, Michael, 'Kampagnen gegen Bonn', *Vierteljahrshefte für Zeitgeschichte*, 41 (1993).
Lersch, Edgar, 'Die Thematisierung des Nationalsozialismus im Rundfunk der Nachkriegszeit', *Rundfunk und Geschichte*, 29(1/2) (2003).
Marßolek, Inge, 'Radio in Deutschland 1923–1960', *Geschichte und Gesellschaft*, 27(2) (2001).
Moores, Sean, 'The Box on the Dresser: Memories of Early Radio and Everyday Life' *Media, Culture and Society*, 10 (1988).
Nora, Pierre, 'Between Memory and History: Les Lieux de Mémoire', *Representations*, 26 (1989).
Pietrzynski, Ingrid, 'Die Gegenwart zwingt zur Besinnung: Die Thematisierung von Kriegsschuld in Kommentaren und Betrachtungen des DDR-Rundfunks der 50er Jahre' *Rundfunk und Geschichte*, 26(1/2) (2000).
Sandford, John, 'What are the Media for? Philosophies of the Media in the Federal Republic and the GDR', in *Contemporary German Studies Occasional Papers No. 5* (Glasgow: University of Strathclyde, 1988).
Thompson, E.P., 'Time, Work-Discipline and Industrial Capitalism', *Past and Present*, 38 (1967).
Wittmann, Rebecca, 'The Wheels of Justice Turn Slowly: The Pretrial Investigations of the Frankfurt Auschwitz Trial 1963–65', *Central European History*, 35(3) (2002).
Yablonka, Hanna, 'The Development of Holocaust Consciousness in Israel: The Nuremberg, Kapos, Kastner and Eichmann Trials', *Israel Studies*, 8(3) (2003).

Books

Åberg, Carin, 'Radio Analysis? Sure! But How?', in Andreas Stuhlmann (ed.), *Radio Kultur und Hör -Kunst – Zwischen Avantgarde und Populärkultur 1923–2001* (Würzburg: Königshausen & Neumann, 2001).
Adorno, Theodor W., *Critical Models* (New York: Columbia University Press, 1998).
Adorno, Theodor W., 'The Psychological Technique of Thomas' Radio Addresses', in *Gesammelte Schriften 9.1; Soziologische Schriften II* (Frankfurt/Main: Suhrkamp Verlag, 1975).
agenda, *Nationalsozialismus und Justiz: Die Aufarbeitung von Gewaltverbrechen damals und heute* (Münster: Agenda Verlag,1993).
Ahrends, Martin, *Klirrende Wörter. Kleiner Sprachführer in ein dahingehendes Deutsch* (Frankfurt/Main: Fischer Verlag, 1990).
Alexander, Maximillian, *Das Chamaeleon: Der Mann, der sich Gaston Oulmán nannte* (Hamburg: Glöß Verlag, 1978).
Apitz, Bruno, *Naked Among Wolves*, transl. Edith Anderson (Berlin: Seven Seas Books, 1960).

Article 19, *Broadcasting Genocide: Censorship, Propaganda and State-Sponsored Violence in Rwanda 1990–1994* (London: Article 19, 1996).
Assmann, Aleida, *Erinnerungsräume: Formen und Wandlungen des kulturellen Gedächtnisses* (Munich: C. H. Beck, 2003).
Baudrillard, Jean, *Selected Writings* (Stanford: Stanford University Press, 1988).
Bauer, Fritz, *Die Humanität der Rechtsordnung* (Frankfurt/Main: Campus Verlag, 1998).
Bausch, Hans, *Rundfunk in Deutschland; Band 3 Rundfunkpolitik nach 1945; Erster Teil* (Munich: dtv, 1980).
Behrens, Roger, 'Die Stimme als Gast empfangen – Walter Benjamins Überlegungen zur Radioarbeit' in Andreas Stuhlmann (ed.), *Radio Kultur und Hör-Kunst*.
Benjamin, Walter, 'Zweierlei Volkstümlichkeit', *Gesammelte Schriften IV.2* (Frankfurt/Main: Suhrkamp 1972).
Benjamin, Walter, *Illuminations* (London, Collins, 1973).
Benzien, Hans, 'Wer besitzt das bessere System? – Zum Selbstverständnis des DDR Journalisten', in Heide Riedel (ed.), *Mit uns zieht die neue Zeit... 40 Jahre DDR Medien*.
Berg, Nicolas, *Der Holocaust und die Westdeutschen Historiker* (Göttingen: Wallenstein Verlag, 2003).
Bergmeier, Horst J.P. and Rainer E. Lotz, *Hitler's Airwaves: The Inside Story of Nazi Radio Broadcasting and Propaganda Swing* (New Haven: Yale University Press, 1997).
Bessler, Hansjörg, *Hörer- und Zuschauerforschung – Rundfunk in Deutschland Band 5* (Munich: dtv, 1980).
Bloxham, Donald, *Genocide on Trial* (Oxford: Oxford University Press, 2001).
Borowski, Tadeusz, *This Way for the Gas, Ladies and Gentlemen* (London: Penguin, 1976).
Brandt, Heinz, *Ein Traum, der nicht entführbar ist. Mein Weg zwischen Ost und West* (Frankfurt/Main: Fischer Taschenbuch Verlag, 1985).
Brecht, Bertolt, *Gesammelte Werke 18 – Schriften zur Literatur und Kunst I* (Frankfurt/Main: Suhrkamp, 1967).
Bürger, Peter, *Theory of the Avant-garde*, translated by Jochen Schutte-Sasse (Manchester: Manchester University Press, 1984).
Classen, Christoph, '"Guten Abend und Auf Wiederhören". Faschismus und Antifaschismus in Hörfunkkommentaren der frühen DDR', in Martin Sabrow (ed.), *Die Verwaltete Vergangenheit. Geschichtskultur und Herrschaftslegitimation in der DDR* (Leipzig: Akademische Verlagsanstalt, 1997).
Classen, Christoph, 'Zum öffentlichen Umgang mit der NS-Vergangenheit in der DDR. Das Beispiel des Radios', in Axel Schildt (ed.), *Dynamische Zeiten*.
Classen, Christoph, *Faschismus und Antifaschismus: Die Nationalsozialistische Vergangenheit im ostdeutschen Rundfunk 1945–1953* (Cologne: Böhlau Verlag, 2004).
Claussen, Detlev, 'Die Banalisierung des Bösen', in Michael Werz (ed.), *Antisemitismus und Gesellschaft: Zur Diskussion um Auschwitz, Kuturindustrie und Gewalt* (Frankfurt/Main: Verlag Neue Kritik, 1995).
Crisell, Andrew, *Understanding Radio*, 2nd edn (London: Routledge, 1994).
Deutschkron, Inge, *Ich trug nun den gelben Stern* (Munich: dtv, 2003).
Deutschkron, Inge, *Mein Leben nach dem Überleben* (Munich: dtv, 2001).
Diller, Ansgar and Werner Mühl-Benninghaus (eds), *Berichterstattung über den Nürnberger Prozess gegen die Hauptkriegsverbrecher 1945/46–Edition und Dokumentation ausgewählter Rundfunkquellen* (Potsdam: Verlag Berlin-Brandenburg, 1998).

Diner, Dan, *Beyond the Conceivable: Studies on Germany, Nazism and the Holocaust* (Berkeley: University of California Press, 2000).

Dussel, Konrad, *Hörfunk in Deutschland Politik, Programm, Publikum (1923–1960)* (Potsdam: Verlag für Berlin-Brandenburg, 2002).

Dussel, Konrad and Lersch, Edgar, *Quellen zur Programmgeschichte des deutschen Hörfunks und Fernsehens* (Göttingen: Muster Schmidt Verlag, 1999).

Dussel, Konrad, 'Vom Radio- zum Fernsehalter. Medienumbrüche in sozialgeschichtlicher Perspektive', in Axel Schildt, *Dynamische Zeiten*.

Dutschke, Rudi, *Die Revolte: Wurzeln und Spuren eines Aufbruchs* (Hamburg: Reibek, 1983).

Eberhard, Fritz, *Der Rundfunkhörer und sein Programm – Ein Beitrag zur empirischen Sozialforschung* (Berlin: Colloquium Verlag, 1962).

Eggebrecht, Axel (ed.), *Die zornigen alten Männer: Gedanken über Deutschland seit 1945* (Hamburg: Rowohlt Verlag, 1979).

Eggebrecht, Axel, *Der Halbe Weg: Zwischenbilanz einer Epoche* (Hamburg: Rowohlt Verlag ,1984).

Ermarth, Fritz, *Volk und Staat: Zehn ausgewählte Rundfunkvorträge* (Karlsruhe, 1947).

Farndale, Nigel, *Lord Haw Haw: the Tragedy of William and Mary Joyce* (London: Macmillan, 2005).

Faulenbach, Bernd, 'Erinnerungsarbeit und demokratische Kultur heute', in Claudia Lenz, Jens Schmidt and Oliver von Wrochem (eds), *Erinnerungskulturen im Dialog – Europäische Perspektiven auf die NS-Vergangenheit* (Hamburg: Unrast Verlag, 2002).

Felman, Shoshanna and Dori Laub, *Testimony: The Crisis of Witnessing in Literature, Psychoanalysis and History* (London: Routledge, 1992).

Fest, Joachim C., *The Face of the Third Reich* (London: Weidenfeld and Nicolson, 1970).

Fischer, E. Kurt, *Dokumente zur Geschichte des deutschen Rundfunks und Fernsehens* (Göttingen: Musterschmidt Verlag, 1957).

Frei, Norbert, *Adenauer's Germany and the Nazi Past: The Politics of Amnesty and Integration* (New York: Columbia University Press, 2002).

Frei, Norbert, van Laak, Dirk and Stolleis, Michael (eds), *Geschichte vor Gericht: Historiker, Richter und die Suche nach Gerechtigkeit* (Munich: C.H. Beck, 2000).

Fritz Bauer Institut, *Auschwitz Prozeß 4Ks 2/63 Frankfurt am Main* (Frankfurt/Main: Campus Verlag 2004).

Fritz Bauer Institute (ed.), *'Gerichtstag halten über uns selbst' – Geschichte und Wirkung des ersten Frankfurter Auschwitz Prozesses* (Frankfurt/Main: Campus Verlag, 2001).

Fritz Bauer Institut (ed.), *Im Labyrinth der Schuld* (Frankfurt/Main: Campus Verlag, 2003).

Fritz Bauer Institut/Staatliches Museum Auschwitz Birkenau, *Der Auschwitz Prozeß – Tonbandmitschnitte, Protokolle, Dokumente*. DVD-ROM (Berlin: Digitale Bibliothek, 2005).

Fröhlich, Claudia and Michael Kohlstruck, *Engagierte Demokraten: Vergangenheitspolitik in kritischer Absicht* (Münster: Westfälisches Dampfboot, 1999).

Galle, Petra, *RIAS Berlin und Berliner Rundfunk 1945–1949. Die Entwicklung ihrer Profile in Programm, Personal und Organisation vor dem hintergrund des beginnenden Kalten Krieges* (Münster: LIT Verlag, 2003).

Giddens, Anthony, *The Consequences of Modernity* (Cambridge: CUP, 1990).
Greve, Michael, 'Von Auschwitz nach Ludwigsburg: Zu den Ermittlungen der "Zentralen Stelle der Landesjustizverwaltungen zur Aufklärung nationalsozialistescher Gewaltverbrechen" in Ludwigsburg', in Fritz Bauer Institut (ed.), *Im Labyrinth der Schuld.Täter – Opfer – Ankläger*. (Frankfurt am Main, New York: Campus Verlag, 2003).
Grimme, Adolf, *Selbstbesinnung* (Braunschweig: Georg Westermann Verlag, 1947).
Groehler, Oskar. 'Verfolgten- und Opfergruppen in den politischen Auseinandersetzungen in der SBZ und DDR', in Jürgen Danyel (ed.), *Die geteilte Vergangenheit* (Berlin: Akademie Verlag, 1995).
Hackett, David A. (ed.) *The Buchenwald Report* (Boulder, CO: Westview Press, 1995).
Halbwachs, Maurice, *On Collective Memory* (Chicago: University of Chicago Press, 1992).
Hartewig, Karin, 'Wolf unter Wölfen? Die prekäre Macht der kommunistischen Kapos im Konzentrationslager Buchenwald', in *Abgeleitete Macht – Funktionshäftlinge zwischen Widerstand und Kollaboration*, Beiträge zur Geschichte der nationalsozialistischen Verfolgung in Norddeutschland; Heft 4 (Bremen: Edition Temmen, 1998).
Herf, Jeffrey, *Divided Memory: The Nazi Past in the Two Germanys* (London: Harvard University Press, 1997).
Heym, Stefan, *Wege und Umwege* (Munich: Wilhelm Goldmann Verlag, 1985).
Horkheimer, Max and Adorno, Theodor W., *The Dialectic of Enlightenment (1947)* (Stanford: Stanford University Press, 2002).
Horkheimer, Max, *Gesammelte Schriften 8* (Frankfurt/Main: Fischer Taschenbuch Verlag, 1985).
Humphreys, Peter J., *Media and Media Policy in Germany: The Press and Broadcasting since 1945* (Oxford: Berg, 1994).
Izyumov, N. and Linde, D., *Fundamentals of Radio* (Moscow: Mir Publishers, 1976).
Jäger, Herbert, *Verbrechen unter totalitärer Herrschaft: Studien zur nationalsozialistischen Gewaltkriminalität* (Frankfurt: Suhrkamp, 1967).
Jaspers, Karl, *Die Schuldfrage* (Zurich: Artemis Verlag, 1946).
Jay, Martin, *The Dialectical Imagination* (Berkeley: University of California Press, 1996).
Jensen, Olaf, *Geschichte machen: Strukturmerkmale des intergenerationellen Sprechens über die NS-Vergangenheit in deutschen Familien* (Tübingen: edition discord, 2004).
Kaienburg, Hermann, '"Freundschaft, Kameradschaft...Wie kann das möglich sein?' Solidarität, Widerstand und die Rolle der "rotten" Kapos in Neuengamme', in *Abgeleitete Macht*.
Kansteiner, Wulf, *In Pursuit of German Memory – History, Television and Politics after Auschwitz* (Athens, OH: Ohio University Press, 2006).
Kästner, Erich, *Notabene 45. Ein Tagebuch* (Munich: dtv, 1993).
Kenny, Mary, *Germany Calling* (Dublin: New Island, 2003).
Kluge, Alexander, *Neue Geschichten: Hefte 1–18, 'Unheimlichkeit der Zeit'* (Frankfurt/Main: Suhrkamp Verlag, 1977).

Koenen, Gerd, *Das rote Jahrzehnt: Unsere kleine deutsche Kulturrevolution* (Cologne: Kiepenheuer & Witsch, 2001).

Kohlstruck, Michael, *Zwische Erinnerung und Geschichte – Der Nationalsozialismus und die jungen Deutschen* (Berlin: Metropol Verlag, 1997).

Komitee der antifaschistischen Widerstandskämpfer in der DDR, *Auschwitz mahnt: Stellungnahme der ehemaligen politischen Gefangenen des Konzentrationslagers Auschwitz in der DDR zum Prozess gegen Windeck und Bonitz in Frankfurt am Main* (East Berlin: Komitee der antifaschistischen Widerstandskämpfer in der DDR, 1968).

Koselleck, Reinhart, *The Practice of Conceptual History* (Stanford: Stanford University Press, 2002).

Krause, Peter, *Der Eichmann-Prozeß in der deutschen Presse* (Frankfurt/Main: Campus Verlag, 2002).

Kresing-Wulf, Felix (ed.), *Judenverfolgung und jüdisches Leben unter den Bedingungen der nationalsozialistischen Gewaltherrschaft, II: Tondokumente und Rundfunksendungen 1947–1990*, 2 vols (Verlag für Berlin-Brandenburg; Potsdam, 1997).

LaCapra, Dominick, *Representing the Holocaust: History, Theory, Trauma* (Ithaca, NY: Cornell University Press, 1994).

LaCapra, Dominick, *History and Memory after Auschwitz* (Ithaca, NY: Cornell University Press, 1998).

Lacey, Kate, *Feminine Frequencies: Gender, German Radio and the Public Sphere* (Ann Arbor: University of Michigan Press, 1996).

Laclau, Ernesto and Mouffe, Chantal, *Hegemony and Socialist Strategy: Towards a Radical Democratic Politics*, 2nd edn (London, Polity, 2001).

Lamm, Hans (ed.) *Der Eichmann Prozess in der deutschen öffentlichen Meinung* (Frankfurt: Ner-Tamid-Verlag, 1961).

Langbein, Hermann, *Der Auschwitz Prozess: Eine Dokumentation*, 2 vols (Frankfurt/ Main: Verlag Neue Kritik, 1995).

Laternser, Hans, *Die andere Seite im Auschwitz-Prozeß 1963–65* (Stuttgart: Seewald Verlag, 1966).

Lazarsfeld, Paul, *Radio Listening in America: The People Look at Radio* (Chapel Hill: University of North Carolina Press, 1946).

Lewis, Derek, *Contemporary Germany* (London: Arnold, 2001).

Lichtenstein Heiner, 'NS-Prozesse und Öffentlichkeit', in *Juristische Zeitgeschichte*, vol. 4 (Justizministerium des Landes Nordrhein-Westfalen, 1996).

Luhmann, Niklas, *The Reality of the Mass Media* (Stanford: Polity, 2000).

Lutz, Benedict and Wodak, Ruth, *Information für Informierte – Linguistische Studien zur Verständlichkeit und Verstehens von Hörfunknachrichten* (Vienna: Verlag der Österreichischen Akademie der Wissenschaften – Philosophisch – Historische Klasse 488.Band, 1987).

Maechler, Stefan, *The Wilkomirski Affair: A Study in Biographical Truth* (New York: Schocken Books, 2001).

Mann, Thomas, *Beobachtungen eines Unpolitischen* (Frankfurt/Main: S. Fischer, 1919); trans. *Reflections of a Non-political Man* (New York: F. Unger, 1983).

Marchand, Phillip, *Marshall McLuhan: The Medium and the Messenger* (Cambridge, MA: MIT Press, 1998).

Marcuse, Herbert, *Negations: Essays in Critical Theory* (London: Free Association, 1988).

Marßolek, Inge, 'Vertraute Töne und Unerhörtes. Radio und Gedächtnis im Nachkriegsdeutschland', in Elisabeth Domansky and Harald Welzer (eds), *Eine Offene Geschichte. Zur kommunikativen Tradierung der nationalsozialistischen Vergangenheit* (Tübingen: edition discord, 1999).

McLuhan, Marshall, *Understanding Media* (London: Routledge, 2002).

McQuail, Denis (ed.), *A Reader in Mass Communication Theory* (London: Sage, 2001).

Meusch, Matthias, *Von der Diktatur zur Demokratie: Fritz Bauer und die Aufarbeitung der NS-Verbrechen in Hessen 1956–1968* (Wiesbaden: Historische Kommission für Nassau, 2001).

Miquel, Marc von, 'Wir müssen mit den Mördern zusammenleben! NS-Prozesse und politische Öffentlichkeit in den sechziger Jahren', in Fritz Bauer Institut (ed.), *'Gerichtstag halten über uns selbst'. Geschichte und Wirkung des ersten Frankfurter Auschwitz Prozesses* (Frankfurt/Main: Campus Verlag, 2001).

Mitscherlich, Alexander and Margarete, *Die Unfähigkeit zu trauern: Grundlagen Kollektiven Verhaltens* (Munich: Piper, 1977).

Moeller, Robert G., *War Stories: The Search for a Usable Past in the Federal Republic of Germany* (Berkeley: University of California Press, 2003).

Mosler, Peter, *Was wir wollten, was wir wurden* (Hamburg: Reibek, 1988).

Mühl-Benninghaus, Wolfgang, 'Medienpolitische Probleme in Deutschland zwischen 1945 und 1989', in *Mit uns zieht die neue Zeit... 40 Jahre DDR Medien* (Berlin: Vistas Verlag, 1993).

Mühlberg, Liselotte, 'Hörerforschung des DDR-Rundfunks', in *Mit uns zieht die neue Zeit... 40 Jahre DDR Medien*.

Müller, Ingo, *Furchtbare Juristen: Die unbewältigte Vergangenheit unserer Justiz* (Munich: Kindler Verlag, 1987).

Naumann, Bernd, *Auschwitz: A Report on the Proceedings against Robert Karl Ludwig Mulka and Others before the Court in Frankfurt* (London: Pall Mall, 1966).

Niethammer, Lutz, *Der gesäuberte Antifaschismus; Die SED und die roten Kapos von Buchenwald* (Berlin: Akademie Verlag, 1994).

Norden, Albert, *An Appeal to the Conscience to the World* (English; no date – date-stamped by Bodleian Library, Oxford, 7 April 1960).

Pätzold, Kurt, 'NS-Prozesse in der DDR', in agenda: *Nationalsozialismus und Justitz*.

Pendas, Devin O., *The Frankfurt Auschwitz Trial 1963–1965* (Cambridge, MA: Cambridge University Press, 2005).

Peukert, Detlef, *The Weimar Republic: The Crisis of Classical Modernity* (London: Penguin, 1991).

Pietrzynski, Ingrid, 'Die Menschen und die Verhältnisse verbessern' Literaturermittlung in Literatursendungen des DDR-Rundfunks', in Monika Estermann and Edgar Lersch (eds), *Buch, Buchhandel, Rundfunk 1950–1960* (Wiesbaden: Harrasowitz Verlag, 1999).

Podewin, Norbert (ed.), *Braunbuch – Kriegs und Naziverbrecher in der Bundesrepublik und Berlin(West). Reprint der 1968 Ausgabe* (Berlin: Edition Ost, 2002).

Podewin, Norbert, *Albert Norden. Ein Rabbinersohn im Politbüro* (Berlin: Edition Ost, 2001).

Pollock, Friedrich, *Gruppenexperiment: Ein Studienbericht* (Frankfurt/Main: Europäische Verlagsanstanstalt, 1955).

Presse- und Informationsamt der Bundesregierung, *Die Verfolgung nationalsozialistischer Straftaten in der Bundesrepublik* (Bonn: Presse- und Informationsamt der Bundesregierung, 1963).

Reisch, Linda, 'Gleitwort' in Hanno Loewy (ed.), *Holocaust: Die Grenzen des Verstehens. Eine Debatte über die Besetzung der Geschichte* (Hamburg: Rowohlt, 1992).

Reitlinger, Gerhard, *Die Endlösung: Hitlers Versuch der Ausrottung der Juden Europas 1939–1945* (Berlin: Colloquium Verlag, 1956).

Riedel, Heide (ed.), *Mit uns zieht die neue Zeit... 40 Jahre DDR Medien* (Berlin: Vistas Verlag, 1993).

Rogasch Wilfried, 'Kalter Krieg im Äther', in Katharina Klotz, Winfried Ranke and Wilfried Rogasch (eds), *Deutschland im Kalten Krieg – Eine Ausstellung des Deutschen Historischen Museums* (Berlin: Argon, 1992).

Roller, Walter and Höschel, Susanne (eds), *Judenverfolgung und jüdisches Leben unter den Bedingungen der nationalsozialistischen Gewaltherrschaft, Band 1: Tondokumente und Rundfunksendungen 1930–1946* (Potsdam: Verlag für Berlin-Brandenburg, 1996).

Rosskopf Annette, 'Anwalt antifaschistischen Offensiven – Der DDR Nebenklagevertreter Friedrich Karl Kaul', in Fritz Bauer Institute (ed.), *'Gerichtstag halten über uns selbst'.*

von Saldern, Adelheit and Inge Marßoleck (eds), *Zuhören und Gehörtwerden I, Radio im Nationalsozialismus: Zwischen Lenkung und Ablenkung* (Tübingen: edition discord, 1998).

von Saldern, Adelheit and Marßoleck, Inge (eds), *Zuhören und Gehörtwerden II: Radio in der DDR der 50er Jahre. Zwischen Lenkung und Ablenkung* (Tübingen: edition discord, 1998).

Scannell, Paddy, *Radio, Television and Modern Life: a Phenomenological Approach* (Oxford: Blackwell, 1996).

Schildt, Axel, 'Zwei Staaten-eine Hörfunk- und Fernsehnation. Überlegungen zur Bedeutung der elektronischen Massenmedien in der Geschichte der Kommunikation zwischen der Bundesrepublik und der DDR', in Arndt Bauerkämper, Martin Sabrow and Bernd Stöver (eds), *Doppelte Zeitgeschichte. Deutsch-deutsche Beziehungen 1945–1990* (Bonn: Verlag J.H.W. Dietz Nachfolger, 1998).

Schildt, Axel, Siegfried, Detlef and Lammers, Christian, *Dynamische Zeiten* (Hamburg: Hans Christians Verlag, 2003).

Schildt Axel, *Moderne Zeiten: Freizeit, Massenmedien und der 'Zeitgeist' der Bundesrepublik der 50er Jahre* (Hamburg: Christians Verlag, 1995).

Schiller-Lerg Sabine, *Walter Benjamin und der Rundfunk: Programmarbeit zwischen Theorie und Praxis* (Munich: K. G. Saur, 1984).

Schmaltz, Florian, 'Das Historische Gutachten Jürgen Kuczynskis zur Rolle der I.G. Farben und des KZ Monowitz im ersten Frankfurter Auschwitz-Prozess', in Fritz Bauer Institut (ed.), *Gerichtstag halten über uns selbst. Geschichte und Wirkung des ersten Frankfurter Auschwitz Prozesses* (Frankfurt/Main: Campus Verlag, 2001).

Schmidt, Regina and Becker, Egon, *Reaktionen auf Politische Vorgänge – Drei Meinungsstudien aus der Bundesrepublik* (Frankfurt/Main: Europäische Verlagsanstanstalt, 1967).

Schneider, Christof, *Nationalsozialismus als Thema im Programm des Nordwestdeutschen Rundfunks 1945–1948* (Potsdam: Verlag für Berlin Brandenburg, 1999).

Sebastian, Mihail, *Journal 1935–1944* (London: Heinemann, 2000).

Sereny, Gitta, *Into that Darkness: From Mercy Killing to Mass Murder* (London: Pimlico, 1995).
Sofsky, Wolfgang, *The Order of Terror: The Concentration Camp* (Princeton: Princeton University Press, 1993).
Steinbach, Peter, 'Nationalsozialistische Gewaltverbrechen in der deutschen Öffentlichkeit nach 1945', in Jürgen Weber and Peter Steinbach (eds), *Vergangenheitsbewältigung durch Srafverfahren? NS-Prozesse in der BRD* (Munich: Olzog Verlag, 1984).
Steinert, Heinz, *Die Entdeckung der Kulturindustrie* (Münster: Westfälisches Dampfboot, 2003).
Stone, Dan, *Constructing the Holocaust: A Study in Historiography* (London: Valentine Mitchell, 2003).
Streim, Alfred, 'Die Verfolgung von NS-Gewaltverbrechen in der Bundesrepublik Deutschland', in agenda (ed.), *Nationalsozialismus und Justitz*.
Unverhan, David, *Das 'NS- Archiv' des Ministeriums für Staatssicherheit* (Berlin: LIT Verlag, 1998).
Voloshinov, V.N., *Marxism and the Philosophy of Language (1929)* (New York: MIT, 1973).
Weinke, Annette, *Die Verfolgung von NS-Tätern im geteileten Deutschland* (Paderborn: Ferdinand Schöningh, 2002).
Weiß, Christoph, *Auschwitz in der geteilten Welt – Peter Weiss und die 'Ermittlung' im Kalten Krieg*. (St Ingbert: Röhrig Universitätsverlag, 2000).
Weiss, Peter, *The Investigation – Oratorio in 11 Cantos* (London: Calder and Boyars, 1965).
Welzer, Harold, Moller, Sabine and Tschuggnall, Karoline, *Opa war kein Nazi – Nationalsozialismus und Holocaust im Familiengedächtnis* (Frankfurt/Main: Fischer Taschenbuch 2002).
Werle, Gerhard and Wanders, Thomas, *Auschwitz vor Gericht: Völkermord und bundesdeutsche Strafjustiz* (Munich: C.H. Beck. 1995).
Wittmann, Rebecca, *Beyond Justice: The Auschwitz Trial* (Cambridge, MA: Harvard University Press 2005).
Wojak, Irmtrud, 'Im Labyrinth der Schuld: Fritz Bauer und die Aufarbeitung der NS-Verbrechen nach 1945', in Fritz Bauer Institut (ed.), *Im Labyrinth der Schuld* (Frankfurt/Main: Campus Verlag, 2003).
Wolf, Helga Maria (ed.), *Auf Ätherwellen – Persönliche Radiogeschichte(n)* (Vienna: Böhlau Verlag, 2004).
Wolf, Markus, *Memoirs of a Spymaster* (London: Pimlico, 1997).
Young, James E., *Writing and Rewriting the Holocaust* (Bloomington: Indiana University Press, 1990).
Žižek, Slavoj, 'The Spectre of Ideology', in Slavoj Žižek (ed.), *Mapping Ideology* (London: Verso, 1994).
Žižek, Slavoj, *Did Somebody Say Totalitarianism?* (London: Verso, 2001).

Index

Adenauer, Konrad   116
Adler, H.G., Dr   139, 140, 141, 143–4
Adorno, T.W.   10, 15, 25, 30, 43–4, 152, 193
Arendt, Hannah   56, 59
Auschwitz Trials   192
Auschwitz Trials, First (1963–5)   6, 13, 97–137
Auschwitz Trials, Second (1966)   208
Auschwitz Trials, Third (1968)   1, 202–14

Bamm, Peter   163
Bathrick, David   41
Bauer, Fritz, Dr   14, 62, 66, 67, 100, 104
Benjamin, Walter   9, 22–4
Berghaus, Margot   55
Bischoff, Friedrich   165
Boger, Willhelm   66, 67, 101
Bolkowiak, Alev, Col.   89, 91–2, 94
Bonitz, Berhard, (Kapo)   2, 208–10
Brandt, Heinz   110
Brecht, Bertholt   9, 20–2
Broszat, Dr Martin   114
Buchenwald Oath   73–4
Buchheim, Dr Hans   114
Bütefisch, Dr Heinrich   114

Capesius, Dr Victor   116
Carleton-Greene, Hugh   163
Crissell, Andrew   199

Deml, Hermann   52–3
Deutsche Welle   1, 167, 202
Die Ermittlung   137, 218
Diner, Dan   149–50
Dost, Wolfgang   105
Deutsches Rundfunk Archiv   69
Duchrow, Alfred   155
Düx, Dr Heinz   139, 140, 141

Eberhard, Prof. Fritz   176
Edel, Peter   95
Eggebrecht, Axel   14, 126–37, 163
Ehrenmänner, radio programme   115
Eichmann Trial   7, 12, 83–4, 190, 191
Eisler, Gerhart   154
Ermarth, Fritz   49–50
Ernenputsch, Werner   107, 108–10

Fleischhacker, Manfred   156
Fr. Roth, catholic priest   82–3

Galinski, Dr Heinz   82
Gemmeker, Albert   79–81
Gershon, Karen   106
Globke, Dr Hans Maria, Dr   12, 85–96
Glowacki, Dr   101
Gnielka, Thomas   101
Goebbels, Josef   25
Goldstein, Kurt   112
Grimme, Adolf   160, 161–2
Großmann, Johannes F.   124
Gruppenexperiment   15, 182–6
Guthmann, Siegurt   1, 5

Harold Welzer   173
Hessischer Rundfunk   5, 101
Heym, Stefan   39
Hinter der Mauer des Schweigens, radio programme   76–83, 186–9
Hofmeyer, Hans, presiding judge First Auschwitz Trial   105, 108
Horkheimer, Max   10, 25, 82, 98

I.G. Farben   103, 104, 106, 112
Ideology   34

Jäger, Prof. Herbert   139, 141
Jaspers, Karl   60

Kansteiner, Wulf   151, 198
Kapos   202–12

Kästner, Erich 31
Kaul, Friedrich Karl 68
Klehr, Josef 101
Kluge, Alexander 97
Koch, Thilo 76, 186
Koselleck, Reinhart 17, 18, 148
Krausnick, Dr Helmut 77
Krüger, Horst 120
Kuchardzyck, Richard 74
Kuczynski, Prof. Jürgen 114

LaCapra, Dominick 150
Langbein, Hermann 66, 67, 138, 140, 141, 143–4
Laub, Dori 150
Lazarsfeld, Paul 147
Ley, Robert 28–9
Lichtenstein, Heiner 65
Ludendorff, Dr Mathilde 81
Luhmann, Niklas 35, 199

Mann, Thomas 16
Mark, Prof. Bernard 93–4
Marßolek, Inge 162
McLuhan, Marshall 10, 32–4
Mitscherlich, Alexander and Margarete 43, 152, 194–6
Modernity 17, 218
Mühl-Benninghaus, Wolfgang 147
Mulka, Robert 67

NDR (*Norddeutscher Rundfunk*) 12, 126, 182
Nora, Pierre 148
Norden, Albert 66, 75, 86
Nuremberg Trials 47–59
NWDR (Nordwestdeutscher Rundfunk) 46, 163

O'Rourke, Richard 107
Oberländer, Prof. Theodor 85
Ormond, Henry 68
Oulman, Gaston 47

Paczula, Tadeusz 2, 102–3, 202
Pätzold, Kurt 145
Pendorf, Robert 190
Peukert, Detlef 17
Pollock, Friedrich 15, 182

Radmann, Martin 115
Reger, Erik 50
Reich-Ranicki, Marcel 120
Reisch, Linda 149
Rossmann, Erich 165

Sammelpunkt Shelesnastrasse, radio programme 91, 116
Schatz-Weinkranz, Noemi, (Szac–Wajnkranc) 93
Schier-Gribowsky, Peter 76, 186
Schnabel, Ernst 163
Schönberger, Gerhard 104
Schüle, Erwin 63, 69
Schütz, Eberhard 47, 49, 51
Seydewitz, Max 53–4
Staatliches Rundfunkkomittee, GDR state radio committee 154, 157, 167
Stachynskij case 213
Staudte, Wolfgang 61
Streicher, Julius 26–7, 28
SWF (*Südwestfunk*) 120
SWR (Südwestdeutscher Rundfunk) 22

The Children of Zamosc, radio programme 87–91, 116
Thomas, Martin Luther 29–30

Van Dam, Dr Hendrik 78
Vergangenheitsbewältigung 7, 13, 147
Volksempfänger (radio receiver) 9, 27
Voloshinov, V.N. 38
Von Schnitzler, Karl Eduard 99–100, 156
Von Zahn, Peter 163, 164

Waldheim Trials 64
WDR (*Westdeutscher Rundfunk*) 124
Weiss, Peter 14, 137
Wiegenstein, Roland H. 104
Windeck, Josef (Kapo) 2, 210
Wolf, Markus 50, 56
Wulf, Dr Josef 120

Žižek, Slavoj 36–7